ʾAggabāb according to the Qəne School Tradition

Gorgias Handbooks

48

Gorgias Handbooks provides students and scholars with reference books, textbooks and introductions to different topics or fields of study. In this series, Gorgias welcomes books that are able to communicate information, ideas and concepts effectively and concisely, with useful reference bibliographies for further study.

ʾAggabāb according to the Qəne School Tradition

Adverbs, Conjunctions, Prepositions, Relative Pronouns, Interrogative Pronouns, Interjections and Particles in Gəʿəz (Classical Ethiopic)

Hiruie Ermias

2020

Gorgias Press LLC, 954 River Road, Piscataway, NJ, 08854, USA

www.gorgiaspress.com

2020 ܒܪ

ISBN 978-1-4632-4206-0 **ISSN 1935-6838**

Library of Congress Cataloging-in-Publication Data

A Cataloging-in-Publication Record is available at the Library of Congress.

Printed and bound by CPI Group (UK) Ltd, Croydon, CR0 4YY

Table of Contents

ACKNOWLEDGMENTS

First of all, I would like thank my Lord for His compassion, protection and provision.

Then, I sincerely thank Univ. Prof. Dr. Alessandro Bausi for his kind support to successfully accomplish this research. I also thank Univ. Prof. Roland Kießling, Univ. Prof. Dr. Henning Schreiber and Dr. Denis Nosnitsin.

My kind gratitude goes to the members of the TraCES project team of the University of Hamburg: Susanne Hummel, Andreas Ellwardt, Wolfgang Dickut, Dr. Vitagrazia Pissni, Eugenia Sokolinski, Magdalena Kryzanowska and Dr. Cristian Vertan. I am also thankful for my dear colleagues Dr. Solomon Gebreyes, Dr. Antonnella Brita, Dr. Gete Gelaye, Elias Feleke, Dr. Maja Pries, Martin Harras, Hewan Simon Marye, Leonard Bahr, Sisay Sahile, Daria Elagina, Sophia Dege, Dr. Pietro Maria Liuzzo, Francesca Panini, Thomas Rave and Dr. Ebrahim Abdu.

Many thanks to Dorothtea Reule, Nafisa Valieva and all the peoples who supported me.

List of Tables

Transliteration

ሀ *h*

ለ *la*

ሐ *ḥa*

መ *m*

ሠ *śa*

ረ *ra*

ሰ *sa*

ሸ *ša*

ቀ *qa*

በ *ba*

ተ *ta*

ቸ *ča*

ኀ *ḫa*

ነ *na*

ኘ *ňa*

አ *ʾa*

ከ *ka*

ኸ *ḵa*

ወ *wa*

ዐ *ʿa*

ዘ *za*

ዠ *ža*

የ *ya*

ደ *da*

ጀ *ǧa*

ገ *ga*

ጠ *ṭa*

ጨ *č̣a*

ጸ *ṣa*

ፀ *ḍa*

ፈ *fa*

ፐ *pa*

ጰ *ṗa*

ቈ *q*^{w}*a*

ኈ *ḫ*^{w}*a*

ኰ *k*^{w}*a*

ጐ *g*^{w}*a*

List of Abbreviations

Biblical Texts

Acts - Acts of the Apostles
Amos - The Prophecy of Amos
Baruch - The Book of Baruch
Coloss. - Paul's Epistle to Colossians
1 Cor. - Paul's First Epistle to the Corinthians
2 Cor. - The Second Epistle of Paul to the Corinthians
1 Chr. - The First Book of Chronicles
2 Chr. - The Second Book of Chronicles
Dan. - The Prophecy of Daniel
Deut. - Deuteronomy
Eph. - Paul's Epistle to the Ephesians
Esther - The Book of Esther
Exod. - Exodus
Ezek. - The Prophecy of Ezekiel
Ezra - The Book of Ezra
Gal. - Paul's Epistle to the Galatians
Gen. - Genesis
Hab. - The Prophecy of Habakkuk
Heb. - Paul's Epistle to the Hebrews
Hos. - The Prophecy of Hosea
Isa. - The Prophecy of Isaiah
Jas. - The Epistle of James
John - The Gospel of John
1 John - The First Epistle of John
2 John - The Second Epistle of John
Jer. - The Prophecy of Jeremiah
Job - The Book of Job

Joel - The Prophecy of Joel
Josh. - The Book of Joshua
Jude - The Epistle of Jude
Judg. - The Book of Judges
Jonah - The Prophecy of Jonah
1 Kgs - The First Book of kings
2 Kgs - The Second Book of Kings
Lam. - The Lamentation of Jeremiah
Lev. - Leviticus
Luke - The Gospel of Luke
Mic. - The Prophecy of Micah
Mark - The Gospel of Mark
Matt. - The Gospel of Mathew
Neh. - The Book of Nehemiah
Num. - Numbers
1 Pet. - The First Epistle of Peter
2 Pet. - The Second Epistle of Peter
3 Pet. - The Third Epistle of Peter
Obad. - The Prophecy of Obadiah
Phil. - Paul's Epistle to the Philippians
Philem. - Paul's Epistle to Philemon
Ps. - Psalms of David
Rev. - The Book of Revelation
Rom. - The Epistle of Paul to the Romans
Ruth - The Book of Ruth
1 Sam. - The First Book of Samuel
2 Sam. - The Second Book of Samuel
Sir. - The Book of Sirach
S. of S. - The S. of S. of Solomon
1 Thess. - Paul's First Epistle to the Thessalonians
2 Thess. - Paul's Second Epistle to the Thessalonians
1 Tim. - Paul's first Epistle to Timothy
2 Tim. - Paul's Second Epistle to Timothy
Zech. - The Prophecy of Zecharia

EXGETICAL, HAGIOGRAPHICAL AND HYMNODIC BOOKS

Anap.Basil (com.) - The Commentary of the Anaphora of Basil
Anap.Dios (com.) - The Commentary of the Anaphora of Dioscurus
Anap.Eph (com.) - The Commentary of the Anaphora of Epiphany
Anap John (com.) -The Commentary of the Anaphora of John
Anap.Jh.chr (com.) -The Commentary of the Anaphora of John Chrysostom
Anap.Mary (com.) - The Commentary of the Anaphora of Mary
Anap. Nicean (com.) - The Commentary of the Anaphora of Nicean Fathers
Eccles. (com.) -The Commentary of Ecclesiasticus
Gdl.Gebr - The Hagiography of St. *Gabra Manfas Qəddus*
Gdl.Qaw - The Hagiography of St. Qawsṭos
Haym. (com.) -The Commentary of Haymanota ʾAbaw
Liturgy (com).- The Commentary of Liturgy
M.Məśṭir - Maṣḥafa Məśṭir
M.Saʿat - Maṣḥafa Saʿatat
Māḫ. Ṣəge (com) -The Commentary of Māḫleta Ṣəge
M. Ziq - Maṣḥafa ziq
Prov. (com) -The Commentary of the Book of Proverbs
Synod - The Book of Synod
Wed. Mār (com) - The Commentary of Weddāse Māryām
Wis (com) - The Commentary of the Book of Wisdom

IN THE ANNOTATIONS

Acc. - Accusative
Adv. - Adverb
AInt. - Adverbial Interrogative
C - Communis
Conj. - Conjunction
ConSt. - Constructed State
Copu. - Copula
ExAff. - Existential Affirmative
F - Feminine
Imperf. - Imperfective
Impt. - Imperative

Inf. - Infinitive
Int. – Interjection
M - Masculine
NCom. - Common Noun
NPro. - Proper Noun
NumCa. - Cardinal number
NumOr. - Ordinal number
P - Plural
Part. - Particle
PartAcc. - Accusative particle
PartAff. - Affirmative particle
PartInt. - Interrogative Particle
PartNeg. - Negative Particle
Partpres. - Presentational Particle
PartQuot. - Quotative Particle
PartVoc. - Vocative Particle
PDem. - Demonstrative Particle
Perf. - Perfective
PObj. - Object base Pronoun
PPer. - Personal pronoun
PPoss. - Possesive pronoun
PRel. - Relative pronoun
PRel(g) - Relative pronoun expressing genitive relationship
Prep. – Preposition
Pron. - Pronoun
PSt. - Pronominal state
PSub. - Subject based pronoun
PSuff. - Pronominal suffix
PTot. - Pronoun of totality
^{s} - Based on the statement
S - Singular
Subj. - Subjective
Unm. - Unmarked
V – Verb

OTHER

AP. - Active participle
Adj. - Adjective

Etc. - et cetera
Fem. - Feminine
Int. - Interrogative
Lit. - Literary meaning
Masc. - Masculine
PP. - Passive Participle
Pers. – Personal Name

INTRODUCTION

1. GƏʿƏZ AND THE SEMITIC LANGUAGES OF ETHIOPIA

From the context of African languages studies, Ethiopia is the homeland to the highest linguistic diversity in the Horn of Africa. It is believed that more than eighty individual languages and several related dialects which belong to the two major language macro families: Afro-Asiatic and Nilo-Saharan are spoken in the country.[1] In fact, this number includes Gəʿəz and Gafat that do not have native speakers nowadays.

The Afro-Asiatic macro family is represented by more than sixty languages belonging to three distinctive families: Cushitic, Omotic and Semitic. Semitic comprises about twenty-two individual languages. Gəʿəz is a member of this language family and is believed to be one of the most ancient languages spoken in the country since the pre-Aksumite period.

According to the classification of Ethiopian Semitic languages proposed by Wolf Leslau, Gəʿəz is grouped into the North-Ethiopian-Semitic language branch which involves only three languages Təgre, Təgrəññā and Gəʿəz itself.[2]

With regard to its origin, there are different scholarly hypotheses. According to the Encyclopaedia Aethiopica,[3] there were immigrants of South-Arabia in the first millennium BCE and also in the first millennium CE who migrated to Ethiopia by crossing the Red sea and settled in the northern highlands of the country. It also tells

[1] "Ethiopia", *EAe*, II (2005), 393 (D. Crummey); Goldenberg 2013, 16.
[2] Leslau 1989, i; "Gəʿəz", *EAe*, II (2005), 732 (S. Weninger).
[3] "Ethio-Semitic", *EAe*, II (2005), 440-443 (R. Voigt); Hudson 1977, 121.

us that the origin of the present Ethiopian Semitic languages including Gəʿəz goes back to the single language of these South-Arabian immigrants.

In agreement with this, Ullendorff claimed that the South-Arabia immigrants introduced cultural and material civilization, improvements of building and manufacturing in East-Africa. He continues the narration explaining that after a considerable time, the immigrants established a Kingdom at Aksum and the kingdom named its language 'Gəʿəz' after the name of the South Arabian tribe of '*Agʿāzəyān*' that migrated from south Arabia and settled in Ethiopia.[1]

However, some other scholars are not convinced with such a hypothesis which ties the historical background of Gəʿəz with a migratory history of a certain ethnic group. On this regard, Baye Yemam affirms that Gəʿəz is not an imported language but an indigenous language which was born in Aksum, the center of ancient Ethiopia.[2] In support of this statement, Goldenberg stated that Gəʿəz is the only local Semitic language that had been spoken and developed in Africa before the spread of the Arabic language in different countries of the continent that speak Arabic today.[3]

Likewise, the perception of the Ethiopian Gəʿəz scholars about the origin of the language is not the same. Some local scholars claim that Gəʿəz means 'first' or 'the first one', and that was the language of Adam. But many scholars do not have the courage to describe it as the language of Adam as to say 'The first language of all human beings'. They would rather claim that it is genuinely an ancient language spoken in the country since a very ancient time.[4]

However, it is indisputably believed that Gəʿəz is one of the most ancient Semitic languages in Ethiopia. It was the official language of the Aksumite and late Christian Ethiopian kingdom. This is one of the most significant factors why the language in many scholar-

---

1 Ullendorff 1955, 5, 7.
2 Baye Yemam 1992, 1.
3 Goldenberg 2013, 16.
4 'Aklila Bərhān Walda Qirqos 1950, 9.

ly works conducted by European scholars was declared as 'Old Ethiopic' or 'Classical Ethiopic'. Some others named it simply 'Ethiopic'.[1]

As a consequence of the coming of King Yəkunno 'Amlāk to power in 1270 CE, Amharic began to serve as an official court-language. This might have interrupted the permanent use of the language as an official language in all activities of the society. It remained a language of literature and religious activities only.[2] Thus, it is possible to say that from the late thirteenth century onward, Gəʿəz was not spoken as a medium of communication, yet no more native speakers existed anywhere in the country. Nevertheless, the only written language up to the nineteenth century when Amharic literature took ground was Gəʿəz.

In the long history of Ethiopian literature, the fourth century CE was the golden era when the production of vocalized texts began to be produced. The translation of Biblical Scriptures from Greek into Gəʿəz was one of the most valuable literary achievements that makes the epoch most memorable. With this regard, *Abbā* Salāmā kaśāte Bərhān (330-356 CE) the first Bishop of Ethiopia and the Nine Saints who came to Ethiopia from different parts of the Roman Empire during the late fifth century, are always remembered for their great contributions for the availability of Biblical and liturgical texts in Ethiopic language. The translations of early Christian texts such as "The Shepherd of Hermas" and "Enoch" were also the other great literary products of the epoch. The huge hymnodic book which is known as *Dəggʷā* is also believed to be composed by the brilliant composer and adored chanter St. Yared in the sixth Century.

Similarly, the period between the restoration of the so-called Solomonic dynasty (1270 CE) and the invasion of Aḥmad Ibn Ibrahim Al-Ghazi /Aḥmad Gərāñ/ (1528 CE) was the other golden age of Ethiopian literature, by which many eclessiastical and secular texts were translated and composed. The translations of the important historical text Kəbra-Nagaśt, of the Miracle of Jesus, of the Miracle of St. Mary, Synaxarium and of many other Christian texts from

[1] "Gəʿəz", *EAe*, II (2005), 732 (S. Weninger); Goldenberg 2013, 16.
[2] Leslau 1989, vii, *EAe*, III (2007), 505a-b (R. Renate).

Copto-Arabic into Gəʿəz were accomplished in this era. The compositions of the remarkable indigenous texts Maṣḥafa Məśṭir of *Abbā* Giyorgis of Gāsəčča /1365-1425 CE/ and Maṣḥafa Bərhān of Emperor Zarʿa-yā'əqob /1434-1468 CE/ were also some of the literary achievements of the time that should be mentioned alongside with the accomplishments of hagiographies and chronicles.

In general, Gəʿəz is persuasively the only Ethiopic language by which numerous Biblical, doctrinal, theological, canonical, hagiographical, liturgical, philosophical, historical, medical and mathematical texts have been originally composed and translated to from foreign languages both before and after it ceased to be spoken until the introduction of modernization in the late 19th century. It is still extensively used for liturgical and academic services up to the present day.[1] Based on these facts, it will not be an exaggeration if it is said that Gəʿəz is unquestionably the cornerstone of Ethiopian literature.

In Europe, Gəʿəz began to be studied in the 17th century. With this regard, the German scholar Hiob Ludolf (1624-1704 CE) is remembered with honor as the founder of Ethiopian studies, which includes Gəʿəz in Germany. He learned the language from the Ethiopian monk *Abba* Gorgoryos in Rome. In addition to studying and teaching Gəʿəz, Hiob Ludolf has carried out various scientific works. The *Lexicon Aethiopio-Latinum* (London, 1699) and the *Grammatical Aethiopica* (London, 1661) are some of his prestigious works.[2]

The other German scholar Christian Friedrich August Dillmann (1823-1894 CE) was also one of the prominent scholars who contributed much to the development of Gəʿəz studies in Europe. He has edited a number of Gəʿəz manuscripts, including various biblical Scriptures. The *Grammatik der äthiopischen Sprache* (1857), *Lexicon Linguae aethiopicae* (1865) and *Chrestomathia aethiopica* (1866) are some of his remarkable contributions in connection with Gəʿəz study.[3] The Italian scholar Carlo Conti Rossini (1872-1949) has also an excellent record of editing Gəʿəz manuscripts.[4]

---

1 Getachew Haile 1981, 102; "Gəʿəz", *EAe*, II (2005), 732 (S. Weninger).
2 "Hiob Ludolf", *EAe*, III (2007), 601 (S. Uhlig).
3 "Dillmann, Christian Friedrich August", *EAe* II (2005), 160 (M. Kleiner).
4 "Conti Rossini, Carlo", *EAe* I (2003), 791 (L. Rici).

In the 19th and 20th centuries, several academic centres for the study of Gəʿəz were established in various European cities such as Rome, Paris, Naples, Berlin, London, Hamburg, Marburg, Mainz, Warsaw and St. Petersburg. It is obvious that the study in some of the institutions is weakening from time to time. But the majority is still working harder to maintain the study of Gəʿəz by recognizing it as a crucial gateway for various fields of study such as philology, manuscriptology and history.

II. THE *QƎNE* SCHOOLS AS IMPORTANT CENTERS OF GƎʿƎZ STUDY

In the present-day Ethiopia, Gəʿəz is prominently studied in the *Qəne* ('Gəʿəz poetry') Schools of the Ethiopian Orthodox Tawāḥədo Church. So far, the language still serves as a liturgical language in all Church services and as a vehicle language of ecclesiastical knowledge, the Church is highly concerned with its preservation and expansion. Despite the facts that some educational institutes of different levels are devoted to providing irregular workshops as well as regular sessions with regard to Gəʿəz literature and the language itself in a systematic way, the most important centers for intensive Gəʿəz study in Ethiopia are *Qəne* schools that are located in or around parish churches and monasteries.

The *Qəne* schools are particular centers at which Gəʿəz is intensely studied, read, written, spoken, sung and interpreted. The students in the schools especially those who are at the high level are ever committed not only to learn thoroughly how to read Gəʿəz texts and to analyse their contents by elaborating their literal and allegorical messages but also to analyse the nature, significance and role of every minor language element. They are warmly encouraged to criticize, interpret and evaluate various written texts according to the common rules of the language.

Many would strongly believe that the indiginous school methodology used in the *Qəne* schools helps students to become more brilliant and creative. In fact, this is not so easy to deny, because if we look at the background of many influential scholars, writers and thinkers of the 20th century Ethiopia that the country has ever seen, most of them were once *Qəne* students or spent a few hours at one of the schools. Among them, *Ṣaḥafe-Tə'zāz* Gabra Śəllāse Walda

Aragāy (1844-1912 CE)[1], *Bəlātten-Getā* Ḫəruy Walda Śəllāse (1878-1938 CE)[2], Marsəʿe Ḫazan Walda Qirqos (1899-1978 CE)[3], Dr. Kabbada Mikāel (1914-1998 CE)[4], Dr. Ḥāddis 'Alamāyyāhu (1909-2003 CE)[5], *Qaňň-'Azmāč* Yoftāhe Nəguśe (1892-1946 CE)[6] and Prof. Taddase Tamrat (1935-2013 CE)[7] are well known to have exercised this journey.

Through the wisdom and talents of these outstanding scholars, everyone can imagine the value and impact of *Qəne* schools in Ethiopia. Nowadays, many people wish to visit the schools and become a student of *Qəne*, but due to various social challenges and political unsustainability, not everyone who wishes becomes successful. Various social affections have a strong impact on the students and their studies.

In addition to this, like cultural and traditional legacies local education is highly affected by modernization. The tendency of the new generation is to visit secular schools rather than spending a couple of years in the traditional schools studying day and night. Most probably, the students are gathered from far areas and do not have close contact with their families during their stay in the schools. They keep the status of self-sponsored students. So, to get whatever they need to eat or wear, they should collect supports from the inhabitants living around the schools or work for people occasionally to make some money. This is among the factors that makes life difficult for students.

Besides, many parents today are not willing to send their children to the traditional schools or let them stay in the schools until they accomplish their study. For such reasons, many students leave the schools before accomplishing the study. Thus, the number of

[1] "Gäbrä Śəllase Wäldä Arägay" *EAe*, II (2005), 628 (Bairu Tafla).
[2] "Həruy Wäldä Śəllase" *EAe*, III (2007), 20 (S. Kaplan).
[3] "Märse Ḫazan Wäldä Qirqos" *EAe*, III (2007), 798 (Asfaw Damte).
[4] "Käbbädä Mika'el" *EAe*, III (2007), 315 (E. Sohier).
[5] "Haddis ʿAlämayyähu" *EAE*, II (2005), 959 (Asfaw Damte).
[6] "Yoftahe Nəguśe" *EAE*, V (2014), 66 (M. Zabolotskikh).
[7] "Interfece between Philology and History", *Ethiopian Philology* Vol. I, Number I (2008), 52, (Shiferaw Bekele).

students in the traditional schools is decreasing through time. This could endanger the knowledge since the survival of any knowledge highly depends on the presence of pupils who receive, use and relay it to the next generation.

These challenges are not exclusively connected with the *Qəne* Schools or any other specific school; all traditional schools are now under such circumstances. To realize this, it might be enough to see the current state of the study of *ʾAbušākər* which is about arithmetical and calendric system.[1] It faces the risk of extinction like the exegetical study of *maṣāḥəfta liqāwənt* 'commentaries of Patristic texts'. In comparison, the study of *maṣāḥəfta liqāwənt* has a much better hope of revival since a few schools still remain opened, though the students do not number as much as the New or Old Testaments schools. But, the recognizable number of the living scholars who studied and can teach *ʾAbušākər* is at present not more than three, and yet, they do not have students. Perhaps, it would be possible to say that its existence in the future will be through the available manuscripts only if its present status does not change.

Eventhough, with the persistent helps of many peoples who understand the significant role and importance of the wisdom, *Qəne* Schools in thousands are still existing throughout the country providing knowledge.

The study in the School is broadly divided into two major parts called ሰዋስው *sawāsəw* and ቅኔ *qəne* by which students can learn and exercise the language until they become able to compose *Qəne* (Gəʿəz poem) in addition to reading and understanding written texts. The tradition of the schools recommends the students to attend both parts of the study in parallel to get better knowledge and experience of the language concurrently.

Qəne deals with the composition, recitation and interpretation of Gəʿəz poetry called *Qəne*.[2] The term *Qəne* is originally a Gəʿəz term

---

[1] "Abušākər", *EAe*, I (2003), 57 (S. Uhlig).

[2] It has three levels: *Qəne qoṭara* (composing and reciting *Qəne*), *ya-qəne zemā ləkk* (a course concerning the measurements of syllables of words in each line) and *ya-qəne godānā* (a course concerned with different styles of *Qəne*). The last section is also known as ጉት *gutt*.

which literally means 'subjection' or 'service'. *Sawāsəw* is specifically concerned with the study of the language itself. It deals with the grammatical aspects of Gəʿəz language. *Sawāsəw* means literally 'ladder'. According to the tradition, the reason why such a metaphorical title is given to the study is that studying Gəʿəz helps to reach the pinnacle of success in all ecclesiastical studies as much as a ladder helps to go upwards.[1]

Gideon Goldenberg stated in his recent book *Semitic Languages* that *Sawāsəw* is the translation of the Arabic *sullam* which is the name of the Coptic-Arabic vocabularies.[2] Meley Mulugetta also connected its remote origin with these Copto-Arabic vocabularies. By expanding the issue, she elucidated that *Sawāsəw* preserved the structure provided in the grammatical introduction of *sullam* and gave few examples of grammatical terms such as *zar* (Arab.: *aṣl*) 'root' and *səm* (Arab.: *ism*) 'noun' which confirm the connection between the two grammatical traditions.[3] Extensively long before Goldenberg and Meley Moreno who did original large-scale research on *Sawāsəw* speaks about this connection in his pioneering article[4]. He goes in detail on some specific points and finds examples that demonstrate the link. Not far from this, Alessandro Gori affirmed the availability of many Arabic loan-words in the later phases of Gəʿəz.[5]

According to the methodology followed by the *Qəne* schools, *Sawāsəw* is a common term which is used to collectively describe all subjects and lessons concerned about the grammatical aspects of the language. At the end of his comprehensive article, Moreno concludes that *Sawāsəw* deserves a better study as it contains a huge amount of information on the vocabulary, grammar and style of the Geez language.[6]

---

[1] 'Admāsu Ǧambare 1970, 11; Tāyya Gabra Māryām; 1965, 3; Muluken Andualem Sieferew 2013, 2.

[2] Goldenberg 2013, 60.

[3] "Sawāsəw", *EAe*, IV (2010), 562 (M. Mulugetta).

[4] Moreno, 1949. 12-62.

[5] "Arabic", *EAe*, I (2003), 302 (A. Gori).

[6] Moreno 1949, 62.

III. VARIOUS STAGES OF THE STUDY OF GƎʿƎZ GRAMMAR

Sawāsəw, the grammatical study in the *Qəne* schools is deliberately divided into four different sections that keep their own identifications, specializations and scopes. They are ግሥ *gəśś*, ርባ፡ ቅምር *rəbā qəmr*, ርባ፡ ግሥ *rəbā gəśś* and አገባብ *'Aggabāb*.

a) *Gəśś*

The first section in the study of *Sawasəw* is called *gəśś*. The term is equally used as the common designation of all Gəʿəz verbs and nouns. It means simply 'verb' or 'vocabulary'.

It is divided into two, *naṭalā*[1] *gəśś* (ነጠላ፡ ግሥ) and *nabbār*[2] *gəśś* (ነባር፡ ግሥ). *Naṭalā gəśś* refers to each verb which is originated from a verbal root called *zar* (ዘር) which means 'seed' or 'root'. Additionally, the term *'anqaṣ gəśś* (አንቀጽ፡ ግሥ) which is the better known and used term is also given to all verbs in the perfective form of the third person singular masculine (e.g.: ቀተለ *qatala*, ቀደሰ *qaddasa* and ተንበለ *tambala etc.*). *'Anqaṣ* means 'gate'. According to the tradition of *sawāsəw*, the reason why each verb is compared with a gate (*'anqaṣ*) is that as a gate serves as an entrance to the house, verbs serve as an entrance to all conjugational units and nominal derivations. Similarly, the term *nabbār gəśś* represents the nouns that do not have etymological affiliation with verbs.

b) Rəbā qəmr

Rəbā qəmr[3] is studied next to *gəśś* for the reason that it is concerned with verbs. It deals with the classification and derivation of Gəʿəz verbs. The students at this level learn about twenty-eight diverse subtopics that are specifically concerned with the entire aspects of verbs.

---

1 Amharic, lit.: 'single'.
2 Amharic, lit.: 'immovable'.
3 A combination of two different words, *rəbā* (lit.: 'reproduction', 'conjugation', 'declination') and *qəmr* (lit.: 'measurement').

c) Rəbā gəśś[1]

This is also an important section which deals with the systematic ways of conjugating verbs. After having studied this part of the grammatical study, students acquire a proper knowledge of verb conjugation based on various conjugating types that are applied by the conjugations of specific model verbs. It also concerns the polysemantic verbs. By means of revising verbs with their initial and further meanings based on reliable textual evidence and by learning how to conjugate them, students expand their Gəʿəz knowledge and practice as well.

d) 'Aggabāb

This is the last and in fact the most essential part in the study of *Sawāsəw*. Most of the decisive language rules concerned with phonological, syntactical and morphological aspects of different lexical categories are studied in this section with a special focus on the so-called *'Aggabāb* elements. The lexical categories involved in the study of *'Aggabāb* are adverbs, conjunctions, prepositions, relative and interrogative pronouns, interjections and particles (we call them forwardly as 'ACPPIP[2] elements). In the other way round, the study of *'Aggabāb* does not deal with the remaining parts of speech such as verbs, adjectives, nouns and pronouns (aside from the relative and interrogative pronouns).

Moreno points to the correspondence between the Arabic concept of *ḥarf* and the *'Aggabāb* teaching, and describes the latter as the widest part of *Sawāsew*. According to Moreno, *'Aggabāb* defines particles and their positions, functions and meanings. But he means that *'Aggabāb* includes the treatment, syntax and style of any word, and therefore *'Aggabāb* refers also to the ways of introducing words into the speech, to the (syntactical) construction and the style.[3]

---

[1] A combination of two words *rəbā* (lit.: 'reproduction', 'conjugation', 'declination') and *gəśś* ('verb', 'vocabulary').

[2] It is just an acronym of the names of these six lexical categories involved in *'Aggabāb*.

[3] Moreno 1949, 44-45.

Indeed, the study of *ʾAggabāb* touches upon several aspects apart from the origin, meaning and use of ACPPIP elements directly and indirectly. But this does not mean that it deals with all Gəʿəz words and phrases. As explained earlier, all parts of *Sawāsəw* have their own special area of study and scope. There might appear some interferences of issues in each part, including *ʾAggabāb*. But each part of the grammatical study is described according to its main concern; and the main concern of *ʾAggabāb* as a grammatical study is dealing with grammatical aspects related with the so-called ACPPIP elements. This will be proved forwardly in the coming chapters.

To acquire some insights into the state of *ʾAggabāb*, let us discuss some general points here. Like homilies, the treatise begins by invoking the name of the Holy Trinity. The invocation is followed by a very short description of what *ʾAggabāb* is. This is used for all three divisions of *ʾAggabāb* as a common formula. The statements that come after the formula give a hint about which *ʾAggabāb* division is going to be discussed and why the division keeps its identification. It looks like the following:

በስመ፡ አብ፡ ወወልድ፡ ወመንፈስ፡ ቅዱስ፡ ፩ዱ፡ አምላክ፡ አሜን።
ንዌጥን፡ በረድኤተ፡ እግዚአብሔር፡ ነገረ፡ አገባብ።

አገባብ፡ የሚባሉ፡ ፫፡ ናቸው። ማን፡ ማን፡ ናቸው፡ ቢሉ፡ ዐቢይ፣ ንኡስና፡ ደቂቅ፡ ናቸው። ከእነዚህም፡ ውስጥ፡ ዐቢይ፡ አገባብን፡ አሁን፡ እንናገራለን። በነባር፣ በቀዳማይ፡ በካልዐይ፣ በሣልሳይ፡ አንቀጽ፡ እየገባ፡ ማሠሪያ፡ ያፈርሳል። አገባብ፡ መባሉ፡ ከአንቀጽ፡ በፊት፡ ስለተነገረ፡ ነው። አገባብ፡ ማለት፡ እግር፡ ብረት፡ ሰንሰለት፡ ማለት፡ ነው። ዐቢይ፡ ያሰኘው፡ አንቀጽ፡ ስላፈረሰ፡ ነው።

ba-səma ʾab wa-wald wa-manfas qəddus 1 ʾamlāk ʾamen. nəweṭṭən ba-radəʾeta ʾəgziʾabəḥer nagara ʾaggabāb.

ʾaggabāb yamibbalu 3 naččaw. mānn mānn nāččaw bilu ʿabiyy nəʾus daqiq naččaw. ka-ʾənnazihəmm wəsṭ ʿabiyy ʾaggabābə-n ʾahun ʾənnənnagarāllan. ba-nabbār, ba-qadāmāy, ba-kāləʿay, ba-śāləsāy ʾəyyagabbā māśaryā yāfarsāl. ʾaggabāb mabbālu ka-ʾanqaṣ ba-fit səla-tanaggara naw. ʾaggabāb mālat ʾəgr bərat sansalat mālat naw. ʿabiyy yāssaňňaw ʾanqaṣ səlāfarassa naw.

In the name of the Father, of the Son and of the Holy Spirit, one God, Amen. We begin (speaking about) the subject of *ʾAggabāb* with the help of God. What are called

> *'aggabāb* are three. If someone asks what they are, they are *'abiyy* (big) *nə'us* (minor) and *daqiq* (small). Among them, we discuss here *'abiyy 'aggabāb*. It is combined with the perfective, imperfective and subjunctive (verbs) and destructs a verb. It is called *'aggabāb* because it is prefixed to a verb. *'Aggabāb* means shackle (or) chain. It is called *'abiyy* since it destructs a verb (Hiruie, *unpublished 'Aggabāb*, 98).

This is the introductory part of the first division '*'abiyy 'aggabāb*'. In the case of *nə'us 'aggabāb* or *daqiq 'aggabāb*, the introduction preceded by the invocation is focused and specific enough on what *nə'us* or *daqiq 'aggabāb* is. Afterwards, the elements arranged in the categories are discussed consecutively.

The discussion is executed in two ways. The first way is introducing firstly the elements with the same semantic value together and giving an explanation about their meanings and grammatical functions later.

Example: ኀበ፡ አምጣነ፡ ሳ፡ ይሆናሉ፤ በሀሎ፡ በ፯፡ በሀለወ፡ በ፲፡ ሠራዊት፡ ይነገራሉ።

> *ḫaba 'amṭāna sā yəhonāllu, ba-hallo ba-7 ba-hallawa ba-10 śarāwit yənaggarāllu.*
>
> '*Haba* and *'amṭāna* are used as 'without'; they are treated with *hallo* in seven (persons) and with *hallawa* in ten (persons)' (Hiruie, *unpublished 'Aggabāb* 105).

The second way is to mention a concept first and then introducing the elements which keep the concept.

Example: ወደ፡ የሚሆኑ፡ ቀለማት፡ ፲፩፡ ናቸው። ምንና፡ ምን፡ ናቸው፡ ቢሉ፡ ኀበ፣ መንገለ፣ እንተ፣ እለ፣ ውስተ፣ በ፣ እም፣ ግዕዝ፣ ራብዕ፣ ኃምስ፣ ሳብዕ፡ ናቸው።

> *wada yamihonu qalamāt 11 naččaw. mənənnā mən nāččaw bilu ḫaba, mangala, 'ənta, 'əlla, wəsta, ba, 'əm, gə'əz, rābə', ḫaməs, sābə' nāččaw.*
>
> The words which are used as 'to' are eleven. If someones ask what they are, they are *ḫaba, mangala, 'ənta, 'əlla, wəsta, ba, 'əm, gə'əz, rābə', ḫaməs* and *sābə* (Hiruie, *unpublished 'Aggabāb*, 104).

In the example above, *gəʿəz, rābəʿ, ḫaməs* and *sābəʿ* are not ACPPIP elements. They are numerals referring to the first, fourth, fifth and seventh order radicals respectively; that is why in the explanation, they are called *qalamā*t 'words'. Quite surely, such a description makes the treatise not easily achievable. Even though the medium is Amharic, the Amharic speakers with less knowledge of Gəʿəz face a big challenge to understand it sufficiently because of technical terms, old Amharic words and the less systematic arrangement of elements and explanations.[1]

Like the numerals, some other words are also included in some versions of the tradition such as ሐዊሳ *ḥawisā* 'Greetings', በሐ *baḥa* (Greetings), ነዓ *naʿā* (come) and ህንክ *hənk* (take). The inclusion of such words makes one out of the *ʾAggabāb* framework. To have a precise understanding of *ʾAggabāb* with special focus on ACPPIP elements, it is necessary to single out the exact ACPIP elements and to put aside the non-ACPPIP elements. Thus, making a careful selection of elements was a crucial task in implementing this work. As mentioned above, such language elements are habitually described in the tradition as *qalamāt* 'words' instead of *ʾaggabāboč* 'ACPPIP elements.' This kind of description helped much for realizing the selection.

The other challenging factor is the presentation of evidence. Moreno affirms that the great display of phrases are taken from sacred texts[2] but most often, the evidence is provided without authentic references. Besides, the evidence is sometimes presented succeedingly without distinction. Much of the evidence is also presented being mingled with simple examples. Let us look at the following example.

> በ፡ ጊዜ፡ ይሆናል። በሳቢ፡ ዘር፡ በንኡስ፡ አንቀጽ፡ በጥሬ፡ ዘር፡ ይገባል፤ በጽሒፈ፡ መጽሐፍ፡ በጽሕፈተ፡ መጽሐፍ፡ ወታቀንተኒ፡ ኀይለ፡ በጸብዕ፡ እንዲል።
>
> *ba gize yəhonāl ba-sābi zar ba-nəʾus ʾanqaṣ ba-ṭəre zar yəgabāl ba-ṣʿəḥifa maṣḥaf ba-ṣəḥfata maṣḥaf wa-tāqannəta-nni ḫayla ba-ṣabʿə*

---

[1] Moreno 1949, 60.

[2] Ibid, 44, 62.

> *ba* serves as 'at' ('during'); it can be attached to a verbal noun, infinitive and deverbal as it says "during writing a book, during composition of a book, and you gird me at a war" (Hiruie, *unpublished 'Aggabāb* 113).

This explanation consists of there different readings without separation. The textual evidence is just one i.e *wa-tāqannəta-nni ḫayla ba-ṣabʿə* which is quoted from Psalm 17:39. *Ba-ṣʿəḥifa maṣḥaf* and *ba-ṣəḥfata maṣḥaf* are two different examples provided to show how the element can be treated with different derivatives. This is however not easily achievable, yet, too difficult to differentiate the evidence from the examples. Thus, sorting out the evidence from the examples, examining its reliability and finding the reference are the principal tasks in realizing this research before moving to analyzing and making a comparison of related observations. If the evidence is not fitting enough or unavailable in the attainable sources, the equivalent textual evidence must be investigated and replace it.

When we come to its value, in the *Qəne* schools, producing a couple of new compositions in the form of poetry (ቅኔ *qəne*), *hymn* (አርኬ *'arke*), or of a prosaic text is the daily key activity of students.[1] Such kind of competence cannot be a result of a mere accumulation of verbs and nouns in mind. That is why the students shall study *'Aggabāb* to develop their knowledge to the high extent by learning all rules and characteristics of the language even after being able to recite new compositions with an excellent ability. This shows evidently what a key role *'Aggabāb* plays in the study of Gəʿəz language or Gəʿəz literature.

According to the academic tradition of the schools, without studying *'Aggabāb*, no one can be a graduate of *Qəne* because it is strongly believed that only those who study *'Aggabāb* can know and understand the language well and its entire characteristics. This means, a perfect knowledge of *'Aggabāb* in the *Qəne* schools is one of the most important requirements to graduate in the study of *Qəne* and Gəʿəz language. Thus, every candidate has to study *'Aggabāb* at the final stage of his study. To finalize, this specific part of the

---

1 Alemayehu Moges 1973, 92.

grammatical study draws a huge attention of both the instructors and the students.

IV. SIGNIFICANCE OF THE STUDY

The production of various outstanding scholarly works concerned with Gəʿəz and Gəʿəz literature in a massive number is certainly a testimony confirming that the language is one of the well-studied Semitic languages in Ethiopia.[1] Putting aside the early productions, yet, since nineteenth century onwards, many scholarly works were carried out by various local and European scholars on different aspects of the language. However, the grammar which is regularly studied in the *Qəne* schools i.e. *ʾAggabāb* is still unpublished.[2]

The importance of conducting deep investigations on the contents of the grammatical study of *ʾAggabāb* is notably connected with preservation of the knowledge as an oral heritage and to do some contribution to developing the used grammars with more additional issues from different points of view. With regard to the number of ACPPIP elements, classifications and reasonable evidence for the metaphoric meanings and various features of polysemantic elements, the printed grammars differ one from the other in most cases.

Even if we compare each with *ʾAggabāb*, a number of ACPPIP elements included in the printed grammars excluding that of Dillmann is fewer than the number of ACPPIP elements involved in *ʾAggabāb*. This means a couple of ACPPIP elements are not yet studied as well from the perspectives of *ʾAggabāb*.

The improper classification of some critical elements may also lead to a serious confusion. Moreno indicates that the classification of the elements according to their function is neither complete nor explicit; the elements may be grouped according to the corresponding Amharic words.[3] Contrarily, the *ʾAggabāb* tradition clarifies that the classification is mainly based on the use and role of the elements

---

[1] Weninger 1999, 1.
[2] Andualem Muluken Sieferew 2013, 5.
[3] Moreno 1949, 50.

in the language and is yet believed that it can simply prove their grammatical function.

Similarly, on providing evidence for the explanations particularly for the metaphorical meanings and other grammatical functions of the elements, the model grammars mentioned earlier follow different ways. For instance, August Dillmann provides short textual evidence intensively for the elements that he collects in each lexical category with sufficient references. Incoherently, Kidāna Wald Kəfle (*'Alaqā*) provides textual evidence, but it is not often that he mentioned references.

On the other hand, Tāyya Walda Māryām (*'Alaqā*) and Yətbārak Marša (*Mal'aka 'Arəyām*) give their own examples alongside with rare textual readings. Even for the textual readings they mention, references are not provided satisfactorily. Of course, from this angle, the *'Aggabāb* tradition is also not irreproachable as mentioned earlier.

Thus, the composition of this work is indisputably important to fill such a gap, including that of the *'Aggabāb* tradition itself.

Such an investigation is expected to play an important role in the pertinent fields, in particular, in philology and linguistics. It will provide inputs to understand Gəʿəz language well from different perspectives of Ethiopian scholarship. It also furnishes a potential to check other works done earlier by linguists and philologists and to compare their approaches. Even for Gəʿəz lexicographers, it may offer various less-known meanings of the polysemous ACPPIP elements.

V. OBJECTIVES OF THE STUDY

The main objective of this study is to analyse what *'Aggabāb* is about, its origin and transmission and to discuss its issues focusing on the etymology, meaning, grammatical function and position of each linguistic element included in the study in comparison with different publications. Providing textual evidence for each theory is also an important task.

VI. STATEMENT OF THE PROBLEM

As mentioned earlier, this research aims principally to deal with the major issues of *ʾAggabāb*. To achieve this, I put the following questions into consideration:

- What is *ʾAggabāb*?
- How many distinctive *ʾAggabāb* (s) is (are) studied in the *Qəne* schools?
- What is the significance of studying *ʾAggabāb*?
- What are the main issues comprised in *ʾAggabāb*?
- On which issues do scholars have argumentative ideas, and what are the arguments?

VII. RESEARCH METHODOLOGY

For the successful achievement of the main goals of this study, I did the following tasks deliberately:

- I collected some handwritten copies of *ʾAggabāb* belonging to the three *Qəne* houses Wādlā, Wāšarā and Gonǧ. Of course, there are some manuscripts of *Sawāsəw* such as EMML 2092 (14 folios) and 2817 (38 folios).[1] They consist of some *ʾAggabāab* issues allied with uncodified points of other sections of *Sawāsəw*. The information they give specifically on *ʾAggabāb* tradition is not complete. Thus, I used the collected handwritten copies as primary sourses since they are fitting with the pertinent oral tradition.
- I sorted out the main issues of *ʾAggabāb* and proposed explanations and analyses on the ACPPIP elements focusing on their origins, meaning, grammatical function and a worthwhile position in a sentence. I carried out the task being apprehended in this framework.
- I searched if there is an argumentative point of view on any issue discussed in the tradition among those *Qəne* houses or individual scholars. Nonetheless, no serious argumentative point of view is captured since the central difference between the traditions of the houses is related with the extent

[1] "Sawāsəw", *EAe*, IV (2010), 562 (M. Mulugetta).

of ACPPIP elements and the state of linguistic analysis. In my assessment, I realized that among the houses, the grammar tradition of Wādlā and Wāšarā is substantially wider than that of Gonǧ.

- On the critical points, numbers and types of elements, I gathered scholarly approaches by making interviews and discussions.
- I made a review of some randomly selected publications of Gəʿəz grammars. This mostly focuses on the number and types of ACPPIP elements as well as on how to categorize them into different lexical categories and how to describe them in terms of origin, meaning and grammatical function.
- I made a comparison between the *'Aggabāb* tradition and the perspectives of various scholars on each issue, and all relevant perspectives, I indicated briefly.
- I provided textual evidence for the analyses without evidence and references for the evidence without references.
- I annotated and translated each textual evidence mentioned in the study to make their translation and the linguistic value of every single element involved in the sentences well understandable and unambiguous.
- For use of Abbreviations of Biblical texts, I have consulted the New Oxford Style Manual.
- I listed all local terms in the glossary and gave short explanations for each. I also presented an index.

CHAPTER ONE: GENERAL INTRODUCTION TO *'AGGABĀB*

1.1. ITS ORIGIN AND MEANING OF THE TERM

'Aggabāb is a polysemous Amharic word which is equivalent to the Gəʿəz words መፍትው *maftəw*, ድልወት *dəlwat* and ሥርዐት *śərʿat*. It has an etymological relation with the verbs ገባ *gabbā* 'enter' and ተገባ *tagabbā* 'be allowed', 'be right'. It literally means 'right', 'lawful', 'the way how to enter or how to be conducted'. In a modern spoken language, particularly in Amharic, it is mostly used as an adjective to express the legitimacy or the rightfulness of any idea or activity. But from the perspective of language studies, *'Aggabāb* refers to a study of grammar because it deals with the grammatical aspects of a language.[1]

'Abbā Gabra Mikā'el discussed *'Aggabāb* briefly in his Maṣḥafa sawāsəw published in 1886, and this can be regarded as its earliest mention in well-known publications.

The schools' tradition expresses *'Aggabāb* as a common designation of all linguistic elements involved in the lexical categories mentioned earlier. In a sentence, these elements are frequently affixed to verbs, nominal derivations and non-derivational nouns as well as to one another. There are in fact a number of elements which cannot be affixed to any word; such an element might precede or follow a verb. But in all cases, every element has its own impacts on the function of the closest verb as well as on the general idea of the

[1] Keśāte Bərhān Tasammā 1958, 811.

sentence. This is the main reason why the elements are collectively called *'Aggabāb*.

At the same time, the specific part of the study which deals with the grammatical aspects of various parts of speech mentioned above is also called *'Aggabāb*. It could be that it is particularly concerned with dealing with how these elements can occur in a sentence. In addition, the term can be used in the studies of any other language in expression of a comparable grammatical lesson. Nonetheless, it is extensively known and used in the *Qəne* schools to pinpoint the stated part of the grammatical study of Gəʿəz. Therefore, it is possible to describe it as Gəʿəz grammar.

Notwithstanding, *'Alaqā* 'Afawarq Zawde[1] attempts to make a distinction between the designation of individual elements and the title of the specified grammatical study by introducing comparative modifying identifications for the elements such as **ዐቢይ፡ ገብ** *ʿabiyy gabb* or **ዐቢይ፡ ገባዊ** *ʿabiyy gabbāwi*, **ንኡስ፡ ገብ** *nəʿus gabb* or **ንኡስ፡ ገባዊ** *nəʿus gabbāwi*, **ደቂቅ፡ ገብ** *daqiq gabb* or **ደቂቅ፡ ገባዊ** *daqiq gabbāwi*, **ግብአት** *gəb'at* and **አግባብ** *'agbāb*. He uses the term *'Aggabāb* only for identifying this particular part of the grammatical study and the way how words can be constructed.[2]

1.2. DIVISION OF *'AGGABĀB* ACCORDING TO THE TRADITION

According to the tradition, *'Aggabāb* is broadly divided into three major groups, namely **ዐቢይ አገባብ** *ʿabiyy 'Aggabāb*, **ንኡስ፡ አገባብ** *nəʿus 'Aggabāb* and **ደቂቅ፡ አገባብ** *daqiq 'Aggabāb*.

---

[1] He is one of the contemporary scholars of Gəʿəz language and *Qəne*. He claims that he visited the famous *Qəne* schools in Wallo, also in Dima and Dabra 'Elyās of Goǧǧām as a student. *Mal'aka Bərhān* 'Admāsu Ǧambare, who was one of the prominent scholars in Gəʿəz literature, in *Qəne* and in Bible commentaries was one of his instructors. Between the years 1938 and 1958, he had taught Gəʿəz language and *Qəne* at the Theological Seminary of St. Paul in Addis Ababa. He authored about seven books, and one of them is known by the title *wa-'amārəňňā* ሀገረ መጻሕፍት፡ ሰዋስው፡ ግዕዝ፡ ወአማርኛ *hagara maṣāḥəft, sawāsəw Gəʿəz*. 'Afawarq Zawde 1995, 7-8.

[2] Ibid: 10.

1.2.1. ʿAbiyy ʾAggabāb

The adjective *ʿabiyy* in Gəʿəz refers to superiority, greatness, dominance and incomparability. So, the term in general has a literal meaning of 'The major ACPPIP element/s'. The elements involved in this category are mostly employed as conjunctions and relative pronouns. Thus, it is possible to say that the group is compared to the lexical categories of Conjunction and Relative pronoun as well.

Out of two hundred thirty-four linguistic elements included in the study of *ʾAggabāb,* forty-seven elements are categorized in this group. We will see them soon in a table illustrating the entire elements in their classes.

There are three factors that make the elements of *ʿAbiyy ʾAggabāb* (in our case, the group of conjunctional elements and relative pronouns) different from the elements of the other categories. They neither occur alone nor follow verbs with the exceptions of ባሕቱ፡ *bāḥəttu* 'but', አኮኑ *ʾakkonu* 'because' and ዳእሙ *dāʾəmu* 'however'. They can be directly attached to verbs with the exceptions of *bāḥəttu, ʾakkonu,* and *dāʾəmu.* The adverbial element ዓዲ *ʿādi* 'again' is also included in this category.

They play a significant role to make a subordinate clause. Without such an element, it is impossible to build a complex sentence. We can prove this by the following example.

> ደንገጽኩ፡ ጥቀ። ርኢኩ፡ አንበሳ።
>
> *dangaṣ-ku ṭəqqa rəʾiku ʾanbasā*
>
> <V:Perf.1c.s> <Adv> <V:Perf.1c.s> <NCom:unm.s.Acc>
>
> 'I was very scared. I saw a lion'.

The absence of a conjunctional element does not lead us to consider the example as a single complex sentence because no link appears between them. Though, if we insert a possible conjunctional element attaching to the second verb, it becomes a complex sentence. Let us insert for example the particle ሶበ soba which is used as a conjunction and a preposition with the meanings 'while', 'when' or 'since'. Thus, it turns a single complex sentence as follows:

> ደንገጽኩ፡ ጥቀ፡ ሶበ፡ ርኢኩ፡ አንበሳ።
>
> *dangaṣ-ku ṭəqqa soba rəʾiku ʾanbasā*

<V:Perf.1c.s> <Adv> <Prep> <V:Perf.1c.s> <NCom:unm.s.Acc>

'I was very scared when I saw a lion'.

According to the tradition, the main reason why the group is particularly called '*Abiyy 'Aggabāb*' is that every verb to which any element of the group is attached cannot stand by itself as a main verb in a sentence.[1] This is in fact clear since a verb to which any linguistic element of the group gets attached is actually part of a subordinate clause, and not part of the main clause as we have already seen in the given example above.

1.2.2. Nəʿus 'Aggabāb

The adjective *nəʿus* shows inferiority; it means 'little', 'small', 'tiny' and 'mini'. So, it is supposed to mean 'The inferior ACPPIP element'. In a modern linguistic approach, this group is like a bundle of several lexical categories because it comprises adverbs, conjunctions, interrogative pronouns, interjections, and particles (interrogative, negative, vocative, causal and all other types of particles) together.[2]

A characteristic feature of this group is that many of the adjectival and nominal derivations can form one of its elements especially those which are used as adverbs as long as the vowel 'a' is added to them at the end (e.g.: ሕሰው *ḥəssəw* → ሕሰወ *ḥəssəwa*, ሐሰት *ḥassat* → ሐሰተ *ḥassata*)[3]. In such a way, some schools collect an extravagant number of adverbial elements under this section. For the precise accomplishment of this work, I had to single out the adverbial elements which are recognized by the majorities of the schools by collating the most used ones using the available handwritten copies as references. Finally, I just took one hundred thirty-five recognizable elements which are studied in the section of *Nəʿus 'Aggabāb*. Even this

---

[1] Alemayehu Moges 1957, 95; Moreno 1949, 45; Kidāna Wald Kəfle 1955, 86; Yətbārak Maršā 202, 154.

[2] Moreno 1949, 48.

[3] This is to indicate that many of the elements in this group are used in their accusative form.

number causes the group to be recognized as larger than the remaining two groups in terms of a large number of elements.

According to the tradition, the reason why the elements are called '*Nə'us 'Aggabāb*' is not because the elements have less value in the language. There are two reasons for that.

First, apart from the elements with a single character such as ሁ *hu*, ሂ *hi*, መ *ma*, ሰ *sa*, ሶ *so*, ኑ *nu*, ኒ *ni*, አ *ā*, ኢ *'i*, ወ *wa*, የ *ya* and ዮ *yo*, the elements of the group are not attached to verbs or nouns; but rather each occurs alone.

Second, the elements make sentences more expressive and informative by providing ideas about when, where and how incidents happen. But, they do not play any role in making a subordinate clause like the elements in the previous group. That is why all the elements as well as the group itself are acknowledged as *Nə'us 'Aggabāb*.[1]

1.2.3. Daqiq 'Aggabāb

This is the third and the last major group of ACPPIP elements which can be just considered as equivalent to the lexical category of preposition in a modern linguistic approach.

In terms of the number of elements, it takes the second position next to the second group with fifty-one linguistic elements. The word *daqiq* which is etymologically related with the verb ደቀ *daqqa* or ደቀቀ *daqaqa* 'be small' has almost the same conceptual meaning as *Nə'us*. It expresses inferiority. Thus, it can be translated exactly as 'The small ACPPIP element'. However, the concept of inferiority is not concerned with importance and value of the elements. It rather depends on the use and role that they play in a sentence.

The elements of the group are employed being combined with nouns and numerals, but they can neither be attached to verbs directly nor have any influence on a verb. These are the main reasons for the elements to be identified as *daqiq* (lit.: 'little', 'small', 'inferior').

Etymologically, more than half of the elements have clear affiliations with various verbs. They are used as prepositional elements

---

[1] Alemayehu Moges 1957, 99; Kidāna Wald Kəfle1955, 87.

with different meanings.[1] This can also be considered as one of the peculiarities of the elements involved in the group.

Finally, the entire ACPPIP elements which are studied in the study of *'Aggabāb* are provided in the separate tables, according to their own classes. The classification depends on common uses and grammatical functions of the elements in consideration of the following characteristics that the elements keep as standards.

1.3. DIVISION OF *'AGGABĀB* FROM THE PERSPECTIVE OF LINGUISTICS

1.3.1. Adverbs

This lexical category comprises of the linguistic elements which are used to modify verbs or adjectives, occurring alone just before or after them.

1.3.2. Conjunctions

The linguistic elements that are mainly used to make a link between words, phrases, clauses or sentences by keeping a direct or an indirect attachment to verbs are involved in this lexical category. Among the elements of the category, only four individual elements namely, *'akkonu*, *'allā*, *bāḥəttu* and *dā'əmu* can occur alone. This is a common feature they share in how they play their role as conjunctions.

1.3.3. Prepositions

This lexical category consists of the elements that can be attached to nouns, pronouns, adjectives, and numerals to indicate the relationship between them and the verb in a sentence.

1.3.4. Relative Pronouns

This sub-lexical category consists of only three elements that are used to give extra information about the subject or the object in a sentence, and to make a connection between relative and main clauses being attached to verbs. These are namely *'əlla*, *'ənta* and *za*.

---

[1] Moreno 1949, 48.

1.3.5. Interrogative Pronouns

The elements involved in this sub-lexical category are the elements that are used to ask questions with the meanings who, whom, what and which, occurring alone in a sentence.

1.3.6. Interjections

The elements that are used to express an emotion such as sadness, happiness, surprise, disagreement, uncertainty as well as a sensation of pain are sorted in this lexical category.

1.3.7. Particles

In this lexical category are comprised different linguistic elements that are used as interrogative, affirmative, vocative, negative and accusative particles as well as the particles of uncertainty and supplication. The elements that serve to indicate the genitive relation of nouns and the elements that are attached to verbs or nouns at the end to make stress are also involved in the category.

Now, we move to the tables provided in the same arrangement exposed above. There is no special reason for such an arrangement of the lexical categories. It is intended simply to have the categories with a huge number of elements at the top of the list. Hence, the categories of Adverbs, conjunctions and prepositions which embrace more than 80 % of the total number of the entire ACPPIP elements have been arranged in the first places respectively; then, follow the remaining categories of pronouns (Relative and Interrogative pronouns), interjections and particles. Notice that some elements are involved in two or more categories due to their various functionalities.

1.4. ADVERBIAL ELEMENTS ACCORDING TO THE TRADITION OF *'AGGABĀB*

This category is compared to the second group of *'Aggabāb* called *Nə'us 'Aggabāb* which comprises all the elements involved in the category.

1.4.1. Adverbs of Place and Direction

ህየ *həyya* 'there'
ለፌ *lafe* 'at this side'
ላዕለ *lāʿəla* 'above'
ላዕሉ *lāʿəlu* 'above'
ላዕሊተ *lāʿəlita* 'upward'
መንጸረ *manṣara* 'forwardly
ታሕተ *tāḥta* 'under', 'downward'

ታሕቱ *tāḥtu* 'under'
ታሕቲተ *tāḥtita* 'downwardly'
ትርአሰ *tər'asa* 'at the head'
ትርጋጸ *tərgāṣa* 'at the foot'
አንጻረ *'anṣāra* 'forwardly'
ከሃ *kahā* 'there'
ከዋላ *kawālā* 'behind'
ኵለሄ *kʷəllahe* 'everywhere'
ዝየ *zəya* 'here'

1.4.2. Adverbs of Time

ለዝሉፉ *lazəlufu* 'always'
ለፌ *lafe* 'afterward'
ሳኒታ *sānita* 'on the next day'
ቀዳሚ *qadāmi* 'firstly', 'earlier'
ቀዲሙ *qadimu* 'in the beginning', 'earlier'
ቅድመ *qədma* 'before'
ቅድም *qədm* 'before'
ትማልም *təmāləm* 'yesterday', 'earlier'
ትካት *təkāt* 'in ancient time'
አሚረ *'amira* 'at a time'
አቅዲሙ *'aqdimu* 'earlier'
ከመ *kəmma* 'the same'
ወትረ *watra* 'every day'
ውቱረ *wəttura* 'every day'
ዘልፈ *zalfa* 'always'
ዘልፍ *zalf* 'every day'
ይእዜ *yə'əze* 'today', 'now'
ዮም *yom* 'today'
ደኃሪ *daḫāri* 'later'
ድኅረ *dəḫra* 'later'
ጌሠም *geśam* 'tomorrow', 'next time'
ግሙራ *gəmurā* 'ever'

1.4.3. Interrogative Adverbs

ማእዜ *mā'əze* 'when'
ስፍን *səfn* 'how often/ much'
ቦኑ *bonu* 'indeed?'
አይቴ *'ayte* 'where'
እስፍንቱ *'əsfəntu* 'how much' or 'how many'
እፎ *'əffo* 'how'

1.4.4. Other Adverbs

ሕቀ *ḥəqqa* 'a little'
መቅድመ *maqdəma* 'firstly
መፍትው *maftəw* 'right'
ምስብዒተ *məsbə'ita* 'sevenfold'
ምክብዒተ *məkbə'ita* 'doubly'
ምዕረ *mə'ra* 'once'
ሠናየ *śannāya* 'rightly'
ርቱዐ *rətu'a* 'correctly'
ርቱዕ *rətu'ə* 'worthy'
ስብአ *səb'a* 'completely'
ቈልቈሊተ *qʷəlqʷlita* 'downward'
በሕቁ *baḥəqqu* 'extreemly'
በምልዑ *baməl'u* 'fully'
በከ *bakka* 'idly'
ባሕቲቱ *bāḥtitu* 'alone', 'only'
ብዙኀ *bəzuḫa* 'abundantly'
ብዝኀ *bəzḫa* 'largly'
ኅባሬ *ḫubāre* 'unitedly'

ኅቡረ *ḫəbura* 'together'
ኅቡዐ *ḫəbuʿa* 'in secret'
ኅዳጠ *ḫədāṭa* 'a little'
ንስቲተ *nəstita* 'slightly'
አሐተኔ *'aḥattane* 'together'
አማን *'amān* 'right'
አምጣነ *'amṭāna* 'in average'
እሙነ *'əmuna* 'truely'
እምድሩ *'əmmədru* 'completely'
እስኩ *'əsku* 'let...'
እንከ *'ənka* 'then', 'now on'
ከንቱ *kantu* 'in vain'
ካዕበ *kāʿəba* 'again'
ክሡተ *kəśuta* 'plainly'
ክቡተ *kəbuta* 'secretly'
ውኁደ *wəḫuda* 'a little'
ወድአ *waddə'a* 'fully'
ዐውደ *ʿawda* 'around'
ዓዲ *ʿādi* 'again', 'yet'
ዕራቁ *ʿərāqu* 'alone'
ይሙነ *yəmuna* 'abundantly'
ዮጊ *yogi* 'yet'
ገሀደ *gahada* 'openly'
ገጸ *gaṣṣa* 'face to face'
ግብር *gəbr* 'must'
ግብተ *gəbta* 'suddenly'
ደርገ *darga* 'jointly'
ዳግመ *dāgəma* 'again'
ድልወት *dəlwat* 'worthy'
ድርገተ *dərgata* 'conjointly'
ድቡተ *dəbbuta* 'in secret'
ድኅሪተ *dəḫrita* 'backwardly'
ጥንቁቀ *ṭənquqa* 'carefully'
ጥዩቀ *ṭəyyuqa* 'prudently'
ጥቀ *ṭəqqa* 'absolutely'
ጽመ *ṣəmma* 'silently'
ጽሚተ *ṣəmmita* 'in secret'
ጽምሚተ *ṣəməmita* 'secretly'
ፈድፋደ *fadfāda* 'very', 'extremely'
ፍጡነ *fəṭuna* 'quickly'
ፍጹመ *fəṣṣuma* 'absolutely'

1.5. CONJUNCTIONAL ELEMENTS ACCORDING TO THE TRADITION OF *'AGGABĀB*

1.5.1. Copulative conjunctions

ሂ *hi* 'also' ኒ *ni* 'also' ወ *wa* 'and'

1.5.2. Causal conjunctions

አምጣነ *'amṭāna* 'for, since'
አኮኑ *'akkonu* 'because'
እስመ *'əsma* 'for the reason that'

1.5.3. Temporal conjunctions

መዋዕለ *mawāʿla* 'at that time that'
ሰዐ *saʿa* 'at the time that'
ሰዐተ *saʿata* 'at the time'

ሶበ *soba* 'in the event that'
አመ *'ama* 'when'
ዕለተ *'əlata* 'at the day that'
ጊዜ *gize* 'when'
ቅድመ *qədma* 'before'
አመ *'ama* 'when'
እስከ *'əska* 'until'
እንዘ *'ənza* 'while'
ዐመተ *'amata* 'at the year that'
እስከ *'əska* 'until'
ድኅረ *dəḫra* 'after'

1.5.4. Adversative Conjunctions

ሰ *sa* 'but'
ባሕቱ *bāḥəttu* 'however'
አላ *'allā* 'on the contrary'
ዳእሙ *dā'əmu* 'nonetheless'

1.5.5. Disjunctive Conjunctions

ሚመ *mimma* 'or, otherwise'
አው *'aw* 'or'

1.5.6. Consecutive Conjunctions

በዘ *baza* 'that'
ከመ *kama* 'that', 'so that

1.5.7. Place Conjunctions

መንገለ *mangala* 'where'
ኀበ *ḫaba* 'where'

1.5.8. Conjunctions of Condition

እመ *'əmma* 'if'
ወእደ *wa'əda* 'if'

1.5.9. Other Conjunctions

ህየንተ *həyyanta* 'instead'
ለ *la* 'let...'
መጠነ *maṭana* 'as much as'
በቀለ *baqala* 'instead'
በእንተ *ba'ənta* 'for', 'since'
በይነ *bayna* 'since', 'because'
ብሂል *bəhil* 'meaning'
ተውላጠ *tawlāṭa* 'in place of'
አርአያ *'ar'ayā* 'as'
እም *'əm* 'rather'
እንበለ *'ənbala* 'without'
እንበይነ *'ənbayna* 'because'
ዐቅመ *'aqma* 'in the degree that'
ፍዳ *fəddā* 'in charge of'

1.6. PREPOSITIONAL ELEMENTS ACCORDING TO THE TRADITION OF *'AGGABĀB*

1.6.1. Place preposition

ላዕለ *lā'əla* 'above', 'over'
መልዕልተ *mal'əlta* 'upon'

መቅድመ *maqdəma* 'before'
መትሕተ *matḥəta* 'under'
መንገለ *mangala* 'to'
ማእከለ *mā'əkala* 'between'
ማዕዶተ *mā'ədota* 'beyond'
ቅድመ *qədma* 'before'
ታሕተ *tāḥta* 'under'
ትርአሰ *tər'asa* 'at the head of'
ትርጋጸ *tərgāṣa* 'at the foot of'
ኀበ *ḫaba* 'to'
አንጻረ *'anṣāra* 'in front of'
አፍአ *'af'ā* 'outside'
እስከ *'əska* 'till', 'to'
እንተ *'ənta* 'to'
ከዋላ *kawālā* 'after'
ውስተ *wəsta* 'in'
ውስጠ *wəsṭa* 'in'
ውሳጢተ *wəsāṭita* 'in'
ውሳጤ *wəsāṭe* 'in'
ዐውደ *'awda* 'around'
ገቦ *gabo* 'near'
ጎረ *gora* 'near'
ዲበ *diba* 'above', 'upon'
ድኅረ *dəḫra* 'after', 'behind'
ጥቃ *ṭəqā* 'near'

1.6.2. Prepositions of Time

ሳኒታ *sānitā* 'on the next day of'
ሶበ *soba* 'when'
አመ *'ama* 'on'
አፈ *'afa* 'around', 'at'
ዕድሜ *'ədme* 'in the age of'
ጊዜ *gize* 'during'
ፍና *fənnā* 'at', 'around'

1.6.3. Comparative Prepositions

መጠነ *maṭana* 'in the degree of'
አምሳለ *'amsāla* 'in the form of'
አምጣነ *'amṭāna* 'similar to'
አርአያ *'ar'ayā* 'like'
አያተ *'ayāta* 'in the manner of'
እም *'əm* 'from'
ከመ *kama* 'like'

1.6.4. Other Prepositions

ህየንተ *həyyant*a 'instead of'
ለ *la* 'to'
ምስለ *məsla* 'together'
በ *ba* 'in', 'by'
በእንተ *ba'ənta* 'for', 'about'
በይነ *bayna* 'about', 'for'
እንበይነ *'ənayna* 'about', 'for'
ቤዛ *bezā* 'for', 'in ransom of'
ተከለ *takla* 'instead of'
ተውላጠ *tawlāṭa* 'in place of'
እንበለ *'ənbala* 'without'

1.7. Relative and Interrogative Pronouns according to *'Aggabāb*

1.7.1. Relative Pronouns

እለ *ʾəlla* 'who', 'which', 'that'
እንተ *ʾənta* 'who', 'which', 'that'
ዘ *za* 'who', 'which', 'that'

1.7.2. Interrogative Pronouns

መኑ *mannu* 'who'
ሚ *mi* 'what', 'which'
ምንት *mənt* 'what'
አይ *ʾay* 'what', 'which'

1.8. Interjections according to the Tradition of *'Aggabāb*

ሰይ *say* 'woo!'
አህ *ʾah* 'ah!'
አሌ *ʾalle* 'woo!'
እንቋዕ *ʾənqʷāʿ* 'aha!'
ወይ *way* 'woo!'
ወይሌ *wayle* 'woo!'
ዬ *ye* 'woo!'

1.9. Particles according to the Tradition of *'Aggabāb*

1.9.1. Interrogative Particles

ሁ *hu* 'is…?', 'shall…?'
ኑ *nu* 'is…?', 'shall…?'

1.9.2. Affirmative Particles

እወ *ʾəwwa* 'yes', 'yeah'
ጓ *gʷā* 'certainly'
ኦሆ *ʾoho* 'ok'

1.9.3. Presentational particles

ነያ *nayā* 'now', 'behold'
ነዋ *nawā* 'now', 'behold'
ናሁ *nāhu* 'now', 'behold'

1.9.4. Particles of uncertainty

እንዳዒ *ʾəndāʿi* 'not sure'
እንጋ *ʾəngā* 'maybe'

1.9.5. Vocative particles: ኦ *'o* 'o!'

1.9.6. Particles of supplication: እግዚኦ *'əgzi'o* (please)

1.9.7. Negative Particles

አል *'al* 'not, non-'	ኢ *'ī* 'non-', 'un-'
አኮ *'akko* 'not'	እንብ *'ənb* 'no'

1.9.8. Accusative Particle: ሃ *ha*

1.9.9. Particles indicating genitive relation

ለ *la* 'of...'	እንተ *'ənta* 'of...'
እለ *'əlla* 'of...'	ዘ *za* 'of...'

1.9.10. Other Particles

These all are particles to make stress:

መ *ma*	ኣ *'ā*	ዮ yo
ሰ *sa*	ኬ *ke*	
ሶ *so*	ያ *ya*	

As a result of studying these sections of the grammar study, students will be able to know the origin, importance and use of each element arranged in the table as well as the difference between the primary and secondary features and roles of the elements that are explicitly used as either conjunctions and prepositions or adverbs and prepositions.

1.10. ON THE AUTHORSHIP OF *'AGGABĀB*

Many scholarly researches affirm that Gəʿəz is one of the most ancient Semitic languages that had been spoken in Ethiopia for several centuries even before the introduction of Christianity until the third quarter of thirteenth century CE.[1] However, it is difficult to trace back to the actual time when it began to be studied in a formal

[1] "Gəʿəz", *EAe*, II (2005), 732 (S. Weninger).

school as well as in the Church as one of the usual ecclesiastical educations as it occurs today.

Indeed, a large number of literary productions whether original local compositions or translations that have been done before and after its replacement by Amharic, the contemporary official court-language around 1270 CE, would testify that a persistent study of the language had been running without interruption. It was also the prominent language of Ethiopian literature until the Amharic literature was well introduced in nineteenth century.

Moreover, the replacement of the language by Amharic is expected to be one of the paramount factors for the growth of Gəʿəz study from thirteenth century onward.

On its introduction, Meley Mulugetta stated that *Azzaž* Sinoda the royal historiographer of eighteenth century is traditionally celebrated as a composer of *Sawāsəw*. She has not mentioned which specific part he composed, but affirmed that no manuscript of *Sawāsəew* bears his name. She also indicates that the earliest *Sawāsəw* manuscripts date from seventeenth to eighteenth century, or even earlier.[1] In agreement with this, Alessandro Bausi presumed that Wansleben probably copied one *Sawāsəw* in the seventeenth century.[2] So, how could the eighteenth century historiographer compose a seventeenth or sixteenth century treatise?

However, according to the historical tradition of the *Qəne* schools, the introduction of the existing Gəʿəz grammar *'Aggabāb* goes back to the fifteenth century scholars. Concerning the introducer, the tradition held by the Gonǧ[3] scholars recognizes Tawānāy as the first introducer of both *Qəne* and *'Aggabāb* during the reign of King 'Əskəndər (1471-1494 CE) about whom it is said that he learned *Qəne* from Tawānay. The tradition states again that Tawānay visited

[1] "Sawāsəw", *EAe*, IV (2010), 562 (M. Mulugetta).

[2] "I manoscritti etiopice di J.M", RSE 33 (1989), 17 (A. Bausi).

[3] It is one of the three houses of *Qəne* which follows the philosophy and tradition of the popular *Qəne* master Tawānāy. It received the name 'Gonǧ' from Gonǧ Dabra Ṭəbab Tewodros the monastery which is located in western Goǧǧam and was the center of the house. "Gonǧ Tewodros", *EAe*, II (2005), 848 (A. Wion).

Greece. There, he learnt seven different languages. Then, on his return home, he introduced *Qəne* and *'Aggabāb.*[1]

Nevertheless, the widely accepted tradition which is followed by the Wādlā[2] scholars gives the credit to the other popular *Qəne* scholar of early fifteenth century whose name was Yohannəs of Gablon. He is also known as Yoḥannəs *Gablāwi*.

According to the scholars, Yoḥannəs had firstly recognized that the wisdom of *Qəne* was revealed to Saint Yāred after he examined his hymns that keep the basic structure of *Qəne* with the names, ሚ በዝኁ *mi-bazḫu*, ዋዜማ *wāzemā*, ሥላሴ *śəllāse*, ዘይእዜ *za-yə'əze*, መወድስ *mawaddəs*, ክብር ይእቲ *kəbr yə'əti* and ዕጣነ ሞገር *'əṭāna mogar* which are still used. Then, he spent a week alone to offer supplications toward the Lord in the town of Dabra Tābor[3] which is said to have been founded by King Yəkunno 'Amlāk (1270-1285 CE) between the provinces of Borena and Amhara Sāyənt so that the Lord might reveal the wisdom to him. Finally, he was able to compose and recite *Qəne*. At the same time, he authored and introduced the grammar. His immediate successor was *'Abbā* Walda Gabrə'el who was succeeded later by Śamra 'Ab. Śamra 'Ab was also one of the most influential scholars to whom the development of *Qəne* is attributed in collaboration with king Ba'da Māryām (1448-1478 CE).

After Śamra 'Ab, his first and second successors Ləhib and 'Elyāb have acquired the responsibility and dignity of the *Qəne* master one after the other. After 'Elyāb, his pupils *Dədq* Walda Māryām and Tawānay have been teaching both subjects jointly. But later when the Christian kingdom of Ethiopia lost power to control the

---

1 'Admāsu Ǧambare1970, 11.

2 It is the one and perhaps the leading house of *Qəne* which follows the tradition of *Dədq* Walda Māryām. The house received its name from its former center which is located in Amḥarā Sāyənt of Wallo. There is no more a well-established *Qəne* school today in the place, but a lot of *Qəne* schools in different parts of the country would always bear the name as long as they follow the tradition and philosophy of the house.

3 It is different from the famous town of Dabra Tābor which is located in Bagemədr and is said to have been founded in the first decade of nineteenth century by Ras Gugsa Maršā. "Dabra Tābor", *EAe*, II (2005), 50. (R. Pankhurst).

country because of Ahmad Ibn Ibrāhim's[1] Jihad,[2] they left their places. *Dədq* Walda Māryām moved to Yačạraqā which is located in Dāwənt and continued teaching. But Tawānay entered the island of Daqq 'Əsṭifā in lake Tānā and stayed there until the time when the persecution ceased as a result of Grañ Ahmad's death in 1537 CE.

When he returned after fifteen years, he only preserved *Qəne* while disregarding the grammatical teachings. At that time, his teacher (Ɛlyāb) was not alive. He felt inferior to be trained by his fellow. Thus, he could not repair it at all, and simply continued teaching focusing on *Qəne*. The scholars would mention this as the main factor why a very short grammar is available in the *Qəne* house of Gonǧ which is believed to be founded by Tawānay.

The tradition tells again that the school founded by *Dədq* Walda Māryām flourished more, and his six successors had received the scholarly title ድ:ድ:ቅ *dədq*[3] to remember him, also to honor their intelligence and efficiency comparing it with that of their master. It affirms again that at the time of the sixth *Dədq*, there had been introduced about seven diverse *'Aggabāb* and *Rəbā qəmr* due to the expansion of the schools. Nonetheless, every school keeps just one *'Aggabāb* as a standardized manual for the grammar lessons. Some differences might occur among the scholars at any time. The difference is gradually decreasing; it seems that the schools attempt to nar-

1 Gəraň 'Ahmad.

2 1522-1537 CE.

3 Both *Liqa Ṭabbabt* 'Aklila Bərhān Walda Qirqos and *Mal'āka Bərhan* 'Admāsu Ǧambare recognized it as a scholarly title in expression of great intelligence, cleverness and shrewdness as to say 'smart', 'clever', 'intelligent' and 'winner'. Admāsu Ǧambare 1970, 11; 'Aklila Bərhān Walda Qirqos 1950, 18. However, it is not clear that in which language the word means 'clever' or 'intelligent'. To be frank, such a title or a mere word does not exist in modern Amharic. There is in fact the same word in Gəʿəz, but its meaning is totally different from what the scholars claimed. In Gəʿəz ድ:ድ:ቅ *dədq* is a noun which does have an etymological relation with the verb ተዳደቀ/ ደደቀ *tadādaqa/ dadaqa* 'meet', 'fight', 'endanger', 'harm'. In This respect, it means 'accident', 'bad incident', 'evil occurrence' etc. Kidāna Wald Kəfle 1955, 341; Leslau 1989, 111. So, if it is a Gəʿəz word, it will be surprising to use it as a scholarly title.

row the gap between them by exchanging and sharing ideas. Currently, the central difference is mostly concerned with number of elements involved in the lesson and with the categorization of some critical elements in different lexical categorization.

I.II. ON THE TRANSMISSION OF *'AGGABĀB*

Like the other disciplines in all ecclesiastical schools of the Ethiopian Orthodox Tewāḥədo Church, *'Aggabāb* was transmitted from generation to generation through oral lectures. It is still studied orally in face to face communication. This might be undoubtedly one of the reasons why some differences appear among the scholars. Even if a few works on Gəʿəz grammar were published by different foreign and local scholars of the language, almost all the existing schools follow still the unpublished grammar (i.e. *'Aggabāb*) which was inherited from former scholars and kept by heart. According to the tradition of the schools, it is not allowed to use handwritten copies or to take notes during the lecture.

The methodology of the schools permits only to hear the lecture attentively and try to memorize by reciting repeatedly during and after the lecture. Due to the complexity of the study, new students are not advised to take part during the session of *'Aggabāb*. The matured students who accomplished the lesson are expected to assist the master by giving tutorials for junior students. The aim is that they should not forget it soon but rather to develop their experience. Lastly, before leaving the school, they would write everything they learnt. For this reason, several handwritten copies of *'Aggabāb* can be found everywhere. Nonetheless, each handwritten copy needs to be checked in terms of quality, reliability and entirety.

Chapter Two: Review of some printed Gəʿəz Grammars

As claimed in the previous chapter, since nineteenth century onward, many scholarly works have been done by different scholars with regard to the study of Gəʿəz. In fact, some of the works are lexicons and dictionaries. But there are also some grammars dealing with different grammatical aspects of the language

To have a clear idea on the importance of studying *ʾAggabāb* and how its approaches look like in comparison with different scholarly approaches, it is good to briefly review various grammars conducted by both local and foreign scholars. Among the grammars listed earlier, the following five grammars are chosen to be under review:

1. Dillmann, C.F.A. 1907. *Ethiopic Grammar*, ed. C. Bezold (London: Williams and Norgate, 1907).
2. Conti Rossini 1941. *Grammatica elementare della lingua etiopica*, Pubblicazioni dell'Istituto per l'Oriente (Roma: Istituto per l'Oriente, 1941).
3. Tropper, J. 2002. *Altäthiopisch: Grammatik des Geʿez mit Übungstexten und Glossar*, Elementa Linguarum Orientis (Münster: Ugarit-Verlag, 2002).
4. Kidāna Wald Kəfle (*ʾAlaqā*) 1955. መጽሐፈ፡ ሰዋስው፡ ወግሥ፡ ወመዝገበ፡ ቃላት፡ ሐዲስ (*maṣḥafa sawāsəw wa-mazgaba-qālāt ḥaddis*) (Artistic Publishing press, 1955).
5. Weninger, S. 1999. *Geʿez (Classical Ethiopic)*, Languages of the World, Materials, 1, (2nd edition.) (München: Lincom Europa, 1999).

There is no particular reason for the selection of these grammars for the review. They are mostly known and used by many students and researchers in the study area, and considered as model grammars among the early and the most recent works. The review specifically focuses on the main topics of *ʾAggabāb* which are the lexical categories of adverbs, conjunctions, prepositions, interrogative and relative pronouns, interjections and various types of particles.

In terms of the number and type of ACPPIP elements that can be involved in those lexical categories, most of the printed grammars mentioned earlier keep different approaches. Moreover, some grammars exclude some of the lexical categories. Even on the way of categorizing some elements, a clear dissimilarity is perceived between the *ʾAggabāb* tradition and some of the grammarians. In some cases, a tendency to reintroduce the same elements in different way of employment by combining them with some appropriate prepositions is executed by some grammarians.

To examine some more points in detail, let us see the perspectives of these scholars individually.

2.1. ACPPIP ELEMENTS AND THEIR CLASSES ACCORDING TO AUGUST DILLMANN

The outstanding Gəʿəz grammar of August Dillmann[1] provides almost the bulk of the lexical categories provided in the previous table. Interestingly, the total number of the ACPPIP elements involved in his grammar is closer to the total number of ACPPIP elements which *ʾAggabāb* is concerned about than the number of elements in the

[1] Dillmann, Christian Friedrich August (1823 - 1894) was a German citizen Ethiopisant of the nineteenth Century. He came to the field of Ethiopian Studies after he got his PhD in Theology from the University of Tübingen in 1846. From the year 1846 - 1848, he studied the Ethiopian manuscript collections at the Libraries of London, Oxford and Paris. Then, in 1848, he became an instructor of Old Testament and Oriental Languages in Tübingen. He taught also in these fields of studies with the rank of Professor in the universities of Kiel, Gießen and Berlin until his last days. Besides, Dillmannn did a great contribution for the growth of modern day Ethiopian studies through his plentiful scholarly works. Among his enormous scholarly achievments, the following publications are mentioned: Gəʿəz Grammar, Gəʿəz Lexicon, the book of Enoch, the book of Jubilees and Job. Dillmann 1907, V-VII; "Dillmann, Christian Friedrich August", *EAe,* II (2005), 160-61 (M. Kleiner).

other grammars under review. About two hundred thirty-one ACPPIP elements are distributed into six major lexical categories as follows: (Dillman 1907, 332–338, 375–406, 410–420, 468–471).

2.1.1. Adverbial elements

As mentioned at the beginning, Dillmann's list of the Adverbial elements has a larger number of elements than all the remaining lists provided in this chapter, including the Adverbs' list of *ʾAggabāb*.

Nonetheless, some differences regarding types of elements is clearly observed between Dillmann's grammar and *ʾAggabāb*.

Under the same category, Dillmann has provided one hundred thirty-one elements while the total number of Adverbial elements comprised in *ʾAggabāb* is ninety-seven. Furthermore, the elements included in Dillmann are not always identical with the elements in *ʾAggabāb*. Each provides a considerable number of elements which are not available in the other.

Precisely, Dillmann has forty-six adverbial elements which are absent in *ʾAggabāb* while *ʾAggabāb* keeps thirty-four elements which are not included in Dillmann.

2.1.1.1. Adverbs of Presentation

ነ *na* 'behold'
ነያ *nayā* 'behold'
ነዋ *nawā* 'behold her'
ናሁ *nāhu* 'behold'
እንከሙ *ʾənkəmu* 'take', 'behold'

2.1.1.2. Place and Time Adverbs

ህየ *həyya* 'there'
አሜሃ *ʾamehā* 'at that time'
ከሐ *kaḥa* 'away yonder'
ዝየ *zəya* 'here'
ይእዜ *yəʾəze* 'now'

2.1.1.3. Interrogative Adverbs

ሁ *hu* 'is...?'
መኑ *mannu* 'who'
ሚ *mi* 'what'
ሚመ *mimma* 'or?'
ማእዜ *māʾəze* 'when'
ኑ *nu* 'is...?'
ምንት *mənt* 'what'
አይ *ʾay* 'which'
አይቴ *ʾayte* 'where'
እስፍንቱ *ʾəsfəntu* 'how many'
እፎ *ʾəffo* 'how'

2.1.1.4. Other Adverbs

ህልወ *həlləwa* 'in reality'
ለዓለም *la'ālam* 'for ever'
ለዝሉፉ *lazəlufu* 'for ever'
ለዝላፉ *lazəlāfu* 'for ever'
ለፌ *lafe* 'side'
ላዕሉ *lā'əlu* 'above'
ላዕለ *lā'əla* 'above'
ሌሊተ *lelita* 'by night'
ልዑለ *lə'ula* 'upward'
ሐሰተ *ḥassata* 'falsely'
ሕቀ *ḥəqqa* 'by degrees'
መልዕልተ *mal'əlta* 'above'
መሪረ *marira* 'bitterly'
መትልወ *matləwa* 'in succession'
መትሕተ *matḥəta* 'below'
መዐልተ *ma'alta* 'by day'
መጠነ *maṭana* 'the bigness of'
ሚመጠነ *mimaṭana* 'how greatly'
ማእከለ *mā'əkala* 'in the midst'
ማዕዶተ *māa'dota* 'beyond'
ምክብዕተ *məkbə'ta* 'repeatedly'
ሠናየ *śannāya* 'well'
ርኁቀ *rəḫuqa* 'for distant'
ርቱዐ *rətu'a* 'rightly'
ሰርከ *sarka* 'in the evening'
ስንአ *sən'a* 'unanimously'
ስፍነ *səfna* 'how often'
ቀዳሚ *qadāmi* 'in the first place'
ቀዲሙ *qadimu* 'earlier'
ቅድመ *qədma* 'in front of'
ቈልቈሊተ *qʷəlqʷəlita* 'downward'
በሕሡም *ba-ḥəśum* 'miserably'
በሕቁ *ba-ḥəqqu* 'considerably'
እንዳዒ *'əndā'i* 'perhaps'
እኩየ *'əkkuya* 'badly'
ከንቱ *kantu* 'in vain'
ከዋላ *kawālā* 'behind'
ካዕበ *kā'əba* 'again'
ካዕበተ *kā'əbata* 'repeatedly'
ኵለሄ *kʷəllahe* 'in every direction'
ክዑበ *kə'uba* 'doubly'
ወትረ *watra* 'continually'
ውስጠ *wəsṭa* 'in'
ውቱረ *wəttura* 'entirely'
ዐቢየ *'abiya* 'highly'
ዐውደ *'awda* 'around'
ዓዲ *'ādi* 'yet'
ዘልፈ *zalfa* 'continually'
ዝሉፈ *zəlufa* 'continually'
ይምነ *yəmna* 'on the right hand'
ዮም *yom* 'today'
ግሙራ *gəmurā* 'wholly'
ግድመ *gədma* 'awry'
ግብተ *gəbta* 'suddenly'
ጌሠመ *geśama* 'tomorrow'
ጕንዱየ *gʷənduya* 'a long time'
ደርግ *darg* 'together'
ደቡበ *dabuba* 'northward'
ዳእሙ *dā'əmu* 'however'
ዳግመ *dāgəma* 'again'
ድሙረ *dəmmura* 'jointly'
ድሩገ *dəruga* 'at the same time'
ድኅረ *dəḫra* 'behind'
ድንጉፀ *dənguḍa* 'scaredly'
ድኅሪተ *dəḫrita* 'backward'
ጥንቁቀ *ṭənquqa* 'exactly'
ጥዩቀ *ṭəyyuqa* 'exactly'
ጥቀ *ṭəqqa* 'properly'
ጽሚተ *ṣəmmita* 'secretly'
ጽሚምተ *ṣəmimta* 'secretly'
ጽሩዐ *ṣəru'a* 'idly'
ጽኑዐ *ṣənu'a* 'strongly'
ጽፉቀ *ṣəfuqa* 'frequently'
ፅግመ *ḍəgma* 'on the left'

ፈድፋደ *fadfāda* 'very'
ፍጡነ *fəṭuna* 'quickly'
ፍጹመ *fəṣṣuma* 'perfectly'
ፍፅመ *fəḍma* 'in front'

The elements that Dillmann has uniquely are the following:

ʿabiyya 'highly'
ḫəyyula 'powerfully'
ʾaddāma 'beautifully'
kāʿəbata 'repeatedly'
ba-daḫn 'in safety'
kəʿuba 'doubly'
ba-faqād 'voluntarily'
laʿālam 'forever'
ba-fəṣṣāme 'lastly'
lelita 'by night'
ba-ḫəśum 'miserably'
ləʿula 'high'
ba-kʷəllu 'gradually'
maʿalta 'by day'
ba-kʷərh 'by constraint'
māʿədota 'beyond',
ba-nəṣuḥ 'innocently
marira 'bitterly'
ba-śannāy 'friendly'
matləwa 'in succession'
ba-ṣəbāḥ 'in the morning'
mimaṭana 'how greatly'
ba-təʿbit 'proudly'
nagha 'early in the morning'
dabuba 'northward'
nawwiḫa 'far'
dəmmura 'jointly'
nəṣuḥa 'innocently'
dənguḍa 'scaredly'
rəḫuqa 'for distant'
dəruga 'at the same time'
sarka 'in the evening'
ʾəkkuya 'badly'
ṣəfuqa 'frequently'
gədma 'awry'
ḍəgma 'on the left'.
gʷənduya 'a long time'
sənʾa 'unanimously'
ḫarifa 'this year'
ṣənuʿa 'strongly'
həlləwa 'in reality'
ṣəruʿa 'idly'
tāḥətya 'under'
təḥuta 'humbly'
tāḥtu 'under'
yəmna 'on the right hand'

Similarly, the elements included in *ʾAggabāb*, but not in Dillmann are the following:

ʾamira 'at a time'
ʾanṣāra 'forwardly'
ʾaqdimu 'before'
baməlʿu (fully)
bəzḫa 'largely'
bonu 'indeed?'
daḫāri 'later'
dəbbuta 'in secret'
dəlwat 'worthy'
dərgata 'conjointly'
ʾəmmədru 'completely'
ʾəmuna 'truly'
ʿərāqu 'alone'
gahada 'openly'
gaṣṣa 'face to face'
gəbr 'must'

ḫəbuʿa 'in secret'
ḫubāre 'unitedly'
kawālā 'behind', 'later'
kəbuta 'secretly'
kəmma 'the same'
kəśuta 'plainly'
lāʿəlita (upward)
maftəw 'right'
manṣara 'forwardly'
məʿra 'once'
məsbəʾita 'sevenfold'
sānitā 'on the next day'
səbʾa 'completely'
ṣəmma 'silently'
tərʾasa 'at the head'
tərgāṣa 'at the foot'
waddəʾa 'fully'
wəḫuda 'a little'
yəmuna 'abundantly'

Now, let us come to the next step of enquiring the approaches of *'Aggabāb* behind the unavailability of these forty-six elements in its list of adverbial elements. According to the tradition of the *Qəne* Schools, *laʿālam* 'for ever', *ba-ḥəśum* 'miserably', *ba-śannāy* 'in friendly way', *ba-təʿbit* 'proudly', *ba-nəṣuḥ* 'innocently', *ba-kʷəllu* 'gradually', *ba-kʷərh* 'by constraint', *ba-dāḫn* 'in safety', *ba-ṣəbāḥ* 'in the morning', *ba-faqād* 'voluntarily' and *bafəṣṣāme* 'lastly' are compounds of two different linguistic items (*la* + *ʿālam*, *ba* + *ḥəśum*, *ba* + *śannāy*...).

The prepositions *la* and *ba* are regularly treated for converting the nouns into adverbial phrases. In fact, like other linguistic elements, nouns are important linguistic elements in the language. However, *'Aggabāb* does not comprise them except the prepositional elements *la* and *ba* because the aim of *'Aggabāb* is to specifically deal with individual elements that are used as frequently as ACPPIP elements. Nouns are studied at the first level of the study which is called *Gəśś*.

The remaining thirty-five elements are also unrecognized as adverbial elements in the tradition of the schools unless they are considered as nouns and studied at the early level mentioned above.

2.1.2. Conjunctional elements

ሂ *hi* 'also'
መ *ma* '-'
ሚ *mi* 'how'
ሰ *sa* 'but'
ሶበ *soba* 'when'
በዘ *baza* 'while'
ባሕቱ *bāḥəttu* 'only'
ኒ *ni* 'also'
ኀበ *ḫaba* 'where'
አ *'a* '-'
አላ *'allā* 'but'
አመ *'ama* 'when'

አምጣነ *ʾamṭāna* ‘as long as’
አው *ʾaw* ‘or’
እመ *ʾəmma* ‘if’
እም *ʾəm* ‘-from’
እስመ *ʾəsma* ‘because’
እስከ *ʾəska* ‘until’
እንበለ *ʾənbala* ‘without’
እንከ *ʾənka* ‘again’
እንዘ *ʾənza* ‘while’
እንጋ *ʾəngā* ‘then indeed’
ከመ *kama* ‘that’
ኬ *ke* ‘now’
ወ *wa* ‘and’
ዘ *za* ‘that’
ዮጊ *yogi* ‘lest’
ዳእሙ *dāʾəmu* ‘rather’

Out of twenty-eight elements gathered in the Dillmann category of Conjunctions, only eight elements are not available in its equivalent category of *ʾAggabāb*. The elements are:

ʾa ‘-’,
ʾəngā ‘then indeed’
ʾənka ‘again’
ke ‘now’
ma ‘-’
mi ‘how’
yogi ‘lest’
za ‘that’

The difference depends on the way of classifying the elements. As we saw above, Dillmann has collected these elements in the category of conjunctions. But in *ʾAggabāb*, *ma, ʾa, ʾəngā* and *ke* are parts of the lexical category of Particles while *mi, ʾənka* and *yogi* are mainatined in the category of Adverbs. The actual meaning of *yogi* in *ʾAggabāb* is ‘still’, ‘yet’ and ‘again’.

The lexical function of *za* (that) as a conjunction is recognized in *ʾAggabāb* too. However, as an important element of the sub-category of Relative pronoun, all its lexical meanings and functions are studied there together with the functions of *ʾəlla* and *ʾənta*. That is why it does not appear in the equivalent category of *ʾAggabāb*.

On the other way, out of forty-four elements of the *ʾAggabāb* category of Conjunctional elements, the following fourteen elements are excluded in Dillmann.

ʿaqma ‘as’
ʾakkonu ‘because’
ʿāmata ‘at the time of’
ʾamsāla ‘as’
ʾarʾayā ‘as’
baqala ‘in stead’
bəhil ‘meaning’
ʿəlata ‘at the day of’
ʾənbayna ‘because’
gize ‘when’
maṭana ‘as much as’
mawāʿəla ‘at the time of’
tawlāṭa ‘in place of’
saʿata ‘at the time of’

2.1.3. Prepositional elements

ህየንተ *həyyanta* 'in place of'
ለ *la* 'to'
ላዕለ *lāʿəla* 'upon'
መልዕልተ *malʿəlta* 'above'
መቅድመ *maqdəma* 'before'
መትሕተ *matḥəta* 'underneath'
መንገለ *mangala* 'towards'
መንጸረ *manṣara* 'over-against'
ማእከለ *māʾəkala* 'between'
ማዕዶተ *māʿədota* 'beyond'
ምስለ *məsla* 'with'
ምእኀዘ *məʾḫaza* 'beside'
ሶበ *soba* 'when'
ቅድመ *qədma* 'before'
በ *ba* 'in'
በበይነ *babayna* 'interval'
በእንተ *baʾənta* 'about'
በዕብሬት *baʿəbret* 'because of'
ቢጸ *biṣa* 'beside'
ቤዛ *bezā* 'in ransom of-'
ተክለ *takla* 'in place of-'
ተውላጠ *tawlāṭa* 'for'
ታሕተ *tāḥta* 'under'
ኀበ *ḫaba* 'with'
አመ *ʾama* 'at the time of'
አምሳለ *ʾamsāla* 'like'
አምጣነ *ʾamṭāna* 'as long as'
አርአያ *ʾarʾayā* 'like'
አንጻረ *ʾanṣāra* 'in front of-'
አፍአ *ʾafʿā* 'outside'
እምነ *ʾəmnna* 'from'
እስከ *ʾəska* 'till'
እንበለ *ʾənbala* 'without'
እንተ *ʾənta* '-wards'
ከመ *kama* 'like'
ከዋላ *kawālā* 'behind'
ውስተ *wəsta* 'in'
ውእደ *wəʾda* 'along'
ዐውደ *ʿawda* 'around'
ጊዜ *gize* 'at that time'
ዲበ *diba* 'upon'
ድኅረ *dəḫra* 'after'
ጥቃ *ṭəqā* 'close to'
ፍና *fənnā* 'towards'
ፍዳ *fəddā* 'in charge of'

Dillmann's Category of Prepositions consists of forty-five elements while fifty-one prepositional elements are comprised in *ʾAggabāb*. The elements that are available in Dillmann but not in *ʾAggabāb* are:

baʿəbret 'because of'
biṣa 'beside'
manṣara 'over-against'
məʾḫaza 'beside'

In the tradition of *ʾAggabāb, manṣara* 'over-against' is considered as an adverbial elements and occurs alone. Thus, *ʾAggabāb* does not recognise it a preposition. As usual, the reason of the absence of *məʾḫāza, ba-ʿəbret* and *biṣa* in *ʾAggabāb* is that the schools' tradition considers them as nouns excluding the preposition *ba* which is initially added to *ʿəbret.* Even as a noun *ʿəbret* and *biṣ* are known in the tradition with the meanings 'alteration' 'turn and 'fellow' respectively. The meaning given to them in Dillmann is strange to the schools' tradition.

Contrarily, among the prepositional elements of *ʾAggabāb*, the following ten elements are not available in Dillmann:

ʾafa 'during'
ʾayāta 'like'
ʿədme 'the time of'
gabo 'near'
gora 'near'
sānitā 'on the next day'
tərʾasa 'at the head of'
tərgāṣa 'at the foot of'
wəsāṭe 'in'
wəsāṭita 'in'

2.1.4. Interjections, Relative pronouns and Particles

2.1.4.1. Interjections

ሰይል *sayl* / ሰይ *say* 'ah'
አሀ *ʾah* 'ah'
አ *ʾa* '-'
አሌ *ʾalle* 'woe'
አዒ *ʾaʿi* 'come'
እንቋዕ *ʾənqwāʿ* 'ha!'
ሰይል *sayl* / ሰይ *say* 'ah'
አሀ *ʾah* 'ah'
አ *ʾa* '-'
አሌ *ʾalle* 'woe'
አዒ *ʾaʿi* 'come'
እንቋዕ *ʾənqwāʿ* 'ha!'
ከመ *kəmma* 'thus'
ወይ *way* 'woe'
ወይሌ *wayle* 'howling'
ዬ *ye* 'Alas'
ዮ *yo* 'Alas'
ጸጥ *ṣaṭṭ* 'call to silence'

2.1.4.2. Relative Pronouns

እለ *ʾəlla* 'who'
እንተ *ʾənta* 'who'
ዘ *za* 'who'

2.1.4.3. Particles

2.1.4.3.1. Affirmative Particles

ሶ *so* 'now'
እወ *ʾəwwa* 'yes'
አሆ *ʾoho* 'Oh'
እስኩ *ʾəsku* 'o now!'

2.1.4.3.2. Negative Particles

አልቦ *ʾalbo* 'no'
አኮ *ʾakko* 'not'
ኢ *ʾi* 'not'
እንብየ *ʾənbəya* 'no'

2.1.4.3.3. Particles indicating Genitive Relation

ለ *la* 'of-'	እንተ *'ənta* 'of-'
እለ *'əlla* '-of'	ዘ *za* 'of-'

In the category of Relative Pronoun as well as in the sub-category of Particles indicating a genitive relation, there is no difference between Dillmann and *'Aggabāb*; both provide the similar number and kinds of elements. On the contrary, the sub-category of Interrogative Pronoun which is part of the lexical category of Pronouns in the *'Aggabāb* tradition is excluded in Dillmann since the elements that can be provided under it *'ay* 'which', 'what', *mannu* 'who', *mənt* 'what', 'which' are already mentioned in the category of Adverbs.

Again, the elements *kəmma* and *yo* included in the category of Interjections, in the *'Aggabāb* tradition, are categorised into the categories of Adverbs and Particles respectively. There is also a semantic difference between them in the case of *kəmma*. In Dillmann, it keeps the meaning 'thus' as it can be seen from the table while *'Aggabāb* confirms it as 'always', 'ever'. On the element አዒ *'a'i* 'come' *'Aggabāb* is unaware. ጸጥ *ṣaṭṭ* 'silence!' is treated as a noun, it mostly goes with various forms of the verb ብህለ *bəhla* 'say'.

The other difference which is observed in the category of Particles is that the interrogative particles *hu* 'is...?', 'shall...?' and ኑ *nu* 'is...?', 'shall...?', *gʷā* 'certainly' which is initially particle of certainity and the particle of supplication *'əgzi'o* 'please' that involve in *'Aggabāb* are not available in Dillmann. Yet, *'əsku* 'let...' which is an adverbial element in *'Aggabāb* keeps a different meaning and function in Dillmann ('thus', affirmative Particle). In the case of the remaining elements, both share almost similar approaches.

2.2. ACPPIP ELEMENTS AND THEIR CLASSES ACCORDING TO CARLO CONTI ROSSINI

Carlo Conti Rossini[1] who was one the prominent Ethiopisants of the late nineteenth and twentieth Century, has dealt with the grammatical functions of several ACPPIP elements in his grammar. The number of the elements involved in his grammar is relatively smaller than the number of ACPPIP elements included in *'Aggabāb* and also in Dillmann.

Nevertheless, he provides one hundred eighteen elements in ten classes as follows (Conti Rossini 1939, 17-27, 86-107, 119-124, 134):

2.2.1 Adverbial elements

ሀየ *həyya* 'there'
ምዕረ *məʿra* 'once'
ለፌ *lafe* 'this side'
ላዕለ *lāʿəla* 'above', 'over'
ታሕተ *tāḥta* 'under'
ሕቀ *ḥəqqa* 'little'
መቅድመ *maqdəma* 'before'
ማእዜ *māʾəze* 'when'
ሶቤሃ *sobehā* 'at that time'
ቀዲሙ *qadimu* 'earlier', 'in the beginning'
አይቴ *ʾayte* 'where'
ከሐ *kaḥa* 'over there'
ከመ *kama* 'like'
ዓዲሁ *ʿādihu* 'yet'
ዘልፈ *zalfa* 'always'
ዝየ *zəya* 'here'
ጌሠመ *geśama* 'tomorrow'
ይእዜ *yəʾəze* 'today'
ቅድመ *qədma* 'before'
ባሕቲቱ *bāḥtitu* 'alone'
ብዙኀ *bəzuḫa* 'much'
ትማልም *təmāləm* 'yesterday'
ኅቡረ *ḫəbura* 'together'
ንስቲተ *nəstita* 'a little'
አሐተኔ *ʾaḥattane* 'together'
አሜሃ *ʾamehā* 'at that time'
አምጣነ *ʾamṭāna* 'as much as'
ዮም *yom* 'now', 'today'
ዮጊ *yogi* 'yet'
ድኅረ *dəḫra* 'later'
ጥቀ *ṭəqqa* 'very'
ጽሚተ *ṣəmmita* 'silently'
ጽሚምተ *ṣəmimta* 'secretly'
ፈድፋደ *fadfāda* 'abundantly'

This list consists of thirty-four adverbial elements. Except *ʾamehā* 'at that time' *sobehā* 'at that time', and *kama* 'like', all the lements are

---

[1] 1872-1949. He was born in North Italy and learned law at the University of Rome at which he became later a professor of History and Languages of Abyssinia in 1920. His office as a Director of Civil Affairs in the local Italian administration in Eritrea between the time 1899 and 1903 gave him a good opportunity to study better the languages and cultures of Ethiopia. He also acquired a chance to collect and search various manuscripts. He edited and translated several chronicles and hagiographical texts such as Gadla ʾAnorewos, Gadla Filip̣os, Gadla Yoḥannəs and the chronicle of Sarṣa Dəngəl etc. These and his many other scholarly contributions regarding literary heritages, traditions and different Semitic and non-Semitic languages of Ethiopia make him considered as one of the most prominent figures in the history of modern Ethiopian studies. "Conti Rossini, Carlo", *EAe*, I (2003) 791-92 (L. Ricci).

present in the same lexical category of *'Aggabāb*. In the case of *sobehā* and *'amehā*, the *'Aggabāb* tradition does not deny their functionality as Adverbs in such a way. Nevertheless, they are still categorized as Conjunctions and Prepositions without the suffixation of *hā* as *soba* and *'ama*. Similarly, the suffixation of *hu* to *'ādi* 'yet' is not shown at the first stage in *'Aggabāb* unless it can be rendered while realizing the suffixations of Determining Particles.

The involvement of ከመ *kama* 'like' in the category of Adverbs is not clear at all because its function is to be used as either a Conjunction or a Preposition, but not as an Adverb. In all other cases, Conti Rossini's list of Adverbs provides elements in more similar ways to *'Aggabāb* though it puts aside seventy-two adverbial elements from the *'Aggabāb* list of Adverbial elements. This will be shown soon in the final table at the end of the chapter. When we compare it with the same list proposed by Dillmann, we find it shorter since Dillmann's list of Adverbial elements comprises ninety-seven elements more. However, apart from *mə'ra* 'once', all elements provided in Conti Rossini are present in Dillmann without serious orthographic or semantic dissimilarities.

Conti Rossini's special focus on the non-derivational elements is supposed to be the main reason for the occurrence of such a huge difference between them. Because he did not intend to render many nominal derivations such as *lə'ula* 'high', *marira* 'bitterly', *'abiyya* 'highly', *gʷənduya* 'a long time' time', *yəmna* 'on the right hand', *ḍəgma* 'on the left' and *dabuba* 'northward' etc. ... in his lexical category of Adverbs as it has been done in Dillmann.

He also did not attempt to introduce some adverbial elements by combining certain prepositions, especially '*ba*' with nouns as Dillmann had already done.

2.2.2 Conjunctional elements

ሂ *hi* 'and', 'also'
ለ *la* 'to'
መ *ma* '-'
ሰ *sa* 'but'
ሶበ *soba* 'when'
በዘ *baza* 'that'
ቅድመ *qədma* 'before'

ባሕቱ *bāḥəttu* 'but'
ኀበ *ḫaba* 'where'
ኒ *ni* 'and', 'also'
አላ *'allā* 'but'
አው *'aw* 'or'
አመ *'ama* 'when'
አምጣነ *'amṭāna* 'since'

እመ *ʾəmma* 'if'
እም *ʾəm* 'from'
እምዘ *ʾəmza* 'as'
እስመ *ʾəsma* 'because'
እስከ *ʾəska* 'until'
እንተ *ʾənta* 'which'
እንበለ *ʾənbala* 'without'
እንከ *ʾənka* 'now on'
እንዘ *ʾənza* 'while'
እፎ *ʾəffo* 'how'
ከመ *kama* 'so that'
ኬ *ke* '-'
ወ *wa* 'and'
ወሚመ *wamimma* 'otherwise'
ድኅረ *dəḫra* 'after'
ዳእሙ *dāʾəmu* 'but'

Except *ma* '-', *ʾəffo* 'how', *ʾənka* 'now on' and *ke* '-', all the conjunctional elements involved in the list are available in *ʾAggabāb* too. According to the *ʾAggabāb* tradition, *ʾəffo* and *ʾənka* are parts of the category of Adverbs while *ma* and *ke* are considered as particles. The initial *wa* in *wa-mimma* is also not originally part of the ACPPIP element *mimma*.

Finally, on one hand, the list (of thirty elements) is smaller than its equivalent category of *ʾAggabāb* (forty-four elements) by fourteen elements. The elements are the same conjunctional elements that are excluded in Dillmann too, including *mangala*, *həyyanta*, *baʾənta*, *ʿādi* and *fəddā*. On the other hand, it is longer than Dillmann's list of Conjunctions (twenty-eight) by two elements. Beside the number of elements, it maintains the following seven elements that are not available in Dillmann:

dəḫra 'after'
ʾəmza 'as'
ʾəffo 'how'
la 'to'
ni 'and' and. 'also'
qədma 'before'
wamimma

Likewise, Dillmann also has seven elements which are excluded in Conti Rossini. They are as follows:

ʾa '-'
ʾənbala 'without'
ʾəngā 'indeed'
ma '-'
mi 'how'
yogi 'lest'.
za 'that'

2.2.3 Prepositional elements according to Conti Rossini

ሀየንተ *həyyanta* 'in stead of'
ለ *la* 'to'
ለዓለመዓለም *laʿālamaʿālam* 'forever'
ላዕለ *lāʿəla* 'above', 'over'

መልዕልተ *mal'əlta* 'above'
መቅድመ *maqdəma* 'before'
መትሕተ *matḥəta* 'under'
መትልወ *matləwa* 'next'
መንገለ *mangala* 'to'
ምስለ *məsla* 'together'
ማእከለ *mā'əkala* 'between'
ማዕዶተ *mā'ədota* 'beyond'
ሶበ *soba* 'when'
ቅድመ *qədma* 'before'
በ *ba* 'in', 'by'
በይነ *bayna* 'for', 'instead of'
በእንተ *ba'ənta* 'because of'
ተክለ *takla* 'instead of'
ታሕተ *tāḥta* 'under'
ኀበ *ḫaba* 'to'
አመ *'ama* 'when'
አምሳለ *'amsāla* 'like'
አንጻረ *'anṣāra* 'in front of'
እም *'əm* 'from'
እስከ *'əska* 'until'
እንበለ *'ənbala* 'without'
እንተ *'ənta* 'to'
ከመ *kama* 'like'
ውስተ *wəsta* 'in', 'to'
ዐውደ *'awda* 'around'
ዲበ *diba* 'over'
ድኅረ *dəḫra* 'after', 'behind'
ጥቃ *ṭəqā* 'near'

The number of prepositional elements maintained in the list above is fewer than the number of elements in the same categories of *'Aggabāb* and Dillmann by eighteen and twelve elements, respectively. If we compare its elements with that of *'Aggabāb*, it keeps exclusively three elements *la'alama'alam* 'forever', *maqdəma* 'before' and *matləwa* 'next'. The *'Aggabāb* tradition considers *la'ālama'ālam* as a compound of the preposition *la* and two identical nouns (*'ālam*). In fact, it does not have a negative attitude against the employment of the combination to function as an Adverb. However, in the study, each is studied alone in its own class.

Matləwa is regarded as an accusative form of the nominal *matləw* 'follower'. It is of course added to nouns like other prepositions, but it is used to express the noun before as an adjective.

Contrarily, the following twenty elements involved in *'Aggabāb* are not available in Conti Rossini's list of prepositions:

'afa 'during'
'af'ā 'outside'
'amṭāna 'like'
'ayāta 'like'
bayna 'about', 'for'
bezā 'for', 'in ransom of'
'ədme 'the time of'
fənnā 'during'
gabo 'near'
gize 'during'
gora 'near'
maṭana 'like'
sānitā 'on the next day'
tawlāṭa 'in place of'
tər'asa 'at the head of'
tərgāṣa 'at the foot of'

wəsāṭe 'in' *wəsāṭita* 'in'	*wəsṭa* 'in'

The elements included in Dillmann, which are not present in Conti Rossini are the following:

ʾafʾā 'outside' *fəddā* 'in charge of' *ʾamṭāna* 'as long as' *fənnā* 'towards' *ʾarʾayā* 'like' *kawālā* 'behind'	*baʿəbret* 'because of' *manṣara* 'over-against' *bezā* 'in ransom of-' *məʾḫaza* 'beside' *biṣa* 'beside' *tawlāṭa* 'for'

The only two elements from Conti Rossini that are not available in Dillmann are *laʿālamaʿālam* and *matləwa*. Otherwise, all the remaining elements are kept in Dillmann though there is a minor difference in providing the elements *bayna* and *ʾəm*. Dillmann has provided them as *babayna* and *ʾəmənna*. Of course, this makes no semantic difference except that it shows an attachment of additional elements to them, *ba* (*ba* + *bayna*) and *na* (*ʾəm* + *ənna*.). In this case, Conti Rossini and the *ʾAggabāb* tradition share an identical perspective.

2.2.4 Interrogative and Relative pronouns

2.2.4.1. Interrogative Pronouns

መኑ *mannu* 'who' ሚ *mi* 'what', 'which' ምንት *mənt* 'what'	አይ *ʾay* 'which' እስፍንቱ *ʾəsfəntu* 'how much'

2.2.4.2. Relative Pronouns

እለ *ʾəlla* እንተ *ʾənta*	ዘ *za* : 'who', 'which' that'

2.2.5 Interjections and Particles

2.2.5.1. Interjections

ሐሰ *ḥassa* 'wrong' ሐዊሳ *ḥawisā* 'greetings' አሌ *ʾalle* 'woe!'	ወይ *way* 'Woe!' ጸት *ṣāt* 'silence'

2.2.5.2. Vocative Particles

ኦ *'o* 'O'	እግዚኦ *'əgzi'o* 'O', 'behold'

2.2.5.3. Particles

2.2.5.3.1. Particles indicating genitive relation

ለ *la* 'of...'	ዘ *za* 'of...'

2.2.5.3.2. Interrogative Particles

ሁ *hu* 'is?'	ኑ *nu* 'is?' 'shall?'

2.2.5.3.3. Negative Particles

አኮ *'akko 'no'*	እንቢ *'ənbi* 'no'
ኢ *'i* 'not', 'un-'	

The elements provided in both tables are recognised in *'Aggabāb* except *ḥassa* 'wrong', *ḥawisā* 'greetings' and *ṣat* 'silence' that have been involved in the category of Interjections. Dillmann also did not keep the first two elements in his equivalent category. He indeed mentioned *ṣat* 'silence' in a geminated form, but it is in a different category of Prepositions. In the sub-category of Particles indicating a genitive relation, the two important elements *'əlla* and *'ənta* are excluded.

2.3. ACPPIP ELEMENTS INCLUDED IN JOSEF TROPPER'S GRAMMAR

Josef Tropper is one of the specialists of the twentieth century in Ethiopic and other Semitic languages. *Altäthiopisch: Grammatik des Ge'ez* is one of his scholarly productions in which he provided various important remarks on different linguistic aspects of Gəʿəz language.

With regard to ACPPIP elements, Tropper proposed the following one hundred seventy-nine elements in four lexical categories and sub-categories as follows (Tropper 2002, 138-53):

2.3.1 Adverbial elements

ህየ *həyya* 'there'	ለምዕር *lamə'r* 'once'
ለምንት *lamənt* 'why'	ለከንቱ፡ *lakantu* 'freely'

ለዝላፉ *lazəlāfu* 'always'
ለግሙራ *lagəmurā* 'completely'
ለፌ *lafe* 'this side'
ለፌ ወለፌ *lafe walafe* 'this and that side'
ላዕለ *lāʿəla* 'above'
ሌሊተ *lelita* 'in the night'
ሕቀ *ḥəqqa* 'a little'
ሚ *mi* 'what'
ማእዜ *māʾəze* 'when'
ምዕረ *məʿra* 'once'
ሶቤሃ *sobehā* 'at that time'
ቀዲሙ *qadimu* 'first', 'before'
ቀዳሚ *qadāmi* 'firstly'
ቀዳሚሁ *qadāmihu* 'in the beginning'
በምንት *bāmənt* 'why'
በኅዳጥ *baḫdāṭ* 'slightly'
በአማን *baʾamān* 'truly'
በእንተ፡ ምንት *baʾənta-mənt* 'why'
በእንተዝ *baʾəntazə* 'therefore'
በእንተዝንቱ *baʾənta-zəntu* 'therefore'
በከንቱ *bakantu* 'for free'
በጊዜሃ *begizehā* 'at that time'
በይነምንት *bayna-mənt* 'for what'
በይነዝ *baynazə* 'therefore'
ብዙኅ *bəzuḫ* 'many'
ትካት *təkāt* 'ancient time'
ኅዳጠ *ḫədāṭ* 'little'
ንስቲተ *nəstita* 'little'
አልቦ *ʾalbo* 'no'
አሜሁ *ʾamehu* 'at that time'
አማነ *ʾamāna* 'truly'
አሜሃ *ʾamehā* 'at that time'
አይቴ *ʾayte* 'where'
አፍአ *ʾafʿā* 'outside'
እምህየ *ʾəmhəyya* 'from there'
እምቀዲሙ *ʾəmqadimu* 'from the beginning'
እምዝ *ʾəmz* 'then'
እምድኅረዝ *ʾəmdəḫrazə* 'after that'
እምድኅረ፡ ዝንቱ *ʾəmdəḫra zənttu* 'later'
እስከ፡ ምንት *ʾəska mənt* 'what extent'
እንበይነዝ *ʾənbaynaz* 'because of this'
እንበይነዝንቱ *ʾənbayna-zənttu* 'therefore'
እንዳዒ *ʾəndāʿi* 'maybe'
እወ *ʾəwwa* 'or'
እፎ *ʾəffo* 'how'
ኦ *ʾo* 'o'
ከሃ *kahā* 'there'
ከመ፡ ምንት *kama mənt* 'like what'
ከማሁ *kamāhu* 'likewise'
ከንቶ *kantto* 'for free'
ከዋላ *kawālā* 'later'
ካዕበ *kāʿəba* 'again'
ክመ *kəmma* 'always'
ኵለሄ *kʷəllahe* 'always'
ወትረ *watra* 'everyday'
ውቱረ *wəttura* 'everyday'
ዓዲ *ʿādi* 'still'
ዘልፈ *zalfa* 'always'
ዛቲ፡ ዕለት *zātti ʿəllat* 'this day'
ዝየ *zəya* 'here'
ዝሉፉ *zəlufu* 'always'
ይእዜ *yəʾəze* 'today'
ዮም *yom* 'today'
ግሙራ *gəmurā* 'every time'

ጌሰም *gesam* 'tomorrow'
ግብተ *gəbta* 'suddenly'
ጥቀ *ṭəqqa* 'very'
ፈድፋደ *fadfāda* 'a lot'
ፍጡነ *fəṭuna* 'quickly'

2.3.2 Conjunctional elements

ሂ *hi* 'and'
ለለ *lalla* 'whenever'
ለእመ *la'əmma* 'if'
መጠነ 'as long as'
ሚመ 'or'
ሶበ *soba* 'when'
በአምጣነ *ba'amṭāna* 'so far as'
ባሕቱ *bāḥəttu* 'but'
ባሕቲቱ *bāḥtitu* 'alone'
እንበለ፡ ዳእሙ *'ənbala dā'əmu* 'but not'
እንዘ *'ənza* 'when'
አው *'aw* 'or'
ከመ *kama* 'that', 'so that'
ኀበ *ḫaba* 'where'
ኒ *ni* 'and'
አላ *'allā* 'but'
አመ *'ama* 'when'
እመ *'əmma* 'when'
እም *'əm* 'from'
አምጣነ *'amṭāna* 'as much as'
እስመ *'əsma* 'because'
እስከ *'əska* 'until'
ወ *wa* 'and'
በዘ *baza* 'as'
በእንተዘ *ba'əntaza* 'because'
ጊዜ *gize* 'when'
ዳእሙ *dā'əmu* 'but'
ድኅረ *dəḫra* 'after'

2.3.3 Prepositional elements

ህየንተ *həyyanta* 'instead'
መልዕልተ *mal'əlta* 'over'
ለ *la* 'to', 'for'
መቅድመ *maqdəma* 'before'
ላዕለ *lā'əla* 'over'
መትሕተ *matḥəta* 'under'
መንገለ *mangala* 'to'
መንጸረ *manṣara* 'in front of'
ምስለ *məsla* 'with'
ማእከለ *mā'əkala* 'between'
ማዕዶተ *mā'ədota* 'beyond'
ቅድመ *qədma* 'before'
በ *ba* 'in', 'by'
በላዕለ *bālā'əla* 'above'
በማእከለ *bamā'əkala* 'in between'
በኀበ *baḫaba* 'near'
በታሕተ *batāḥta* 'under'
በአፍአ *ba'af'ā* 'outside'
በእንተ *ba'ənta* 'because of'
በከመ *bakama* 'as'
በዕብሬት *ba'əbret* 'for the sake of'
በዕዳ *ba'ədā* 'through'
በዕዳወ *ba'ədāwa* 'through'
በበይነ *babayna* 'for the sake of'
በወዕደ *bawa'əda* 'by'
ቤዛ *bezā* 'for'
ታሕተ *tāḥta* 'under'

ኀበ *ḫaba* 'to'
አመ *ʾama* 'when'
አንጻረ *ʾanṣāra* 'in front of'
እም *ʾəm* 'from'
እምነ *ʾəmənna* 'from'
እምላዕለ *ʾəmlāʿəla* 'from'
እምቅድመ *ʾəmqədma* 'before'
እምኀበ *ʾəmḫaba* 'from'
እምአመ *ʾəmʾama* 'since'
እምአፍአ *ʾəmʾafʿā* 'from outside'
እምውስተ *ʾəmwəsta* 'among'
እስከ *ʾəska* 'until'
እስከለ *ʾəskala* 'until'
እስከ፡ አመ *ʾəska-ʾama* 'till'
እንበለ *ʾənbala* 'without'
እንበይነ *ʾənbayna* 'because of'
እንተ *ʾənta* 'via'
እንተመንገለ *ʾənta-mangala* 'through ... to'
እንተቅድመ *ʾənta-qədma* 'ahead'
እንተውስተ *ʾənta-wəsta* 'through'
እንተዲበ *ʾənta-diba* 'over'
እንተድኅረ *ʾənta-dəḫra* 'behind'
ከመ *kama* 'like'
ከዋላ *kawālā* 'behind'
ውስተ *wəsta* 'in'
ዐውደ *ʿawda* 'around'
ዘበእንተ *za-baʾənta* 'because of'
ፍና *fənnā* 'to'

2.3.4 Particles

2.3.4.1. Part. of negative reaction

እንብ *ʾənb* 'no'
እንበለ *ʾənbala* 'without'
እንዳዒ *ʾəndāʿi* 'I do not know'

2.3.4.2. Presentational particles

ነይ *nay* 'behold'

2.3.4.3. Negative Particles

አልቦ *ʾalbo* 'there is no'
አኮ *ʾakko* 'not'
ኢ *ʾi* 'not', 'un-'

2.3.4.4. Vocative particles

አሌ *ʾalle* 'woe!
ወይ *way* 'woe!'

2.3.4.5. Admiring Part.

ሚ *mi* 'how'

2.3.4.6. Other Particles

ሁ *hu* 'is?', 'shall?'
ሂ *hi* 'also'
ሄ *he* '-'
ኒ *ni* 'still'

መ *ma* '-'
ሰ *sa* 'on the other hand'
ኑ *nu* 'is?', 'shall?'
አ *'a* '-'
እንከ *'ənka* 'now on'
እንጋ *'əngā* 'so'
ኦ *'o* 'O!'
ኬ *ke* '-'
ከመ *kəmma* 'then'

In terms of quantity of elements involved in the lexical categories, Tropper's grammar contains the largest list of ACPPIP elements next to Dillmann and Kidāna Wald. The following two factors made his contribution larger.

The first factor is the repeated mention of some elements, with and without pronominal suffixes. For example, he mentioned *soba* 'when', *'ama* 'when' and *gize* 'when' the prepositional and conjunctional elements in their original forms. At the same time, he implemented *sobehā* 'at that time', *'amehā* 'at that time', *'amehu* 'at that time' and *begizehā* 'at that time' as individual elements in the same circumstances. The adverbial element *qadāmi* 'firstly' is also mentioned again with a suffix as *qadāmi-hu* 'in the beginning'.

The second factor is the reintroduction of different elements combined with other ACPPIP elements. He mainly used *la*, *ba*, *ba'ənta*, *'əm* and *'ənta* as important components for the reintroduction. Thirty-eight of the listed elements are the results of this tendency of reintroducing elements in different forms.

Generally, Tropper has mostly listed the same elements involved in Dillmann's grammar though his list consists of a smaller number of elements. Astonishingly, the noun '*əlat*' preceded by a demonstrative pronoun '*zātti*' is introduced as an individual element in the lexical category of Adverbs.

Furthermore, the elements *ba'əda* 'through', *ba'ədāwa* 'through' and *bawa'əda* 'by' are not recognized as adverbial elements in the tradition of *'Aggabāb*. Even the other scholars who have been mentioned in this work have not included them in their lists. It is supposed to be newly introduced by Tropper himself.

2.4. ACPPIP ELEMENTS INVOLVED IN *'ALAQĀ* KIDĀNA WALD KEFLE'S GRAMMAR

One of the outstanding Gəʿəz grammarians of the early twentieth century *'Alaqā* Kidāna Wald Kəfle[1] has collected 193 ACPPIP elements in his Gəʿəz grammar and dictionary. His way of categorization of the elements is completely different from the way carried out by the scholars whose approaches we discussed up to now. He just followed the tradition of *'Aggabāb* and categorized the elements in three major groups of *ʿAbiyy 'Aggabāb*, *Nəʿus 'Aggabāb* and *Daqiq 'Aggabāb*.

However, the elements are recategorized in six lexical categories to discern his approach on the standing points comparing with the scholarly approaches detected above (Kidāna Wald Kəfle 1955:86-88, 126-159).

[1] Kəfle (1869–1944) was one of the most popular Ethiopian scholars of the nineteenth and twentieth century. He was 20 years old when he left Ethiopia and joined the Ethiopian monastic community in Jerusalem where he spent the next 30 years. He was a highly motivated person of intelligence; he spent much time by searching and copying manuscripts. The arrival of *Mamhər* Kəfla Giyorgis (1825-1908) in 1897 in Jerusalem gave him a good opportunity to bring up his intellectuality to the highest level. Within a couple of years at which he lived with him, he could study the Gəʿəz grammer as well and the commentaries of O.T scriptures including the commentaries of Qerlos, John Chrysostom, Ephiphany, and Abušākər. *Mamhər* Kəfla Giyorgis motivated him to improve his knowledge of Hebrew, Syriac, Greek and Arabic languages and to realize the preparation of his Gəʿəz-Amharic Lexicon. He also gave him his own preliminary draft. In 1919, he was invited by Emperor Hayla Sellāse I and returned to Ethiopia to prepare the commentary of Ezkiel. Besides, he has prepared some other exegeses such as Mār Yəsḥaq, Aragāwi Manfasāwi, Filksəyus, Qəddāse, Haymānota 'Abaw and Hebrew grammar in Gəʿəz syllabary. Kidāna Wald 1955: Preface; "Kidāna Wald Kəfle" *EAe,* III (2007), 399-400 (Baye Yemam).

2.4.1. Adverbial elements

2.4.1.1. Adverbs

ህልወ *həlləwa* 'existingly'
ህዱአ *hədua* 'silently'
ለዝላፉ *lazəlāfu* 'always'
ለፌ *lafe* 'this side', 'here'
ለፍጻሜ *lafəṣṣāme* 'at the end'
ሐዊሳ *ḥawisā* 'Greetings'
ሕቀ *ḥəqqa* 'a little'
መ *ma* '-'
መቅድም *maqdəm* 'before'
መፍትወ *maftəwa* 'willingly'
ርቱዐ *rətuʿa* 'uprightly'
ሶ *so* '-'
ቀዳሚ *qadāmi* 'firstly', 'before'
ቀዲሙ *qadimu* 'at first', 'in old time'
ቅድመ *qədma* 'before', 'firstly'
ቅድም *qədm* 'before'
ብዙኀ *bəzuḫa* 'much'
ታሕተ *tāḥta* 'under'
ትማልም *təmāləm* 'yesterday', 'earlier'
ትርአስ *tərʾas* 'at the top of'
ሳኒታ *sānitā* 'on the next day
ትካት *təkāt* 'in ancient time'
ኀሪፍ *ḫarif* 'next year'
ኅቡአ *ḫəbua* 'secretly'
ኅዳጠ *ḫədāṭa* 'a little'
ናሁ *nāhu* 'now', 'behold'
ንሕኑሐ *nəḥnuḥa* 'extravagantly'
ንስቲተ *nəstita* 'slightly'
አሚር *'amir* 'time'
አምጣነ *'amṭāna* 'in average'
አስፌር *'asfer* 'last year'
አቅዲሙ *'aqdimu* 'before'
አ *'ā* (-),
እስኩ *'əsku* 'let...'
እንከ *'ənka* 'now on'
እንጋ *'əngā* 'then indeed?'
እንዳዒ *'əndāʿi* 'not surely'
ከሃ *kahā* 'there'
ከዋላ *kawālā* 'behind', 'later'
ኵለሄ *k^wəllahe* 'wherever', 'whenever'
ኬ *ke* '-'
ክመ *kəmma* 'always'
ክሡተ *kəśuta* 'plainly'
ክቡተ *kəbuta* 'in secret'
ወትረ *watra* 'everyday'
ወትር *watr* 'everyday'
ውኁደ *wəḫuda* 'a little'
ዘልፈ *zalfa* 'always'
ዘልፍ *zalf* 'always'
ዝየ *zəya* 'here'
የማን *yamān* 'right'
ይምን *yəmn* 'right'
ይእዜ *yəʾəze* 'today', 'now'
ዮም *yom* 'now', 'today'
ዮጊ *yogi* 'yet'
ገጽ *gaṣṣ* 'face'
ግሙራ *gəmurā* 'everytime'
ጌሠም *geśam* 'tomorrow'
ግሁደ *gəhuda* 'in public'
ግንጽሊተ *gənṗəlita* 'the wrong way'
ግድመ *gədma* 'not straightly'
ግፍትዒተ *gəftəʿita* 'perversely'
ጓ *g^wā* 'also'

ድልወ *dəlləwa* ‘readily’
ድቡተ *dəbbuta* ‘in secret’
ደኃሪ *daḫāri* ‘later’
ድኅር *dəḫr* ‘later’, ‘back’
ድኅሪተ *dəḫrita* ‘backward’
ጥንቁቀ *ṭənquqa* ‘carefully’
ጥዩቀ *ṭəyyuqa* ‘exactly’
ጥቀ *ṭəqqa* ‘absolutely’
ጽመ *ṣəmma* ‘totally’
ጽሚተ *ṣəmmita* ‘silently’
ፀጋም *ḍagām* ‘left’
ፅግም *ḍəgm* ‘left’
ፈድፋደ *fadfāda* ‘extremely’
ፍጹመ *fəṣṣuma* ‘absolutely’

2.4.1.2. Interrogative Adverbs

ሚመ *mimma* ‘otherwise’
ማእዜ *māʾəze* ‘when’
ስፍን *səfn* ‘how much’
አይቴ *ʾayte* ‘where’
እፎ *ʾəffo* ‘how’

2.4.2 Conjunctional elements

ሂ *hi* ‘and’, ‘also’
ሕገ *ḥəgga* ‘as’
ህየንተ *həyyanta* ‘because’
መንገለ *mangala* ‘where’
መዋዕለ *mawāʿəla* ‘at the time of’
መጠነ *maṭana* ‘as much as’
ሰ *sa* ‘but’
ሰዓ *sʿā* ‘at the time of’
ሰዐተ *saʿata* ‘at the time of’
በዘ *baza* ‘as’
ሶበ *soba* ‘when’
በቀለ *baqala* ‘as’, ‘for’
በእንተ *baʾənta* ‘because’
በይነ *bayna* ‘because’
እምዘ *ʾəmza* ‘as’
እምይእዜ *ʾəmyəʾəze* ‘from now on’
እምዮም *ʾəmyom* ‘from this day on’
እስመ *ʾəsma* ‘because’
እስከ *ʾəska* ‘until’
እንበለ *ʾənbala* ‘without’
እንበይነ *ʾənbayna* ‘since’
እንዘ *ʾənza* ‘while’
ከመ *kama* ‘as’
ብሂል *bəhil* ‘meaning’
ባሕቱ *bāḥəttu* ‘however’
ተውላጠ *tawlāṭa* ‘in place of’
ኀበ *ḫaba* ‘to’
ኒ *ni* ‘and’, ‘also’
አላ *ʾallā* ‘but’
አመ *ʾama* ‘when’
አምሳለ *ʾamsāla* ‘like’
አምጣነ *ʾamṭāna* ‘because’
አርአያ *ʾarʾayā* ‘as’
አኮኑ *ʾakkonu* ‘because’
አው *ʾaw* ‘or’
እመ *ʾəmma* ‘if’
እም *ʾəm* ‘from’
ወ *wa* ‘and’
ወእደ *waʾda* ‘as’, ‘if’
ዐቅመ *ʿaqma* ‘as much as’
ዓለም *ʿālam* ‘ever’
ዓመተ *ʿāmata* ‘annually’
ዓዲ *ʿādi* ‘again’
ዕለተ *ʿəlata* ‘daily’, ‘in a day’
ጊዜ *gize* ‘when’, ‘at a time of’

ዳእሙ *dāʾəmu* 'but'
ድኅረ *dəḫra* 'after'
ፍዳ *fəddā* 'in place of'

2.4.3. Prepositional elements

ለ *la* 'to'
ላዕለ *lāʿəla* 'above', 'over'
ሐይቅ *ḥayq* 'boundary'
መልዕልተ *malʿəlta* 'above'
መትሕተ *matḥəta* 'under'
ምስለ *məsla* 'together'
ማእከለ *māʾəkala* 'between'
ቅድመ *qədma* 'before', 'firstly'
በ *ba* 'by', 'in'
በይነ *bayna* 'because of'
ቤዛ *bezā* 'for', 'in the ransom of'
ብሔር *bəḥer* 'during', 'dawn'
ተክለ *takla* 'for', 'on behalf of'
ታሕተ *tāḥta* 'under'
አርአያ *ʾarʾayā* 'in the form of', 'like'
አድያም *ʾadyām* 'area', 'surrounding'
አያተ *ʾayāta* 'about', 'for'
አፈ *ʾafa* 'at the edge of'
አፍአ *ʾafʾā* 'outside'
ከመ *kama* 'like'
ከንፈር *kanfar* 'rim'
ክንፍ *kənf* 'wing'
ውስተ *wəsta* 'in'
ውሳጤ *wəsāṭe* 'in'
ዐስበ *ʿasba* 'in compensation of'
ዐውድ *ʿawd* 'around'
ዕሴተ *ʿəsseta* 'in charge of'
ዘዘ *zaza* '-'
ገበዝ *gabaz* 'border', 'seashore'
ደወል *dawal* 'area', 'province'
ዲበ *diba* 'over'
ድንጋግ *dəngāg* 'border', 'hedge'
ጽላሎተ *ṣəlālota* 'in the likeness of'
ጽንፍ *ṣənf* 'border'
ፍና *fənnā* 'at', 'on the way of'

2.4.4 Interjections, Relative Pronouns and Particles

2.4.4.1. Interjections

ሰይ *say* 'woe!'
አህ *ʾah* 'ʾah'
አሀሀ *ʾahah* 'ah'
አሌ *ʾalle* 'woe!'
እንቋዕ *ʾənqʷaʿ* 'aha!'
ወይ *way* 'woe!'
ወይሌ *wayle* 'Woe!'
ዬ *ye* 'Woe!'

2.4.4.2. Relative Pronouns

እለ *ʾəlla* 'who', 'that', 'which'
እንተ *ʾənta* 'who', 'that', 'which'
ዘ *za* 'who', 'that', 'which'

2.4.4.3. Particles

2.4.4.3.1. Affirmative Particles

አሆ *ʾoho* 'ok'

2.4.4.3.2. Negative Particles

አል *ʾal* 'no', 'not'	ኢ *ʾi* (not, un-, dis-)
አኮ *ʾakko* (not)	

2.4.4.3.3 Vocative Particles

ኦ ʾo 'o'

2.4.4.3.4. Interrogative Particles

ሁ *hu* 'is…?'	ቦኑ *bonu* '-'
ኑ *nu* 'shall?', 'is…?	

2.4.4.3.5. Particles indicating Genitive relation

ለ *la* 'of…'	እንተ *ʾənta* 'of…'
እለ *ʾəlla* (of…)	ዘ *za* 'of…'

In terms of quantity, Kidāna Wald's list of ACPPIP elements is similar with that of Dillmann. But on the types of elements, there is an unambiguous difference between them. Particularly in the lexical categories of Adverbs and Prepositions, each has collected several elements which do not exist in the list of the other. For instance, the elements *lelita, ləʿula, ḥassata, maʿalta, maṭana, ḫəyyula* and *ʾəkkuya* which are listed only in Dillmann, and again, the elements *maqdəma, manṣara* and *maʿədota* involved in the category of Prepositions are not included in Kidāna Wald's list of elements.

Likewise, the elements *tərʾas* 'at the top of', *tərgāḍ* 'at the foot of', *gənṗəlita* 'the wrong way', *gəftəʿita* 'perversely', *yamān* 'right', 'area', 'surrounding', *ḍagām* 'left', *bəḥer* 'during', 'dawn', *ʾadyām kanfar* 'rim', and *kənf* 'wing' which Kidāna Wald collected in the categories of Adverbs and Prepositions are excluded in Dillmann.

Furthermore, Kidāna Wald has added two combined phrases to the elements in the lexical category of Conjunction as single elements *ʾəmyəʾəze* and *ʾəmyom*. However, in accordance with the tradition of *ʾAggabāb*, such combinations of two elements which still keep their own meanings in the combination are not considered as single ACPPIP elements. Even, the nouns such as *lelita, bəḥer, yamān, yəmn, ḍagām, ḍəgām, 'adyām, kanfar* and *kənf* are not given attention in the study of *'Aggabāb* like the other ACPPIP elements unless they are studied as nouns. To be precise, out of one hundred sixteen elements provided in the categories of Adverbs and Prepositions twenty-eight elements are not involved in the *'Aggabāb* tradition since they are not considered as ACPPIP elements. The elements provided in their classes are as follows:

Adverbial elements (sixteen):

'asfer 'last year'
dəlləwa 'readily'
gədma 'not straightly'
gəftəʿita 'perversely'
gənṗəlita 'the wrong way'
ḫarif 'next year'
ḥawisā 'Greetings'
hədu'a 'silently'
həlləwa 'existingly'
lafəṣṣāme 'at the end'
maftəwa 'willingly'
nəḥnuḥa 'extravagantly'
rətuʿa 'uprightly'
ḍəgm 'left'
yamān 'right'
yəmn 'right'

Prepositional elements (twelve):

ʿasba 'in compensation of'
bəḥer 'during', 'dawn'
dawal 'area', 'province'
dəngāg (border)
ʿəsseta 'in charge of'
gabaz 'border'
ḥayq 'boundary'
kanfar 'rim'
kənf 'wing'
ṣəlālota 'in the likeness of'
ṣənf 'border'
zaza '-'

Regarding the elements listed in the categories of Conjunctions and Particles, no element is involved in the *'Aggabāb* tradition except *'əmyə'əze* 'from now on' and *'əmyom* 'from this day onward'.

2.5. ACPPIP ELEMENTS AND THEIR CLASSES ACCORDING TO STEFAN WENINGER

A short grammar of Gəʿəz published by Stefan Weninger who is a reknown Semitist and Ethiopianist of the day contained at least four lexical categories and some ACPPIP elements from each category. The elements are twenty-two all in all. He presented them in their classes as follows (Weninger 1993, 16-17, 32- 33):

2.5.1 Relative Pronouns

እለ *ʾəlla* 'who', 'that', 'which'	ዘ *za* 'who', 'that', 'which'
እንተ *ʾənta* 'who', 'that', 'which'	

2.5.2 Interrogative pronouns

መኑ *mannu* 'who?'	ምንት *mənt* 'what?'

2.5.3 Prepositions

ለ *la* 'to'	ኀበ *ḫaba* 'to', 'where'
ላዕለ *lāʿəla* 'above', 'over'	እምኀበ *ʾəmḫaba* 'from...where'
መልዕልተ *malʿəlta* 'above'	እምነ *ʾəmənna* 'from'
ምስለ *məsla* 'with'	እስከ *ʾəska* 'to', 'until'
ማእከለ *māʾəkala* 'between'	ከመ *kama* 'like'
ቅድመ *qədma* 'before'	ውስተ *wəsta* 'in'
በ *ba* 'by', 'in'	በዲበ *badiba* 'above', 'over'
በእንተ *baʾənta* 'because of'	

2.5.4 Particles indicating Genitive relation

ለ *la* 'of'	ዘ *za* 'of'

As anyone can observe, this list provides a very few number of ACPPIP elements. In the grammars under review as well as in the tradition of *ʾAggabāb*, the lexical categories of Adverbs and Conjunctions are the most important lexical categories that consists of a considerable number of elements. However, he did not include them in his work since it is designed to provide only a short overview.

The other significant lexical category of Particles is also represented only by two elements indicating a genitive relation (*la* and *za*). He paid a better attention to the lexical category of Prepositions. But, this also cannot be considered as completely done because it involves less than one third of the prepositional elements that can be listed in the category.

With regard to the elements involved in the list, they do not show a serious orthographic or semantic difference from their state in *ʾAggabāb*. The only differences that can be mentioned here is that he provides the elements ኀበ *ḫaba* 'to', 'where' and ዲበ *diba* 'above', 'over' with the combination of other prepositional elements እም *ʾəm* 'from' በ *badiba* 'above', 'over'. In the *'Aggabāb* tradition, each element is studied as an individual prepositional element though the combination is grammatically possible.

Table 1. Adverbial Elements

Remarks: A = Absent, P = Present, - = unknown

	Adverbial Elements	*'Aggabāb*	Dillmann	Conti-Rossini	Tropper	Kidāna Wald	Weninger
1	*'a* 'ኣ'	A	A	A	A	P	-
2	*'abiyya* 'highly'	A	P	A	A	A	-
3	*'addāma* 'beautifully'	A	P	A	A	A	-
4	*'ādi* 'yet'	P	P	P (*'adihu*)	P	A	-
5	*'af'ā* 'outside'	P	P	A	P	A	-
6	*'aḥattane* 'in one'	P	P	P	A	A	-
7	*'albo* 'no'	A	A	A	P	A	-
8	*'amān* 'truly'	P	P	A	P (*'amāna*)	A	-
9	*'amehā* 'at that time'	A	P	P	P	A	-
10	*'amehu* 'at that time'	A	A	A	P	A	-
11	*'amira* 'time'	P	A	A	A	P (*'amir*)	-
12	*'amṭāna* 'in average'	A	P	P	A	P	-
13	*'anṣāra* 'forwardly'	P	A	A	A	A	-
14	*'aqdimu* 'before'	P	A	A	A	P	-
15	*'asfer* 'last year'	A	A	A	A	P	-
16	*'awda* 'around'	P	P	A	A	A	-

17	*ʾay* 'which'	A	P	A	A	A	-
18	*ʾayte* 'where'	A	P	P	P	P	-
19	*badāḫn* 'in safety'	A	P	A	A	A	-
20	*baʾənta-mənt* 'why'	A	A	A	P	A	-
21	*baʾəntaz* 'therefore'	A	A	A	P	A	-
22	*baʾənta-zəntu* 'therefore'	A	A	A	P	A	-
23	*bafaqād* 'volunerly'	A	P	A	A	A	-
24	*bafəṣṣāme* 'lastly'	A	P	A	A	A	-
25	*begizehā* 'at that time'	A	A	A	P	A	-
26	*baḥəqqu* 'considerably'	P	P	A	A	A	-
27	*baḫəśum* 'miserably'	A	P	A	A	A	-
28	*bāḫtitu* 'alone', 'only'	P	P	P	A	A	-
29	*bāḫəttu* 'only'	A	P	A	A	A	-
30	*bakka* 'in vain'	P	P	A	A	A	-
31	*bakʷəllu* 'gradually'	A	P	A	A	A	-
32	*bakʷərh* 'by constraint'	A	P	A	A	A	-
33	*baməlʿu* 'fully'	P	A	A	A	A	-
34	*banəṣuḥ* 'innocently'	A	P	A	A	A	-
35	*baśannāy* 'in friendly way'	A	P	A	A	A	-
36	*baṣəbāḥ* 'in the morning'	A	P	A	A	A	-

37	*batə'bit* 'proudly'	A	P	A	A	A	-
38	*beyna-mənt* 'for what'	A	A	A	P	A	-
39	*baynaz* 'therefore'	A	A	A	P	A	-
40	*bəzḫa* 'largly'	A	A	A	A	A	-
41	*bəzuḫa* 'much'	A	P	P	P (*bəzuḫ*)	P	-
42	*bonu* 'indeed?'	P	A	A	A	A	-
43	*dabuba* 'northward'	A	P	A	A	A	-
44	*dā'əmu* 'however'	A	P	A	A	A	-
45	*dāgəma* 'again'	P	P	A	A	A	-
46	*daḫāri* 'later'	P	A	A	A	P	-
47	*darga* 'together'	P	P (*darg*)	A	A	A	-
48	*dəbbuta* 'in secret'	P	A	A	A	P	-
49	*dəḫra* 'later, behind'	P	P	P	A	P (*dəḫr*)	-
50	*dəḫrita* 'backward'	P	P	A	A	P	-
51	*dəlləwa* 'readily'	A	A	A	A	P	-
52	*dəlwat* 'worthy'	P	A	A	A	A	-
53	*dəmmura* 'jointly'	A	P	A	A	A	-
54	*dənguḍa* 'scaredly'	A	P	A	A	A	-
55	*dərgata* 'conjointly'	P	A	A	A	A	-
56	*dəruġa* 'at the same time'	A	P	A	A	A	-
57	*'əffo* 'how'	A	P	A	P	P	-

58	*ʾəkkuya* 'badly'	A	P	A	A	A	-
59	*ʾəmmədru* 'completely'	P	A	A	A	A	-
60	*ʾəmdəḫraz* 'after that'	A	A	A	P	A	-
61	*ʾəmdəḫrazənttu* 'later'	A	A	A	P	A	-
62	*ʾəmhəyya* 'from there'	A	A	A	P	A	-
63	*ʾəmuna* 'truely'	P	A	A	P (*baʾ amān*)	A	-
64	*ʾəmqadimu* 'from the beginning'	A	A	A	P	A	-
65	*ʾəmz* 'then'	A	A	A	P	A	-
66	*ʾəndāʿi* 'perhaps'	A	P	A	P	P	-
67	*ʾənbaynaz* 'because of this'	A	A	A	P	A	-
68	*ʾənbayna-zənttu* 'therefore'	A	A	A	P	A	-
69	*ʾənka* 'now on'	P	A	A	A	P	-
70	*ʾənkəmu* 'take', 'behold'	A	P	A	A	A	-
71	*ʾəngā* 'then indeed?'	P	A	A	A	P	-
72	*ʾərāqu* 'alone'	P	A	A	A	A	-
73	*ʾəsfəntu* 'how many'	A	P	A	A	A	-
74	*ʾəskamənt* 'to what extent'	A	A	A	P	A	-
75	*ʾəsku* 'let...'	P	A	A	A	P	-
76	*ʾəwwa* 'or'	A	A	A	P	A	-
77	*fadfāda* 'very'	P	P	P	P	P	-

78	*fəṣma* 'in front'	P	P	A	A	A	-
79	*fəṣṣuma* 'absolutely'	P	P	A	A	P	-
80	*fəṭuna* 'quickly'	P	P	A	P	A	-
81	*gahada* 'openly'	P	A	A	A	P (*gəhuda*)	-
82	*gaṣṣa* 'face to face'	P	A	A	A	P (*gaṣṣ*)	-
83	*gədma* 'awry'	A	P	A	A	P	-
84	*gəbr* 'must'	P	A	A	A	A	-
85	*gəbta* 'suddenly'	P	P	A	P	A	-
86	*gəftəʿita* 'perversely'	A	A	A	A	P	-
87	*gəmurā* 'every time'	P	P	A	P+ *lagəmurā*	P	-
88	*gənpəlita* 'the wrong way'	A	A	A	A	P	-
89	*geśam* 'tomorrow'	P	P (*geśama*)	P (*geśama*)	P	P	-
90	*gʷā* 'also'	A	A	A	A	P	-
91	*gʷunduya* 'a long time'	A	P	A	A	A	-
92	*ḫarifa* 'this year'	A	P	A	A	P (*ḫarif*)	-
93	*ḫassata* 'falsely'	A	P	A	A	A	-
94	*ḫawisā* 'Greetings'	A	A	A	A	P	-
95	*ḫəbuʿa* 'secretly'	P	A	A	A	P	-
96	*ḫəbura* 'all together'	P	P	P	A	A	-
97	*ḫəduʾa* 'silently'	A	A	A	A	P	-
98	*ḫədāṭa* 'a little'	P	P	A	P+ (*baḫədāṭ*)	P	-

99	*həlləwa* 'existingly'	A	P	A	A	P	-
100	*ḥəqqa* 'by degrees', 'a little'	P	P	P	P	P	-
101	*həyya* 'there'	P	P	P	P	A	-
102	*ḫəyyula* 'powerfully'	A	P	A	A	A	-
103	*hu* 'is...?'	A	P	A	A	A	-
104	*ḫubāre* 'unitedly'	P	A	A	A	A	-
105	*kāʿəba* 'again'	P	P	A	P	A	-
106	*kāʿəbata* 'repeatedly'	A	P	A	A	A	-
107	*kahā* 'away'	P	P (*kaḥa*)	P (*kaḥa*)	P	P	-
108	*kama* 'like'	A	A	P	A	A	-
109	*kamāhu* 'likewise'	A	A	A	P	A	-
110	*kama-mənt* 'like what'	A	A	A	P	A	-
111	*kantu* 'in vain'	P	P	A	P (*ba/la-kantu*)	A	-
112	*kawālā* 'behind', 'later'	P	P	A	P	P	-
113	*kʷəllahe* 'where', 'whenever'	P	P (every direction)	A	P	P	-
114	*ke* '-'	A	A	A	A	P	-
115	*kəbuta* 'in secret'	A	A	A	A	P	-
116	*kəʿuba* 'doubly'	A	P	A	A	A	-
117	*kəmma* 'always'	P	A	A	P	P	-
118	*kəśuta* 'plainly'	P	A	A	A	P	-
119	*laʿālam* 'for ever'	A	P	A	A	A	-

120	*lāʿəla* ‘above’	P	P	P	P	A	-
121	*lāʿəlita* ‘above’	P	P	A	A	A	-
122	*lāʿəlu* ‘upward’	P	A	A	A	A	-
123	*lafe* ‘this side’, ‘here’	P	P	P	P+(*lafe walafe*)	P	-
124	*lafəṣṣāme* ‘at the end’	A	A	A	A	P	-
125	*lelita* ‘by night’	A	P	A	P	A	-
126	*lazəlāfu* ‘always’	P + *lazəlāfu*	P	A	P	P	-
127	*ləʿula* ‘upward’	A	P	A	A	A	-
128	*ma* ‘-’	A	A	A	A	P	-
129	*maʿalta* ‘by day’	A	P	A	A	A	-
130	*māʾəze* ‘when’	P	P	P	P	P	-
131	*maftəw* ‘right’	P	A	A	A	P (*maf-təwa)*	-
132	*māʿədota* ‘beyond’	A	P	A	A	A	-
133	*māʾəkala* ‘in the midst’	A	P	A	A	A	-
134	*malʿəlta* ‘above’	A	P	A	A	A	-
135	*manṣara* ‘forwardly’	P	A	A	A	A	-
136	*mannu* ‘who’	A	P	A	A	A	-
137	*maqdəma* ‘firstly’	P	A	P	A	P (*maq-dəm)*	-
138	*marira* ‘bitterly’	A	P	A	A	A	-
139	*maṭana* ‘the bigness of’	A	P	A	A	A	-
140	*matḥəta* ‘below’	A	P	A	A	A	-

141	*matlǝwa* 'in succession'	A	P	A	A	A	-
142	*mǝnt* 'what'	A	P	A	P (*ba/ lamǝnt)*	A	-
143	*mǝkbǝʿta* 'repeatedly'	P	P	A	A	A	-
144	*mǝʿra* 'once'	P	A	P	P + *lamʿǝr*	A	-
145	*mǝsbǝʿita* 'sevenfold'	P	A	A	A	A	-
146	*mi* 'what'	A	P	A	P	A	-
147	*mimma* 'otherwise'	A	P	A	A	P	-
148	*mimaṭana* 'how greatly'	A	P	A	A	A	-
149	*na* 'behold'	A	P	A	A	A	-
150	*nagha* 'early in the morning'	A	P	A	A	A	-
151	*nāhu* 'now', 'behold'	A	P	A	A	P	-
152	*nawā* 'behold her'	A	P	A	A	A	-
153	*nawwiḫa* 'far'	A	P	A	A	A	-
154	*nayā* 'behold'	A	P	A	A	A	-
155	*nǝḥnuḥa* 'extravagantly'	A	A	A	A	P	-
156	*nǝṣuḥa* 'innocently'	A	P	A	A	A	-
157	*nǝstita* 'slightly'	P	P	P	P	P	-
158	*nu* 'is...?'	A	P	A	A	A	-
159	*ʾo* 'o'	A	A	A	P + *qadāmi hu*	A	-
160	*qadāmi* 'firstly', 'before'	P	P	A	P	P	-
161	*qadimu* 'at first', 'earlier'	P	P	P	P	P	-

162	*q̣ədma* 'before', 'firstly'	P	P	P	A	P	-
163	*q̣ədm* 'before'	P	A	A	A	P	-
164	*q̣ʷəlq̣ʷlita* 'downward'	A	P	A	A	A	-
165	*rəḫuq̣a* 'for distant'	A	P	A	A	A	-
166	*rətuʿə* 'worthy'	P	A	A	A	A	-
167	*rətuʿa* 'uprightly'	P	P	A	A	P	-
168	*śannāya* 'rightly'	P	P	A	A	A	-
169	*sānitā* 'on the next day'	P	A	A	A	P	-
170	*sarka* 'in the evening'	A	P	A	A	A	-
171	*ṣəfuqa* 'frequently'	A	P	A	A	A	-
172	*səfna* 'how often'	P	P	A	A	P (*səfn*)	-
173	*ṣəmma* 'totally'	P	A	A	A	P	-
174	*ṣəmmita* 'silently'	P	P	P	A	P	-
175	*ḍagām* 'left'	A	P (*ṣəgma*)	A	A	P + *ṣəgm*	-
176	*səbʾa* 'completely'	P	A	A	A	A	-
177	*sənʾa* 'unanimously'	A	P	A	A	A	-
178	*ṣənuʿa* 'strongly'	A	P	A	A	A	-
179	*ṣəruʿa* 'idly'	A	P	A	A	A	-
180	*ṣəmimta* 'secretly'	P	P	P	A	A	-
181	*so* '-'	A	A	A	A	P	-
182	*sobehā* 'at that time'	A	A	P	P	A	-

183	*tāḥta* 'below'; 'under'	P	P	P	A	P	-
184	*tāḥətya* 'under'	A	P	A	A	A	-
185	*tāḥtita* 'downwardly'	P	A	A	A	A	-
186	*tāḥtu* 'under'	P	P	A	A	A	-
187	*təḥuta* 'humbly'	A	P	A	A	A	-
188	*təkāt* 'once'	P	P	A	P	P	-
189	*təmāləm* 'yesterday', 'earlier'	P	P	P	A	P	-
190	*ṭənquqa* 'carefully', 'fully'	P	P	A	A	P	-
191	*ṭəyyuqa* 'exactly'	P	P	A	A	P	-
192	*ṭəqqa* 'absolutely'	P	P	P	P	P	-
193	*tər'asa* 'at the top of'	P	A	A	A	P (*tər'as*)	-
194	*tərgāṣa* 'at the foot of'	P	A	A	A	P (*tərgāṣ*)	-
195	*waddə'a* 'fully'	P	A	A	A	A	-
196	*wəḫuda* 'a little'	P	A	A	A	P	-
197	*watra* 'everyday'	P	P	A	P	P + *watr*	-
198	*wəsṭa* 'in'	P	P	A	A	A	-
199	*wəttura* 'every day'	P	P	A	P	A	-
200	*yə'əze* 'now', 'today'	P	P	P	P	P	-
201	*yəmna* 'on the right hand'	A	P	A	A	P (*yəm* (*ā*)*n*)	-
202	*yəmuna* 'abundantly'	P	A	A	A	A	-
203	*yogi* 'yet'	P	A	P	A	P	

203	*yom* 'today'	P	P	P	P	P	-
204	*zalfa* 'continually', 'always'	P + *zalf*	P	P	P	P + *zalf*	-
205	*zātti* ʻəlat 'this day'	A	A	A	P	A	-
206	*zəlufa* 'continually'	A	P	A	P (*zəlufu*)	A	-
207	*zəya* 'here'	P	P	P	P	P	-
		97	131	34	73	78	-

Table 2. Conjunctional elements

	Conjunctional Elements	*ʼAggabāb*	Dillmann	Conti Rossini	Tropper	Kidāna Wald	Weninger
1	*ʼa* ʻ-ʼ	A	P	A	A	A	
3	*ʼakkonu* 'because'	P	A	A	A	P	
4	*ʻālam* 'ever'	A	A	A	A	P	
5	*ʼallā* 'but'	P	P	P	P	P	
6	*ʼama* 'when'	P	P	P	P	P	
7	*ʼamsāla* 'as'	P	A	A	A	P	
8	*ʻāmata* 'annually'	P	A	A	A	P	
9	*ʼamṭāna* 'as long as'	P	P	P	P + *baʼamṭāna*	P	
10	*ʻaqma* 'as much as'	P	A	A	A	P	
11	*ʼarʼayā* 'as'	P	A	A	A	P	
12	*ʼaw* 'or'	P	P	P	P	P	
13	*baʼənta* 'because'	P	A	A	P (*baʼəntaza*)	P	

14	*bāḥətitu* 'alone'	A	A	A	P	A	
15	*bāḥəttu* 'but'	P	P	P	P	P	
16	*baqala* 'as', 'for'	P	A	A	A	P	
17	*bayna* 'because'	P	A	A	A	P	
18	*baza* 'that'	P	P	P	P	P	
19	*bəhil* 'meaning'	P	A	A	A	P	
20	*dāʾəmu* 'rather'	P	P	P	P	P	
21	*dəḫra* 'after'	P	A	P	P	P	
22	*ʾəffo* 'how'	A	A	P	A	A	
23	*ʿəlata* 'in the day of'	P	A	A	A	P	
24	*ʾənbala* 'without'	P	P	P	P (*ʾənbala dāʾəmu*)	P	
25	*ʾənbayna* 'since'	P	A	A	A	P	
26	*ʾəngā* 'then', 'indeed'	A	P	A	A	A	
27	*ʾənka* 'again'	A	P	P	A	A	
28	*ʾənta* 'which'	A	A	P	A	A	
29	*ʾənza* 'while'	P	P	P	P	P	
30	*ʾəm* 'from', 'rather'	P	P	P	P	P	
31	*ʾəmma* 'if'	P	P	P	P (*laʾəmma*)	P	
32	*ʾəmyəʾəze* 'from now on'	A	A	A	A	P	
33	*ʾəmyom* 'from this day on'	A	A	A	A	P	
34	*ʾəmza* 'as'	A	A	P	A	P	

35	*'əska* 'until'	P	P	P	P	P	
36	*'əsma* 'because'	P	P	P	P	P	
37	*fədda* 'in place of'	P	A	A	A	P	
38	*gize* 'when', 'at a time of'	P	A	A	P	P	
39	*ḫaba* 'where'	P	P	P	P	P	
40	*ḫəgga* 'as'	A	A	A	A	P	-
41	*ḫəyyanta* 'because'	P	A	A	A	P	
42	*ḫi* 'also'	P	P	P	P	P	-
43	*kama* 'that'	P	P	P	P	P	-
44	*ke* 'now'	A	P	P	A	A	
45	*la* 'to'	P	A	P	P (*lalla*)	A	-
46	*ni* 'also'	P	P	P	P	P	
47	*ma* '-'	A	P	P	A	A	-
48	*mangala* 'where'	P	A	A	A	P	-
49	*mawāʿəla* 'at the time of'	P	A	A	A	P	-
50	*maṭana* 'as much as'	P	A	A	P	P	-
51	*mimma* 'or', 'otherwise'	P	P (*mi*-how)	P (*wamim-ma*)	P	A	-
52	*qədma* 'before'	P	A	P	A	A	
53	*sa* 'but'	P	P	P	A	P	-
54	*sāʿata* 'at the time of'	P	A	A	A	P	-
55	*ṣaṭṭ* 'silence'	A	A	A	A	A	
56	*soba* 'when'	P	P	P	P	A	-

57	*tawlāṭa* ‘in place of’	P	A	A	A	P	-
58	*wa* ‘and’	P	P	P	P	P	-
59	*wa’əda* ‘as’, ‘if’	P	A	A	A	P	-
60	*yogi* ‘lest’	A	P	A	A	A	-
61	*za* ‘that’	A	P	A	A	A	-
		44	28	30	27	47	-

Table 3. Prepositional elements

	Preposition-al Elements	*’Aggabāb*	Dillmann	Conti Ros-sini	Tropper	Kidāna Wald	Weninger
1	*’adyām* ‘area’, ‘surrounding’	A	A	A	A	P	A
2	*’afa* ‘during’	P	A	A	A	P	A
3	*’af‘ā* ‘outside’	P	P	A	P (*ba’af‘ā*, *’əm’af‘ā*)	P	A
4	*’ama* ‘since’	P	P	P	P + *’əska/ ’əm-’ama*	A	A
5	*’amsāla* ‘in the form of’	P	P	P	A	A	A
6	*’amṭāna* ‘like’	P	P	A	A	A	A
7	*’anṣāra* ‘in front of’	P	P	P	P	A	A
8	*’ar’ayā* ‘like’	P	P	A	A	P	A
90	*‘asba* ‘in com-pensation of’	A	A	A	A	P	A
10	*‘awda* ‘around’	P	P	P	P	P (‘awd)	A
11	*’ayāta* ‘like’	P	A	A	A	P	A

12	*ba* 'in', 'by'	P	P	P	P	P	P
13	*ba'əbret* 'because of'	A	P	A	P	A	A
14	*ba'ədāwa* 'through'	A	A	A	P + *ba'ədā*	A	A
15	*ba'ənta* 'for', 'about'	P	P	P	P + *zaba'ənta*	A	P
16	*bayna* 'about', 'for'	P	P (*babayna*)	P	P (*babayna*)	P	A
17	*bəḥer* 'during', 'dawn'	A	A	A	A	P	A
18	*bezā* 'for', 'in ransom of'	P	P	A	P	P	A
19	*biṣa* 'beside'	A	P	A	A	A	A
20	*dawal* 'area', 'province'	A	A	A	A	P	A
21	*dəḫra* 'after', 'behind'	P	P	P	P + *'əntadəḫra*	A	A
22	*dəngāg* 'border', 'hedge'	A	A	A	A	P	A
23	*diba* 'above', 'upon'	P	P	P	P (*'əntadiba*)	P	P (*badiba*)
24	*'ədme* 'the time of'	P	A	A	A	A	A
25	*'əm* 'from'	P	P (*'əmənna*)	P	P + *'əmənna*, *'əmḫaba*	A	P (*'əmənna*)
26	*'ənbala* 'without'	P	P	P	P	A	A
27	*'ənbayna* 'beacuse of'	P			P	A	A
28	*'ənta* 'to'	P	P	P	P	A	A
29	*'əsseta* 'in charge of'	A	A	A	A	P	A
30	*'əska* 'till', 'to'	P	P	P	P + *'əskala*	A	P
31	*fəddā* 'in charge of'	A	P	A	A	A	A
32	*fənnā* 'during'	P	P	A	P	P	A

33	*gabaz* 'border', 'seashore'	A	A	A	A	P	A
34	*gabo* 'near'	P	A	A	A	A	A
35	*gize* 'during'	P	P	A	A	A	A
36	*gora* 'near'	P	A	A	A	A	A
37	*ḫaba* 'to', 'toward', 'near'	P	P	P	P + *baḫaba*	A	P + *ʾəmḫaba*
38	*ḫayq* 'boundary'	A	A	A	A	P	A
39	*ḫəyyanta* 'in stead of'	P	P	P	P	A	A
40	*kama* 'like'	P	P	P	P + *bakama*	P	P
41	*kanfar* 'rim'	A	A	A	A	P	A
42	*kawālā* 'after'	P	P	A	P	A	A
43	*kənf* 'wing'	A	A	A	A	P	A
44	*la* 'to'	P	P	P	P	P	P
45	*laʿālamaʿālam* 'forever'	A	A	P	A	A	A
46	*lāʿəla* 'above', 'over'	P	P	P	P + *ba/ ʾəm lāʿəla*	P	A
47	*māʿədota* 'beyond'	P	P	P	P	A	A
48	*māʾəkala* 'between'	P	P	P	P + *bamāʾəkala*	P	P
49	*malʿəlta* 'upon'	P	P	P	P	P	P
50	*maqdəma* 'before'	P	P	P	P	A	A
51	*matḥəta* 'under'	P	P	P	P	P	A
52	*matləwa* 'next'	A	A	P	A	A	A
53	*mangala* 'to'	P	P	P	P + *ʾəntamangala*	A	A

54	*manṣara* 'over against'	A	P	A	P	A	A
55	*maṭana* 'like'	P	A	A	A	A	A
56	*mə'ḫaza* 'beside'	A	P	A	A	A	A
57	*məsla* 'together'	P	P	P	A	P	P
58	*qədma* 'before'	P	P	P	P + *'əntaqədma*	P	P
59	*sānitā* 'on the next day of'	P	A	A	A	A	A
60	*ṣəlālota* 'in the likeness of'	A	A	A	A	P	A
61	*ṣənf* 'border'	A	A	A	A	P	A
62	*soba* 'during'	P	P	P	A	A	A
63	*tāḥta* 'under'	P	P	P	P + *batāḥta*	P	A
64	*takla* 'in stead of'	P	P	P	A	P	A
65	*tawlāṭa* 'in place of'	P	P	A	A	A	A
66	*ṭəqā* 'near'	P	P	P	A	A	A
67	*tər'āsa* 'at the head of'	P	A	A	A	A	A
68	*tərgāṣa* 'at the foot of'	P	A	A	A	A	A
69	*wəsta* 'in', 'to', 'through'....	P	P	P	P + *ənta/* ***'əm-wəsta***	P	A
70	*wəsṭa* 'in'	P	A	A	A	A	P
71	*wəsāṭita* 'in'	P	A	A	A	A	A
72	*wəsāṭe* 'in'	P	A	A	A	P	A
73	*wə'da* 'along'	A	P	A	P (*bawə'da*)	A	A
74	*zaza* '-'	A	A	A	A	P	A
		51	**45**	**33**	**55**	**35**	**14**

Table 4. Relative and Interrogative Pronouns

	Elements	*'Aggabāb*	Dillmann	Conti Rossini	Tropper	Kidāna Wald	Weninger
1	*'ay* 'what', 'which'	P	A	P	-	A	A
2	*'əlla* 'who', 'which', 'that'	P	P	P	-	P	P
3	*'ənta* 'who', 'which', 'that'	P	P	P	-	P	P
4	*'əsfəntu* 'how much'	A	A	P	-	A	A
5	*mannu* 'who'	P	A	P	-	A	P
6	*mənt* 'what'	P	A	P	-	A	P
7	*mi* 'what', 'which'	P	A	P	-	A	A
8	*za* 'who', 'which', 'that'	P	P	P	-	P	P
		7	3	8	-	3	5

Table 5. Interjections

		'Aggabāb	Dillmann	Conti Rossini	Tropper	Kidāna Wald	Weninger
1	*'a* '-'	A	P	A	-	A	A
2	*'aʿi* 'come'	A	P	A	-	A	A
3	*'ah* 'ahh!'	P	P	A	-	P + *'ahah*	A
4	*'alle* 'woo!'	P	P	P	-	P	A
5	*'ənqʷā'* 'aha!'	P	P	A	-	P	A

6	*ḫassa* ‘wrong’	A	A	P	-	A	A
7	*ḫawisā* ‘greetings’	A	A	P	-	A	A
8	*kəmma* ‘thus’	A	P	A	-	A	A
9	*ṣaṭṭ* ‘silence’	A	P	P (*ṣat*)	-	A	A
10	*say* ‘woo!’	P	P (sayl)	A	-	P	A
11	*way* ‘woo!’	P	P	P	-	P	A
12	*wayle* ‘woo!’	P	P	A	-	P	A
13	*ye* ‘woo!’	P	P	A	-	P	A
14	*yo* ‘alas’	A	P	A	-	A	A
		7	**12**	**5**	**-**	**8**	

Table 6. Particles

	Particles	*’Aggabāb*	Dillmann	Conti Rossini	Tropper	Kidāna Wald	Weninger
1	*’a* ‘-’	P	A	A	P	P	A
2	*’akko* ‘not’	P	P	P	P	A	A
3	*’al* ‘not’, ‘non-’	P	P (*’albo*)	A	P (*’albo*)	P	A
4	*’alle* ‘woo!’	A	A	A	P	A	A
5	*bonu* ‘is ... indeed... ?’	A	A	A	A	P	A
6	*’əgzi’o* ‘please’	P	A	P	A	A	A
7	*’əlla* ‘of...’	P	P	A	A	P	A

8	*ʾənb* 'no'	P	P (*ʾənbəya*)	P	P	A	A
9	*ʾənbala* 'without'	A	A	A	P	A	A
10	*ʾəndāʿi* 'not sure'	P	A	A	P	A	A
11	*ʾəngā* 'maybe'	P	A	A	P	A	A
12	*ʾənka* 'now on'	A	A	A	P	A	A
13	*ʾənta* 'of...'	P	P	A	A	P	P
14	*ʾəsku* 'now!'	A	P	A	A	A	A
15	*ʾəwwa* 'yes', 'ja'	P	P	A	A	A	A
16	*gʷā* 'certainly'	P	A	A	A	A	A
17	*hā* '-'	P	A	A	A	A	A
18	*he* '-'	A	A	A	P	A	A
19	*hi* 'also'	A	A	A	P	A	A
20	*hu* 'is... ?'	P	A	P	P	P	A
21	*ʾi* 'non-', 'un-'	P	P	P	P	P	A
22	*la* 'of...'	P	P	P	A	P	P
23	*ma* '!'	P	A	A	P	A	A
24	*mi* 'how'	A	A	A	P	A	A
25	*nāhu* 'now', 'behold'	P	A	A	A	A	A
26	*nawā* 'now', 'behold'	P	A	A	A	A	A
27	*nayā* 'now', 'behold'	P	A	A	P	A	A
28	*ni* 'still'	A	A	A	P	A	A
29	*nu* 'is?', 'shall?'	P	A	P	P	P	A

30	*'o* 'o!'	P	A	P	P	P	A
31	*'oho* 'ok'	P	A	A	A	P	A
32	*sa* '!'	P	A	A	P	A	A
33	*so* '!'	P	P	A	A	A	A
34	*ke* '!'	P	A	A	P	A	A
35	*kəmma* 'then'	A	A	A	P	A	A
36	*way* 'woo!'	A	A	A	P	A	A
37	*yā* '!'	P	P	A	A	A	A
38	*yo* '!'	P	P	A	A	A	A
39	*za* 'of...'	P	P	P	A	P	A
		28	**12**	**9**	**23**	**12**	**2**

CHAPTER THREE: ADVERBS

This chapter deals with the linguistic elements which are used as adverbs focusing on their etymology, meaning and use. Ninety-seven individual elements are provided in three separate sections. The majorities are originally nouns which are placed in their accusative forms so that they may play the role of an adverb, and very few elements have neither other origins nor clear relations with verbs or nouns. Let us see each in detail.

3.1. ADVERBS OF PLACE

3.1.1. ህየ *həyya*, ለፌ *lafe*, ከሃ *kahā* and ዝየ *zəya*

On their origin, Dillmann claimed that *həyya* comes from ሄ *he*, and *zəya* from ዜ *ze* which is also used in the case of ይእዜ *yəʾəze*. This seems to mean that the core elements are *he* and *ze* and *ya* is a suffix in both cases. He also expressed *kahā* (*kaḥā*) as a combination of *ka* and *hā* of direction while connecting *lafe* with the verb ለፈየ *lafaya* 'separate' or 'divide'.[1] These last two expressions are supported by Leslau.[2] However, according to the tradition of *ʾAggabāb*, all are independent linguistic elements with no etymological affiliation with verbs or nouns. Their grammatical function is to be used as adverbs of locality.[3] In a sentence, each can either precede or follow a verb.

---

[1] Dillmann 1865, 65, 1344; 1907, 377.
[2] Leslau 2006, 154, 278, 646.
[3] Dillmann 1865, 13, 65, 823; Kidāna Wald Kəfle 1955, 158; Leslau 1989, 3, 13, 188.

ህየ *həyya* and ዝየ *zəya* have theoretically contrary meanings 'there' and 'here' respectively. They have similar orthographic structure and number of syllables. Nonetheless, they are pronounced in different ways, *həyya* is pronounced with a weak tone which tends to calm down at the ending point like the tone of a noun which ends with a second or a third order radical. On the contrary, *zəya* is pronounced with a strong tone, pushing out the air powerfully like a perfective or an imperfective verb. According to the tradition of the schools, the pronunciation mode of *həyya* is called ወዳቂ ንባብ *wadāqi nəbāb* while that of *zəya* is known as ተነሽ ንባብ *tanaš nəbāb.*

ለፌ *lafe* as an adverb of place is mostly used to indicate directions and sites with the meanings 'this/ that way', 'this/ that direction', 'this/ that side', 'this/ that place' and 'here'/ 'there'.

ከሃ *kahā* refers to a distant place with the precise meanings 'over there', 'that place', 'beyond' and 'the other side'.

Textual evidence:

3.1.1.1. ወእምዝ፡ ሰከበ፡ ወኖመ፡ ህየ፡ ታሕተ፡ ዕፅ። (1 Kgs 19:5).

wa-'əmz sakaba wa-noma həyya tāḥta 'əṣ́

<Conj-Adv> <V:Perf.3m.s> <Conj-V:Perf.3m.s> <Adv> <Prep> <NCom:unm.s.Nom>

'And then, he lay down and slept at that place under a tree'.

3.1.1.2. ወይትሀወኩ፡ ለፌ፡ ወለፌ። (Enoch (com.) 42:4).

wa-yəthawwaku lafe wa-lafe

<Conj-V:Imperf.3m.p> <Adv> <Conj-Adv>

'And they had been moving here and there'.

3.1.1.3. ትብልዎ፡ ለዝ፡ ደብር፡ ፍልስ፡ እም፡ ዝየ፡ ኀበ፡ ከሃ፡ ወይፈልስ። (Matt. 17:20).

təblə-wwo la-zə dabr

<V:Imperf.2.m.p-PSuff:3m.s> <Prep-PDem:m.s.Nom> <NCom:m^s.Nom>

fələs 'əm zəya ḫaba kahā wa-yəfalləs

<V:Impt.2m.s> <Prep> <Adv> <Prep> <Adv> <Conj-V:Imperf.3m.s>

'You will say to this mountain 'Move from here to there', and it will move'.

3.1.1.4. ነዋ፡ ሀለዉ፡ ክልኤቱ፡ መጣብሕ፡ ዝየ። (Luke 22:38).

nawā hallawu kəl'ettu maṭābəḥ zəya

<PartPres> <V:Perf.3m.p> <NumCa.Nom> <NCom:ms.p> <Adv>

'Behold there are two swords here'.

Further references: Ezek.11:18, 32:23; Matt. 24:33; Mark 14:32, 34; Luke 19:24; John 18:1,2 19:18; Acts 22:5, 19.

The elements which are recognized as prepositions of place or direction such as መንገለ *mangala,* በ *ba,* ኀበ *ḫaba,* እም *'əm,* እስከ *'əska* and እንተ *'ənta* can be attached to each one of the elements, keeping or not keeping their own ordinary meaning

Textual evidence:

3.1.1.5. አንሰኬ፡ በህየ፡ ተወለድኩ። (Acts 22:28).

'ansa-ke ba-həyya tawaladku

<PPer:1c.s-Part> <Prep-Adv> <V:Perf.1c.s>

'But I was actually born there' (here no word representing ba).

3.1.1.6. ፀቊን፡ እም፡ ለፌ፡ ወፀቊን፡ እም፡ ለፌ። (Num. 22:24).

ḍaqwan 'əm lafe wa-ḍaqwan 'əm lafe

<NCom:unm.s.Nom> <Prep> <Adv> <Conj-NCom:unm.s.Nom> <Prep> <Adv>

'A wall on this side and a wall on that side...'.

3.1.1.7. ተንሥኡ፡ ንሑር፡ እም፡ ዝየ። (John 14:31).

tanś'ə'u nəḥur 'əm zəya

<V:Impt.2m.p> <V:Subj (Impt).2c.p> <Prep> <Adv>

'Get up, let us go from here'.

Further references: Neh. 3:30 Ps. 131:17; Job 13:9; S. of S. 7:12, 8:5; Jer. 38:9; Ezek. 8:4,14, 29:31; Acts 27:12.

But even in the absence of the above-mentioned elements, the elements by themselves can introduce the concept of any possible element in translation.

Textual evidence:

3.1.1.8. ወበጺሖ፡ ህየ፡ ይቤሎሙ፡ ጸልዩ። (Luke 22:40).

wa-baṣiḥo həyya yəbel-omu ṣalləyu

<Conj-V:Ger.3m.s> <Adv> <V:Perf.3m.s-PSuff:3m.p> <V:Impt.2m.p>

'And having been arrived at the place, he said them 'pray!''

3.1.1.9. ረቢ፡ ማእዜ፡ በጻሕከ፡ ዝየ። (John 6:25).

Rabbi māʾəze baṣāḥ-ka zəya

<NCom.m.s> <AInt> <V:Perf.2m.s-PSuff:2m.s> <Adv>

'Rabbi, when did you come up to this place?'

Further references: Job 3:17; Ps. 131:14; Jer. 37:12; Mark 14:69, 15:35, 16:6; Luke 19:27.

ለፌ *lafe* and ከሃ *kahā* can take pronominal suffixes to determine persons in both singular and plural forms. As usual the pronominal suffixes are *hu* (3m.s), *ka* (2m.s), *ha* (3f.s), *ki* (2f.s), *homu* (3m.p), *kəmu* (2m.p), *hon* (3f.p), *kən* (2f.p), *ya* (1c.s) and *na* (1c.p).

3.1.2. ላዕለ *lāʿəla*, ላዕሉ *lāʿəlu* and ላዕሊተ *lāʿəlita*

ላዕለ *lāʿəla* in such a specific case is the accusative form of the noun ላዕል *lāʿəl* which is etymologically related with the verb ለዐለ *laʿala*, ተለዐለ *talaʿala*, ተልዕለ *talʿəla* 'go upward', 'be great', 'be superior', 'be the highest one'.

ላዕሊተ *lāʿəlita* is also the accusative form of ላዕሊት *lāʿəlit* 'the highest one' (feminin). The elements of the same category ታሕተ *tāḥta*, ታሕቱ *tāḥtu*, ታሕቲተ *tāḥətita* and መትሕተ *matḥəta* are their negative counterparts.

They are used as adverbs in expression of place or position with the meanings 'above', 'greatly', 'superiorly', 'upward' and 'upwardly'.[1] In a sentence, each occurs alone either before or after a verb. *Lāʿəlu* exceptionally takes an initial attachment of a possible place preposition such as *ba* and *əm*.

Textual evidence:

3.1.2.1. ወንስአል፡ አንቃዕዲወነ፡ ላዕለ። (Haym. (com.) 10:2).

wa-nəsʾal ʾanqāʿədiwana lāʿəla

<Conj-V:Subj.2m.p> <V:Ger.1c..p> <Adv>

'And we may pray gazing upward'.

3.1.2.2. ተፋቀዱ፡ ዘእም፡ እስራ፡ ዓም፡ ወላዕሉ። (Num. 26:4).

tafāqadu za-ʾəm ʾəsrā ʿām wa-lāʿəlu

<V:Impt.2m.p> <PRel-Prep> <NumCa> <NCom:unm.s> <Conj-Part>

'Take a census of those who are twenty years old and over'.

3.1.2.3. አልቦ፡ ከማከ፡ አምላክ፡ በሰማይ፡ በላዕሉ፡ ወበምድር፡ በታሕቱ። (1 Kgs 8:21).

ʾalbo kamā-ka ʾamlāk ba-samāy

<ExNeg-Verb> <Prep-PSuff:2m.s> <NCom:m.s.Nom> <Prep-NCom:unm.s.Nom>

ba-lāʿəlu wa-ba-mədr ba-tāḥtu

<Prep-Prep-Psuff:3m.s> <Conj-Prep-NCom:unm.s.Nom> <Prep-Prep-Psuff:3m.s>

'There is no God like you in heaven above or on earth beneath'.

Further references: Sir. 43.1; 2 Chr. 25:5

---

[1] Dillmann 1865, 56, 59; Kidāna Wald Kəfle 1955, 89; Leslau 2006, 304.

3.1.3. መንጸረ *manṣara* and አንጸረ *'anṣara*

Both elements share the same root with the verb ነጸረ *naṣṣara* 'see', 'look' and 'watch'. They are the accusative forms of the substantives መንጸር *manṣar* and አንጸር *'anṣār* respectively. The elements have the same grammatical function and meaning even if different affixes (መ *ma* and አ *'a*) are added to their roots ንጸር *nəṣar* and ንጸር *nəṣār* initially. They are used equally as adverbial elements with the meanings 'forward', 'forwardly', 'opposite facing' and 'parallel' concerned with the notions of direction, position and site.[1]

Theoretically, as adverbs, they occur alone either before or after a verb without being convinced to any word attachment.

Textual evidence:

3.1.3.1. ኢሖረ፡ በከመ፡ ያለምድ፡ መንጸረ፡ ቅድሜሁ፡ ለአስተቃስሞ። (Num. 24:1).

'i-ḥora ba-kama yālammәd manṣara qәdme-hu

<PartNeg-V:Perf.3m.s> <Prep> <Conj-V:Imperf.3m.s> <Adv> <Prep-PSuff:3m.s>

la-'astaqāsәmo

<Prep-V:Inf.Nom>

'He did not go forward before him to seek omens as he was accustomed'.

3.1.4. መትሕተ *matḥәta*, ታሕተ *tāḥta* and ታሕቲተ *tāḥtita*[2]

Tāḥt is the the noun which is etymologically affiliated with the substantives *matḥәt* and *tāḥtit* including the verb ተትሕተ *tatḥәta* 'be humble', 'be lower'. Leslau claimed that the original form of the verb is ትሕተ *təḥta* or ተሐተ *taḥata* but not *tatḥәta*.[3] But it is difficult to find any textual reading in these forms.

[1] Dillmann 1865, 702-703; Kidāna Wald Kәfle 1955, 650; Leslau 1989, 130.
[2] Dillmann 1865, 319; Kidāna Wald Kәfle 1955, 895; Leslau 1989, 106, 107.
[3] Leslau 2006, 572.

The elements are used as adverbs in expression of place and position. They occur alone before or after a verb with the meanings 'under', 'down', 'downward' and 'beneath'.

Textual evidence:

3.1.4.1. ወታሕተ፡ ውስተ፡ ምድር፡ ትሬእዩ። (Isa. 8:22).

wa-tāḥta wəsta mədr təreʼəyu

<Conj-Adv> <Prep> <NCom:unm.s.Nom> <V:Imperf.2m.p>

'And you look downward to the earth'.

3.1.5. ትርአሰ *tərʼasa* and ትርጋጸ *tərgāṣa*

ትርአሰ *tərʼasa* is the accusative form of the noun ትርአሰ *tərʼas* which is etymologically affiliated with the verb ተተርአሰ *tatarʼasa* 'lie on a cushion'. Similarly, the noun ትርጋጸ *tərgāṣa* is the accusative form of ትርጋጽ *tərgāṣ* which is related with the verb ረገጸ *ragaṣa* 'trample'.[1]

Both are not considered as parts of the adverbial elements by almost all grammarians whose works are mentioned in the review. However, according to the tradition of *ʼAggabāb*, they are used as adverbs in expressing a position with the meanings 'at the head'/ 'at the top' and 'at the foot'/ 'at the bottom' respectively. They occur alone. Their frequent position is after the verb.

Textual evidence:

3.1.5.1. ወይነብሩ፡ አሐዱ፡ ትርአሰ፡ ወአሐዱ፡ ትርጋጸ። (John 20:12).

wa-yənabbəru ʼaḥadu tərʼasa wa-ʼaḥadu tərgāṣa

<Conj-V:Imperf.3m.p> <NumCa> <Adv> <Conj-NumCa> <Adv>

'They were sitting, one at head and the one at the feet'.

---

1 Dillmann 1865, 1389; Kidāna Wald Kəfle 1955, 157; Leslau 1989, 64, 107.

3.1.6. ፍጽመ *fəṣma*

ፍጽመ *fəṣma* is initially the accusative form of ፍጽም the noun which is related with the verb ፈጸመ *faṣṣama* 'finish', 'accomplish', 'complete'. Its grammatical function is to be used as an adverb in expression of place with the meanings 'before', 'face-to-face', 'in front' and 'personally'.[1]

Textual evidence:

3.1.6.1. ወአቅምዎ፡ ፍጽመ፡ ወተመየጡ፡ ወኅድግዎ፡ ይቀስል፡ ወይሙት። (2 Sam. 11:16).

wa-'aqəmə-wwo fəṣma wa-tamayaṭu

<Conj-V:Impt.2m.p-PSuff:3m.s> <Adv> <Conj-V:Impt.2m.p-PSuff: 3m.s>

wa-ḫədgə-wwo yəqʷəsəl wa-yəmut

<Conj-V:Impt.2m.p-PSuff:3m.s> <V:Subj.3m.s> <Conj-V:Subj.3m.s>

'Place him in front and come back leaving him alone so that he shall be wounded and die'.

3.1.6.2. እስመ፡ ተቃወምከ፡ ፍጽመ፡ አመ፡ ጼወውዎሙ፡ ካልእ፡ ሕዝብ። (Obad.1:11).

'əsma taqāwamka fəṣma...'ama ṣewawə-wwomu

<Conj> <V:Perf.3m.s-PSuff:2m.s> <Adv> <Prep-V:Perf-3m.p-PSuff:3m.p>

kālə' ḥəzb

<NumOr.Nom> <NCom:m[s].p.Nom>

'...because you opposed him personally when stranger people captured them'.

---

[1] Dillmann 1907, 383; Leslau 2006, 169.

3.2. ADVERBS OF TIME

3.2.1. ለፌ *lafe*

In the previous sub-section, we have seen its function as an adverb of place. The following textual reading indicates how it can be used in expression of time[1] in collaboration with እም *ʾəm* with the meanings: 'from .... on' and 'afterwards'.

Textual evidence:

3.2.1.1. ፎጢኖስ፡ ይቤ፡ ለፌ፡ እማርያም፡ ህላዌሁ፡ ለወልደ፡ እግዚአብሔር፡ ወአኮ፡ እም፡ ትካት። (M. Məśṭir 1:14).

foṭinos yəbe lafe ʾəm-mārəyam həllāwe-hu

<NPro.m.s.Nom> <V:Perf.m.s> <Adv> <Prep-NPro.f.s.Nom> <NCom:unm.s.PSuff:3m.s>

la-walda ʾəgziʾabəḥer wa-ʾakko ʾəm təkāt

<Prep-NCom:m.s.ConSt> <NCom.m.s.Nom> <Conj> <ExNeg> <Prep-Adv>

'Photinus said, the existence of the Son of God is from Mary onward, but not from the ancient time'.

Leslau focused on its function as an adverb of place; he did not mention while explaining about the element as it works also as expressing time. But Dillman put consciously both functions of the element in his lexicon.[2]

3.2.2. መቅድመ *maqdəma*, ቀዲሙ *qadimu*, ቀዳሚ *qadāmi*, ቅድመ *qədma*, ቅድም *qədm* and አቅዲሙ *ʾaqdimu*

Etymologically, all these elements are related with one another; *qdm* (*qədm*) which is the root of all the remaining elements including the verb ቀደመ *qadama* 'be first', 'take ahead' and 'proceed'. *Qədma* is its accusative form as *maqdəma* is the same to the nominative *maqdəm*. *Qadimu* is also a substantive while *qadāmi* is the active participle of

---

[1] Dillmann 1865, 65; Kidāna Wald Kəfle 1955, 570; Leslau 1989, 13.

[2] Dillmann 1865, 65-66; Leslau 2006, 306-307.

qadama. Only *maqdəma* and *qədma* are formed exclusively in accusative form.

They are precisely concerned with time and sequence; this leads them to be regarded as adverbial elements of time and progression with the meanings 'at first', 'at the beginning', 'before', 'earlier', 'firstly', 'formerly', 'in ancient time', 'previously' and 'primarily'.[1] The elements of the same group ከዋላ *kawālā*, ዮም *yom*, ይእዜ *yə'əze* , ዳኅሪ *dahāri* and ድኅረ *dəhra* are recognized to be their negative counterparts.

They (except *qədm)* frequently occur alone unless when they need to take the initial attachment of a viable preposition such as *ba* and *'əm*. For *qədm*, the initial attachment of one of the aforementioned elements is apparently unavoidable to be used as an adverb.[2]

Textual evidence:

3.2.2.1. ቀዳሚኒ፡ ነገርኩክሙ። (John 8:25).

qadāmi-ni nagarku-kəmu

<Adv-Part> <V:Perf.1c.s:PSuff:2m.p>

'Even in the beginning, I have told you'.

3.2.2.2. ዘቅድመ፡ ሀሎ፡ ወይሄሉ፡ እስከ፡ ለዓለም። (Haym. (com.) 2:3).

za-qədma hallo wa-yəhellu 'əska-la'ālam

<PRel-Adv> <V:Perf.3m.s> <Conj-V:Imperf.3m.s> <Prep-Adv>

'He who was before, and who lives forever...'.

3.2.2.3. ሀሎከኑ፡ ቀዲሙ፡ አመ፡ ይፈጥር፡ ኵሎ፡ ዓለመ። (Job 11:6).

halloka-nu qadimu'ama yəfaṭṭər kʷəllo 'ālama

<V:Perf.2m.s-Part> <Adv> <Conj> <V:Imperf.3m.s> <PTot.Acc> <NCom:unm.s.Acc>

---

[1] Dillmann 1865, 462-463; Kidāna Wald Kəfle 1955, 89, 150, 158; Leslau 1989, 90.

[2] Dillmann 1907, 385-386.

'Have you existed in ancient time when he was creating the entire world?'

Further references: Ezra 9:2 Sir. 37:8; Job 13:10, 42:11; John 1:1; Rom. 11:30.

* Note that every employment of *qadāmi* cannot represent its nature of adverbial element. As an active participle in origin, it can also be used to express a noun. Example: ቀዳሚ፡ ወርኅ፡ *qadāmi warḫ* 'the first month' Josh 4:19. So, in such cases, it cannot be declared as an adverbial element.

3.2.3. ሳኒታ *sānitā*, ትማልም *təmāləm*, ትካት *təkāt*, ይእዜ *yə'əze*, የዮም *yom* and ጌሠም *geśam*

All these elements are used as adverbs in expression of time. All except *sānitā* and *təkāt* are not related originally with verbs or other nouns. *Sānitā* has a connection with the noun ሰኑይ *sanuy* 'two' or 'second', which is also the name of the second day of the week (monday). So, *sānit* is a feminine equivalent of the masculine *sanuy* and *-ā* is a prenominal suffix of the third person feminine singular. Leslau claimed ሳንይ *sānəy* 'The next day' to be its equivalent.[1] He has also connected *geśam* with ጋይስ *gays* 'journey'.[2]

Similarly, the origin of *təkāt* is related with that of the verb *takata* 'be ancient' or 'be late'. It literally means 'ancient' or 'old time'.[3] Again, on the formation of *yə'əze* , Dillmann stated that it is a compound of *yə* and *ze*, and that it at once refered to place and was transferred to time.[4] But in the tradition of *'Aggabāb* acknowledges it only as an adverb of time.

Due to their meaning, they can be sub-divided into three:

3.2.3.1. Elements concerned with a past time: ትማልም *təmāləm* and ትካት *təkāt*

3.2.3.2. Elements concerned with a present time: ይእዜ *yə'əze* and ዮም *yom*

[1] Leslau 2006, 509.
[2] Leslau 2006, 208.
[3] Dillmann 1865, 566; Kidāna Wald Kəfle 1955, 898; Leslau 2006, 574.
[4] Dillmann 1907, 377.

3.2.3.3. Elements concerned with a future time: ሳኒታ *sānitā* and ጌሠም *geśam*

Let us see each sub-category one by one.

3.2.3.1. Elements concerned with a past time: ትማልም *təmāləm* and ትካት *təkāt*

ትማልም *təmāləm* means literally 'yesterday', and ትካት *təkāt* means 'before', 'earlier', and 'ancient time'.[1] As adverbs, their function is not edged only with a particular day, but rather they can express days, seasons, years, ages and a period of time in the past

Thus, they can be translated as follows 'yesterday', 'at/ during/ on the day' 'before the present day', 'before', 'earlier', 'in ancient time', 'previously', 'at the time in the past'. Even if both have the same dimension, and can demonstrate the time which has already passed, there is still a difference between them regarding a degree; *təmāləm* refers to the recent past time while *təkāt* is mainly to demonstrate the non-recent time. That means its use is interrelated especially with the ancient time or with the beginning time of any incident.

Textual evidence:

3.2.3.1.1. (*təmāləm* 'yesterday') በከመ፡ ቀተልካሁ፡ ትማልም፡ ለግብጻዊ። (Exod. 2:14).

ba-kama qatalkā-hu təmāləm la-gəbṣāwi

<Prep-Conj> <V:Perf.2m.s-Suff:3m.s> <Adv> <Prep-NCom:m.s.Nom>

'As you killed the Egyptian yesterday...'.

3.2.3.1.2. (*təmāləm* 'as unfixed time') ዘትማልም፡ ወዮም። (Heb. 13:8).

za-təmāləm wa-yom

<PRel:m.s-Adv> <Conj-Adv>

'He who was before and is today'.

---

[1] Dillmann 1865, 555, 566; Kidāna Wald Kəfle 1955, 151; Leslau 1989, 107, 109.

3.2.3.1.3. (*təkāt* 'beginning') ወአንትሙኒ፡ ሰማዕትየ፡ እስመ፡ እም፡ ትካት፡ ሀለውክሙ፡ ምስሌየ። (John 15:27).

wa-'antəmu-hi samāʿtə-ya 'əsma 'əm

<Conj-PPer:2m.p-Part> <NCom:m[s].P.PSt-PSuff:1c.s> <Conj> <Prep>

təkāt hallawkəmu məsle-ya

<Adv> <V:Perf.2m.p> <Prep-Psuff:1c.s>

'You are also my witnesses for you have been with me from the beginning'.

3.2.3.1.4. (*təkāt-* as unfixed ancient time) እም፡ ትካት፡ አእመርኩ፡ ስምዐከ። (Ps. 118:152).

'əm təkāt 'a'əmarku səmʿa-ka

<Prep> <Adv> <V:Perf.1c.s> <NCom:unm.s.Acc-PSuff:2m.s>

'From old, I have known your testimony'.

Further references: Gen. 31:42; Josh. 4:17; PS. 76:5, 76:11, 77:2; Wisd. (com.) 8:17; Sir. 37:25; Eph. 5:8; Heb. 1:1.

3.2.3.2. Elements concerned with a present time: ይእዜ *yə'əze* and ዮም *yom*

Their literal meaning is 'today'. However, as adverbs of time, they can indicate the present day and yet the unfixed time and will be determined as follows 'today', 'this day/ age/ period/ time', 'currently', 'at present' and 'nowadays'.[1]

Textual evidence:

3.2.3.2.1. (*yə'əze* - as a present day) ናሁ፡ እም፡ ይእዜሰ፡ ያስተበፅዑኒ፡ ኵሉ፡ ትውልድ። (Luke 1:48).

Nāhu 'əm yə'əze -ssa yastabaḍəʿu-ni kʷəllu təwlədd

---

[1] Dillmann 1865, 189, 1072; Kidāna Wald Kəfle 1955, 151; Leslau 1989, 189, 190.

<Adv> <Prep> <Adv-Part> <V:Imperf.3m.p-PSuff:1c.s> <PTot.Nom> <NCom:unm.p^{s}.Nom>

'Behold, from this day on, all generations will bless me'.

3.2.3.2.2. (*yom-* as a present day) ወናሁ፡ አሰምዕ፡ ለክሙ፡ ዮም፡ በዛቲ፡ ዕለት...። (Acts 20:26).

wa-nāhu ʾasammǝʿ la-kǝmu yom ba-zātti ʿǝlat

<Conj-Adv> <V:Imperf.1c.s> <Prep-PSuff:2m.p> <Adv> <Prep-PDem:f.s.Nom> <NCom: unm.s.Nom>

'And now, I testify today, this very day...'

3.2.3.2.3. (*yǝʾǝze* - as unfixed time) ወይእዜኒ፡ አማኅፀንኩክሙ፡ ኀበ፡ እግዚአብሔር። (Acts 20:32).

wa-yǝʾǝze -ni ʾamāḫḍanku-kǝmuḫaba ʾǝgziʾabǝḥer

<Conj-Adv-Part> <V:Perf.1c.s-PSuff:2m.p> <Prep> <NCom:m.s.Nom>

'And now, I entrust you to God'.

3.2.3.2.4. (*yom-* as unfixed time) ወእም፡ ዮምሰ፡ ያፈቅረኒ፡ ምትየ። (Gen. 30:19).

wa-ʾǝm yom-ssa yāfaqqǝra-nni mǝṭǝ-ya

<Conj-Prep> <Adv-Part> <V:Imperf.3m.s-PSuff:1c.s> <NCom:m.s. Nom-PSuff:1c.s>

'From now on, my husband will love me'.

Further references: Gen. 24:12, 30:15, 31:43, 35:4; Josh. 4:9, 5:10; Ps. 2:7, 10, 94:8; Prov. (com.) 22:20; Luke 13:32, 19:5; Acts 20:28, 22:3; Heb. 3:15; Anp.Ath (com.) verse 3.

The elements under the first and the second sub-categories are not going to be combined with other words and phrases except some appropriate elements such as: ቅድመ *qǝdma*, እም፡ ቅድመ *ʾǝm-qǝdma*, አንተ *ʾǝnta*, እለ *ʾǝlla*, ዘ *za*, እም *ʾǝm* and እስከ *ʾǝska*. Their ending vowels remain the same in all cases.

3.2.3.3. Elements concerned with a future time : ሳኒታ *sānitā* and ጌሠም *geśam*[1]

These are concerned with a time in the future to a short extent with the meanings 'the next day' and 'tomorrow' respectively. However, as adverbs, they are used to indicate the day and at the same time the unfixed age or time which has to come.

Textual evidence:

3.2.3.3.1. ብሉየ፡ መዋዕል፡ ዘእንበለ፡ ዮም፡ ወጌሠም። (Anp. Gry (com.) verse 22).

bəlluya mawāʿəl za-ʾənbala-yom wa-geśam

<NCom:m.s.Nom.ConSt> <NCom:unm.c.Nom> <PRel-Conj-Adv> <Conj-Adv>

'The ancient of days without today and tomorrow'.

Each element has its own feature which is not shared by the others. For example: *sānitā* can receive a pronominal suffix of the third person singular male ሁ *hu*, and the preposition በ *ba* is mostly used to be attached to it initially to form a fixed phrase 'On the next day'. Likewise, *geśam* is the only element which exceptionally changes and adds the vowel 'a' at the end in the case of accusative phrases. The initial attachment of the viable prepositions mentioned earlier still works even in the cases of *sānitā* and *geśam.*

Textual evidence:

3.2.3.3.2. ወይቤ፡ ጌሠመ፡ ይገብር፡ እግዚእ፡ ዘ፡ ነገረ። (Exod. 9:5).

wa-yəbe geśama yəgabbər ʾəgziʾ za nagara

<Conj-V:Perf.3m.s> <Adv> <V:Imperf.3m.s> <NCom:m.s.Nom> <PDem.Acc><Ncom :unm.s.Acc>

'And he said: tomorrow, I will do this thing'.

---

[1] Kidāna Wald Kəfle 1955, 151; Leslau 1989, 73, 211.

3.2.3.3.3. ወበሳኒታ፡ ፈቀደ፡ መልአክ፡ ያእምር፡ ጥዩቀ፡ በእንተ፡ ምንት፡ ያስተዋድይዎ፡ አይሁድ። (Acts 22:30).

wa-basānitā faqada malak yāʾmər ṭəyyuqa

<Conj-Prep-Adv> <V:Perf.3m.s> <NCom:m.s.Nom> <V:Subj.3m.s>

baʾənta-mənt yastawāddəyə-wwo ʾayhud

<Adv> <Prep-AInt> <V:Imperf.3m.p-PSuff:3m.s> <NCom:m.p.Nom>

'On the next day, the commander wanted to know why the Jews accuse him'.

In narrating a story, *sānitā* can be used exceptionally to express a day in the past. Its meaning, however, remains the same even in such cases.

3.2.3.3.4. ወገብረ፡ እግዚአ፡ ዘ፡ ነገረ፡ በሳኒታሁ። (Exod. 9:5).

wa-gabra ʾəgziʾabəḥer za nagara ba-sānitā-hu

<Conj-V:Perf.3m.s> <NCom:m.s.Nom> <PDem.Acc> <NCom:unm.s.Acc> <Prep Adv-Psuff:3m.s>

'And the Lord did this thing on the next day'.

Further references: John 1:29; Acts 22:30.

3.2.4. አሚረ *ʾamira*

It is originally the accusative form of the noun አሚር *ʾamir* (lit.: 'time', 'moment', 'occasion' and 'point').[1] Its function is to be used as adverb of time in nominative or in accusative form. If ውእቱ *wəʾətu* or ይእቲ *yəʾəti* combined with a certain preposition such as ለ *la*, በ *ba* and እም *ʾəm* precedes it, it should keep a nominative form. Otherwise, it is employed in an accusative form to be parallel to the accusative

[1] Dillmann 1865, 731; Kidāna Wald Kəfle 1955, 228. Leslau gives it the meanings of 'sun', 'day' and 'time'. Leslau 2006, 26. 'Day' and 'time' are corresponding to its functionality of an adverb. But the concept 'sun' does not go together. This might be አሜር *ʾamer* (acc.: *ʾamera*) 'sun' or 'sun's light' - ለመልክእኪ፡ ዘተሠርገወ፡ አሜረ *selām la-malkəʾə-ki za-taśargawa ʾamera* 'Greetings to your image which shines like a sun' Malkəʾa Maryam - Hymn 52.

form of *wəʾətu, yəʾəti* or ኵሉ *kʷəllu* (wəʾəta, *yəʾəta* and *kʷəllo*). These demonstrative pronouns are expected to occur together and can clearly express it as to which specific time or moment it refers.

If it comes together with *wəʾətu* or *yəʾəti,* it refers to a specific time, but if it comes after *kʷəllo,* it is to mean 'all day-time', 'always' or 'continually'.

Textual evidence:

3.2.4.1. ወእም፡ ይእቲ፡ አሚር፡ ተፈወሰ፡ ውእቱ፡ ማይ። (2 Kgs 2:22).

wa-ʾəm yəʾəti ʾamir tafawwasa wəʾətu māy

<Conj-Prep> <PPer:3f.s> <Adv> <V:Perf.3m.s> <PPer:3m.s> <NCom:unm.s.Nom>

'And since that very time, the water was healed'.

3.2.4.2. ወተሰብሩ፡ ሠራዊቶሙ፡ ይእተ፡ አሚረ። (1 Kgs 22:34).

wa-tasabru śarāwit-omu yəʾta ʾamira

<Conj-V:Perf.3m.p> <NCom:unm.p.Nom:PSuff:3m.p> <PPer:3f.Acc> <Adv>

'And at that moment, their armies fled back'.

3.2.4.3. ወትጼዕረኒ፡ ልብየ፡ ኵሎ፡ አሚረ። (Ps. 12:2).

wa-təṣeʿəra-nni ləbbə-ya kʷəllo ʾamira

<Conj-V:Imperf.3f.s-PSuff:1c.s> <NCom:unm.s.Nom:Psuff:1c.s> <PTot.Acc> <Adv>

'And my heart suffers all the time'.

Further references: Ps. 77:34; Sir. 18:6; John 14:20.

3.2.5. ከዋላ *kawālā*, ደኃሪ *daḫāri* and ድኅረ *dəḫra*

ከዋላ *kawālā* is a noun related with the verb ተከውለ *takawla.* ደኃሪ *daḫāri* is also a substantive related with the verb ተድኅረ *tadḫəra* while ድኅረ *dəḫra* is the accusative form of the noun *dəḫr* which is related with the same verb. Both verbs have almost similar meanings 'remain behind', 'go back', 'reverse', 'be behind', 'be last' and 'be late.[1] Leslau presented the verbs in the form of ከወለ *kawala* and ደኀረ *dahara* by dropping the initial *ta*.[2] But in accordance with the Qəne Schools' tradition, *kawla* and *dahara* are studied as variants but not taken as formal forms since the variants that are frequently attested in various texts are *takawla* and *tadhəra*.

The elements are used as adverbs in expression of time, position, schedule and sequence with the meanings 'after', 'lastly', 'afterward', 'behind', 'at the end', 'later', 'next' and 'subsequently'.[3] The elements of the same category መቅድመ *maqdəma*, ቀዲሙ *qadimu*, ቀዳሚ *qadāmi*, ቅድመ *qədma* and አቅዲሙ *'aqdimu* are their negative counterparts due to their lexical meanings.

In another way of functionality, ደኃሪ *dahāri* can keep an initial attachment of the prepositions *ba* and *'əm*. In such cases, it is often expected to be followed by a certain noun which indicates time (e.g.: ዘመን *zaman*, ዓመት *'āmat*, መዋዕል *mawā'əl*, ዕለት *'əlat* and ጊዜ *gize*). However, in such employment it plays the role of adjective, but not of an adverb since it is used to express the noun.

When it functions as an adverb, it occurs always alone like its fellow *kawālā* and *dəhra*.

Textual evidence:

3.2.5.1. (Elem. - verb) ተዐገሣ፡ ለመዐት፡ ወድኅረ፡ ታስተፌሥሐከ። (Sir. 1:22).

ta'agass-ā la-ma'at wa-dəhra tastafeśśəha-kka

<V:Impt.2m.s> <Prep-NCom:unm.s.Nom> <Conj-Adv> <V:Imperf.3f.s-PSuff:2m.s>

'Be patient on anger, and it will please you later'.

3.2.5.2. (verb - part) ለኪሰ፡ ወለወልድኪ፡ ትገብሪ፡ ድኅረ። (1 Kgs 17:12).

la-ki-ssa wa-la-waldə-ki

---

1 Leslau 1989, 156, 196.

2 Leslau 2006, 129, 299.

3 Dillmann 1865, 860, 1109-1110; Kidāna Wald Kəfle 1955, 158-159; Leslau 1989, 156.

<Prep-PSuff:2f.s-Part> <Conj-Prep-NCom:m.s.Nom-PSuff:2f.s>

təgabbəri dəḫra

<V:Imperf:2f.s> <Adv>

'But for you and your son, you may make later'.

Further references: Prov. (com.) 5:11; Luke 13:30; Anap.Eph (com.) verse 24.

3.2.6. ኵሉሄ *kʷəllahe*, ወትረ *watra*, ውቱረ *wəttura*, ዘልፈ *zalfa*, ዝላፉ *zəlāfu*, ለዝሉፉ *la-zəlufu* and ግሙራ *gəmurā*

ኵሉሄ *kʷəllahe* and ግሙራ *gəmurā* have not an etymological relation with verbs. On the origin of *kʷəllahe*, Dillmann announced that it is a compound of *kʷəll* and *he*, the *he* which corresponds in meaning to *ne* in *ʾaḥattane*.[1] Tropper indicated that this *he* is to mean 'here' and 'there'.[2]

Leslau has also realised a relation between ግሙራ *gəmurā* and ገመረ *gamara*/ አግመረ *ʾagmara* 'accomplish' or 'complete'.[3] There is indeed an immense graphic and phonetic similarity between ኵሉሄ *kʷəllahe* and ኵሉ *kʷəllu*, and between ግሙራ *gəmura* and the adjective ግሙር *gəmur*. However, in accordance with the *ʾAggabāb* tradition, they are different in pattern and in grammatical function.

In contrast, the remaining five elements are etymologically related with the verbs አውተረ *ʾawtara* and አዝለፈ *ʾazlafa* 'continue' and 'keep continually', they share the same root. Specifically, *watra* and *wəttura* are related with *ʾawtara*, and *zalfa*, *zəlāfu*, and *la-zəlufu* are similarly related with *ʾazlafa*. In many texts ለዝላፉ *lazəlāfu* is treated instead of *lazəlufu*. However, this does not make any change on its meaning.

They can plausibly precede or follow verbs, but do not entertain a combination of other words in the state of adverbial elements except the initial attachment of possible elements that can be used as

---

1 Dillmann 1907, 377.

2 Tropper 2002, 153.

3 Leslau 2006, 194-195.

prepositions or conjunctions such as አምጣነ *ʾamṭāna*, ከመ *kama*, እስመ *ʾəsma* and እንዘ *ʾənza*. This means every attestation of the elements as combined with nouns specifically keeping the second position in the combination cannot be recognized as a feature of an adverb.

Example:

3.2.6.1. መሥዋዕተ፡ ዘልፍ፡ ዘለለሠርቀ፡ ወርኀ። (Ezra 3:5).

maśwāʿəta zalf za-lalla-śarqa warḫ

<NCom:unm.s.ConSt> <NCom:unm.s.Nom> <PRel-Prep-Prep-NCom:unm.s.ConSt> <NCom:unm.s.Nom>

'Daily sacrifice of each first day of a month'.

Kʷəllahe and *gəmurā* have random tendency of keeping the attachment of *ba* and *la* respectively. Such a combination introduces the most used fixed phrases በኵለሄ *ba-kʷəllahe* and ለግሙራ *la-gəmurā*. Otherwise, each must be employed individually.

The most important grammatical function that all these elements share is to be used as an adverb in expression of frequency or continuity with the meanings 'all the time', 'always', 'constantly', 'ever', 'forever', 'frequently' and 'often'.[1]

Textual evidence:

3.2.6.2. እንዘ፡ ሀሎከ፡ ኵለሄ። (Anap.John (com.) verse 28).

ʾənza halloka kʷəllahe

<Conj> <V:Perf.2m.s-PSuff:2m.s> <Adv>

'Since you live all the time....'.

3.2.6.3. ወብፁዓን፡ አግብርቲከ፡ እለ፡ ይቀውሙ፡ ቅድሜከ፡ ወትረ። (1 Kgs 10:8).

wa-bəṣuʿān ʾagbərti-ka ʾəlla yəqawwəmu

<Conj-NCom:m.p.Nom> <NCom:m.p.Nom-PSuff:2m.s> <PRel>

[1] Dillmann 1865, 816, 915, 1035, 1147; Kidāna Wald Kəfle 1955, 151, 157, 203. Leslau described it specifically as an adverb of place with the meanings 'everywhere' and 'wherever' Leslau 2006, 281.

qədme-ka watra

<V:Imperf.3m.p> <Prep-PSuff:2m.s> <Adv>

'Blessed are your servants who stand before you continually'.

3.2.6.4. ወንሄሉ፡ እንከ፡ ዘልፈ፡ ኀበ፡ እግዚእነ። (1 Thess. 4:17).

wa-nəhellu 'ənka zalfa ḫaba 'əgzi'ə-na

<Conj-V:Imperf.1c.p> <Adv> <Adv> <Prep-NCom:m.s.Nom-PSuff:1c.p>

'And then, we will be always with our Lord'.

3.2.6.5. ኢትትአመኖ፡ ለጸላኢከ፡ ለዝላፉ። (Sir. 12:10).

'i-tət'amann-o la-ṣalā'i-ka la-zəlāfu

<PartNeg-V:Subj.2m.s> <Prep-NCom:m.s.Nom-PSuff:2m.s> <Adv>

'You shall not trust your enemy any longer'.

3.2.6.6. ወኢተአብስ፡ ለዝሉፉ። (Sir. 7:36).

wa-'i-ta'abbəs lazəlufu

<Conj-PartNeg-V:Imperf:2m.s> <Adv>

'And you shall not sin always'.

3.2.6.7. እስከ፡ ማእዜኑ፡ እግዚኦ፡ ትረስአኒ፡ ለግሙራ። (Ps. 12:1).

'əska mā'əze-nu 'əgzi'o tərassə'a-nni la-gəmurā

<Prep> <AInt-PartInt> <PartSup> <V:Imperf.2m.s-PSuff:1c.s> <Adv>

'How long, O Lord will you forget me forever?'

Further references: Ps. 24:15; Wisd. (com.) 11:18; Sir. 17:19, 20:17; Ezra 9:14; Sir. 24:9; Matt. 9:33 Luke 15:29 John 1:18; Heb. 3:6.

Moreover, *kʷəllahe* and *gəmurā* have extra functions with their own diverse meanings, *kʷəllahe* 'everywhere' and *gəmurā* 'absolutely'.

Textual evidence:

3.2.6.8. በኵሉሄ፡ በኀበ፡ ትነብሩ። (Lev. 3:17).

ba-kʷəllahe ba-ḫaba-tənabbəru

<Prep-Adv> <Prep-Conj> <V:Imperf.2m.p>

'Everywhere you dwell'.

3.2.6.9. ወኢትምሐሉ፡ ግሙራ። (Jas. 5:12).

wa-'i-təmḥalu gəmurā

<Conj-PartNeg-V:Subj.2m.p> <Adv>

'But do not swear at all'.

Further references: Matt. 9:33; Mark 16:20; Luke 15:29; Luke 15:29, 19:43; John 1:18; Acts 10:14.

3.3. INTERROGATIVE ADVERBS

3.3.1. ማእዜ *mā'əze*

ማእዜ *mā'əze* seems to have etymologically a strong connection with ይእዜ *yə'əze* 'now', 'nowadays' and 'today'. The replacement of ይ *y* by ማ *mā* shifted its pattern from being a noun to be an interrogative adverb. Dillmann claimed that it is formed from *'əze by means of ma.*[1] It is concerned with time with the precise meanings 'when', 'at what time', 'on which day'.

In a sentence, it can precede or follow a verb. እም *'əm* and እስከ *'əska* can be added to it initially. Particularly, the combination of እስከ *'əska,* ማእዜ *mā'əze* and ኑ *nu* introduces the most attainable interrogative of extent እስከ፡ ማእዜኑ *'əska-mā'əze-nu* 'until what time', 'until which period', 'how long'.[2] Though, most frequently, it occurs alone.

---

[1] Dillmann 1907, 379.

[2] Dillmann 1865, 197; Kidāna Wald Kəfle 1955, 142, 575; Leslau 1989, 40.

Textual evidence:

3.3.1.1. (*māʾəze*) ማእዜ፡ ይከውን፡ ዝንቱ። (Matt. 24:3).

māʾəze yəkawwən zəntu

<AInt> <V:Imperf.3m.s> <PPer:m.s.Nom>

'When will this happen?'

3.3.1.2. (*ʾəm + māʾəze*) ቀዳማዊ፡ ዘኢይብልዎ፡ እማእዜ። (Anp. Epi (com.) verse 3).

qadāmawi za-ʾi-yyəblə-wwo ʾəm-māʾəze

<NCom:m.s.Nom> <PRel-PartNeg-V:Imperf.3m.p-PSuff:3m.s> <Prep-AInt>

'The foremost one who is not said 'since what time?'

3.3.1.3. (*ʾəska + maʾəze + nu*) እስከ፡ ማእዜኑ፡ ረሲዓን፡ ታፈቅሩ፡ ስሕተተ። (Prov. (com.) 1:22).

ʾəska māʾəze-nu rasiʿān tāfaqqəru səḥtata

<Prep> <AInt-PartInt> <NCom:m.p.Nom> <V:Imperf.2m.p> <NCom:unm.s.Acc>

'How long, O the wicked ones, will you love inaccuracy?'

Further references: Gen. 30:30; Neh. 2:6; Ps. 4:2, 93:3; Prov. (com.) 6:9; Matt. 17:17; Luke 15:29; Acts 10:14.

3.3.2. ስፍን *səfn* and እስፍንቱ *ʾəsfəntu*

Both are initially adverbial elements which are concerned with amount and rate of recurrence with the meanings 'how much', 'how many' and 'how often'.[1] According to Dillmann, *ʾəsfənttu* is a combination of the interrogative *ʾə* and *səfəntu* 'what is the size of it'.[2]

In poetic proses, they are sometimes positioned after a verb. But their frequent position is before the verb.

---

[1] Dillmann 1865, 405-406; Kidāna Wald Kəfle 1955, 91, 142; Leslau 1989, 78, 138; Yətbārak Maršā 2002, 188.
[2] Dillmann 1907, 361.

When they are employed with accusative phrases, the vowel ‘a’ is added to them at the end. Nonetheless, the modes of their pronunciations are not similar; ስፍነ *səfna* is pronounced by the mode of *tanaš nəbāb* while the pronunciation of እስፍንተ *ʾəsfənta* keeps the mode of *wadāqi nəbāb*.

The possible verb forms that can come after those elements are perfective, imperfective, subjunctive, infinitive and gerendium.

Textual evidence:

3.3.2.1. (Part – perf.) እስፍንተ፡ ነፍሳተ፡ ሰብእ፡ ኀይለ፡ ተአምርኪ፡ ዘመሠጠ። (Māḫ̮l.ṣəge (com.) verse 74).

ʾəsfənta nafsāta sabʾ ḫ̮ayla

<AInt> <NCom:unm.p.ConSt> <NCom:unm.p^{s}.Nom> <NCom:unm.s.ConSt>

taʾammərə-ki za-maśaṭa

<NCom:unm. s.Nom-PSuff:2f.s> <PRel-V:Perf.3.m.s>

‘How many souls of men did the power of your miracle take away?’

3.3.2.2. (Part – imperf.) ስፍነ፡ ድንግል፡ ለጽጌኪ፡ ተአምራቲሁ፡ እዜኑ። (Maḫ̮ ṣəge (com.) verse 72).

Səfna dəngəl la-ṣəge-ki

<AInt> <NCom:c.s.Nom> <Prep-NCom:unm.s.Nom-PSuff:2f.s>

taʾammərati-hu ʾəzennu

<NCom:unm.p.Nom-PSuff:3m.s> <V:Imperf.1c.s>

‘O, Virgin, how many (times) would I tell the miracles of your flower (son)?’

3.3.3. ቦኑ *bonu*

To trace its origin, we split the two elements ቦ *bo* and ኑ *nu*, and then, we take courage in considering it as a constructed phrase out of these two elements that have their own patterns, meanings and uses.[1] በ *bo* is an existential affirmative which is recognized by the tradition as an alternative of the verb ሀሎ *hallo*/ ሀለወ *hallawa*. ኑ *nu* is also as usual an interrogative particle.

Not far from these conceptions, the element as a fixed interrogative phrase is used to form questions about the presence, existence, attendance or being of somebody or something with the meaning 'is/ are there...?', 'do/ does... exist?'.[2] The questions may be either in the past tense or in the present continuous form, but surely, ቦኑ *bonu* is fairly used in both possibilities. Its frequent position in a sentence is before the verb.

Textual evidence:

3.3.3.1. ቦኑ፡ እመላእክት፡ ወእም፡ ፈሪሳውያን፡ ዘአምነ፡ ቦቱ። (John 7:48).

bo-nu 'əm-malā'əkt wa-'əm-farisāwəyān

<ExAff:3m.s-PInt> <Prep-NCom:m.p.Nom> <Conj-Prep-NCom:m.p.Nom>

za-'amna b-ottu

<PRel-V:Perf.3m.s> <Prep-PSuff:3m.s>

'Is there anyone who believes in him from the rulers of the Pharisees?'

Furthermore, it is used to support questions by giving an emphasis on the certainty of the issue mentioned in the question with the meanings 'in fact', 'indeed', 'just', 'really' and 'truly'. In this case, it must not always precede or follow a verb, but it can also come together with a noun without mention of a copula (ውእቱ *wə'ətu*) or its possible relative.

Textual evidence:

3.3.3.2. (bonu - verb) ቦኑ፡ ለከንቱ፡ ፈጠርኮ፡ ለእጓለ፡ እመ፡ ሕያው። (Ps. 88:47).

bonu la-kantu faṭark-o la-'əgʷala

---

[1] Dillmann 1907, 347; Leslau 2006, 82; Tropper 2002, 153,

[2] Kidāna Wald Maršā 1955, 255; Leslau 1989, 94.

<AInt> <Prep-Adv> <V:Perf.1m.s-PSuff:3m.s> <Prep-NCom:m.c.ConSt>

ʾəmma ḥəyāw

<NCom:f.s.ConSt> <NCom:m.s.Nom>

'Have you (indeed) created the sons of men in vain?'

3.3.3.3. ቦኑ፡ ዐቃቢሁ፡ አነ፡ ለእኁየ። (Gen. 4:9).

bonu ʿaqābi-hu ʾana la-ʾəḫu-ya

<AInt> <NCom:m.s-PSuff:3m.s> <PPers.1c.s> <Prep-NCom:m.s.Nom-PSuff: 1c.s>

'Am I the keeper of my brother?'

3.3.3.4. ቦኑ፡ ለሙሴ፡ ባሕቲቱ፡ ተናገሮ፡ እግዚአብሔር። (Num. 12:2).

bonu la-muse bāḥətit-u tanāgar-o

<AInt> <Prep-NPro:m.s.Nom> <Adv> <V:Perf.3m.s:PSuff:3m.s>

ʾəgziʾabəḥer

<NPro:m.s.Nom>

'Has the Lord indeed spoken only to Moses?'

3.3.3.5. ቦኑ፡ እም፡ ዛቲ፡ ኰኵሕ፡ ናወጽእ፡ ለክሙ፡ ማየ። (Num. 20:10).

bonu ʾəm zātti kʷakʷḥ nāwaṣṣəʾ

<AInt> <Prep> <PDem:f.s.Nom> <NCom:unm.s.Nom> <V:Imperf.1c.p>

la-kəmu māya

<Prep-PSuff:2m.p> <NCom:unm.s.Acc>

'Do we indeed bring forth water out of this rock?'

Further references: Luke 15:29; Acts 10:14.

3.3.4. አይቴ *ʾayte*

It is originally an element with no etymological relation with any verb or noun. Dillmann's observation about its origin is to consider it as an element formed from the interrogative አይ *'ay* and ቴ *te* which means in '*here*'. Leslau also explained it the same way while Tropper wanted saying nothing on the issue[1] This *te* however is not recognised in the *'Aggabāb* tradition as an individual element for it is difficult to find out its individual attestation in the well-known texts.

Its grammatical function is to be used as an interrogative adverb of place with the meaning 'where?'[2] The elements which are recognized as place prepositions can be added initially to it keeping their own meaning. Example: በአይቴ *ba-'ayte* 'at which place', 'where'; ኀበ፡ አይቴ *ba-'ayte,* መንገለ፡ አይቴ *mangala-'ayte-* 'to...where'; እም፡ አይቴ *'əm-'ayte* 'from...where'. Likewise, the particles ኑ *nu* and መ *mma* individually or jointly (in that order) can be added to it at the end. In the absence of a verb, the element itself fills the gap by putting forward the possible relative of a copula.

Textual evidence:

3.3.4.1. (*'ayte* - verb) አይቴ፡ ተኀድር። (John 1:39).

'ayte taḫaddər

<AInt> <V:Imperf.2m.s>

'Where do you dwell?'

3.3.4.2. (*'əm* + *'ayte*) ኢየአምረክሙ፡ እም፡ አይቴ፡ አንትሙ። (Luke 13:25).

'i-yya'ammǝra-kkəmu 'əm 'ayte 'antəmu

<PartNeg-V:Imperf.3m.s-PSuff:2m.p> <Prep> <AInt> <PPer:2m.p>

'I do not know (you) where you are from'.

3.3.3.3. (*'ayte* + *nu-mma*) አይቴኑመ፡ አማልክቲከ፡ ዘገበርከ፡ ለከ። (Jer. 2:28).

'ayte-nu-mma 'amālәkti-ka za-gabarka la-ka

<AInt-PartInt-Part> <NCom:unm.p.Nom:PSuff:2m.s> <PRel-V:Perf.2m.s> <Prep-PSu ff:2m.s>

---

[1] Dillmann 1907, 379; Leslau 2006, 51; Tropper 2002, 140.

[2] Dillmann 1865:795; Kidāna Wald Kəfle 1955, 142; Leslau 1989, 145.

'Where are your gods that you made for yourself?'

Further references: Deut. 32:37; S. of S. 1:7; John 8:10.

3.3.5. እፎ *ʾəffo*

According to Dillmann, እፎ *ʾəffo* is originally formed from እ *ʾə* (አይ *ʾay*) and ፎ *fo* 'here'.[1] But as to the *ʾAggabāb* tradition, it is initially a grammatical element with no other origin nor an etymological affiliation with verbs or nouns.

It is used as an interrogative adverb with the meaning 'how?' or 'in what manner?'[2] In a sentence, it regularly precedes verbs and adjectival phrases. In an interrogative sentence, it is employed most of the time only once with a single verb; but in some cases, it does appear repetitively corresponding with a single verb. In the same way, in a sentence with two or more verbs linked by ወ *wa*, it can be employed either once at the beginning or as much as the number of verbs treated in a sentence.

Textual evidence:

3.3.5.1. (single intr.) ኦ፡ ሞት፡ እፎ፡ መሪር፡ ዝክርከ። (Sir. 41:1).

ʾo mot ʾəffo marir zəkrə-ka

<PartVoc> <NCom:unm.s.Nom> <AInt> <NCom:m.s.Nom> <NCom: unm.s.Nom-PSuff: 2m.s>

'O death, how bitter is your memory?'

3.3.5.2. (single intr.) ወእፎ፡ ነግሠ፡ አዶንያስ። (1 Kgs 1:13).

wa-ʾəffo nagśa ʾadonəyas

<Conj-AInt> <V:Perf.3m.s> <NPro:m.s.Nom>

'How then has Adonijah become a king?'

---

[1] Dillmann 1907, 379.

[2] Dillmann 1865:806; Kidāna Wald Kəfle 1955:143; Leslau 1989, 147.

3.3.5.3. (repetitive intr.) እፎ፡ እፎ፡ አግመረተከ፡ ድንግል፡ ወእፎ፡ እንዘ፡ አምላክ፡ ሰከብከ፡ በጎል። (M. Ziq I, 107).

ʾəffo ʾəffo ʾagmaratta-kka dəngəl wa-ʾəffo

<AInt> <PartInt> <V:Perf.3f.s-PSuff:2m.s> <NCom:unm.s.Nom> <Conj-PartInt>

ʾənza ʾamlāk sakabka ba-gol

<Conj> <NCom:m.s.Nom> <V:Perf.2m.s> <Prep-NCom:unm.s.Nom>

'How did the virgin carry you, and how did you sleep in the cave since you are the Lord?'

Further references: Eccles. 3:7; Luke 20:5; Gal. 2:6.

The prepositions በ *ba* and ከመ *kama* (ዘከመ *za-kama*) can be attached to it initially without affecting its right meaning. Likewise, the particles such as: መ *ma*, ኑ *nu* (or their combination *nu* + *mma*) and ኬ *ke* are frequently added to it at the end.[1] Even in this case, there will be no effect that appears due to the combination.

Textual evidence:

3.3.5.4. እፎመ፡ ዘኢያምጻእክምዎ። (John 7:45).

ʾəffo-mma za-ʾi-yyāmṣāʾkəmə-wwo

<AInt-Part> <PRel-PartNeg-V:Perf.2m.p-PSuff:3m.s>

'Why did you not bring him?'

3.3.5.5. በእፎ፡ እንከ፡ ታጠምቅ፡ ለእመ፡ ኢኮንከ፡ ክርስቶስሃ። (John 1:25).

ba-ʾəffo ʾənka tāṭamməq la-ʾəmma ʾi-konka

<Prep-AInt> <Adv> <V:Imperf.2m.s> <Prep-Conj-V:PartNeg-V:Perf.2m.s>

krəstosə-hā

<NPro:m.s-PartAcc>

'How would you then baptize if you are not the Christ?'

[1] Leslau 2006, 9.

3.3.5.6. እፎኑመ፡ ይከውን፡ በይቡስ። (Luke 23:32).

ʾəffo-nu-mma yəkawwən ba-yəbus

<AInt-PartInt-Part> <V:Imperf.3m.s> <Prep-NCom:m.s.Nom>

'How will it happen with the dry one?'

3.3.5.7. እፎኑ፡ እሠውቀከ፡ ኤፍሬም። (Hos. 11:8).

ʾəffo-nu ʾəśawwəqa-kka ʾefrem

<AInt-PartInt> <V:Imperf:2m.s-PSuff:2m.s> <NPro:m.s.Nom>

'How can I sustain you, Ephraim?'

Further references: Isa. 36:9; John 7:45; Acts 23:4.

To determine persons, *ʾəffo* can take the pronominal suffixes mentioned earlier.

3.4. OTHER ADVERBS

3.4.1. ሐሰተ *ḥassata* and ሕስወ *ḥəssəwa*

ሐሰተ *ḥassata* is the accusative form of ሐሰት *ḥassat* the noun which is etymologically affiliated with the verb ሐሰወ *ḥassawa* 'lie', 'deceive' and 'tell untrue'. ሕስወ *ḥəssəwa* is also the accusative form of the passive participle ሕስው *ḥəssəw*. Both are used as adverbs with the meanings 'by mistake', 'deceitfully', 'falsely', 'untruly', 'untruthfully' and 'wrongly'.[1] The adverbial elements in the same category ርቱዐ *rətuʿa*, እሙነ *ʾəmuna* and ጽድቀ *ṣədqa* are their negative counterparts.

Like many adverbial elements, they take the immediate position either before or after a verb.

---

[1] Dillmann 1865:94; Kidāna Wald Kəfle 1955:466; Leslau 1989, 19; Tropper 2002, 139.

Textual evidence:

3.4.1.1. ወእለሰ፡ የዐቅቡ፡ ከንቶ፡ ወሐሰተ፡ ገደፉ፡ ሣህሎሙ። (Jonah 2:9).

wa-ʾəlla-ssa yaʿaqqəbu kanto wa-ḥassata gadafu śahəl-omu

<Conj-Prel-Part> <V:Imperf.3m.p> <Adv> <Conj-Adv> <V:Perf.3m.p> <NCom:unm.s. Acc-Psuff:3m.p>

'But those who regard in vain and wrongly left their mercy'.

Həssəwa is employed in all cases without any morphological change. But *ḥassata* can be used alternatively either in the root form or by taking a pronominal suffix.

3.4.2. ሕቀ *ḥəqqa*, ንስቲተ *nəstita*, ኅዳጠ *ḫədāṭa* and ውኁደ *wəḫuda*

ሕቀ *ḥəqqa* and ኅዳጠ *ḫədāṭa* have no etymological relation with any verb. By contrast, ንስቲተ *nəstita* and ውኁደ *wəḫuda* are substantives that have the same root with the verbs ንእሰ *nəʾsa* ('be small', 'be little', 'be few' and 'be younger') and ውኅደ *wəḫda* ('decrease', 'diminish' and 'be less') respectively. However, all are used as adverbial phrases as particularly connected with duration of events and with a quantity of any countable or measurable thing. They express a less amount or a short duration. The following adverbial phrases are supposed to be their equivalents 'at least', 'a little', 'minimally', 'shortly', 'slightly' and 'insignificantly'.

The elements of the same category ምልዐ *məlʿa*, ምሉዐ *məluʿa*, በምልዑ *baməlʿu*, ብዙኅ *bəzuḫa*, ብዝኅ *bəzḫa* and ፈድፋደ *fadfada* are their counterparts. In a sentence, they can be employed either before or after a verb.

Textual evidence:

3.4.2.1. (preceding a verb) ሕቀ፡ ትነውም፡ ወሕቀ፡ ትነብር። (Prov. (com.) 6:10).

ḥəqqa tənawwəm wa-ḥəqqa tənabbər

<Adv> <V:Imperf.2m.s> <Conj-Adv> <V:Imperf.2m.s>

'You sleep a little and sit a little'.

3.4.2.2. (preceding a verb) እስመ፡ ዓዲ፡ ኅዳጠ፡ ኢይቌርር፡ መዓትየ። (Isa. 10:25).

ʾəsma ʿādi ḫədāṭa ʾi-yyəqʷarrər maʿat-əya

<Conj> <Adv> <Adv> <PartNeg-V:Imperf.3m.s> <NCom:unm.s.Nom-PSuff:1c.s>

'For my anger is not yet getting calm a little'.

3.4.2.3. (following a verb) ወስኅትነ፡ ሕቀ፡ እምነ፡ ቅኔነ። (Ezra 9:8).

wa-səḫətna ḥəqqa ʾəmnna qəne-na

<Conj-V:Perf.1c.p> <Adv> <Prep> <NCom:unm.s.Nom-PSuff:1c.p>

'And we rested a little from our bondage'.

3.4.2.4. (following a verb) አሥረቀ፡ ንስቲተ፡ መለኮቶ። (Anap. Nicean (com) verse 101).

ʾaśraqa nəstita malakot-o

<V:Perf.3m.s> <Adv> <NCom:unm.s.Acc-PSuff:3m.s>

'He slightly revealed his Divinity'.

3.4.2.5. አክአብሰ፡ ውኁደ፡ ተቀንየ፡ ለበአል፡ ወኢዩሰ፡ ብዙኀ፡ ይትቀነይ፡ ሎቱ። (2 Kgs 10:18).

ʾakəʾab-ssa wəḫuda taqanya la-baʾal

<NPro.m.s.Nom-Part> <Adv> <V:Perf.3m.s> <Prep-NCom:unm.s.Nom>

wa-ʾiyyu-ssa bəzuḫa yətqannay l-otu

<Conj-NPro.m. s.Nom-Part> <Adv> <V:Imperf.3m.s> <Prep-PSuff:3m.s>

'Ahab served Baal a little; but Jehu will serve him much'.

Further references: Ps. 8:5, 72:2; Eccles. 1:63; Isa. 28:13; Mark 14:35; John 16:16,19; Heb. 2:9.

The preposition *ba* can be attached to their nominative forms like በሕቅ *ba-ḥəqq*, በንስቲት *ba-nəstit*, በኅዳጥ *ba-ḫədāṭ* and በውኁድ *ba-wəḫud.*

A multiplication of *ba* in such an attachment is also practicable and predictable. In fact, it does make a slight difference because it rather shows an ongoing process which is not completed at once. Hence, in the case of a double *ba* (በበ *ba-bba*) attachment to them, we should add descriptive phrases such as 'gradually', 'progressively', 'steadily', 'successively', 'little by little' or 'step by step' to the actual meanings of the elements.

Textual evidence:

3.4.2.6. በበሕቅ፡ ልሀቀ፡ በሠላሳ፡ ክረምት፡ በዮርዳኖስ፡ ተጠምቀ። (Anap.Dios (com.) verse 17).

babba-ḥəqq ləhqa ba-śalasā

<Prep-NCom:unm.s.Nom> <V:Perf.3m.s> <Prep-NumCa.Nom>

kramt ba-yordānos taṭamqa

<NCom:unm.s.Nom> <Prep-NPro:pl.s.Nom> <V:Perf.3m.s>

'He grew gradually; at (his) thirty, he was baptized at Jordan'.

3.4.2.7. ወሖረ፡ ወኀለፈ፡ በበንስቲት፡ በብሔረ፡ ፍርግያ። (Acts 18:23).

wa-ḥora wa-ḫalafa babba-nəstit ba-bəḥera fərgəyā

<Conj-V:Perf.3m.s> <Conj-V:Perf.3m.s> <Prep-NCom:unm.s.Nom> <Prep-NCom:unm.s.ConSt> <NPro:pl.s.Nom>

'Then, he left and passed successively through Phrygia'.

Besides, there is a possibility to use each element as an adjectival phrase to express a less amount or size of things or a short duration of occasions. This is of course richly practicable in the tradition of Gəʿəz literature. For this, we can achieve much evidence.

However, to digest the point, we will examine some textual evidence. The main thing is to make known that all kinds of *ḥəqqa, nəstita, ḫədāṭa* and *wəhuda* are not able to play the role of adverbs. Because, with the same structure and position in a sentence, the accusative forms of the nouns ንስቲት *nəstit,* ኅዳጥ *ḫədaṭ* and ውኁድ *wəḫud* can be used as the adjectival phrases with the meanings: 'little', 'small', 'miniature'.

Textual evidence:

3.4.2.8. ወበሳብዕት፡ ርእየ፡ ሕቀ፡ ደመና፡ መጠነ፡ ሰኰና፡ ብእሲ። (1 Kgs 18:44).

wa-ba-sāb'ət rə'ya ḥəqqa

<Conj-Prep.NumOr:f.Nom> <V:Perf.3m.s> <NCom:unm.s.Acc>

dammanā maṭana sakʷanā bə'si

<NCom:unm.s.Acc> <Prep> <NCom:unm.s.ConSt> <NCom:m.s.Nom>

'And at the seventh (time), he saw a cloud as small as a man's heel'.

3.4.2.9. ይዘርዕ፡ ኅዳጠ፡ መለንሰ። (Isa. 28:25).

yəzarr' ḫədāṭa malansa

<V:Perf.3m.s> <NCom:unm.s.Acc> <NCom:unm.s.Acc>

'(he) sows a little cumin'.

3.4.3. መፍትው *maftəw*, ሠናየ *śannāya*, ርቱዕ *rətu'* and ድልወት *dəlwat*[1]

All are originally substantives which share the same roots with the verbs ፈተወ *fatawa* 'like', 'love', ሠነየ *śannaya* 'be good', ረትዐ *rat'a* 'be right' and ደለወ *dalawa* 'be worthy', 'be lawful', respectively.

They function in two different ways. The first way is specifically concerned with *maftəw, rətu'* and *dəlwat*. In this way, each is employed in a nominative form, and co-acts the role of the main verb with a copula *wə'ətu* which is not apparent in a sentence.

In a sentence, they fairly take the position before the verb. The preposition ለ *la* followed by an applicable pronominal suffix (ሎቱ *l-ottu*, ለከ *la-ka*, ላቲ *l-ātti*, ለኪ *la-ki*, ሎሙ *l-omuu*, ለክሙ *la-kəmu*, ሎን *l-on*, ለክን *la-kən*, ሊተ *l-ita* and ለነ *la-na*) is advised to intervene between the element and the verb. Nonetheless, it is not obligatory in every case. The verb form which can be used in such cases is only the sub-

[1] Dillmann 1865:252, 1082, 1369; Kidāna Wald Kəfle 1955:88; Leslau 1989, 52, 59, 60, 191.

junctive form because only this kind of construction allows the phraseological conception 'it is worthy to me/ you .... to do/ be ....'.
Textual evidence:

3.4.3.1. መፍትው፡ ዝኒ፡ ትግበሩ። (Matt. 23:23).

maftəw zə-ni təgbaru

<NCom:m.s.Nom> <PDem.Nom-Part> <V:Subj.2m.p>

'This is worthy so that you have to do'.

3.4.3.2. ርቱዕ፡ ሊተ፡ እግበር፡ ግብሮ፡ ለዘፈነወኒ። (John 9:4).

rətuʿ li-ta ʾəgbar gəbr-o la-za-

<NCom:m.s.Nom> <Prep-PSuff:1c.s> <V:Subj.1c.s> <NCom:unm.s.Nom>

fannawa-nni

<Prep-Prel-V:Perf.3m.s>

'It is worthy to me to perform the deeds of he who sent me'.

Further references: Matt. 14:16, 18:33; Rom. 11:20; 2 Cor. 12:11; Heb. 2:1.

The second way of functionality includes *śannāya*, and its state as well as the state of the remaining two elements (*rətuʿ* and *dəlwat*) must remain accusative. At this time, any possible verb form can occur after the elements since they are usually used as adverbs, and it is the common features of adverbs to magnify verbs by adding some expressive ideas. In this case, they can have the following meanings: 'rightly', 'truly', 'straightly', 'trustfully' = ርቱዐ *rətuʿa*; 'rightfully', 'lawfully' = ድልወተ *dəlwata* and 'accurately', 'beautifully', 'correctly', 'in a good way' = ሠናየ *śannāya*.
Textual evidence:

3.4.3.2. (*rətuʿa* – Infin.) ወኢትክል፡ ርቱዐ፡ ቀዊመ። (Luke 13:11).

wa-ʾi-təkəl rətuʿa qawima

<Conj-PartNeg-V:Imperf.2m.s> <Adv> <V:Inf.Acc>

'And she could not stand straightly'.

3.4.3.3. (*śann'āya* - Imperf) ቁሙ፡ ሠናየ፡ ቁሙ። (Anap.Basil (com.) verse 3).

qumu śannāya qumu

<V:Impt.2m.p> <Adv> <V:Impt.2m.p>

'Stand up accurately!'

3.4.3.4. (*śannāya* - perf.) አኮኑ፡ ሠናየ፡ ንቤለከ፡ ከመ፡ ሳምራዊ፡ አንተ፡ ወጋኔን፡ ብከ። (John 8:50).

'akko-nu śannāya nəbela-kka kama sāmrāwi 'anta

<PartInt> <Adv> <V:Imperf.1c.p> <Conj> <NCom:m.s.Nom> <PPer: m.s>

wa-gānen bə-ka

<Conj-NCom:unm.s.Nom> <ExAff:PSuff:2m.s>

'Do we say rightly that you are a Samaritan and have a Demon?'

Further references: Esther 10:8 Jer. 3:1.

3.4.4. ምክብዒተ *məkbə'ita* and ምስብዒተ *məsbə'ita*[1]

Both elements are initially the accusative forms of the substantives ምክብዒት *məkbə'it* and ምስብዒት *məsbə'it* that share similar roots with the verbs አመከዐበ *'amakə'aba*[2] 'double' and ሰብዐ *sabbə'a*[3] 'multiply seven times' respectively. They are used as adverbs in expression of the multiplication of a certain amount, number and extent. The precise meanings of *məkbə'ita* are 'twofold' or 'doubly'. Likewise, the actual concept of *məsbə'ita* can also be determined by 'sevenfold'. They mostly follow the verb.

1 Dillmann 1865, 206, 363, 867; Kidāna Wald Kəfle 1955:541, 847; Leslau 1989, 71, 156.
2 "Denominative from *məkbə'it*" Leslau 2006, 339.
3 "Denominative". Leslau 2006, 482.

Textual evidence:

3.4.4.1. ወበኵለሄ፡ ተሐረትም፡ ምክብዒተ። (Sir. 21:5).

wa-ba-kʷəllahe taḥarattəm məkbəʿita

<Conj-Prep-Adv> <V:Imperf.2m.s> <Adv>

'And all the time, you shall be doubly afflicted'.

3.4.4.2. ወአዘዘ፡ ያንድዱ፡ እሳተ፡ ምስብዒተ። (Dan. 3:22).

wa-ʾazzaza yāndədu ʾəsāta məsbəʿita

<Conj-V:Perf.3m.s> <V:Subj.3m.p>
<NCom:unm.s.Acc> <Adv>

'And he ordered to burn a fire sevenfold'.

Further references: 1 Kgs 1:42; Prov. (com.) 23:23; Esther 3:9; Matt. 15:7; Luke 7:43, 10:28 Anap.John (com.) verse 59.

3.4.5. ምዕረ *məʿra*

ምዕረ *məʿra* is originally a polysemantic element; it has two different functions. On one side, it is used as an adverb in expression of excellence and entirety with the meanings 'absolutely', 'ultimately', 'totally', 'in general' and 'completely'. On the other hand, it is used as an adverb in expression of frequency with the precise meaning 'once' ('only one time', 'for a moment').[1] If ለ *la*, or ለእንተ *la-ʾənta* gets attached to it initially, the ending vowel 'a' will be detached.[2]

Textual evidence:

3.4.5.1. ምዕረ፡ አውሢአከ፡ ሶቤሃ፡ ፈጽም፡ ቃለከ። (Sir. 35:8).

məʿra ʾawśiʾa-ka sobehā faṣṣəm qāla-ka

<Adv> <V:Gern.2m.s> <Adv> <V:Impt.2m.s>
<NCom:unm.s.Acc-PSuff:2m.s>

'Having answered once, finish your conversation at a time'.

---

[1] Dillmann 1865, 206; Kidāna Wald Kəfle 1955:603; Leslau 1989, 42.
[2] Tropper 2002, 138.

3.4.5.2. ወበከመ፡ ጽኑሕ፡ ለሰብእ፡ ምዕረ፡ መዊት.... ። (Heb. 9:27).

wa-ba-kama ṣənuḥ la-sab’ mə‘ra mawit...

<Conj-Prep-Prep> <NCom:m.s.Nom> <Prep-NCom:unm.c.Nom> <Adv> <NCom: unm.s.Nom>

‘And as it is appointed for men to die once....’.

3.4.5.3. ወይትበላዕ፡ ቆዑ፡ ለምዕር። (Job 15:27).

wa-yətballā‘ qo‘u la-mə‘r.

<Conj-V.Imperf.3m.s> <NCom:m.s.Nom> <Prep-Adv>

‘And its fruit will be eaten once’.

3.4.5.4. ለእንተ፡ ምዕር፡ ይቀውም፡ ምስሌከ፡ ወእስከ፡ ትትመየጥ፡ኢትሬእዮ፡ እንከ። (Sir. 12:15).

la-’ənta mə‘r yəqawwəm məsle-ka wa-’əska-tətmayyaṭ

<Prep-Prep> <Adv> <V:Imperf.3m.s> <Prep-PSuff:2m.s> <Conj-Conj-V:Imperf.2m.s>

’i-tre’əy-o ’ənka

<PartNeg-V:Imperf.2m.s:Psuff:3m.s> <Adv>

‘For a moment, he stands together with you, but when you return, you do not see him any longer’.

Further references: Sir. 18:26; Job 40:5; Matt. 3:15.

3.4.6. ሰብዐ *səb‘a*, ጥቀ *ṭəqqa*, ወድአ *waddə’a*, ጽመ *ṣəmma* and ፍጹመ *fəṣṣuma*

These elements except ጥቀ *ṭəqqa* have an etymological relation with verbs; ሰብዐ *səb‘a* is the accusative form of ሰብዕ *səb‘* the noun which is related with the verb ሰብዐ *sabbə‘a* ‘make seven’. ወድአ *waddə’a* is also related with the verb ወድአ *waddə’a* ‘complete’, ‘finish’, and ‘accomplish’. Alike, ጽመ *ṣəmma* and ፍጹመ *fəṣṣuma* are related with the verb ፈጸመ *faṣṣama* which has almost the same meanings with *waddə’a.*

Only ጥቀ *ṭəqqa* is uniquely without another origin. Leslau has connected it with the verb *ṭanqaqa* 'be exact' or 'be accurate'.[1]

Each is used as an adverb with the meanings 'absolutely', 'abundantly', 'a lot', 'at all', 'completely', 'fully', 'highly', 'lavishly', 'much' and 'ultimately'.[2]

The literal meaning of the accusative *səbʿa* or the nominative *səbʿ* is 'seven'. The factor that enables it to be considered as a particle is the scholarly conviction towards the number 'seven' itself. According to the scholars of *Qəne* and Bible commentaries, the number seven in Hebrew (שבע-Sheva) is a perfect number and a numerical sign of perfection. For this reason, all numerical derivations which represent the number 'seven' are considered as signs of completeness, fullness, perfection, absolutism and blamelessness. It seems that for this very reason it is used as an adverb with the meanings indicated above.

In constructing sentences, all the elements will independently take their own places after or before a verb or any adjectival phrase to boldly express the verb or the adjectival phrase. There will be no possible attachment to them as far as they play the role of adverbs. Their presence in a sentence expresses not only the certainty of the message, but also the confidence of the speaker or the writer on the issue he is expressing about.

Textual evidence:

3.4.6.1. (verb - element) ወበእንተዝ፡ አዕበዮ፡ እግዚአብሔር፡ ጥቀ። (Phil. 2:9).

wa-ba'əntazə 'aʿəbay-o 'əgzi'abəḥer ṭəqqa

<Conj-Conj> <V:Perf.3m.s-PSuff:3m.s> <NCom:m.s.Nom> <Adv>

'Therefore, God highly exalted him'.

---

[1] Leslau 2006, 594.

[2] Dillmann 1865, 363, 932, 1223, 1388; Kidāna Wald Kəfle 1955, 146, 166, 759, 729, 847; Leslau 1989, 71, 216, 247; Tropper 2002, 139; Yətbārak Maršā 2002, 194-5.

3.4.6.2. (element - adjective) ጥቀ፡ ኄር፡ እግዚአብሔር። (Ps. 72:1).

ṭəqqa ḫer 'əgzi'abəḥer

<Adv> <NCom:m.s.Nom> <Ncom.m.s.Nom>

'God is extremely good'.

3.4.6.3. (element+ element - verb) ወድአኑ፡ ሞተ። (Mark 15:44).

waddə'a-nu mota

<Adv-PartInt> <V:Perf.3m.s>

'Did he completely die?

Further references: 1 Kgs 1:4; Ps. 8:9; Wisd. (com.) 4:13; Matt. 17:12; Mark 16:4; John 18:28.

Besides, ጥቀ *ṭəqqa* can separately have the meaning of 'even'; it shows the greater degree to which the action extends.

Textual evidence:

3.4.6.4. ለመላእክቲሁ፡ ጥቀ፡ አቢሶሙ፡ ኢመሐኮሙ። (2 Pet. 2:4).

la-malā'əkti-hu ṭəqqa 'abbisomu 'i-maḥak-omu

<Prep-NCom:m.p.Nom-PSuff:3m.s> <Adv> <V:Gern.3m.p-PSuff:3m.p> <PartNeg-V: Perf.3m.s>

'He did not spare even his angles having (they) sinned'.

3.4.6.5. እዴክሙ፡ ጥቀ፡ ኢሰፋሕክሙ፡ ላዕሌየ። (Luke 22:53).

'əde-kəmu ṭəqqa 'i-safaḥ-kəmu lā'le-ya

<NCom:unm.s.Acc-PSuff:2m.p> <Adv> <PartNeg-V:Perf.2m.p PSuff:2m.p> <Prep-PSuff:1c.s>

'Even your hand, you did not lay on me'.

Further references: Matt. 6:29; John 8:52.

3.4.7. በምልዑ *bamǝl'u* and እምድሩ *'əmmədru*

They are originally the nominal derivations related with the verbs መልአ *mal'a* 'fill', 'become full', 'be complete' and መደረ *madara* 'become solid' with a suffix 'u' and with the initial affixation of the prepositions በ *ba* and እም *'əm* respectively. It is just this way of construction (በ *ba* + ምልዕ *məl'* + ኡ *u* = በምልዑ *baməl'u*; እም *'əm* + ምድር

mədr + ኡ *u* = እምድሩ *'əmmədru*) that produced these fixed elements.[1] They are used as adverbs in expression of completeness, absolutism and comprehensiveness. The following adverbial phrases express them as 'absolutely', 'completely', 'generally', 'entirely', 'fully' and 'wholly'.[2]

Their advisable position in a sentence is just after a noun which is magnified thoroughly by one of the particles. In fact, እምድሩ *'əmmədru* can uniquely take the closer position to the verb. However, their main function is to express to what extent the action which is determined through the verb goes on.

Textual evidence:

3.4.7.1. እስመ፡ ዚአየ፡ ውእቱ፡ ኵሉ፡ ዓለም፡ በምልዑ። (Ps. 49:13).

'əsma zi'a-ya wə'ətu kʷəllu 'ālam ba-məl'u

<Conj> <PPoss-Psuff:1c.s> <Copu> <PTot.Nom> <NCom:unm.s.Nom> <Adv>

'For the entire world is mine'.

In some cases, ኵሉ *kʷəllu* as combined with the same preposition *ba* can fully represent በምልዑ *bamlə'u* depending on the nature and characteristics of the closest noun. Let us see the following textual evidence:

3.4.7.2. እገኒ፡ ለከ፡ እግዚኦ፡ በኵሉ፡ ልብየ። (Ps. 9:1).

'əganni la-ka 'əgzi'o ba-kʷəllu ləbbə-ya

<V:Perf.1c.s> <Prep-PSuff:2m.s> <PartVoc> <Prep-Pron> <NCom:unm .s.Nom-Psuff:1c.s>

'I will praise you, O Lord, with my whole heart'.

3.4.7.3. በኵሉ፡ ነፍስከ፡ ፍርሆ፡ ለእግዚአብሔር። (Sir. 7:29).

ba-kʷəllu nafsə-ka fərh-o la-'əgzi'abəḥer

[1] Leslau 2006, 342.
[2] Kidāna Wald Kəfle 1955, 225.

<Prep-Pron> <NCom:unm.s.Nom-PSuff:2m.s>
<V:Impt.2m.s> <Prep-NCom:m.s.Nom>

'Fear unto the Lord in your whole soul (body)'.

This is not to say 'in all heart/s of mine' as it can be translated literally. But rather, one can easily understand that he wants to express the absolute subjection of his heart or his absolute subjection from the heart.

በምልዑ *ba-məlʿu* has distinctively a variant በምልዓ *ba-məlʿā* which is purposely drawn from it to go parallel with the nouns of a feminine gender as ኵላ *kʷəlla* and በኵላ *ba-kʷəllā* goes parallel with the masculine ኵሉ *kʷəllu* and በኵሉ *ba-kʷəllu.*

Textual evidence:

3.4.7.4. ለእግዚአብሔር፡ ምድር፡ በምልዓ። (Ps. 23:1).

la-'əgzi'abəḥer mədr ba-məlʿā

<Prep-NCom:m.s.Nom> <NCom:unm.s.Nom> <Adv>

'The whole earth is the Lord's'.

3.4.8. ባሕቲቱ *bāḥtitu* and ዕራቁ *ʿərāqu*

ባሕቲቱ *bāḥtitu* is a nominal derivation related with the denominal verb ባሕተወ *bāḥtawa*/ ተባሕተወ *tabāḥətawa* 'become alone'. Dillmann proposed ባሕቲት *bāḥtit* 'solitude' as its origin. Leslau used the form በሐተ *baḥata* and ብሕተ *bəḥta* instead of *bāḥtawa* or *tabāḥətawa* .[1] ዕራቁ *ʿərāqu* is also a derivation affiliated with the verb ዐረቀ *ʿaraqa*/ ተዐርቀ *taʿarqa* 'be naked', 'be empty', 'be alone', 'become destitute' and 'be isolated'. At the end, both receive the pronominal suffix 'u'. As ACPPIP elements, their function is to be used as adverbs with the precise meanings 'alone', 'solely', 'only' and 'merely'.[2]

[1] Dillmann 1907, 363; Leslau 2006, 92.

[2] Dillmann 1865, 496, 962; Kidāna Wald1955, 92, 263; Leslau 1989, 96. When they are employed as adjectives in expression of aloneness, individuality, isolation, loneliness and uniqueness, they will be expressed as follows: 'the only', 'the one and the lonely'. 'ዕራቁ፡ ደመና፡ አልባቲ፡ ሙስና፡ *ʿəraqu dammanā 'al-bātti musənnā* 'the only cloud (that) has no defilement' Maṣ.Ziq, 56.

The relative pronouns እንተ *ʾənta*, እለ *ʾəlla* and ዘ *za* can be attached to them initially. Moreover, *bāḥtitu* can distinctively keep the attachments of *la*, *ba* and *ʾəm* initially. But theoretically, this kind of superfluous attachment does not make any change on the actual meaning that the element has.

These particles can be attached to them only when the elements take pronominal suffixes. Their accusative forms do not need an additional particle to be combined with.

Textual evidence:

3.4.8.1. (*za* + Part) ዘባሕቲትከ፡ ሀሎከ፡ ለዓለመ፡ ዓለም። (Haym. (com.) verse 57).

za-bāḥtitə-ka halloka la-ʿālama ʿālam

<PRel-Adv-Psuff:2m.s> <V:Perf.2m.s> <Prep-NCom:unm.s.ConSt> <NCom: unm.s.Nom >

'You, who live alone forever'.

3.4.8.2. (*la* + Part) ወይትከሀኑ፡ ሎሙ፡ ለባሕቲቶሙ። (Haym. (com.) 10:10).

wa-yətkahanu lo-mu la-bāḥətit-omu

<Conj-V:Imperf.3m.p> <Prep-PSuff:3m.p> <Prep-Adv-PSuff:3m.p>

'And they will serve alone for them'.

3.4.8.3. (*ba* + Part) ወአእመንከሙ፡ ከመ፡ ሀለውከሙ፡ ቦቱ፡ በባሕቲቱ። (Haym. (com.) 5:10).

wa-ʾaʾəman-kəmu kama hallawkəmu b-ottu

<Conj-V:Perf:2m.p-PSuff:2m.p> <Conj> <V:Perf.2m.p-PSuff:2m.p>

ba-bāḥətit-u

<Prep-Psuff:3m.s> <Prep-Adv-Psuff:3m.s>

'You still believe that you are in him only'.

3.4.8.4. (Part.fem.) ትሬእዩኑ፡ ከመ፡ ይጸድቅ፡ ሰብእ፡ በምግባሩ፡ ወአኮ፡ በሃይማኖቱ፡ ባሕቲታ። (Jas. 2:24).

təreʾəyu-nu kama yəṣaddəq sabʾ ba-məgbār-u

<V:Imperf.2m.p-PartInt> <Conj> <V:Imperf.3m.s>
<NCom:c.s> <Ncom:unm.s.Nom.PSt-Psuff:3m.s>

wa-'akko ba-haymānot-u bāḥətit-ā

<Conj-ExNeg> <Prep-NCom:unm.s. Nom>
<Adv-Psuff:3f.s>

'Do you see that a man is justified by his deed and not by his faith alone?'

Further references: 1 Kgs 18:7; Prov. (com.) 5:17.

As indirectly mentioned earlier, both elements can take pronominal suffixes in both nominative and accusative forms.

3.4.9. በሕቁ *bahəqqu*, ብዝኀ *bəzḫa*, ብዙኀ *bəzuḫa*, ይሙነ *yəmuna* and ፈድፋደ *fadfāda*

ብዝኀ *bəzḫa* and ብዙኀ *bəzuḫa* are originally the accusative forms of ብዝኅ *bəzḫ* and ብዙኅ *bəzuḫ* the nouns which are etymologically related with the verb በዝኀ *bazḫa*. Alike, ይሙነ *yəmuna* is the accusative passive participle of the verb የመነ *yamana*. ፈድፋደ *fadfāda* is also the accusative form of ፈድፋድ *fadfād* which is affiliated with the verb ፈድፈደ *fadfada*. All these verbs have the same meaning 'become abundant', 'be many', 'be much' and 'become plentiful'. The elements also have identical meanings such as 'abundantly', 'more', 'much', 'a lot', 'in a large number' and 'superfluously'.[1] In order to function as adverbs, each is formed in accusative form excluding በሕቁ *bahəqqu* which seems to be the combination of the preposition በ *ba* and the substantive ሕቍ *həqq^w* 'much' or 'many' with the suffix *-u*.[2]

Besides, *fadfāda* can be used as an adverb in expression of preference with the meaning 'rather'. In all cases, they occur before or after verbs, and attempt to express the high degree of the action or the incident expressed through the verbs.

---

[1] Dillmann 1865, 97, 533, 1070, 1381; Kidāna Wald Kəfle 1955, 88, 152, 515; Leslau 1989, 103, 189, 245.
[2] Dillmann 1907, 386.

Textual evidence:

3.4.9.1. (verb – Part) ወኮኑ፡ ወዐልት፡ ይጸፍዕዎ፡ በሕቁ። (Mark 14:65).

wa-konu wa'alt yəṣaff'ə-wwo ba-ḥəqqu

<Conj-V:Perf.3m.p> <NCom:unm.p.Nom> <V:Imperf.m.p-PSuff:3m.s> <Adv>

'And the officers used to slap him much'.

3.4.9.2. (Part - verb) ብዙኀ፡ ትረድእ፡ ጸሎቱ፡ ለጻድቅ። (Jas. 5:16).

bəzuḫa təradd' ṣalot-u la-ṣādəq

<Adv> <V:Imperf.3f.s> <NCom:unm.s.Nom.PSt-PSuff:3m.s> <Prep-NCom:m.s.Nom>

'The prayer of a righteous helps much'.

3.4.9.3. (verb – Part) ወሰሚዖ፡ ጲላጦስ፡ ዘንተ፡ ነገረ፡ ፈርሀ፡ ፈድፋደ። (John 19:8).

wa-sami'o p̣ilaṭos zanta nagara farha fadfāda

<Conj-V:Gern.3m.s> <NPro:m.s.Nom> <PDem.m.s.Acc> <NCom: unm.s.Acc> <V:Perf.3m.s> <Adv>

'When Pilate heard this thing, he was more afraid'.

3.4.9.4. (Part - verb) ወፈድፋደሰ፡ አበድኩ፡ ላዕሌሆሙ፡ እንዘ፡ እዴግኖሙ፡ ውስተ፡ አህጉር። (Acts 26:11).

wa-fadfāda-ssa 'abadku lā'le-homu 'ənza 'ədeggən-omu

<Conj-Adv-Part> <V:Perf.1c.s> <Prep-PSuff:3m.p> <Conj> <V:1c.s-PSuff:3m.p>

wəsta-'ahgur

<Prep-NCo m:unm.p.Nom>

'But rather, I was furious at them while pursuing (them) in cities'.

Further references: Gen. 29:30; 1 Kgs 18:3; 2 Chr. 33:12; Neh. 5:6; Prov. (com.) 21:3; Eccles. (com.) 10:10; Sir. 31:9,11; Matt. 10:15; John 21:15. 16; Acts 16:16, 22:2.

However, it is important to put into consideration that *bəzḫa* and *bəzuḫa* are not to be used only as adverbs. *Bəzḫa* can be utilized as a noun being combined with another word/s. Likewise, *bəzuḫa* is frequently employed as an adjective to semantically specify the state of a noun that precedes or follows it.

Textual evidence:

3.4.9.5. ወነበርነ፡ ብዙኀ፡ መዋዕለ፡ ኀቤሁ። (Acts 21:10).

wa-nabarna bəzuḫa mawāʿəla ḫabe-hu

<Conj-V:Perf.1c.p> <Adv> <Adv> <Prep-PSuff:3m.s>

'And we did stay much time with him'.

Therefore, whenever they function as adverbs, they occur alone like their associate element *fadfāda*.

3.4.10. በከ *bakka* and ከንቱ *kantu*

በከ *bakka* is the accusative form of በከ *bakk* which is initially related with the verb በከ *bakka*/ በከከ *bakaka* 'be damaged', 'be spoiled', 'remain vain', 'remain useless', 'be idle'. ከንቱ *kantu* has almost identical meanings. *ʾAggabāb* states that it has no different origin nor an etymological relation with any verb like *bakk*. But according to Dillmann's implication, it is a compound of a noun *kant* with a suffix *-u*.[1]

In this form, they are rather used to give expressions about the nouns that are closer to them from both sides. Their employment as adverbs take place in two possibilities, either when they are combined with one of the possible prepositions such as *la* and *ba* (በበከ *ba-bakk*, ለከንቱ *la-kantu*, በከንቱ *ba-kantu*) or if they are used in their accusative forms በከ *bakka* and ከንቶ *kanto*.[2] With this regard, the fixed phrases: 'invain', 'vainly', 'futilely', 'unnecessarily', 'unreasonably' and 'worthlessly' are supposed to be their English equivalents.[3]

1 Dillmann 1907, 363.

2 Tropper 2002, 139.

3 Dillmann 1865, 523, 853; Kidāna Wald Kəfle 1955:270, 540; Leslau 1989, 100, 155.

Textual evidence: (used as adverbs)

3.4.10.1. እስመ፡ በከ፡ ለሊነ፡ ተፈጠርነ። (Eccles. (com.) 2:2).

ʾəsma bakka lalina tafaṭarna

<Conj> <Adv> <PSub:1c.p> <V:Perf.1c.p>

'Since we have been created in vain'.

3.4.10.2. በከንቱ፡ ዘነሣእክሙ፡ በከንቱ ፡ ሀቡ። (Matt. 10:8).

ba-kantu za-naśāʾəkəmu ba-kantu habu

<Prep-Adv> <PRel-V:Perf.2m.p-PSuff:2m.p>
<Prep-Adv> <V:Impt. 2m.p>

'What you freely received, give freely'.

3.4.10.3. ወኢትፍቅድ፡ ተጻልዮ፡ በከንቱ። (Prov. (com.) 3:30).

wa-ʾi-təfqəd taṣāləʿo ba-kantu

<Conj-PartNeg-V:Subj.2m.s> <V:Inf.Acc> <Prep-Adv>

'Do not like disputing in vain'.

Textual evidence: (used as a noun and adjective)

3.4.10.4. ወለከንቱ፡ ተክል፡ ኢይትአመር፡ ላቲ፡ ሥርዋ። (Eccles. (com.) 2:5).

wa-la-kantu talk ʾi-yyətʾammar

<Conj-Prep-NCom:unm.s.Nom>
<NCom:unm.s.Nom> <PartNeg-V:Imperf:3m.s>

l-atti śərw-ā

<Prep-PSuff:3f.s> <NCom:unm.s.Nom-PSuff:3f.s>

'But (to) the worthless plant, its root is not known'.

3.4.10.5. ወከንቶ፡ ምግባሪሁ፡ ይጸልዕ። (Prov. (com.) 22:9).

wa-kanto məgbāri-hu yəṣalləʿ

<Conj-Adv> <NCom:unm.s.Acc-PSuff:3m.s>
<V:Imperf.3m.s>

'And he dislikes his worthless deed'.

3.4.10.6. ወየማንከ፡ እንተ፡ ፈጠረት፡ ዓለመ፡ እምነ፡ ከንቱ። (Eccles. (com.) 7:41).

wa-yamānə-ka 'ənta faṭarat

<Conj-NCom:unm.s.Nom-PSuff:2m.s> <PRel> <V:Perf.3f.s-PSuff:3f.s>

'ālama 'əmənna kantu

<NCom:unm.s.Acc> <Prep> <NCom:unm.s.Nom>

'And your right hand that created the world from nothing'.

3.4.11. ኅቡሬ *ḫubāre*, ኅቡረ *ḫəbura*, ኅብረ *ḫəbra*, አሐተኔ *'aḥattane*, ደርገ *darga* and ድርገተ *dərgata*

ኅብረ *ḫəbra* is the accusative form of the noun ኅብር *ḫəbr* which is connected with the noun ኅቡሬ *ḫubāre* while ኅቡረ *ḫəbura* is of ኅቡር *ḫəbur*. All are related with the verb ኀበረ *ḫabara*/ ኅብረ *ḫabra* 'unite', 'come together' or 'cooperate'. Similarly, ደርገ *darga* is the accusative form of the noun ደርግ *darg* which has a clear connection with the substantive ድርገት *dərgat* and with the reciprocal verb ተዳረገ *tadāraga*[1] 'become one', 'go together', 'be united'.

አሐተኔ *'aḥattane* is also a linguistic element which shares the same meaning and function with the other elements of the subsection. Dillmann analyses it as a combination of አሐተ *'aḥatta* which is the accusative form of *'aḥatti* and ኔ *ne*. Leslau also connected it with *'aḥatti*.[2]

They all are used as adverbs in expression of companionship, group, connection and togetherness with the meanings: 'together', 'jointly', 'conjointly', 'connectedly' and 'in cooperation with'.

In a sentence, they are employed quite often with a plural subject. But even in a sentence with a singular subject, they are utilized followed by the preposition ምስለ *məsla*. They can precede a verb but most frequently their position is after the verb.

---

[1] Kidāna Wald Kəfle 1955, 361; 211, 471; Leslau 1989, 114, 133, 193; Yetbārak Maršā 2002, 126.

[2] Dillmann 1907, 386; Leslau 2006, 13.

Textual evidence:

3.4.11.1. ወእምዝ፡ ተጋብኡ፡ ሕዝብ፡ ውስተ፡ ኢየሩሳሌም፡ ኅቡረ። (Ezra 3:1).

wa-ʾəmz agābəʾu ḥəzb wəsta

<Conj-Prep> <V:Perf.3m.p> <NCom:unm:p.Nom> <Prep>

ʾiyyarusālem ḫəbura

<NPro.pl.s.Nom> <Adv>

'Then, the people were gathered together in Jerusalem'.

3.4.11.2. ወመላእክትኒ፡ ተጋብኡ፡ ምስሌሆሙ፡ ኅቡረ። (Ps. 2:2).

wa-malāʾəktə-ni tagābəʾu məsle-homu ḫəbura

<Conj-NCom:m.p.Nom-Part> <V:Perf.3m.p> <Prep-PSuff:3m.p> <Adv>

'And the rulers took council together with them'.

3.4.11.3. ከመ፡ ያስተጋብኦሙ፡ ለውሉደ፡ እግዚአብሔር፡ እለ፡ ተዘርዉ፡ አሐተኔ። (John 11:52).

kama-yāstagabəʾ-omu la-wəluda ʾəgziʾabəḥer

<Conj> <V:Subj.3m.s-PSuff:3m.p> <Prep-NCom:m.p.Const> <NCom:m.s.Nom>

ʾəlla-tazarwu ʾaḥattane

<PRel-V:Perf.3m.p> <Adv>

'So that he may gather together the sons of God who are scattered'.

Further references: Ps. 2:2 Prov. (com.) 22:2, 22:18; Wisd. (com.) 9:29; John 20:4; Acts 12:20; Synod I verse 8.

3.4.12. ኅቡዐ *ḫəbuʿa*

It is the accusative form of the passive participle ኅቡዕ *ḫəbuʿ* which is initially related with the verb ኀብዐ *ḫabʿa* 'hide' or 'put in secret'. It is used as an adverb with the meanings 'in a hidden way', 'secretly' and 'not in public'.[1] It can keep the position before or after the verb. The combination of *ba* and its nominative form ኅቡዕ *ḫəbuʿ* (በኅቡዕ *ba-ḫəbuʿ*) introduces the same notion.

3.4.13. አማን *'amān* and እሙነ *'əmuna*

አማን *'amān* is a noun which is related with the verb አምነ *'amna* 'believe'. እሙነ *'əmuna* is also the accusative form of እሙን *'əmun* the noun from the same root. Both are used as adverbs in expression of certainty, authenticity and confidence with the meanings 'accurately', 'truly', 'just', 'really', 'unquestionably', 'indeed', 'in fact' and 'truthfully'.

Regarding a position in a sentence, they follow a diverse scheme; *'amān* takes most frequently a position before the verb or an adjectival phrase while for *'əmuna*, it is equally possible to come before or after the verb/ an adjectival phrase in any range of distance. Dillmann mentioned *'amān* as one of the adverbs which are originally nouns, and used without special termination for it does not need to change its state like many of the other adverbial elements.[2]

Textual evidence:

3.4.13.1. ወካዕበ፡ አማን፡ እኅትየ። (Gen. 20:12).

wa-kāʿəba 'amān 'əḫtə-ya

<Conj-Adv> <Adv> <NCom:f-s-Nom-PSuff:1c.s>

'And again, she is truly my sister'.

Based on the tradition of biblical texts, the repetition of *'amān* is supposed to give more validation to the reality of the message. But *'əmuna* is not to be employed more than once referring to the same verb.

Textual evidence:

3.4.13.2. አማን፡ አማን፡ እብለከ፡ ከመ፡ ዘነአምር፡ ንነግር። (John 3:11).

'amān 'amān 'əbəla-kka kama za-na'ammər nənaggər

---

[1] Dillmann 1865, 600, 737; Kidāna Wald Kəfle 1955, 469; Leslau 1989, 114.

[2] Dillmann 2006, 386.

<Adv> <Adv> <V:Imperf.1c.s-PSuff:2m.p> <Conj> <PRel-V:Imperf. 1c.p> <V:Imperf. 1c.p>

'Truly, truly, I say to you, we tell what we know'.

3.4.13.3. እሙነ፡ ይበጽሕ። (Sir. 31:8).

ʾəmuna yəbaṣṣəḥ

<Adv> <V:Imperf.3m.s>

'It will truly take place'.

በ *ba* is the only prepositional element which can be attached initially to *ʾamān* without affecting its lexical meaning. Its graphic structure will not be affected due to the attachment (በአማን *ba-ʾamān*).

3.4.14. እስኩ *ʾəsku*

እስኩ *ʾəsku* has a large graphic and phonetic similarity with the preposition እስከ *ʾəska*. Nevertheless, they have no semantic affiliation. It is not only the ending vowel 'u' the marks the difference between them, but their exact meanings and functions are also quite different. እስከ *ʾəska* is a preposition with the meaning 'till/ until' while *ʾəsku* is an element helping the imperative verbs or a subjunctive which is used in the place of an imperative in the expression of commands, requests and permissions with the meaning 'may' or 'let'. Dillmann proposed 'O now!' to be its equivalent phrase.[1]

In a sentence, it can alternatively come just before or after the verb. The intervention of some other nouns or terms between the particle and the verb is possible. ኬ *ke* is the only particle that can be added to it at the end without affecting its lexical meaning and grammatical function at all.

Textual evidence:

3.4.14.1. (verb - *ʾəsku*) ንግረኒ፡ እስኩ። (Acts 5:8).

nəgrə-nni ʾəsku

---

1 Dillmann 1865, 751; Kidāna Wald Kəfle 1955, 145; Leslau 1989, 138.

<V:Impt:2f.s-PSuff:1c.s> <AInt>

'Just tell me'.

3.4.14.2. (*'əsku* + *ke* - verb) አስኩኬ፡ ንርአዮ፨ (Anp. Ath. (com.) verse 156).

'əsku-ke nər'ayy-o

<AInt-Part> <V:Subj.1c.p-PSuff:3m.s>

'Let us see him'.

3.4.15. እንከ *'ənka*

እንከ *'ənka* is an element with no etymological relation with any verb or noun. Dillmann indicated that it is formed from *'ən* and *ka* and its initial meaning was 'thus' and 'now'.[1]

It is one of the significant adverbial elements that can be used to give supplementary expressions on the conceptions of verbs and adjectival phrases. The following phrases can express its lexical meaning: 'then', 'now on', 'onwards', 'forwardly' and 'afterwards'.[2]

Textual evidence:

3.4.15.1. ንጹሕ፡ አነ፡ እንከ፡ እም፡ ይእዜሰ፡ አሐውር፡ መንገለ፡ አሕዛብ፨ (Acts 18:6).

nəṣuḥ 'ana 'ənka 'əm yə'əze-ssa 'aḥawwər

<NCom:m.s.Nom> <PPer:1c.s> <Adv> <Prep> <AInt-Part> <V:Imperf.1c.s>

mangala 'aḥəzāb

<Prep> <NCom:unm-p.Nom>

'Then, I am clean. From now on, I will go to the Gentiles'.

3.4.15.2. ጸሐፍ፡ እንከ፡ ዘትሬኢ፡ ውስተ፡ መጽሐፍ፨ (Rev. 1:11).

ṣaḥaf 'ənka za-təre'i wəsta maṣḥaf

---

[1] Dillmann 1907, 414.

[2] Dillmann 1865, 777; Kidāna Wald Kəfle 1955, 146; Leslau 1989, 142.

<V:Impt.2m.s> <Adv> <PRel-V:Imperf.2m.s> <Prep> <NCom:unm .s.Nom>

'Now on, you may write in a book what you see'.

3.4.15.3. ወኢይሬኢ፡ እንከ፡ ብርሃነ፡ እስከ፡ ለዓለም። (Ps. 48:20).

wa-ʾi-yyəreʾi ʾənka bərhāna ʾəska la-ʿālam

<Conj-PartNeg-V:Imperf.3m.s> <Adv> <NCom:unm.s.Acc> <Prep> <Adv>

'And forward, he shall not see the light forever'.

Further references: Prov. (com.) 24:64; Acts 19:15.

The particle ሰ *sa/ ssa* is attached to *ʾənka* at the end when necessary. About the position in a sentence, like many of the elements of the group, it takes equally the position either before or after the verb. Both arrangements are feasible.

When it is preceded by any adverbial element (eg. መኑ *mannu*, ምንት *mənt*, ቦኑ *bonu*, እፎ *ʾəffo*, ናሁ *nāhu*, እወ *ʾəwwa*, ይእዜ *yəʾəze* and አኮ *ʾakko*), it takes quite often the position before the verb.

Textual evidence:

3.4.15.4. (*ʾənka* - verb) በእፎ፡ እንከ፡ ታጠምቅ፡ ለእመ፡ ኢኮንከ፡ ክርስቶስሃ። (John 1:25).

ba-ʾəffo ʾənka tāṭamməq la-ʾəmma ʾi-konka

<Prep-AInt> <Adv> <V:Imperf.2m.s> <Prep-Conj> <PartNeg-V:Perf.2m.s-PSuff.2m.s>

krəstos-ha

<NPro.m.s-PartAcc>

'How would you then baptize if you are not the Christ?'

3.4.15.5. (*ʾənka* - verb) ሰማዕክሙ፡ ጽርፈቶ፡ ምንተ፡ እንከ፡ ትብሉ። (Mark 14:63).

samāʿəkəmu ṣərfat-o mənta ʾənka təblu

<V:Perf.2m.p-PSuff:2m.p> <NCom:unm.s.Acc> <AInt.Acc> <Adv> <V:Imperf.2m.p>

'You have heard his blasphemy, what do you say then?'

3.4.15.6. (verb - *'ənka*) ትፈቅዱኑ፡ እንከ፡ አሕይዎ፡ ለክሙ፡ ለንጉሠ፡ አይሁድ። (John 18:39).

təfaqəddu-nu 'ənka 'aḥyəw-o la-kəmu

<V:Imperf.2m.p-PartInt> <Adv> <V:Subj.1c.s-PSuff:3m.s> <Prep-PSuff:2m.p>

la-nəguśa 'ayhud

<PrepNCom:m.s. .ConSt> <NProp:c.p.Nom>

'Do you want then that I save the king of the Jews for you?'

3.4.15.7. (*'ənka* - verb) ይእዜኬ፡ እንከ፡ ተሰብሐ፡ ወልደ፡ እጓለ፡ እመ፡ ሕያው። (John 13:31).

yə'əze -ke 'ənka tasabbəḥa walda 'əgʷāla

<AInt-Part> <Adv> <V:Perf.3m.s> <NCom:m.s.ConSt> <NCom:m.p.ConSt>

'əmma ḥəyāw

<NCom:f.s.Nom.ConSt> <NCom:unm.s.Nom>

'Now on, the son of man is glorified'.

3.4.15.8. (verb - *'ənka* + ssa) ኑሙ፡ እንከሰ፡ ወአዕርፉ። (Mark 14:41).

numu 'ənka-ssa wa-'a'rəfu

<V:Impt.2m.p> <Adv-Part> <Conj-V:Impt.2m.p>

'Then, sleep and take rest'.

Further references: Ezra 5:7 John 12:34, 14:9; John 18:21.

3.4.16. ካዕበ *kā'əba*, ዓዲ *'ādi* and ዳግመ *dāgəma*

ካዕበ *kā'əba* and ዳግመ *dāgəma* are the accusative forms of ካዕብ *ka'əb*[1] and ዳግም[2] *dāgəm* which are etymologically related with the verbs አመክዐበ *'amak'aba* ('add' and 'make double') and ደገመ *dagama* ('repeat' or 'say or do something again in the same way'). According to

[1] means, literally, 'two', 'second' and 'the second one' Leslau 1989: 156.
[2] mean literally: 'second' and 'secondary'.

Leslau, *kaʿəb* is an origin of the denominative *kaʿaba* 'make double'.[1] Incoherently, ዓዲ *ʿādi* has no etymological affiliation with any verb.[2] However, all have identical meanings and functions in the language.

Each element is used as an adverb in expression of continuity and repetition with the meanings 'again', 'once more', 'in addition', and 'secondly'.[3]

In a sentence, they can equally precede or follow verbs. None of them goes to be combined with other words except some selective ACPPIP elements such as አምጣነ *ʾamṭāna*, እስመ *ʾəsma*, እለ *ʾəlla*, እንተ *ʾənta*, እም *ʾəm*, ዘ *za*, ከመ *kama*, ሂ *hi*, ኒ *ni*, ሰ *sa*, ወ *wa*, ኑ *nu*, ሁ *hu* and መ *ma** (*excluding ዳግመ *dāgəma*).

Textual evidence:

3.4.16.1. (Part - verb) ወካዕበ፡ ተመየጥኩ፡ ደማስቆ። (Gal. 1:17).

wa-kāʿəba tamayaṭku damāsəqo

<Conj-Adv> <V:Perf.1c.s> <Npro:p.s.Acc>

'And again, I returned to Damascus'.

3.4.16.2. (Part- verb) ዳግመ፡ ይመጽእ፡ በስብሐት። (Anp. śallastu (com.) verse 7).

dāgəma yəmaṣṣəʾ ba-səbḥat

<Adv> <V:Imperf.3m.s> <Prep-NCom:unm.s.Nom>

'He will come again in glory'.

3.4.16.3. (verb – Part) ወርእየቶ፡ ካዕበ፡ ይእቲ፡ ወለት። (Mark 14:69).

wa-rəyatt-o kāʿəba yəʾəti walatt

<Conj-V:Perf.3f.s-PSuff:3m.s> <Adv> <PPers.f.s.Nom> <NCom:f.s. Nom>

'And a servant-girl saw him again'.

---

[1] Leslau 2006, 271.

[2] Dillmann attested ዓድ፡ *ʿād'* as its origin. 1907, 384.

[3] Dillmann 1865, 867, 1008, 1131; Kidāna Wald Kəfle 1955, 150, 339; Leslau 1989, 156, 178, 199.

3.4.17.4. ወዓዲ፡ ይደሉ፡ ከመ፡ ትሥረዩ፡ ሎቱ። (2 Cor. 2:7).

wa-ʿādi yədallu kama-təśrayu l-ottu

<Conj-Adv> <V:Imperf.3m.s> <Conj-Subj.2m.p> <Prep-PSuff:3m.s>

'And again, it is worthy that you might forgive him'.

Further references: Gen. 45:13; 1 Kgs 1:42; Ezra 1:1; Ps. 77:17; Sir. 4:18; 2 Cor. 7:13; M. Məśṭir 4:23.

ዓዲ *ʿādi* can provide some more concepts which are not shared by *kāʿəba* and *dāgəma,* 'still', 'even' and 'yet'.[1]

3.4.16.5. ወዓዲ፡ ቦ፡ መካን። (Luke 14:22).

wa-ʿādi bo makān

<Conj-Adv> <V:Perf.c> <NCom:unm.s.Nom>

'There is still place'.

3.4.16.6. ለእመ፡ ግዝረተ፡ እሰብክ፡ ዓዲ፡ ለምንትኑ፡ እንከ፡ እዴገን። (Gal. 5:11).

la-ʾəmma gəzrata ʾəsabbək ʿādi la-məntə-nu

<Prep-Conj> <NCom:unm.s.Acc> <V:Imperf.1c.s> <Adv> <Prep-AInt-PartInt>

ʾənka ʾəddeggan

<Adv> <V:Imperf.1c.s>

'If I still preach circumsion, why am I then persecuted?'

3.4.16.7. ወበእንቲአሁ፡ መዊቶ፡ ዓዲ፡ ተናገረ። (Heb. 11:4).

wa-baʾəntiʾa-hu mawito ʿādi tanāgara

<Conj-Prep-PSuff:3m.s> <V:Gern.3m.s> <Adv> <V:Perf.3m.s>

'And even after he died, (Lord) has testified about him'.

---

[1] Dillmann 1865, 1008; Kidāna Wald Kəfle 1955, 137; Leslau 1989, 178; Yāred Šiferaw 2009,410.

It can also play the role of ውጥን ጨራሽ *wəṭən ćarrāš* (lit.: 'the one that completes what is already started'). This means, in the absence of a verb in the relative clause, *ʿādi* introduces the same verb mentioned in the main clause in the translation to make it complete.

Textual evidence:

3.4.16.8. ወኵሎ፡ አግረርከ፡ ሎቱ፡ ታሕተ፡ እገሪሁ፡ አባግዐኒ፡ ወኵሎ፡ አልሕምተ፡ ወዓዲ፡ እንስሳ፡ ዘገዳም። (Ps. 8:6).

wa-kʷəllo ʾagrarka l-ottu tāḥta

<Conj-PTot.Acc> <V:Perf.2m.s> <Prep-PSuff:3m.s> <Prep> <NCom:unm.s.Nom-PSuff:3m.s>

ʾəgari-hu ʾabāgəʿa-ni wa-kʷəlllo

<NCom:m.p.Acc-Part> <Conj-PTot.Acc>

ʾaləḥəmta wa-ʿādi ʾənsəsā za-gadām

<NCom:f.p.Acc> <Conj-Adv> <NCom:unm.p[s].ConSt> <PRel (g)-NCom:unm.s.Nom>

'And you make all subject under his feet, sheep and all oxen, you also make all wild animals subject to him'.

3.4.17. ክመ *kəmma*

ክመ *kəmma* seems to have an immense graphic and phonetic similarity with ከመ *kama*. However, it is an individual element which is used as an adverb with the meaning 'the same way', 'similarly'. Dillmann expressed it as an exclamation of restrictive force with the meaning 'thus' and 'like what'.[1]

Textual evidence:

3.4.17.1. ወከማሁ፡ ክመ፡ ተጋደሉ። (Phil. 1:30).

wä-kamāhu kəmma tgādalu

<Conj-Prep> <Adv> <V:Impt:2m.p>

'Likewise, you shall suffer the same way'.

1 Dillmann 1903, 381.

3.4.18. ከሡት *kəśuta,* ዐውደ *ʿawda* and ገሀደ *gahada*

These elements are initially the accusative forms of ከሡት *kəśut,* ዐውድ *ʿawd* and ገሀድ *gahad* the nouns that are etymologically affiliated with the verbs ከሠተ *kaśata* ('reveal', 'open' and 'make clear'), ዖደ *ʿoda* ('go around' or 'revolve') and አግሀደ *'aghada/* ገሀደ *gahada*' ('reveal', 'make something publicly' and 'manifest') respectively.

Their grammatical function is to be used as adverbs with the meanings 'clearly', 'openly', 'plainly', 'publicly' and 'visibly'. Even their nominative forms *kəśut, ʿawd* and *gahad* can keep the same function if they receive the initial attachment of *ba* in the following forms: በከሡት *ba-kəśut,* በዐውድ *ba-ʿawd* and በገሀድ *ba-gahad.*[1]

Otherwise, they usually occur alone. Regarding the position in a sentence, each can be positioned either before or after verbs, both schemes are equally plausible.

Textual evidence:

3.4.18.1. (part - verb) አላ፡ አየድዐከሙ፡ ከሡተ። (John 16:25).

'allā 'ayaddəʿa-kkəmu kəśuta

<Conj> <V:Imperf.1c.s-PSuff-2m.p> <Adv>

'But I tell you plainly'.

3.4.18.2. (Part - verb) ዐውደ፡ የሐውሩ፡ ረሲዓን። (Ps. 11:9).

ʿawda yaḥawwəru rasiʿān

<Adv> <V:Imperf.3m.p> <NCom:m.p.Nom>

'The wicked prowl openly'.

3.4.18.3. (Part - verb) እግዚአብሔርሰ፡ ገሀደ፡ ይመጽእ። (Ps. 49:3).

'əgzi'abəḥerə-ssa gahada yəmaṣṣə'

<NCom:m.s.Nom-Part> <Adv> <V:Imperf.3m.s>

'But the Lord shall come manifestly'.

---

1 Dillmann 1865, 833, 1000; Kidāna Wald Kəfle 1955, 303, 540, 687; Leslau 1989, 151, 177, 201; Yətbārak Maršā 2002, 195.

3.4.18.4. (verb - Part) ወአርአይዋ፡ ለዛቲ፡ መጽሐፍ፡ ገሀደ። (Esther 10:25).

wa-ʾarʾayə-wwā la-zātti maṣḥaf gahada

<Conj-V:Perf.3m.p-PSuff:3f.s> <Prep-PDem.f.s.Nom> <NCom:f.s. Nom> <Adv>

'And they showed the book publicly'.

3.4.19. ዮጊ *yogi*

ዮጊ *yogi* is initially an element which serves as an adverb with the meanings 'maybe' or 'perhaps' (in expression of probability or uncertainty) and 'now' (to indicate the time or an event at hand).[1] Dillmann testified that its origin is obscure.[2] It can take the position either before or after a verb.

Textual evidence:

3.4.19.1. (verb - *yogi*) ወባሕቱ፡ እፈርህ፡ ዮጊ፡ ከመ፡ አርዌ፡ ምድር፡ ዘአስሐታ፡ ለሔዋን፡ በጕሕሉት . . .። (2 Cor. 11:3).

wa-bāḥəttu ʾəfarrəh yogi kama ʾarwe

<Conj-Conj> <V:Imperf.1c.s> <Adv> <Prep> <NCom:m^{s}.s.Nom.PSt>

mədr za-ʾasḥat-ā la-ḥewān ba-g^{w}əḥlut

<NCom:unm.s.Nom> <PRel-V:Perf.3m.s-PSuff:3f.s> <Prep-NPro.f.s. Nom> <Prep-NCom:unm.s. Nom>

'But I am afraid that the serpent that deceived Eve in his deceitfulness maybe...'

3.4.19.2. (yogi - *verb*) ዮጊ፡ ካዕበ፡ መጺእየ፡ ኀቤክሙ፡ የሐምመኒ፡ እግዚአብሔር፡ በእንቲአክሙ። (2 Cor. 12:21).

yogi kāʿəba maṣiʾəya ḫabe-kəmu yaḥamməma-nni

<Adv> <Adv> <V:Gern:1c.s> <Prep-PSuff:2m.p> <V:Imperf.3m.s-PSuff:1.c.s>

ʾəgziʾabəḥer baʾənti-akəmu

---

[1] Dillmann 1865, 1075; Kidāna Wald Kəfle 1955, 145; Leslau 1989, 145.

[2] Dillmann 1907, 417.

<NCom:m.s.Nom> <Prep-PSuff:2m.p>

'Now again when I come to you, perhaps God may cause me sorrow for your sake'.

Further references: Gen. 20:11, 24:39, 27:12; Josh. 9:6; Sir. 19:13.

3.4.20. ገጸ *gaṣṣa*

Originally, it is the accusative form of ገጽ *gaṣṣ* which relates to the verb ገጸወ *gaṣṣawa* 'differentiate', 'separate' and 'put each by one'.

Its function is to be used as an adverb in expression of direction or position with the meanings 'ahead', 'before', and 'personally'.[1] The noun *gaṣṣ* can also keep the same function even if *ba* is attached to it initially. In some cases, they occur together in the form of ገጸ፡ በገጽ *gaṣṣa ba-gaṣṣ*.[2] But in this case, it will be better to explain the combination as 'face to face'.

Textual evidence:

3.4.20.1. ርእዮዎ፡ ነቢያት፡ ለእግዚአብሔር፡ ወተናጸሩ፡ ገጸ፡ በገጽ። (Anp. Mar (com.) verse 159).

rəy'ə-wwo nabiyāt la-'əgzi'abəḥer wa-tanāṣṣaru

<V:Perf:3m.p-PSuff:3m.s> <NCom:m.p.Nom> <Prep-NCom:m.s.Nom>

gaṣṣa ba-gaṣṣ

<Conj-V:Perf:3m.p> <Adv>
<Prep:NCom:unm.s.Nom>

'The prophets have seen the Lord, and they have seen each other face to face'.

3.4.21. ግብር *gəbr*

ግብር *gəbr* is originally a noun which is etymologically related with the verb ገብረ *gabra* 'work', 'do', 'perform' and 'make'. In its grammatical

[1] Dillmann 1865, 1209; Kidāna Wald Kəfle 1955:329.
[2] Leslau 2006, 205.

aspect, it helps a verb with the meanings 'must', 'shall', 'ought to' and 'has/ have to…'.[1]

The appropriate verb form which can follow it is the imperfective one. Some significant ACPPIP elements such as በእንተ *ba'ənta*, ህየንተ *həyyanta*, ከመ *kama*, አምጣነ *'amṭāna'* and እስመ *'əsma* can be attached to it, initially. But the element itself cannot be attached to other linguistic elements as long as it functions as an adverb.

Textual evidence:

3.4.21.1. እስመ፡ ግብር፡ ይከውን፡ ከማሁ። (Matt. 24:6).

'əsma-gəbr yəkawwən kamā-hu

<Conj-Aux> <V:Imperf.3m.s> <Prep-PSuff:3m.s>

'Because it must happen like this'.

3.4.22. ግብተ *gəbta*

ግብተ *gəbta*[2] is originally the accusative form of the noun ግብት *gəbt* 'sudden'.[3] Kidāna Wald Kəfle claimed that it is derived from the verb ወገበ *wagaba* 'come sudden', 'happen sudden'. Leslau reformed the verb as *'awgaba* 'arrive suddenly' or 'attack suddenly'.[4] As a nominative noun, *gəbt* receives the combination of any noun,[5] indicating a similar concept with what the accusative *gəbta* reflects. However, this does not enable it to be recognized as an adverbial element like its accusative form *gəbta*.

The principal function of *gəbta* is to be employed as an adverb in expression of suddenness and precipitousness with the meanings 'suddenly', 'straight away', 'unexpectedly' and 'at/ on the unexpected moment or situation'.

As many of the elements in the same category, it can precede or follow verbs. But in the case of nominalized verbs and adjectival

---

[1] Dillmann 1865, 1163; Kidāna Wald Kəfle 1955:298.

[2] Dillmann 1865, 938; Kidāna Wald Kəfle 955, 376; Leslau 1989, 167.

[3] Kidāna Wald Kəfle 1955, 376.

[4] Leslau 2006, 608.

[5] Example: ሞተ፡ ግብት *mota-gəbt* 'sudden death', ሐተታ፡ ግብት *ḥatatā-gəbt* 'sudden examination'.

phrases, it is most likely employed after the nominalized verb or the adjective is already mentioned.

Textual evidence:

3.4.22.1. (*gəbta* - verb) ግብተ፡ በረቀ፡ መብረቅ፡ ዐቢይ፡ እም፡ ሰማይ፡ ላዕሌየ። (Acts 22:6).

gəbta baraqa mabraq ʾəm samāy lāʿle-ya

<Adv> <V:Perf.3m.s> <NCom:unm.s.Nom> <Prep> <NCom:m.s. Nom> <Prep-PSuff:1c.s>

'A lightening suddenly flashed from heaven on me'.

3.4.22.2. ግርማ፡ ሌሊት፡ ወመጽዓም፡ ይመጽኦ፡ ለሰብእ፡ ግብተ። (Job 4:13).

gərma lelit wa-maṣʿāmo

<NCom:m.s.ConSt> <NCom:unm.s.Nom> <Conj-NCom:m.s.Nom>

yəmaṣṣə-ʾo la-sabʾ gəbta

<V.Imperf.3m.s-PSuff:3m.s> <Prep-NCom:m.s.Nom> <Adv>

'Awe of the night and deep sleep comes suddenly to a man'.

Further references: Job 1:20; Prov. (com.) 1:27, 6:15.

3.4.23. ድቡተ *dəbbuta* and ክቡተ *kəbuta*

ድቡተ *dəbbuta* is originally the accusative form of ድቡት *dəbbut* which is related with the verb ደበተ *dabbata* 'be slow', 'bend' and 'put something in secret'. ክቡተ *kəbuta* is also a noun in accusative form. The nominative ክቡት is originally related with the verb ከበተ *kabata* 'hide'. Their function is to be used as an adverb with the meanings 'clandestinely', 'secretly', 'privately' and 'quietly'.[1] Leslau fixed its relation with the ደበወ *dabawa* 'be hidden'.[2]

---

[1] Dillmann 1865,1107; Kidāna Wald Kəfle 1955, 335; Leslau 1989, 195.

[2] Leslau 2006, 122.

As an alternative, the nominative ድቡት *dəbbut* can be used, taking an initial attachment of *ba* (በድቡት *ba-dəbbut*).

Textual evidence:

3.4.23.1. (*ba* + .*dəbbut*) ወይእዜኒ፡ ርቱዕ፡ በድቡት፡ ንግበሮ፡ ለዝ። (Acts 19:36).

wa-yə'əze -ni rətu' ba-dəbbut

<Conj-Adv-Part> <NCom:m.s.Nom> <Prep-NCom:unm.s.Nom-Psuff:3m.s>

nəgbarr-o la-zə

<V:Subj:1c.p> <Prep-PDem:m.s.Nom>

'And now we have to do this thing in secret'.

3.4.24. ድኅሪተ *dəḫrita*

ድኅሪተ *dəḫrita* is originally a noun in accusative form. Its origin is related with that of *dəḫra*. It is used as an adverb with the meaning of 'backward' or 'backwardly'.

Textual evidence:

ወሖሩ፡ ድኅሪተ፡ ወከደኑ፡ ዕርቃነ፡ አቡሆሙ። (Gen. 9:23).

wa-ḥoru dəḫrita wa-kadanu 'ərqāna 'abu-homu

<Conj-V:Perf.3.m.p> <Adv> <Conj-V:Perf.3m.p> <Ncom:unm.s.ConSt> <Ncom:m.s.Nom-PSuff :3m.p>

'They went backward, and covered the nakedness of their father'.

3.4.25. ጥንቁቀ *ṭənquqa*

It is originally the accusative form of the passive participle ጥንቁቅ *ṭənquq*. It has etymological relation with the verb ጠንቀቀ *ṭanqaqa* 'take care', 'well understand', 'complete', 'be exact' and 'generalize'.

It is used as an adverb in expression of carefulness and extensiveness with the meanings 'carefully', 'prudently', 'perfectly', 'understandingly', 'completely', 'touching one by one' and 'entirely'.[1] In a sentence, it can precede or follow a verb.

Textual evidence:

3.4.25.1. ነጊሮታ፡ ኢይትከሀል፡ ጥንቁቀ። (Haym. (com.) 4:3).

nagirot-ā 'i-yyətkahal ṭənquqa

<V:Inf-PSuff:3f.s> <PartNeg-V:Imperf.3m.s> <Adv>

'It is absolutely impossible to talk about it'.

3.4.26. ጥዩቀ *ṭəyyuqa*

It is the accusative form of the noun ጥዩቅ *ṭəyyuq*. It has the same root with the verb ጠየቀ *ṭayyaqa* 'understand', 'comprehend' and 'recognize'. It is used as an adverb in expression of certainty, comprehensiveness and intelligibility with the meanings 'certainly', 'comprehensively' and 'understandably'.[2] It mostly modifies verbs, preceding or following them.

Textual evidence:

3.4.26.1. ፈቀደ፡ መልአክ፡ ያእምር፡ ጥዩቀ፡ በእንተ፡ ምንት፡ያስተዋድዩዎ፡ አይሁድ። (Acts 22:30).

faqada mal'ak yā'mər ṭəyyuqa ba'ənta

<V:Perf.3m.s> <NCom:m.s.Nom> <V:Subj.3m.s> <Adv> <Prep>

mənt yastawāddəyə-wwo 'ayhud

<PInt> <V:Imperf.3m.s.p-PSuff:3m.p> <NCom:unm.p.Nom>

'The commander wanted to know exactly why the Jews accuse him'.

Further references: Esther 5:5; Acts 4:10.

---

[1] Dillmann 1865, 1235; Kidāna Wald Kəfle 1955, 504; Leslau 2006, 594.
[2] Dillmann 1865, 1246; Kidāna Wald Kəfle 1955, 499; Leslau 2006, 600.

3.4.27. ጽሚተ *ṣəmmita* and ጽምሚተ *ṣəməmita*

Both elements are originally the accusative forms of ጽሚት *ṣəmmit* and ጽምሚት *ṣəməmit*[1] which share the same root with the verb ጸመ *ṣamma*/ ጸመመ *ṣamama* 'keep silence', 'be unable to hear'.

The little difference that can be seen structurally is concerned with the number of consonants, i.e.: three consonants with germination (ጽሚተ *ṣəmmita*) and four consonants with no gemination (ጽምሚተ *ṣəməmita*). Otherwise, the conceptions that they convey and the engagement in which they are concerned about are identical. They are used as adverbs with the meanings 'silently', 'mutely', 'secretly' and 'without warning in advance'.[2]

Each can take the position either before or after a verb; there is no restriction.

Textual evidence:

3.4.27.1. ወይእዜኒ፡ ጽሚተ፡ ያውፅኡነ፡ ይፈቅዱ። (Acts 16:37).

wa-yə'əze -ni ṣəmmita yāwḍəu-na yəfaqqədu

<Conj-Adv-Part> <Adv> <V:Subj.3m.p-PSuff:1c.p> <V:Imperf.3m.p>

'And now they want to send us away secretly'.

3.4.27.2. ምንተ፡ ገበርኩ፡ ጽምሚተ፡ ዘትትኀጥአኒ። (Gen. 31:26).

mənta gabarku ṣəməmita za-tətḫaṭṭə'a-nni

<AInt.Acc> <V:Perf.1c.s> <Adv> <Conj-V:2m.s-PSuff:1c.s>

'What did I do wrongly that you flee in secret from me?'

Further references: Exod. 11:2; 2 Sam. 12:12; Ps. 10:3; Sir. 23:19 John 18:20.

---

[1] Dillmann 1907, 384.

[2] Dillmann 1865, 1271; Kidāna Wald Kəfle 1955:146, 759; Leslau 1989, 225.

3.4.28. ፍጡነ *fəṭuna*

Initially, ፍጡነ *fəṭuna* is the accusative form of the noun ፍጡን *fəṭun*. It has the same root with the verb ፈጠነ *faṭana* 'hurry', 'be fast' and 'accelerate'. It is used as an adverb in expression of speed with the meanings 'quickly', 'in hurry', 'immediately', 'as soon as possible', 'hastily' and 'rapidly'.[1] ሕቀ *ḥəqqa,* በበሕቅ *babbaḥəq,* ክብደ *kəbədda*[2] and ድቡተ *dəbbuta* are its negative counterparts. In a sentence, it can precede or follow a verb.

Textual evidence:

3.4.28.1. (*fəṭuna* - verb) ዘፍጡነ፡ የአምን፡ ቀሊል፡ ልቡ። (Sir. 19:4).

za-fəṭuna ya'ammən qalil ləbb-u

<Prel-Part> <V:Imperf.3m.s> <NCom:m.s.Nom> <NCom:unm.s.Nom-NomSuff:3m.s>

'Meek is the heart of the one that believes immediately'.

3.4.28.2. (*verb* - fəṭuna) ጻእ፡ ፍጡነ፡ እም፡ ኢየሩሳሌም። (Acts 22:18).

ṣā' fəṭuna 'əm 'iyyarusālem

<V: Impt.2m.s> <Part> <Prep> <NPro:unm.s.Nom>

'Get out of Jerusalem quickly'.

Further references: 2 Kgs 1:9; Ps. 78:8; Prov. (com.) 23:29; Wisd. (com.) 4:14, 13:32; Luke 14:21.

※ ※ ※

[1] Dillmann 1865, 1386; Kidāna Wald Kəfle 1955, 720; Leslau 2006, 171.

[2] 'ወይእቲሰ፡ ሐመር፡ ክብደ፡ ሖረት። - *wa-yə'əti-ssa ḥamar kəbədda ḥorat* (But the ship had been sailing slowly) Acts 27:6.

CHAPTER FOUR: CONJUNCTIONS

In this part, the grammatical functions of various conjunctional elements are discussed in detail. It is also concerned with tracing the etymology of each element. The elements comprised in nine different sections are forty-four all in all. More than half of the elements have no connection with verbs or nouns while many are of course substantives in their status constructus. Many of the elements are directly prefixed or suffixed to verbs, and this is the common characteristic of the elements comprised in this group which is not shared by five elements only. Let us come to the detail.

4.1. COPULATIVE CONJUNCTIONS

4.1.1. ሂ *hi*, ኒ *ni* and ወ *wa*

As copulative conjunctions, they are used to make grammatical affiliations between two or more words, phrases and nouns with the precise meanings 'and' and 'also'.[1] According to the tradition of the *Qəne* schools, they are known as ዋዌ *wāwe*.[2] Dillamnn claimed ሂ *hi* to be formed from the root ሀ *ha* and ኒ *ni* from ነ *na*. According to him, *ni* is somehow a stronger conjunction than *hi*.[3] *'Aggabāb* does not keep such an implication.

[1] Dillmann 1865, 1, 629, 880; Kidāna Wald Kəfle 1955, 149-150; Leslau 1989, 119, 158.
[2] As to mean 'conjunction'.
[3] Dillmann 1907, 411.

They can be equally attached to nouns, verbs, numerals and other elements in two different ways. *Hi* and *ni* are commonly attached to a word at the end while *wa* is always attached at the beginning of the word.

Textual evidence:

4.1.1.1. (verb + *hi*) ኣአምሮሂ፡ ወቃሎሂ፡ አዐቅብ። (John 8:55).

ʾaʾammər-o-hi wa-qālo-hi ʾaʿaqqəb

<V:Imperf.1c.s-PSuff:3m.s-Conj> <Conj-NCom:unm.s.Acc-Conj> <V:Imperf.1c.s>

'And I know him and keep his word'.

4.1.1.2. (noun + *ni*) ፀሐይኒ፡ ይጸልም፡ ወወርኅኒ፡ ደመ፡ ይከውን። (Joel 2:31).

ḍaḥayə-ni yəṣalləm wa-warḫə-ni

<NCom:unm.s-Conj> <V:Imperf.m.s> <Conj-NCom:unm.s-Conj>

dama yəkawwən

<Ncom:unm.s.Acc> <V:Imperf.3m.s>

'The sun will be darkened, and the moon will be bloody'.

4.1.1.3. (*wa* + verb) ወቀርባ፡ ወአኀዛ፡ እገሪሁ፡ ወሰገዳ፡ ሎቱ። (Matt. 28:10).

wa-qarbā wa-ʾaḫazā ʾəgari-hu

<Conj-V:Perf.3f.p> <Conj-V:Perf.3f.p> <NCom:unm.p.AccPSt-PSuff:3m.s>

wa-sagadā l-ottu

<Conj-V:Perf.3f.p> <Prep.-PSuff:3m.s>

'And they came up and took hold of his feet and worshiped him'.

Further references: Gen. 43:8; 1 Kgs 1:46; 2 Kgs 14:26; Job 7:3; Ps. 22:4, 104:23, 27; Eccles. 1:21; Sir. 1:26, 15:20; Isa. 14:9, 36:17; Jer. 47:4; Ezek. 8:18, 10:17, 24:13, 15:5; Dan. 3:33; Amos 7:3; Mich. 3:11, 5:2, 6:12 Matt. 1:6, 2:16, 21:32; 25:22; John 6:55, 8:57, 14:7 2; Acts 7:13, 10:45, 27:10; Heb. 9:28, 11:31.

ወ *wa* is profoundly engaged in the attachments of ሂ *hi* or ኒ *ni* to various elements.[1] In some cases, the reason for the engagement is concerned with the introduction of a new sentence because new sentences in Gəʿəz mostly begin with the conjunction *wa.* However, in other cases, the reason why it comes jointly with the same valid particle is not quite clear. Nevertheless, we will have only a mere conception of a copulative conjunction in the translation.

Textual evidence:

4.1.1.4. ርእዩኒሂ፡ ወጸልዑኒሂ፡ ኪያየሂ፡ ወአቡየሂ፡፡ (John 15:24).

rə'yuni-hi wa-ṣalʿuni-hi kiyāya-hi

<V:Perf.3m.p-PSuff:1c.s-Conj> <Conj-V:3m.p-PSuff:1c.s-Conj> <PObj:1c.s-Conj>

wa-'abu-ya-hi

<Conj-NCom:m.s.Acc-PSuff:1c.s-Conj>

'They have both seen and hated me, me and my father'.

Further references: Prov. (com.) 1:28, 4:12; Matt. 18:5; Luke 13:26; John 12:50, 14:19; Gal. 1:12.

4.1.1.5. ወዘኒ፡ ይትወለድ፡ እምኔኪ፡ ቅዱስ፡ ውእቱ፡፡ (Luke 1:35).

wa-za-ni yətwallad 'əmənne-ki qəddus wə'ətu

<Conj-PRel:m.s-Conj> <V:Imperf.3m.s> <Prep-PSuff:2f.s> <NCom:m.s. Nom> <Copu>

'And he who will be born from you is holy'.

Further references: Prov. (com.) 2:3, 6:22, 24:21; Sir. 50:33; John 12:47.

With regard to a position in a sentence, *hi* and *ni* have two other common features which are not shared by *wa*.

1. When they make a link between two or more different verbs, nouns or other language elements in the presence of *wa*, they can appear only once being attached to the first element or continually after each component. Both trends are equally plausible.

[1] Tropper 2002, 145.

Textual evidence:

4.1.1.6. (verb + *hi* - *wa* + verb) ወርዘውኩሂ፡ ወረሳእኩ። (Ps. 36:26).

warzawku-hi wa-rasā'ku

<V:Perf.1c.s.PSuff:1c.s-Conj> <Conj-V:Perf.1c.s-PSuff:1c.s>

'I have been young and now I became old'.

Further references: Deut 32:6; 1 Sam. 2:6; Jer. 7:9; Luke 15:24.

4.1.1.7. (verb + *hi* – *wa* + verb + *hi*) ወነገርኩሂ፡ ወአድኀንኩሂ፡ ወገሠጽኩሂ። (Isa. 43:12).

wa-nagarku-hi wa-'adḫanku-hi wa-gaśśaṣku-hi

<Conj-V:1c.s-PSuff:1c.s-Conj> <Conj-V:Perf.1c.s-PSuff:1c.s-Conj> <Conj-V:1c.s.PSuff:1c.s-Conj>

'And I proclaimed and saved and rebuked'.

4.1.1.8. (noun + *hi* – *wa* + noun + *hi*) ወበምንዳቤሂ፡ ወበተሰዶሂ፡ ወበተጽናስሂ። (2 Cor. 12:10).

wa-ba-mənddābe-hi wa-ba-tasaddo-hi

<Conj-Prep-NCom:unm.s.Nom-Conj> <Conj-Prep-V:Inf:s.Nom-Conj>

wa-ba-taṣnāsə-hi

<Conj-Prep-NCom:unm.s.Nom-Conj>

'With trouble and with persecution, again with difficulty'.

Further references: Num. 13:24; Josh. 8:35; Job 28:22; Dan. 2:46, 6:27; Philem. 1:11.

4.1.1.9. (verb + *ni* - *wa*+ verb + *ni*) ወቀተሉነኒ፡ ወዴወዉነኒ፡ ወበርበሩነኒ። (Ezra 9:7).

wa-qatalu-na-ni wa-ḍewawu-na-ni

<Conj-V:Perf.3m.p-PSuf f:1c.p-Conj> <Conj-V:Perf.3m.p-PSuff:1c.p-Conj>

wa-barbaru-na-ni

<Conj-V:Perf.3m.p-PSuff:1c.p-Conj>

'They still gave us to death and made us captives and yet plundered us'.

4.1.1.10. (noun + *ni* – *wa* + noun + *ni*) ንጉሥየኒ፡ ወአምላኪየኒ። (Ps. 5:2).

nəguśə-ya-ni wa-ʾamlāki-ya-ni

<NCom:m.s.Nom-PSuff:1c.s-Conj> <Conj-NCom:m^{s}.s.Nom-PSuff:1c.s-Conj>

'My king and my Lord'.

Further references: Ezra 1:11, 3:7; Neh. 13:12; Job 15:10; Ps. 48:3, 50:21; Dan. 3:52; Luke 15:21.

4.1.1.11. (...*ni* - *wa* + ...*hi*) በሥጋሁኒ፡ ወበእግዚእነሂ። (Philem. 1:16).

ba-śəgā-hu-ni wa-ba-ʾəgziʾə-na-hi

<Prep-NCom:unm.s.Nom-PSuff:3m.s-Conj> <Conj-Prep-NCom:m.s. Nom-PSuff:1c.p-Conj>

'Both in his flesh and in our Lord'.

In connecting proper names preceded or followed by adjectival phrases, the elements are mostly attached only once, to the firstly mentioned element either a noun or an adjectival phrase.

Textual evidence:

4.1.1.12. ወዳዊትኒ፡ ንጉሥ፡ ወለደ፡ ሰሎሞንሃ። (Matt. 1:6).

wa-dāwitə-ni nəguś walada salomonə-hā

<Conj-NPro:m.s.Nom-Conj> <NCom:m.s.Nom> <V:Perf.3m.s> <NPro .m.s-PartAcc>

'And King David begot Solomon'.

Further references: Ezra 1:7, 6:20; Hos. 4:15; Mich. 5:2; John 8:9.

The same can happen when a verb is preceded by a relative pronoun or by another element.

Textual evidence:

4.1.1.13. (pron. + *hi* - verb) ከመ፡ እለሂ፡ ይፈቅዱ፡ ይኅልፉ ፡ እም፡ ለፌ...። (Luke 16:26).

Kama ʾəlla-hi yəfaqqədu yəḫləfu ʾəm lafe

<Conj> <PRel-Conj> <V:Imperf-3m.p> <V:Subj.3m.p> <Prep> <Adv>

'Even those who want to come over from there ...'.

Further references: Matt. 10:27, 33; Luke 12:11; John 9:8.

4.1.1.14. (pron. + *ni* - verb) ወእለኒ፡ ተርፉ፡ አኃዊሆሙ፡ ካህናት....። (Ezra 3:8).

wa-'əlla-ni tarfu 'aḫāwi-homu kāhnat

<Conj-PRel.Conj> <V:Perf.3m.p> <NCom:m.p-PSuff:3m.p> <NCom: m.p>

'And the rest of their brothers the priests...'.

However, it is not unavoidable to use them this way in all cases. They can alternately come after the second component, particularly when the adjectival phrase precedes the noun.

Textual evidence:

4.1.1.15. ወእግዚእ፡ ኢየሱስኒ፡ ሖረ፡ ውስተ፡ ደብረ፡ ዘይት። (John 8:1).

wa-'əgzi' 'iyyasusə-ni ḥora wəsta

<Conj-NCom:m.s.Nom> <NPro:m.s.Nom-Conj> <V:Perf.3m.s> <Prep>

dabra zayt

<NCom:unm.s.ConSt> <NCom:unm.s.Nom>

'And the Lord Jesus went to the Mount of Olives'.

Likewise, in status constructus, the elements are attached to the dependant noun.

Textual evidence:

4.1.1.16. ወበኵረ፡ እንስሳሂ፡ ዘርኩስ፡ ታቤዙ። (Num. 17:15).

wa-bakʷra 'ənsəsā-hi za-rəkus

<Conj-NCom:unm.s.ConSt> <NCom:mˢ.s.Nom-Conj> <PRel-NCom:m.s.Nom>

tābezzu

<V:Im perf.2m.s>

'And the firstborn of unclean animal, you shall redeem.'.

4.1.1.17. ለአህጉረ፡ ሰዶምኒ፡ ወጎሞራ፡ አውዐዮን። (2 Pet. 2:6).

la-'aḫgura sadomə-ni wa-gomorā

<Prep-NCom:f^{s}.p.ConSt> <NPro:unm.s.Nom-Conj> <Conj-NPro:unm.s.Nom-Part>

'aw'ay-on

<V:Perf. 3m.s-PSuff:3f.p>

'He burnt the cities of Sodom and Gomorrah'.

Further references: Num. 26:57; Ezra 2:1, 3:9, 7:7; Neh. 2:8, 9:24, 10:28; Ps. 49:10; 1 Cor. 7:25.

* Notice that the Pronominal suffix of the first person both masculine and feminine singular ኒ *nni* (በደረኒ *badara-nni*, ቀደመተኒ *qadamatta-nni* etc.) is not the same in function with the conjunction ኒ *ni* that we discussed up to now.

4.2. CONJUNCTIONS EXPRESSING CAUSE

4.2.1. አምጣነ *'amṭāna*, አኮኑ *'akkonu* and እስመ *'əsma*

አምጣነ *'amṭāna* is originally the accusative form of አምጣን *'amṭān* which does have an etymological connection with the verb መጠነ *maṭṭana* 'measure' or 'weigh' and with the noun መጠን *mṭan*. አኮኑ *'akkonu* is believed to be a combination of the negative particle አኮ *'akko* and the interrogative particle ኑ *nu* while እስመ *'əsma* is neither a derivation nor a combined phrase, according to *'Aggabāb*. But In accordance with Dillmann's observation, *'əsma* as a causal or justificative element is formed from *sa* and *ma*.[1]

However, they all keep a common grammatical function. Their major task is to introduce a subordinate clause by expressing a cause for the action or incidence mentioned in the main clause. Thus, the following conjunctions and idioms are to be their English equivalents 'because', 'for', 'since' and 'for the reason that'.[2]

---

[1] Dillmann 1907, 415.

[2] Dillmann 1865, 222, 781, 746; Kidāna Wald Kəfle 1955, 127, 129; Leslau 1989, 46, 137, 143; Yāred Šiferaw 2009,388; Yətbārak Maršā 2002, 156.

Regarding the syntactical arrangement, as part of the subordinate clause, they occur quite often after the main verb is mentioned. Though, the subordinate clause itself sometimes precedes the main clause. In such cases, the elements occur before the main verbs. However, the change in syntactic arrangement does not affect their meaning and function.

Textual evidence: (after the main verb)

4.2.1.1. ወኢአኀዝዎ፡ እስመ፡ ዓዲ፡ ኢበጽሐ፡ ጊዜሁ። (John 8:20).

wa-ʾi-ʾaḫazəww-o ʾəsma ʿādi ʾi-baṣḥa

<Conj-PartNeg-V:Perf.3m.p-PSuff:3m.s> <Conj> <Part> <PartNeg-V:Perf.3m.s>

gize-hu

<Adv-PS. uff:3m.s>

'But they did not seize him because his time has not yet reached'.

Further references: Josh. 4:14; Ps. 6:2, 11,1, 32:20; Jer. 31:15; Matt. 2:18; John 12:39; 1 Tim. 1:13; 1 Cor. 15:33.

Textual evidence: (before the main verb)

4.2.1.2. እስመ፡ አርመምኩ፡ በልያ፡ አእጽምትየ። (Ps. 31:3).

ʾəsma ʾarmamku balyā ʾaʿṣəmtə-ya

<Conj> <V:Perf.1c.s> <V:Perf:3f.p> <NCom:fˢ.p-PSuff:1c.s>

'For I kept silence, my bones became old'.

Further references: Ps. 31:2; Rom. 2:12.

Moreover, *ʾəsma* can be used solely as a conjunction in expressing a time with the meaning 'when'.

Textual evidence:

4.2.1.3. ተፈሣሕኩ፡ እስመ፡ ይቤሉኒ፡ ቤተ፡ እግዚአብሔር፡ ነሐውር። (Ps. 121:1).

tafaśśāḥku ʾəsma yəbelu-ni beta

<V:Perf.1c.s> <Conj> <V:Perf.3m.p-PSuff.1c.s>
<NCom:unm.s.ConSt>

ʾəgziʾabəḥer naḥawwər

<NCom:m.s.Nom> <V:Imperf.1c.p>

'I was glad when they said to me, 'Let us go into the house of the Lord'.

It is used again as an exclamation of surprise, pleasure or assurance with the meanings 'just', 'indeed', 'oh'.

Textual evidence:

4.2.1.4. ኦ፡ እኁየ፡ እስመ፡ አነ፡ በእንተ፡ ኵሉ፡ እጼሊ፡ ለከ፡ ከመ፡ ትሥራሕ፡ ፍኖተከ። (3 John 1:2).

ʾo ʾəḫu-ya ʾəsma ʾana baʾənta

<Int> <NCom.m.s.Nom-Psuff.1c.s> <Conj>
<PPer:unm.s> <Prep>

kʷəllu ʾəṣelli la-ka kama təśrāḥ

<PTot.Nom> <V:Imperf.1c.s> <Prep-PSuff:2m.s>
<Conj> <V:Subj.2m.s>

fənota-ka

<NCom:unm.s.Acc-PSuff: 2m.s>

'O, brother, I just pray for you concerning all things so that you may be prosperous in your path'.

አኮኑ *ʾakkonu* has at least three basic features. The first one relates to status in a sentence. As it can be seen in the examples above, *ʾamṭāna* and *ʾəsma* shall be attached always to verbs or nouns. But *ʾakkonu* is not attached by nature to any word; it occurs individually.

Second, it can equally occur before or after a verb in the subordinate clause. But in the case of *ʾamṭāna* and *ʾəsma*, the verb in the subordinate clause is preceded by *ʾəsma* or *ʾamṭāna.*

Thirdly, as a conjunction which is featured out of two different particles, አኮኑ *ʾakkonu* can provide answer for the action done by the subject in a question form.

Textual evidence:

4.2.1.5. ምንትኑ፡ ጳውሎስ፡ ወምንትኑ፡ አጵሎስ፡ አኮኑ፡ ከማክሙ፡ ሰብእ። (1 Cor. 3:5).

məntə-nu ṗāwəlos wa-məntə-nu 'aṗəlos

<AInt-PartInt> <Npro:m.s.Nom> <Conj-AInt-PartInt> <NPro:unm.s.Nom>

'akko-nu kamā-kəmu sabə'

<PartNeg-PartInt> <Prep-Psuff:2m.p> <NCom:unm.p^{s}.Nom>

'What is Paul and what is Apollos, are we not men like you?'

Further references: Ps. 38:11, 61:1; Isa. 66:1; Luke 17:17, 22: 27, 48; John 11:8; Jas. 2:4.

In a subordinate clause with two or more verbs each after a conjunction ወ *wa*, the conjunction used to express a cause (*'əsma* or *'akkonu* or *'amṭāna*) does not need to be mentioned repeatedly. Its single employment is enough to serve as a cause conjunction for the subsequent verbs.

Textual evidence:

4.2.1.6. እስመ፡ ተወክፈቶሙ፡ ወኀብአቶሙ። (Heb. 11:34).

'əsma tawakfatt-omu wa-ḫabatt-omu

<Conj> <V:Perf:3f.s-PSuff:3m.p> <Conj-V:Perf:3f.s-PSuff:3m.p>

'Because she received them, and (because) she hid them'.

Further references: 1 Thess. 4:16; Heb. 5:11, 11:31.

4.3 TEMPORAL CONJUNCTIONS

4.3.1. መዋዕለ *mawāʿəla*, ሰዐተ *saʿata*, ሶበ *soba*, አመ *ʾama*, ዕለተ *ʿəlata*, ዐመተ *ʿamata* and ጊዜ *gize*

Only መዋዕለ *mawāʿəla* and ዕለተ *ʿəlata* have etymological affiliation with other words; they have a common root which is related with the verb ወዐለ *waʿala* 'pass the day'.[1] Their grammatical function is to be used as temporal conjunctions with their own concerns. As long as they are used as conjunctions, they do not occur alone, but rather they are added to verbs (perfectives and imperfectives) initially.[2]

ሰዐተ *saʿata*[3] is an important element for expressing time of the day or a specific hour. Sometimes, it is represented by ሰዓ *saʿā*. ዕለተ *ʿəlata* is also used as an expression of a day. Thus, they keep the meanings 'at', 'on', and 'in'. Indeed, all the remaining elements (except ሶበ *soba*) are also used to express time of the day and days. However, their foremost role including that of *soba*[4] is to express seasons, periods, years, and an unfixed time. With this regard, the possible lexical meanings that the elements can keep are the following 'when', 'since', 'during', 'at the time of' and 'in the days of'.

Three elements namely, *ba*, *ʾəm* and *ʾəska* can be attached to the elements initially, keeping their own meanings 'by'/ 'at', 'from' and 'until' respectively.[5] Likewise, the particles ሁ *hu*, ሂ *hi*, ሰ *ssa*, ኒ *ni* and ኬ *ke* can be suffixed to them.

---

1 Dillmann 1865, 389, 925; Kidāna Wald Kəfle 1955,133; Leslau 1989, 76, 165, 211; Yāred Šiferaw 2009,351, 376.

2 በዐመተ፡ ሞተ፡ ዖዝያን፡ ንጉሥ፡ ርኢክዎ፡ ለእግዚአብሔር። (Isa. 6:1) *ba-ʿamata mota ʿozəyān nəguś rəʾikə-wwo la-ʾgziʾabəḥer* 'In the year that king Uzziah died I saw the Lord'. This is a good example to see how these elements get attached to verbs directly. However, this kind of attachment is found very rarely.

3 It is also rarely used to demonstrate unfixed time with the meaning 'short time/ moment'. Ref. እስመ፡ ሕማምነ፡ ዘለሰዐት፡ ቀሊል *ʾəsma ḥəmāmə-na za-la-saʿat qalil* 'for our light affliction, which is for a moment…'. 2 Cor. 4:17

4 "It is formed from ሶ (there) and በ (in)". Dillmann 1907, 405.

5 Leslau 2006, 21.

The elements ሶበ *soba,* አመ *'ama*[1] and ጊዜ *gize* are principally found in written texts having been combined with the elements (ሶበሁ *soba-hu,* አመሁ *'ama-hu,* ጊዜሁ *gize-hu*...). The particles enable them to occur without attachment. Otherwise, they should always be combined with other words particularly with verbs as far as they play the role of adverbs.

Only in such forms, the elements can occur without direct attachment to verbs or nouns.

እንተ *'ənta* is an exceptional element to be added to *soba* and *gize* initially without introducing any grammatical change.

Textual evidence:

4.3.1.1. እንተ፡ ሶበ፡ ጸዋዕኩዎ፡ ለእግዚአብሔር፡ እድኅን፡ እም፡ ፀርየ። (Ps. 17:3).

'ənta soba ṣawwāʿkə-wwo la-'əgzi'abəḥer 'ədəḫən

<PRel> <Conj> <V:Perf.1c.s-PSuff:3m.s> <Prep-NCom:m.s.Nom> <V:Imperf.1c.s>

'əm ḍarə-ya

<Prep > <NCom:unm.s.Nom-Psuff:1c.s>

'When I call to the Lord, I will be saved from my enemy'.

4.3.1.2. እንተ፡ ጊዜ፡ ተንሥአ፡ ሰብእ፡ ላዕሌነ። (Ps. 123:2).

'ənta gizetanśə'a sabə' lāʿle-na

<PRel> <Conj> <V:Perf.3m.s> <NCom:m.s^{s}.s.Nom> <Prep-PSuff:1c.p>

'When man revolted against us'.

As mentioned above, the elements are directly attached to verbs. Though, there is a way by which other verbal or non-verbal elements or a couple of words can come between the element and the verb. Even jussives can split the attachment and take the medial position. Nevertheless, the intercession of a jussive or any other word can never affect the common use and meaning of the elements. The in-

[1] Dillmann analysed it as formed from the interrogative and relative *ma* by prefixing *'a*. Dillmann 1907, 417.

serted word is defined by itself without confusing the actual meaning of the attachment. Let us see the following reading in different syntactical arrangements.

Textual evidence:

4.3.1.3. (*soba* + verb) ሶበ፡ ተንሥአ፡ እግዚአብሔር፡ ለኰንኖ። (Ps 75:9)

soba tanśəʾa ʾəgziʾabəḥer la-kʷannəno

<Conj> <V:Perf.3m.s> <NCom:m.s.Nom> <Prep-V:Inf.Nom >

'When God arose to judge'

4.3.1.4. (*soba* + ... verb) ሶበ፡ ጻድቅ፡ እም፡ ዕፁብ፡ ይድኅን። (Prov. (com) 11:31).

soba ṣādəq ʾəm-ʿəḍub yədəḫən

<Conj> <NCom:m.s.Nom> <Prep-NCom:m.s.Nom> <V:Imperf.3m.s>

'Since a righteous will be saved '.

The conjunction *soba* and the verb which is assigned to relate to *soba* took different positions in each sentence. Nonetheless, the translation of the second sentence is identical with that of the first which from the perspective of *ʾAggabāb* is considered as the standardized one.

So, each can be translated as 'when the Jews took our Lord to crucify him on the cross'.

Soba, ʾama and *gize* are exclusively combined with all other elements, initially. However, only one of them will be often dominant in translation. Even *gize* appears sometimes as combined with *soba, ʾama* and *mawāʿəla.*

Textual evidence:

4.3.1.5. ወሶበ፡ ጊዜ፡ እመጽእ፡ አነ፡ ባዕድ፡ ይቀድመኒ። (John 5:7).

wa-soba gize ʾəmaṣṣəʾ ʾana bāʿəd

<Conj-Conj> <Conj> <V:Imperf.1c.s> <PPer:c.s> <NCom:m.s.Nom>

yəqaddəma-nni

<V:Imperf.3m.s-Vsuff :1c.s>

'But, while I am coming, another (steps down) before me'.

Further references: Num. 27:26; 2 Sam. 11:1; 1 Kgs 2:8, 2:37; Ps. 55:9, 101:2.

Moreover, *soba*, *'ama* and *gize* are important time prepositions. In this case, they are attached to the non-verbal elements አመ፡ ወርኀ፡ መስከረም *'ama warḫa maskaram*, ሶበ፡ ምኑን፡ አነ *soba mənnun*, ጊዜ፡ ንዋም *gize nəwām* etc. (Acts 17:30, 21:26; Anap. Nicean (com) verse 6).

The theory concerning the attachment of the particles *ba*, *'əm* and *'əska* at the beginning yet function in such cases.

Interestingly, the elements with a pronominal suffix of the third person singular feminine ሶቤሃ *sobehā,* አሜሃ *'amehā* and ጊዜሃ *gizehā* are particularly used as adverbs in expression of time with the meanings 'immediately', 'at that very time' and 'directly'. In usage, ጊዜሃ *gize-hā* needs the affixation of *ba* to keep the same function. ሶቤሃ *sobe-hā* and አሜሃ *'ame-hā* can occur alone.

Textual evidence:

4.3.1.6. ወተጠሚቆ፡ እግዚእ፡ ኢየሱስ፡ ሶቤሃ፡ ወፅአ፡ እማይ። (Matt. 3:16).

wa-taṭamiqo 'əgzi'ə 'iyyasus sobehā

<Conj-V:Gern.3m.s> <NCom:m.s.Nom> <Nprop:m.s.Nom> <Adv>

waḍa 'əm-māy

<V:Perf.3m.s> <Prep-NCom:unm.s.Nom>

'Having been baptised, Jesus came up immediately from the water'.

4.3.1.7. ወፈረየ፡ ፍሬ፡ አሜሃ፡ አስተርአየ፡ ክርዳድኒ። (Matt. 13:26).

wa-faraya fəre 'amehā 'astar'aya kərdādə-ni

<Conj-V:Perf.3m.s> <NCom:m.s.Nom> <Adv> <V:Perf.3m.s> <Ncom :m.s.Nom-Conj>

'It bore grain, the tare also became evident at the same time'.

4.3.1.8. ወኀደጋ፡ በጊዜሃ። (Acts 16:18).

wa-ḫadag-ā ba-gizehā

<Conj-V:Perf.3f.s-Psuff:3f.s> <Prep-Adv>
'And it left her immediately'.
Further references: Matt. 21:19, 20, 25:15.

4.3.2. ቅድመ *qədma*

ቅድመ *qədma* in such a case is a noun in status constructus. The nominative ቅድም *qədm* (*qdm*) is the root of the verb ቀደመ *qadama* 'precede', 'be first' and 'come before'.

Interestingly, *qədma* is one of the two exclusive ACPPIP elements that can be categorized into three lexical categories of adverbs, conjunctions and prepositions. Leslau considers it to be a conjunction only when *'əm* is prefixed to it while Dillmann identified it only as preposition and an adverb. [1]

As a conjunctional element, it is added to jussives with or without an initial attachment of እም *'əm*, and as a prepositional element, it is attached to the non-verbal items with or without *ba*. Distinctively, when it is used as an adverb, it occurs alone.[2]

In the state of being a conjunction, it is used in expression of priority and precedence with the meanings 'before', 'at first', 'at the beginning', 'primarily', 'as prior', 'earlier' and 'previously'. When it is used as a preposition expressing location, its meaning will be as follows: 'in front of', 'before', 'in sight of' and 'in the presence of'.

Regarding with the syntactical arrangement, its position in a sentence depends on the role it plays. When it plays the role of an adverb, it can take the place either before or after a verb. As a preposition, it can only be directly attached to a noun initially. But when it is used as a conjunction, the attachment can be either direct or indirect attachment as we have already seen earlier in the case of ሶበ *soba*.

---

[1] Dillmann 1907, 383, 400; Leslau 2006, 421.
[2] Dillmann 1865, 462-463; Kidāna Wald Kəfle 1955, 150-151; Leslau 1989 90; Yāred Šiferaw 2009,351; Yətbārak Maršā 2002,157.

Textual evidence:

4.3.2.1. ዘሀሎ፡ እም፡ ቅድመ፡ ይትፈጠር፡ ዓለም። (Ps. 54:15).

za-hallo 'əm qədma yətfaṭar 'ālam

<PRel-V:Perf.3m.s> <Prep> <Conj> <V:Subj.3m.s> <NCom:m^{s}.s.Nom>.

'He who was before the world was created'.

Further references: Anap. Nicean (com) verse 17; Gdl.Qaw 3:19.

Here, the elements are directly attached to the verbs one after the other. But it is also possible to have the same sentences without the occurrence of direct attachment.

4.3.2.2. ዘሀሎ፡ እም፡ ቅድመ፡ ዓለም፡ ይትፈጠር።

za-hallo 'əm qədma 'ālam yətfaṭar

<PRel-V:Perf.3m.s> <Prep> <Conj> <NCom:m^{s}.s.Nom> <V:Subj.3m.s>

Nonetheless, the core message of the sentences is not affected due to the intercession of words between the elements and the verb.

Apart from this, there are two possibilities by which ቅድመ *qədma* can take place in a sentence as an individual lexical item without being attached to verbs or nouns. The first possibility is if any single particle such as *hi*, *ni* or *ssa* is suffixed to it. Instances, ቅድመሂ *qədma-hi*, ቅድመኒ *qədma-ni*, ቅድመሰ *qədma-ssa.*

The other possibility is if it is used as an adverb of time occurring before or after perfectives, imperfectives, imperatives or a gerund as an individual item helping the verb by indicating an order or a time schedule. In such cases, it will occur individually.

Textual evidence:

4.3.2.3. ቅድመ፡ ተኳነን፡ ምስለ፡ እኁከ። (Matt. 5:24).

qədma tak^{w}ānan məsla 'əḫu-ka

<Adv> <V:Impt.2m.s> <Prep> <NCom:m.s.Nom-PSuff:2m.s>

'First, be reconciled to your brother'.

In all cases, it expresses a contradicting meaning against ድኅረ *dəḫra.*

4.3.3. እስከ *'əska*

እስከ *'əska* is originally an element with dual functions of a conjunction and a preposition. Dillmann suggested that it was originally a conjunction; then, it was extended to be used as a preposition. About its origin, he has stated that it is formed from 'əs and ka.[1]

As a conjunction, it is attached particularly to verbs (perfectives and imperfectives (Gen. 38:17; Enoch (com.) 33:37, 34:13; Job 2:11) while as a preposition, its attachment occurs to the non-verbal language elements. Though, in both cases, it expresses amount, point, scope, range and degree with the meanings 'till', 'until', 'to', 'to the point of' and 'up to'.[2]

In some cases, though, the events demonstrated by the element can have no end or limit. Therefore, it is possible to assume the element in two ways as እስከ *'əska* with and without end.[3] This is specifically concerned with time. In the first case, the time is specified whether in past or in present or in future too. The action or the occurrence demonstrated by the main verb of the sentence has also got or gets or will get an end at a certain point of time. This is a very common case.

---

[1] Dillmann 1907, 395.

[2] Dillmann 1865, 750; Kidāna Wald Kəfle 1955, 244; Leslau 1989, 137; Yətbārak Maršā 2002, 161.

[3] In the tradition, it is known as ፍጻሜ፡ ያለው፡ እስከ *fəṣṣāme yāllaw 'əska* and ፍጻሜ፡ የሌለው፡ እስከ *fəṣṣāme yalellaw 'əska.*

Textual evidence:

4.3.3.1. (Imperf. - *'əska* + Perf.) ወእነብብ።[1] ተዝካረ፡ ስእለቶሙ፡ እስከ፡ ደቀስኩ። (Enoch (com.) 33:37).

wa-'ənabbəb tazkāra sə'lat-omu

<Conj-V:Imperf.1c.s> <NCom:m.s.ConSt> <NCom:unm.s.Nom>

'əska daqqasku

<Conj> <V:Perf. 1c.s>

'I was telling the remembrance of their supplication until I slept'.

Further references: Acts 8:40; Anap. Nicean (com) verse 77; M. Məśṭir 2:30.

4.3.3.2. (Perf. - *'əska* +Imperf.) አኀዝክዎ፡ ወኢየኀድጎ፡ እስከ፡ ሶበ፡ አባእክዎ፡ ውስተ፡ ቤተ፡ እምየ። (S. of S. 3:4).

'aḫazkə-wwo wa-'i-yyaḫaddə-go 'əska soba

<V:Perf.1c.s-PSuff:3m.s> <Conj-PartNeg-V:Imperf.1c.s> <Conj> <Conj>

'aba'əkəww-o wəsta beta 'əmmə-ya

<V:Imperf.1c.s-PSuff:3m.s> <Prep> <NCom:unm.s.ConSt> <NCom:f.s. Nom-PSuff:1c.s>

'I held him, and will never leave him until I will bring him to my mother's house'.

Further references: Prov. (com.) 4:15, 6:27.

---

[1] Describing the ocurences happened is the common use of an imperfective verb in Gəʿəz literature. We can find a lot of readings with the same feature. The coherent factor that enables us to decide as it tells not about the future, but about the past is the verb which comes after *'əska*, if it is in the past form. The following sentence is similarly structured: ወተለውክዋ፡ በድኅሬሃ፡ ወመጻእኩ፡ ኀቤክሙ፡ ዘከመ፡ ትሬእዩኒ። ወኢይትናገር፡ ምስሌሃ፡ እስመ፡ አኀዘኒ፡ ፍርሀት፡ ወድንጋጼ። *wa-talawkəww-ā ba-dəḫre-hā wa-maṣā'ku ḫabe-kəmu za-kama-təre'əyu-ni wa- 'iyyətnāggar məsle-hā 'əsma 'aḫaza-nni fərhat wa-dəngāḍe* 'Then, I followed after her and came to you as you see me. I was not talking with her because I was afraid' Gdl.Qaw 4:46.

4.3.3.3. (Impt. - *ʾəska* + Imperf.) አንትሙሰ፡ ንበሩ፡ ሀገረ፡ ኢየሩሳሌም፡ እስከ፡ ትለብሱ፡ ኀይለ፡ እም፡ አርያም። (Luke 24: 49).

ʾantəmu-ssa nəbaru hagara ʾiyyarusālem

<PPer: 2m.p-Part> <V:Impt:2m.p> <NCom: unm.s.ConSt> <NCom:pl.s.Nom>

ʾəska təlabbəsu ḫayla ʾəm ʾaryā

<Conj> <V:Imperf.2m.p> <NCom:unm.s.Acc> <Prep> <NCom: nm.s.Nom>

'You may stay in the city of Jerusalem until you are closed with power from the high'.

In the above-mentioned readings, the demonstrated occurrences got an end at a certain point of time. So, in the first sentence, we understand that David was not a king any more after getting old; and in the second sentence, we understand that David will leave his kingdom when he gets old.

When we come to the second kind of *ʾəska,* we find the actions or occurrences referred by the main verbs getting no end. The following two textual references are mainly mentioned by the scholars to show the certainty of this theory.

Textual evidence:

4.3.3.4. ኢተመይጠ፡ ቋዕ፡ እስከ፡ አመ፡ ነትገ፡ ማየ፡ አይኅ። (Gen. 8:7).

ʾi-tamayṭa qʷāʿ ʾəska ʾama natga

<PartNeg-V:Perf.3m.s> <NCom:m.s.Nom> <Conj> <Conj> <V:Perf.3m.s>

māya ʾayəḫ

<NCom:mˢ.s.ConSt> <NCom:unm.s.Nom>

'A raven did not come back until the flood was dried up'.

4.3.3.5. ኢወለደት፡ ሜልኮል፡ እስከ፡ አመ፡ ሞተት። (2 Sam. 6:23).

ʾi-waladat meləkol ʾəska ʾama motat

<PartNeg-V:Perf.3f.s> <NPro:f.s.Nom> <Conj> <Conj> <V:Perf.3f.s>

'Michal had no child to the day of her death'.

Further references: Deu. 3:20; Luke 9:4.

Concerning the first example, we know from the history of flood that all animals and beasts including Noah and his families have left the ark (ship) when the flood was dried up and the ark remained alone. Based on this fact, we understand that it is not to mean that the raven returned to the ark since all left the ark and it has remained alone.

Regarding the second sentence, from the common understanding of human nature, we can simply conclude as it is never to mean that Michal was barren until her death; but after death, she gave birth to a child. But instead, it is to mean she was barren entirely since no one can beget a child after death. So, in such cases, *'əska* does not refer to a certain point of time or a limited time; the actions or occurrences are also not to be considered as reaching completion. That is why this kind of *'əska* is called *fəṣṣāme yalellaw 'əska.*

On the attachment to other words, *'əska* can be attached to verbs or nouns either directly or indirectly being accompanied by any one of the following six elements ለ *la*, ሶበ *soba*,[1] ነ *na*, ኀበ *ḫaba*, አመ *'ama;* ኬ *ke* and ጊዜ *gize*. Each particle accompanies *'əska* in different cases, *la* in expression of things and situations; ኀበ *ḫaba* in expression of place and አመ *'ama* in expression of time. Only ነ *na* can come after it in all cases.

Textual evidence:

4.3.3.6. ፍቅር፡ ሰሐቦ፡ ለወልድ፡ ኀያል፡ እመንበሩ፡ ወአብጽሖ፡ እስከ፡ ለሞት። (Anap.Mary (com.) verse 124).

fəqr saḥab-o la-wald

<NCom:m.s.Nom> <V:Perf.3m.s-PSuff:3m.s> <Prep-NCom:m.s.Nom>

ḫayyāl 'əm-manbar-u wa-'abṣəḥ-o

<NCom:m.s.Nom> <Prep-NCom:unm.s.Nom-PSuff:3m.s> <Conj-V:Perf.3m.s-PSuff:3m.s>

'əska la-mot

<Prep> <Prep-NCom:unm.s.Nom>

---

[1] Dillmann 1907, 416.

'Love has drawn the almighty Son from his throne and reached Him until death'.

4.3.3.7. ወናሁ፡ ኮከብ፡ ዘርእዩ፡ በምሥራቅ፡ ይመርሖሙ፡ እስከ፡ ሶበ፡ አብጽሖሙ፡ ቤተልሔም። (Matt. 2:9).

wa-nāhu kokab za-rə'yu ba-məśrāq

<Conj-PartPres> <Ncom:m^{s}.s.Nom> <PRel-V:Perf.3m.p> <Prep-NCom:unm.s.Nom>

yəmarrəḥ-omu 'əska soba 'abṣəḥ-omu

<V:Imperf.3m.s-Psuff:3m.p> <Conj> <Conj> <V:Perf.3m.s-Psuff:3m.p>

betaləḥem

<Npro:unm.s.Acc>

'Behold the star which they saw in the east, had been leading them until it brings them to Bethlehem'.

4.3.3.8. ወእግዚአ፡ አባግዕ፡ አርመመ፡ እስከነ፡ ተዘርዘሩ፡ ኵሉ፡ አባግዕ፡ ገዳመ። (Enoch (com.) 33:17).

wa-'əgzi'a 'abāgʿə 'armama 'əskana

<Conj-NCom:m.s.ConSt> <NCom:m.p.Nom> <V:Perf.3m.s> <Conj>

tazarzaru kʷəllu 'abāgʿə gadāma

<V:Perf.3m.p> <ProTot.Nom> <NCom:m.p.Nom> <NCom:unm.s. Acc>

'And the owner of the sheeps was silent until the sheeps were scatered in the wilderness'.

4.3.3.9. ኢያእመራ፡ ዮሴፍ፡ ለማርያም፡ እስከ፡ አመ፡ ወለደት፡ ወልደ፡ ዘበኵራ። (Matt. 1:21).

'i-yyā'mar-ā yosef la-mārəyām

<PartNeg-V:Perf.3m.s-PSuff:3f.s> <NPro:m.s.Nom> <Prep-NPro:f.s.Nom>

'əska 'ama waladat walda za-bakʷr-ā

<Conj> <Conj> <V:Perf.3f.s> <NCom:m.s.Acc> <PRel-NCom: m.s.nom-PSuff:3f.s>

'Joseph did not know her to the date at which she gave birth to her first born'.

Further references: Gen. 8:7; 1 Sam. 1:11; 2 Sam. 6:22; Ezra 2:63; Acts 7:45.

This is one kind of indirect attachment. There is also another type of indirect attachment which is frequently employed in the tradition of all kinds of Gəʿəz literature. It can be expressed as *ʾəska* + subject/ object + verb.

Textual evidence:

4.3.3.10. **ወርኢኩ፡ እስከ፡ መንበር፡ ተሐንጸ፡ በምድር።** (Enoch (com.) 34:1).

wa-rəʾiku ʾəska manbar taḥanṣa ba-mədr

<Conj-V:Perf.1c.s> <Conj> <NCom:m^{s}.s.Nom> <V:Perf.3m.s> <Prep-NCom:unm.s>

'And I saw until a throne was built on the earth'.

In other words, this is to mean **ወርኢኩ፡ እስከ፡ ተሐንጸ፡ መንበር፡ በምድር።** *wa-rəʾiku ʾəska taḥanṣa manbar ba-mədr.* However, both give the same meaning, 'And I saw until a throne was built on the earth'.

When *ʾəska* is combined with nouns with the intercession of *la* as a mediator, the verb **በጽሐ** *baṣḥa* may appear in the translation. The following textual statement is a good reference for this.

Textual evidence:

4.3.3.11. **ተከዘት፡ ነፍስየ፡ እስከ፡ ለሞት።** (Mark 14:34).

takkazat nafsə-ya ʾəska la-mot

<V:Perf.3f.s> <NCom:m.s.Nom-PSuff.1c.s> <Prep> <Prep-NCom:unm. s.Nom>

'My soul is sad until it reaches to the point of death'.

To construct interrogative statements using *ʾəska,* the interrogative particles **ማእዜ** *māʾəze* and **አይ** *ʾay* are the most important supplementary elements to be attached to the element, initially. In such a combination, the other interrogative particle **ኑ** *nu* can accompany *ʾay* and *māʾəze.* Its combination with *ʿay* concerns time, place, person, thing and situation.

Examples:

> እስከ፡ አይ/ኑ ፡ሰዐት *ʾəska ʾāy/-nu saʿat* → 'until which time?'
> እስከ፡ አይ/ኑ፡ መካን *ʾəska ʾāy/-nu makān* → 'to which place?'
> እስከ፡ አይ/ኑ፡ ብእሲ *ʾəska ʾāy/-nu bəʾsi* → 'up to which person?'
> እስከ፡ አይ/ኑ፡ ደብር *ʾəska ʾāy/-nu dabr* → 'up to which mountain?'
> እስከ፡ አይ/ኑ፡ ድልቅልቅ *ʾəska ʾāy/-nu dələqləq* 'until which disaster?'

The combination with ማእዜ *māʾəze* is concerned with time. However, it expresses an enthusiasm or frustration of the one who asks.

Textual evidence:

4.3.3.12. ደቂቀ፡ እጓለ፡ እመ ፡ ሕያው፡ እስከ፡ ማዕዜኑ፡ ታከብዱ፡ ልበክሙ። (Ps. 4:2).

daqiqa ʾəgʷāla ʾəmma ḥəyʾāw

<NCom:m.p^{s}.ConSt> <NCom:m.s.ConSt> <NCom:m.s.ConSt> <NCom:m.s.Nom>

ʾəska māʾəze-nu tākabbəddu ləbba-kəmu

<Prep> <AInt-PartInt> <V:Perf.2m.p> <NCom:unm.s.Acc-PSuff:2m.p>

'O, sons of men, how long will you harden your heart?'

4.3.3.13. ወእስከ፡ ማእዜኑ፡ እትዔገሠክሙ። (Matt. 17:17).

wa-ʾəska māʾəze-nu ʾətʿeggaśa-kkəmu

<Conj-Prep> <AInt-PartInt> <V:Imperf.1c.s-PSuff:2m.p>

'And how long shall I keep patience on you?'

4.3.4. እንዘ *ʾənza*

Dillmann analaysed it as a compound of *ʾən* 'there' and the relative pronoun *za*.[1] But according to *ʾAggabāb ʾənza*[2] is initially an individual element with no etymological relation with verbs or nouns. Its

---

[1] Dillmann 1907, 419.
[2] Dillmann 1865, 778; Kidāna Wald Kəfle 1955,139; Leslau 1989, 34

grammatical function is to be used as a conjunction and a preposition with the meanings 'although', 'as', 'even', 'even as', 'even though', 'since', 'when', 'whereas', 'while' and 'without' to indicate the way how somebody does something or how something happens as well as the time when things happen. References: Gen. 38:17; Job 2:11; Mark 1:16; Acts 11:5; 2 Cor. 5:4; Rev. 1:10.

The one and only verb which can have a combination with *'ənza* in its perfective form is ሀሎ *hallo*/ ሀለወ *hallawa* 'be', 'exist', 'live'. Otherwise, it is commonly attached to imperfectives only. Its attachment to ሀሎ *hallo*/ ሀለወ *hallawa* is enormously used in different texts. It is also attached to the existential affirmative ቦ *bo* and its negation አልቦ *'albo* as well as to the personal pronoun/ copula ውእቱ *wə'ətu* including its negation አኮ *'akko*.[1] Let us see the following textual accounts.

Textual evidence:

4.3.4.1. እንዘ፡ ሀሎከ፡ ኵሎሄ። (Anap.John (com.) verse 28).

'ənza hallo-ka kʷəllahe

<Conj> <V:Perf.2m.s-PSuff:2m.s> <Adv>

'Since you are existing always'.

Further references: Matt. 5:25; Gdl.Qaw 1:37, 42.

4.3.4.2. ከማሁ፡ ዘይትሌቃሕ፡ ሥርናየ፡ እንዘ፡ ቦ፡ ውስተ፡ ከምሩ። (Prov. (com.) 20:4).

kamā-hu za-yətleqqāḥ śərnāya 'ənza

<Prep-Psuff:3m.s> <PRel-V:Imperf.3m.s> <NCom:unm.s.Acc> <Conj>

bo wəsta kəmr-u

<ExAff.3m.s> <Prep> <NCom:unm.s.Nom>

---

[1] According to the tradition of the *Qəne* Schools, they are considered as special verbs, and are known as ነባር አንቀጽ *nabbar 'anqaṣ*. It literally means 'an immovable gate'. This implies that they are not declined like other verbs albeit they are regarded as verbs.

'Whoever borrows wheat since he has in his heap is like him'.

4.3.4.3. እንዘ፡ አልቦ፡ ዘያድኅን፡ ወዘይባልሖ። (Ps. 7:2).

ʾənzaʾalbo za-yādəḫən wa-za-yəbālləḥ

<Conj> < ExNeg> <PRel-V:Imperf.3m.s> <Conj-PRel-V:Imperf.3m.s>

'While there is no one who saves or who rescues'.

The verb to which *ʾənza* is attached cannot be in any case the main verb of a sentence, but instead gives information how or when the action is done or happens as ideally connected with the main verb which remains disjointed of any ACPPIP element.

Textual evidence:

4.3.4.4. ወቦእኩ፡ ኀበ፡ ሰብእየ፡ እንዘ፡ እባርኮ፡ ለእግዚአ፡ ዓለማት። (Enoch (com.) 27:21).

wa-boʾku ḫaba sabʾə-ya ʾənza

<Conj-V:Perf.1c.s> <Prep> <NCom:unm.p^{s}.Nom-PSuff:1c.s> <Conj>

ʾəbārrək-o la-ʾəgziʾa ʿālamāt

<V:Imperf.1c.s-Psuff:3m.s> <Prep-NCom:m.s.ConSt> <NCom:unm.p. Nom>

'Then, I entered to my households while blessing the Lord of the worlds'.

In the case of a nominal clause when the attachment of *ʾənza* to a nominal derivation takes part without a verb, a copula takes the place of the verb.

Textual evidence:

4.3.4.5. እንዘ፡ ብዙኅ፡ ኀይልከ፡ ሐሰዉከ፡ ጸላዕትከ። (Ps. 65:3).

ʾənza bəzuḫ ḫaylə-ka ḫassawu-ka

<Conj> <NCom:m.s.Nom> <NCom:unm.s.Nom-PSuff:2m.s> <V:Perf.3m.p-PSuff:2m.s>

ṣalāʿtə-ka

<NCom:m.p-PSuff:2m.s>

'While much is your power, your enemies did lie to you'.

The initial attachment of መጠነ *maṭana* and አምጣነ *'amṭāna* to *'ənza* might occur rarely when it is used as a time preposition with the meanings 'while' and 'since'. It is just to give emphasis that the action is too important to happen or to be done frequently. However, it might be difficult to explain the attached element in another language. So, in many cases, only the meaning of *'ənza* will be demonstrated in the translation.

Textual evidence:

4.3.4.7. አምጣነ፡ እንዘ፡ ብክሙ፡ ብርሃን፡ እመኑ፡ በብርሃን። (John 12:36).

'amṭāna 'ənza bə-kəmu bərhān 'əmanu

<Conj> <Conj> <ExAff.PSuff:2m.p> <NCom:unm.s.Nom> <V:Impt:2m.p>

ba-bərhān

<Prep-NCom:unm.s.Nom>

'While you have a light, believe in light'.

During its combination with the verb *hallo/ hallawa*, the concept of the the following verb will be expressed in a gerund or an infinitive form.

Textual evidence:

4.3.4.8. እንዘ፡ ሀሎ፡ ሳኦል፡ ይነግሥ፡ ላዕሌነ። (2 Sam. 5:2).

'ənza hallo sā'ol yənaggəś lā'le-na

<Conj> <V:Perf.3m.s> <Npro:m.s.Nom> <V:Imperf.3m.s> <Prep-PSuff:1c.p>

'Since Saul was still alive being a king over us'.

It sometimes keeps the concept of the conjunction 'as'.
Textual evidence:

4.3.4.9. ወካዕበ፡ ርኢኩ፡ በአዕይንትየ፡ እንዘ፡ እነውም። (Enoch (com.) 30:14).

wa-kā'əba rə'iku ba-'a'əyyəntə-ya 'ənza 'ənawwəm

<Conj-Adv> <V:Perf.1c.s> <Prep-NCom:unm.p.Nom-PSuff:1c.s> <Conj> <V:Imperf.1c.s>

'And again, I saw with my eyes as I slept'.

Its role and meaning remains the same even when it is used as a preposition. The only difference is that the components to which it gets attached as a preposition are the non-verbal elements such as the nominal derivations, nouns, numerals and other ACPPIP elements. References: 1 Cor. 12:2; Anap.John (com.) verse 65; M. Məśṭir 4:34; Gdl.Qaw 1:38.

4.3.5. ድኅረ *dəḫra*

In this case, ድኅረ *dəḫra* is a noun in status constructus. The nominative ድኅር *dəḫr* is related with the verb ደኀረ *daḫara* or ተድኅረ *tadəḫra* 'be late' or 'follow behind'. It is the second element among the entire ACPPIP elements to be categorized into three lexical categories of adverbs, conjunctions and prepositions. Leslau mentioned its function as a preposition only while Dillman identified it as preposition and an adverb.[1] In all cases, ቅድመ *qədma* is its negative counterpart.

As a conjunction, it is attached to verbs (perfectives and imperfectives). In such a case, its meaning is 'after'. The conjunction *'əm* can be attached to it initially. At this time, ድኅረ *dəḫra* shall take the medial position. However, no grammatical change is introduced due to the attachment.

Textual evidence:

4.3.5.1. ኤልያስ፡ አንሥኦ፡ ለወልደ፡ መበለት፡ እም፡ ድኅረ፡ ሞተ። (M. Məśṭir 17:21).

'elyās 'anśə-'o la-walda-maballat

<NPro:m.s.Nom> <V:Perf.3m.s-PSuff:3m.s> <Prep-NCom:m.s.ConSt-NCom:f.s.Nom>

'əm dəḫra mota

<Conj> <Conj> <V:Perf.3m.s>

'Elijah caused the widow's son to arise after he died'.

Further references: Matt. 10:28, 11:6 John 21:14, 15.

---

[1] Dillman 1907, 401; Leslau 2006, 129.

As a preposition, it is used in expression of position or place with the meanings 'after', 'back' and 'behind' as attached with the non-verbal language elements.

On the other hand, when it is used as an adverb with the meaning 'later',[1] it occurs alone without getting attached to other words. It can precede or follow a verb.

Textual evidence:

4.3.5.2. (following a verb) ለኪሰ፡ ወለወልድኪ፡ ትገብሪ፡ ድኅረ። (1 Kgs 17:13).

la-ki-ssa wa-la-waldə-ki təgabbəri dəḫra

<Prep-PSuff:2f.s-Part> <Conj-Prep-NCom:m.s.Nom-PSuff:2f.s> <V:Imperf.2f.s> <Adv>

'And afterward you may make for yourself and for your son'.

4.3.5.3. (preceding a verb) ወድኅረ፡ ፈነወ፡ ኀቤሆሙ፡ ወልዶ። (Matt. 21:37).

wa-dəḫra fannawa ḫabe-homu wald-o

<Conj-Adv> <V:Perf.3m.s> <Prep-PSuff:3m.p> <NCom:m.s.Acc-PSuff: 3m.s.Acc>

'Then, he sent his son to them'.

Further references: Matt. 25:15; John 13:36.

Idiosyncratically, the nominative form *dəḫr* can play the same role if a proper preposition of place such as መንገለ *mangala,* በ *ba*, ኀበ *ḫaba,* እም *'əm* and እንተ *'ənta* is attached to it. The actual concepts of the elements added to it may not move on in terms of the attachment. It may rather have the following meanings መንገለ፡ ድኅር *mangala dəḫr* ኀበ፡ ድኅር *ḫaba dəḫr* 'towards back', በድኅር *ba dəḫr* 'at the back', 'behind', እም፡ ድኅር *'əm dəḫr* 'from behind' and እንተ፡ ድኅር *'ənta dəḫr* 'backward'.

---

1 Dillmann 1865, 1109; Kidāna Wald Kəfle 1955: 134; Leslau 1989, 196; Yətbārak Maršā 2002, 159.

Textual evidence:

4.3.5.4. ሑር፡ እም፡ ድኅሬየ፡ ሰይጣን፡ እስመ፡ ኮንከ፡ ማዕቀፍየ። (Matt. 16:23).

ḥur ʾəm dəḫre-ya sayṭān ʾəsma

<V:Impt.2m.s> <Prep> <prep-PSuff:1c.s> <NPro:m.s.Nom> <Conj>

konka māʿəqafə-ya

<V:Perf.2m.s> <NCom:unm.s.Acc-PSuff:1c.s>

'Go away Satan behind me! You became a stumbling block to me'.

The form with a pronominal suffix of the third feminine singular is eventually attested keeping the status of a preposition of time with the meanings 'after that', 'after a while', 'later' and 'afterward'.

Textual evidence:

4.3.5.5 ተአምሩ፡ ከመ፡ ድኅሬሃ፡ ፈቀደ፡ ይረስ፡ በረከተ። (Heb. 12:17).

taʾamməru kama dəḫre-hā faqada yəras barakata

<V:Imperf.2m.p> <Conj> <Prep-PSuff:3f-s> <V:Perf:3m.s> <V:Subj. 3m.s> <NCom: unm.s.Acc>

'You know that he afterward desired to inherit blessings'.

4.4. ADVERSATIVE CONJUNCTIONS

4.4.1. ሰ *sa* and ወ *wa*

We discussed earlier the primary grammatical function of ወ *wa* as a copulative conjunction. Hence, we examine its further function as an adversative conjunction which is not shared by *hi* and *ni.* In such a case, its fellow element is ሰ *sa*. They are used to add a clause which is semantically contradicting with the meanings 'but', 'contrarily', 'however', 'nonetheless', 'notwithstanding' and 'nevertheless'.[1] The

[1] Dillmann 1865, 321, 880; Kidāna Wald Kəfle 1955:140; Leslau 1989, 64, 198; Tropper 2002, 146.

only difference between them is in fact the position that they take in the attachment; as usual, *wa* takes the first position but ሰ *sa* comes always at the end of the word like ሂ *hi* and ኒ *ni*.

Textual evidence:

4.4.1.1. ትሰምዑ፡ ወኢትሌብዉ። (Matt. 13:14).

təsamməʿu wa-ʾi-təlebbəwu

<V:Imperf.2m.p> <conj-PartNeg-V:Imperf.2m.p>

'You hear but you do not comprehend'.

4.4.1.2. ለወልደ፡ እጓለ፡ እመ፡ ሕያውሰ፡ አልቦቱ፡ ኀበ፡ ያሰምክ፡ ርእሶ። (Matt. 8:20).

la-walda ʾəgʷala ʾəmma

<Prep-NCom:m.s.ConSt> <NCom:unm.p.ConSt> <NCom:f.s.ConSt>

ḥəyāw-ssa ʾalbo-ttu ḫaba yāsamməḵ rəʾso

<NCom:m.s.Nom-Part> <PartNeg-PSuff:3m.s> <Conj> <V:Imperf.3m. s> <NCom:unm.s.Acc>

'But the son of man has nowhere to lay his head'.

4.4.1.3. አንትሙሰ፡ ኢትሰምዑኒ። (John 8:46).

ʾantəmu-ssa ʾi-təsamməʿu-ni

<PPer:2m.p-Conj> <PartNeg-V:2m.p-PSuff:1c.s>

'But you do not listen to me'.

Further references: 2 Kgs 2:19; Matt. 6:6, 9, 23:27, 39; John 1:11, 8:15, 13:10.

As it occurs in the case of *hi* and *ni*, without any clear reason and importance, *wa* can join the attachment of *sa*, keeping the initial position.

Textual evidence:

4.4.1.4. ሰማይ፡ ወምድር፡ የኀልፍ፡ ወቃልየሰ፡ ኢየኀልፍ። (Matt. 24:34).

samāy wa-mədr yaḫalləf

<NCom:unm.s.Nom> <Conj-NCom:unm.s.Nom> <V:Imperf.3m.s>

wa-qālə-ya-ssa ʾi-yyaḫalləf

<Conj-NCom:unm.s.Nom-PSuff:1c.s-Conj> <PartNeg-V:Imperf.3m.s>

'Heaven and earth will pass away but my word will not pass away'.

4.4.1.5. ወዳዊትሰ፡ ንጉሥ፡ ልህቀ፡ ወኀለፈ፡ መዋዕሊሁ። (1 Kgs 1:1).

wa-dāwit-ssa nəguś ləhqa wa-ḫalafa

<Conj-NPro.m.s.Nom-Conj> <NCom:m.s.Nom> <V:Perf.3m.s> <Conj-V:Perf.3m.s>

mawāʿli-hu

<NCom: unm.s.Nom-PSuff:3m.s>

'However, King David became old, and his age passed'.

Further references: 1 Kgs 1:4, 10; Matt. 1:19 Matt. 6:33, 25:30, 26:11 John 7:17,18, 8:14 1 Pet. 1:25.

4.4.2. ባሕቱ *bāḥəttu*, አላ *ʾallā* and ዳእሙ *dāʾəmu*

Leslau connected *bāḥəttu* with the verb በሐተ *baḥta* or ብሕተ *bəḥta* 'be alone'.[1] But in accordance with the *ʾAggabāb* tradition none of them has a relation with any verb or noun. They are used as adversative conjunctions with the meanings 'but', 'however' and 'but rather'.[2]

Bāḥəttu and *ʾallā* are not attached to any word or phrase but occur alone just before or after a verb or a noun. *Dāʾəmu* also occurs quite often alone. But, in some cases, it receives the initial attachment of እንበለ *ʾənbala* or ዘእንበለ *za-ʾənbala* to express the notion of 'unless' or 'otherwise'. None of them can begin a new sentence.

---

[1] Leslau 2006, 92.

[2] Dillmann 1865, 496, 718, 1121; Kidāna Wald Kəfle 1955, 136; Leslau 1989, 96, 132, 198; Yāred Šiferaw 2009,352, 381; Yətbārak Maršā 2002,164.

Textual evidence:

4.4.2.1. ገሥጾሰ፡ ገሠጸኒ፡ እግዚአብሔር፡ ወለሞትሰ፡ ባሕቱ፡ ኢመጠወኒ። (Ps. 117:15).

gaśśəṣo-ssa gaśśaṣa-nni ʾəgziabəḥer wa-la-mot-ssa

<V:Inf.Acc-Conj> <V:Perf.3m.s-Psuff.1c.s> <NPro:m.s.Nom> <Conj-Prep-NCom:unm.s.Nom>

bāḥəttu ʾi-maṭṭawa-nni

<Conj> <PartNeg-V:Perf.3m.s-Psuff:1c.s>

'God has punished me a punishment, but he has not given me over to death'.

4.4.2.2. አኮ፡ ዘሞተት፡ ሕፃን፡ አላ፡ ትነውም። (Matt. 9:24).

ʾakko za-motat ḥəḍan ʾallā tənawwəm

<PartNeg> <Prel-V:Perf.3m.s> <NCom:f^{s}.s.Nom> <Conj> <V: Imperf. 3f.s>

'The child is not dead but sleeping'.

4.4.2.3. ኢመጻእኩ፡ ከመ፡ እስዐሮሙ፡ ለኦሪት፡ ወለነቢያት፡ ዘእንበለ፡ ዳእሙ፡ ከመ፡ እፈጽሞሙ። (Matt. 5:17).

ʾi-maṣāʾəku kama ʾəsʿarr-omu la-ʾorit

<PartNeg-V:Perf.1c.s> <Conj> <V:Subj.1c.s-PSuff.3m.p> <Prep-NCom:m^{s}.s.Nom>

wa-la-nabiyāt za-ʾənbala-dāʾəmu kama

<Conj-Prep-NCom:m.p.Nom> <PRel-Conj-Conj> <Conj>

ʾəfaṣṣəmm-omu

<V:Subj.1c.s-PSuff:3m.p>

'I did not come to abolish the Law and the prophets unless to fulfil them'.

4.4.2.4. አኮ፡ አንትሙ፡ ዘኀረይክሙኒ፡ አላ፡ አነ፡ ኀረይኩክሙ። (John 15:16).

ʾakko ʾantəmu za-ḫaraykəmu-ni ʾallā ʾana

<PartNeg> <PPer:2m.p> <PRel-V:Perf.2m.p-PSuff:1c.s> <Conj> <PPer:1c.s>

ḫarayku-kəmu

<V:Perf.1c.s-PSuff:2m.p>

'You did not choose me, but I chose you'.

Further references: 1 Kgs 2:1; Ps. 61:5; Luke 9:24; Rom. 3:31; 2 Cor. 4:18.

Besides, *dāʾəmu* has especially one more function. It can be used as 'only'.

Textual evidence:

4.4.2.5. እሉኑ፡ ደቂቅከ፡ ዳእሙ። (1 Sam. 16:11).

ʾəllu-nu daqiqə-ka dāʾəmu

<PPer:m.p.Nom-Int> <NCom:m.p-PSuff:2m.s> <Conj>

'Are only these your sons?'

Further references: Luke 6:32; Acts 18:25; Rom. 3:30, 4:9; 2 Cor. 5:9; Gal. 6:13.

4.5. DISJUNCTIVE CONJUNCTIONS

4.5.1. ሚመ *mimma* and አው *ʾaw*

ሚመ *mimma* is supposed to be a combination of the interrogative *mi* 'how' or 'what' and the particle *ma*.[1] አው *ʾaw* an independent element having no affiliation to any noun. They are used as disjunctive conjunctions with the meaning 'or'.[2] Dillmann described *ʾaw* as it is sometimes disjunctive and sometimes explanatory.[3]

In a sentence, they usually take a medial position between two or more components. There is no restriction regarding the pattern of the components; they can be verbs or nouns or other language elements. The crucial difference between them in use is that *mimma* comes most often being preceded by a conjunction *wa* in the form of ወሚመ *wa-mimma.* For *ʾaw,* it is not so important to have the conjunction *wa* even if it is often used. But rather, when it is used twice,

[1] Tropper 2002, 145.

[2] Dillmann 1865, 142; Kidāna Wald Kəfle 1955, 148; Leslau 1989, 28.

[3] Dillmann 1907, 410.

the first *wa* will be translated as 'either'; this means, the continual use of *'aw* gives fully the correlative conjunction 'either ... or'.

Textual evidence:

4.5.1.1. አንተኑአ፡ ዘይመጽእ፡ ወሚመ፡ ቦኑ፡ ካልዕ፡ ዘንሴፈው። (Luke 7:19).

'anta-nu-'a za-yəmaṣṣə' wa-mimma bo-nu

<PPer:2m.s-PartInt-Part> <Prel-V:Imperf.3m.s> <Conj-Conj> <V:c-PartInt>

kālə' za-nəseffaw

<NCom:m.s.Nom> <Prel-V:Imperf.1c.p>

'Are you the one who has to come or is there someone else whom we have to wait for?'

4.5.1.2. አው፡ ለየማን፡ አው፡ ለጸጋም። (1 Kgs 3:42).

'aw la-yamān 'aw la-ṣagām

<Conj> <Prep-NCom:unm.s.Nom> <Conj> <Prep-NCom:unm.s.Nom>

'Either to right or to left...'.

Further references: Gen. 30:28, 31:28; Luke 13:4; Jas. 4:5.

4.6. CONSECUTIVE CONJUNCTIONS

4.6.1. በዘ *baza*

በዘ *baza* has no origin related with a verb. It is just a combination of the preposition በ *ba* and the relative pronoun ዘ *za*.[1] It is mostly added to verbs (perfectives and imperfectives). Its functions are as follows:

[1] Leslau explained it as to mean: 'with which, by which, through which' by considering that two different elements በ *ba* and ዘ *za* with different meanings follow each other and did not recognize it as a single element (Leslau 1989 182). In fact, this is also a feature of the combination of these two elements, but it must be clear the difference between the two natures of በዘ *baza*, as a combination of two different elements with their own meanings, and a compounded በዘ *baza* which stands bearing a single meaning as men-

4.6.1.1. It is used as a conjunction with the meanings ‘so that’, ‘in order that’, ‘because’

እስመ፡ ተድላ፡ ብዙኃን፡ አኀሥሥ፡ በዘየሐይዉ። (1 Cor. 10:33).

ʾəsma tadlā bəzuḫān ʾaḫaśśəś baza-

<Conj> <NCom:unm.s.ConSt-NCom:m.p.Nom> <V:Imperf.1c.s>

yaḥayyəwu

<Conj-V:Imperf.3m.p>

‘For I seek the pleasure of many so that they might be saved’.

Further references: Luke 19:47; Acts 17:27; 2 Cor. 2:3; Gal. 6:4; Eph. 6:11; 2 Pet. 1:4; Rev. 2:21.

4.6.1.2. It is used as a conjunction with the meanings ‘therefore’, ‘for that reason’, ‘after’ and ‘since’.

4.6.1.3. እስመ፡ አሐዱ፡ ሞተ፡ ቤዛ፡ ኵሉ፡ በዘወድአ፡ ሞተ፡ ኵሉ። (2 Cor. 5:14).

ʾəsma ʾaḥadu mota bezā

<Conj> <NumCa:m.s.Nom> <V:Perf.3m.s> <NCom:unm.s.ConSt>

kʷəllu baza-waddəʾa mota kʷəllu

<ProTot:m^{s}.Nom> <Conj-Adv> <V:Perf.3.m.s> <Ptot:m^{s}.s.Nom>

‘For the one has died for the ransom of all since all has completely died’.

4.6.1.4. ይእቲኒ፡ ሣራ፡ ረከበት፡ ኀይለ፡ ታውጽእ፡ ዘርዐ፡ እንዘ፡ መካን፡ ይእቲ፡ በዘረሥአት። (Heb. 11:11).

yəʾəti-ni śārā rakabat ḫayla tāwṣəʾ

<PPer:f.s.Nom-Conj> <Npro:f.s.Nom> <V:Perf.3f.s> <NCom:unm.s.Acc>

---

tioned above. Kidāna Wald Kəfle 1955, 131; Yāred Šiferaw 2009,404; Yətbārak Maršā 2002, 158-9.

zarʿa ʾənza makkān

<V:Subj.3f.s> <NCom:unm.s.Acc> <Conj> <NCom:f^{S}.s.Nom>

yəʾəti baza-raśat

<Copu:f.s> <Conj-V:Perf.3f.s>

'Even that Sarah received power to conceive since she was barren, since she got old'.

4.6.1.5. It is used as a conjunction with the meanings 'how', 'as', 'as much as'.

ወእንተሰ፡ አውሰበት፡ ትኄሊ፡ ንብረተ፡ ዝ፡ ዓለም፡ በዘታደሉ፡ ለምታ። (1 Chr. 7:34).

wa-ʾənta-ssa ʾawsabat təḫelli nəbrata

<Conj-PRel-Part> <V:Perf.f.s> <V:Imperf.3f.s> <NCom:unm.s.ConSt>

zə ʿālam baza-tādallu la-mət-ā

<PDem:m.s.Nom> <NCom:unm.s.Nom> <Conj-V:Imperf.3f.s> <Prep-NCom:m.s.Nom-PSuff:3f.s>

'But she who is married thinks the life of this world how she pleases her husband'.

4.6.1.6. ወከፈለነ፡ በዘሠርዐነ፡ እግዚአብሔር። (Eph. 1:11).

wa-kafala-nna baza-śarʿa-nna ʾəgziʾabḥer

<Conj-V:Perf.3m.s-PSuff.1c.p> <Conj-V:Perf.3m.s-PSuff:1c.p> <NPro:m. s.Nom>

'And we obtained as God appointed for us'.

4.6.1.7.

In a sentence at which በዘ *baza* is attached to the verb, which does not directly refer to the subject but instead to the third person, it leads the verb to keep a gerund expression in translation.

Textual evidence:

እመ፡ ኢረከብከ፡ በዘበልዐ፡ ቤል፡ ንመውት። (Dan. 14:12).

ʾəmma ʾi-rakabka baza-balʿa bel nəmawwət

<Conj> <PartNeg-V:Perf.2m.s> <Conj-V:Perf.3m.s> <NPro:m.s.Nom> <V:Imperf: 1c.p>

'If you do not find Baal eating, we shall die'.

4.6.2. ከመ *kama*

ከመ *kama* has no original affiliation with any verb. It is a linguistic element which can play the role of conjunction and preposition with the meanings 'so that', 'in order that', 'as', 'as if', 'as though', 'if', 'that' and 'how'.[1] It gets attached to verbs (perfectives, imperfectives and subjunctives) when it is used as a conjunction while the components to which it is added as a prepositional element are the non-verbal linguistic elements.

Textual evidence:

4.6.2.1. (with the meanings 'as', 'as if', 'as though')

With a purpose to indicate the way that something happens or is done by comparison (ከመ *kama* + verb/ noun)

ወዝንቱ፡ ተአምር፡ ለከ፡ ከመ፡ አነ፡ እፌንወከ። (Ox. 3:12).

we-zəntu ta'ammər la-ka kama

<Conj-PDem:m.s.Nom> <NCom:ms.s.Nom> <Prep-Psuff:2m.s> <Conj>

'ana 'əfennəwa-kka

<Ppers:1c.s> <V:Impt.1c.s>

'And this is the sign for you as I send you'.

4.6.2.2. (with the meanings 'as' and 'that')

With a purpose to indicate that something was or is surely done.
(ከመ *kama* + perf./ imperf.)

---

[1] Dillmann 1865, 826; Kidāna Wald Kəfle 1955, 130; Leslau 1989, 150; Yāred Šiferaw 2009,351; Yətbārak Maršā 2002, 158.

4.6.2.2.1. እንግርክሙ፡ ክሡተ፡ በእንተ፡ ዳዊት፡ ርእሰ፡ አበው፡ ከመሂ፡ ሞተ፡ ወተቀብረ። (Acts 2:29).

'əngər-kəmu kəśuta ba'ənta dāwit

<V:Subj(Impt).1c.s-PSuff:2m.p> <Adv> <Prep> <Npro:m.s.Nom>

Rəsa 'abaw kama-hi mota wa-taqabra

<NCom:m.s.ConSt> <NCom:m.p.Nom> <Conj-Part> <V:Perf.3m.s> <Conj-V:Perf.3m.s>

'Let me tell you plainly regarding David the patriarch as he died and was buried'.

4.6.2.2.2. ወእግዚአብሔር፡ ሰማዕትየ፡ ከመ፡ አፈቅረክሙ። (Phil. 1:8).

wa-'əgzi'abḥer samā'ətə-ya kama 'afaqqəra-kkəmu

<Conj-NCom:m.s.Nom> <NCom:m.s.Nom-PSuff:1c.s> <Conj> <V:Imperf. 1c.s-PSuff:2m .p>

'God is my witness that I love you'.

Further references: 1 Kgs 2:37; Num. 26:65; M. Məśṭir 3:35.

4.6.2.3. (with the meaning 'as far as')

ወከመሰ፡ ውሉድ፡ አንትሙ፡ ናሁ፡ ፈነወ፡ እግዚአብሔር፡ መንፈሰ፡ ውሉድ፡ ውስተ፡ ልብክሙ። (Gal. 4:6).

wa-kama-ssa wəlud 'antəmu nāhu fannawa

<Conj-conj-Part> <NCom:m.p.Nom> <PPer:2m.p> <Adv> <V:Perf.3m.s>

'əgzi'abḥer manfasa wəlud

<NCom:m.s.Nom> <NCom:unm.s.ConSt> <NCom:m.p.Nom>

wəsta ləbbə-kəmu

<Prep> <NCom:unm.s.Nom-PSuff:2m. p>

'As far as you are sons, now, God has sent the spirit of sons into your hearts'.

4.6.2.4. (with the meaning ‘so that’ or ‘in order that’)[1]

With a purpose to indicate the reason why things happen. (ከመ *kama* + subj)

ወከሠተ፡ ሊተ፡ ወልዶ፡ ከመ፡ እስብክ፡ ለአሕዛብ፡ በስሙ። (Gal. 1:16).

wa-kaśata li-ta wald-o

<Conj-V:Perf.3m.s> <Prep-Psuff:1c.s> <NCom:m.s.Acc-Psuff:3m.s>

kama ʾəsbək la-ʾaḥzāb ba-səmu

<Conj> <V:Subj.1c.s> <Prep-NCom:unm.p.Nom> <Prep-NCom:unm. s.Nom-Psuff:3m.s>

‘And he revealed his son to me so that I may preach to the Gentiles in his name’.

Further references: Gen. 1:16; Prov. (com.) 5:9; John 9:3; Acts 8:37; Anap.Diosc (com.) verse 33.

4.6.2.5. (with the meaning ‘how’)

The combination of *za* and *kama* gives the concept ‘how’, not in a sense of interrogation but of a conjunction.

ወኵሉ፡ ለይትዐቀብ፡ ዘከመ፡ የሐንፅ። (1 Cor. 3:10).

wa-kwəllu la-yətʿaqab za-kama yaḥannəḍ

<Conj-PTot.Nom> <Prep-V:Subj (Impt).3m.s> <PRel-Conj> <V:Imperf. 3m.s>

‘But each man has to be careful how he builds’.

Further references: Judg. 10:15 1; Kgs 2:9; Acts 12:17; 2 Cor. 1:8; M. Məʿṭir 3:31.

In such cases, both direct and indirect attachments of the element are possible. A position does not affect its meaning and use. When occurs indirect attachment, *kama* goes to be combined with preposition, conjunction, adverb, noun or number; the verb comes soon after the attachment.

---

[1] In such cases, Tropper calls it ‘Finale Nuance’. Tropper 2002, 147.

Textual evidence:

4.6.2.6. ከመ፡ እም፡ ፍሬ፡ ከርሡ፡ ያነብር፡ ዲበ፡ መንበሩ። (Acts 2:30).

kama ʾəm fəre karś-u

<Conj> <Prep> <NCom:unm.s.ConSt> <NCom:unm.s.Nom-PSuff:3m.s>

yānabbər diba manbar-u

<V:Imperf.3m.s> <Prep> <NCom:unm.s.Nom-PSuff:3m.s>

'As he places one among his descendants on his throne'.

This can be converted into a sentence with a direct attachment as ከመ፡ ያነብር፡ እም፡ ፍሬ፡ ከርሡ፡ ዲበ፡ መንበሩ። *kama yānabbər ʾəm fəre karś-u diba manbar-u* or እም፡ ፍሬ፡ ከርሡ፡ ከመ፡ ያነብር፡ ዲበ፡ መንበሩ። *ʾəm fəre karś-u kama yānabbər diba manbar-u.* However, the meaning remains the same.

Further references: Acts 8:18; 1 Pet. 3:21.

በ *ba* and ዘ *za* can be affixed to it without affecting its meaning and function in the form of በከመ *ba-kama* and ዘከመ *za-kama.* This does not occur when it is used to indicate a purpose with the meaning of 'so that' or 'in order that'. Likewise, particles ሂ *hi*, ሰ *ssa,* ኒ *ni* and ኬ *ke* can be added to *kama* with and without a pronominal suffix. References: 1 Kgs 3:7; Mark 13:29 Acts 2:29; Rom. 11:25; 1 Cor. 2:1; 2 Cor. 5:11; Jas. 1:11.

The repetition of *kama* in the combination of three elements is possible. Though, both may introduce a single time conjunction 'when' or 'since'.

Textual evidence:

4.6.2.7. ወከመ፡ ከመ፡ ይቀርብ፡ ዓመቲሁ፡ አአምረከ። (Hab. 3:2).

wa-kama kama yəqarrəb ʿāmati-hu

<Conj-Conj> <Conj> <V:Imperf.3m.s> <NCom:mˢ.s.Nom-PSuff:3m.s>

ʾaʾammәra-kka

<V:Imperf.1c.s-PSuff:2m. s>

'And when the time is coming, I will know you'.

In two different cases, *kama* plays the role of a conjunction of condition with the meaning 'if'. First, when it occurs after the combination of እመ *'əmma* + ቦ *bo*; and second, when እም *'əm* is attached to it initially.

Textual evidence:

4.6.2.8. እመቦ፡ ከመ፡ ኢየአክለነ፡ ለነ፡ ወለክን፡ ሑራ፡ ኀቤሆሙ፡ ለእለ፡ ይሣየጡ፡ ወተሣየጣ፡ ለክን። (Matt. 25:9).

'əmma-bo kama 'i-yya'akkəla-nna la-na wa-la-kən

<Conj-ExAff.3m.s> <Conj> <PartNeg-V:Imperf.1c.p> <Prep-PSuff:1c.p>

ḥurā ḫabe-homu la-'əlla

<Conj-Prep-PSuff:2f.p> <V:Impt.2f.p> <Prep-PSuff:3m.p> <Prep-PRel>

yəśśāyyaṭu wa-taśāyāṭā la-kən

<V:Imperf.3m.p> <Conj-V:Impt.2f.p> <Prep-PSuff:2f.p>

'If it might not be enough for us and you, go to the dealers and buy for yourselves'.

4.6.2.9. እብለክሙ፡ እምከመ፡ ትትገዘሩ፡ ክርስቶስ፡ ኢይበቍዐክሙ። (Gal. 5:2).

'əbəla-kkəmu 'əm-kama tətgazzaru krəstos

<V:Imperf.1c.s-PSuff:2m.p> <Conj-Conj> <V:Imperf.2m.p> <NPro:m.s.Nom>

'i-yyəbaqqʷə'a-kkəmu

<PartNeg-V:Imperf.2m.p-PSuff:m.p>

'I say to you, if you are going to be circumcised, Christ will not benefit you'.

Further references: Matt. 5:23; Acts 7:9.

4.7. PLACE CONJUNCTIONS

4.7.1. መንገለ *mangala* and ኀበ *ḫaba*

On their origin, August Dillmann affirms that *mangala* is a derivation from *nagala* ‘be uprooted’ and that *ḫaba* is formed from ኀ and the preposition በ ‘in-there’.[1] His analysis about the formation of *ḫaba* is somehow questionable to Leslau; he stated that the meaning of *ḫ* is not indicated.[2] However, according to the *’Aggabāb* tradition both are linguistic elements with no etymological affiliation with verbs.

Both share similar meaning, importance and role in the language. They have double characteristics of conjunctions and prepositions. As conjunctional elements, they are added to perfectives and imperfectives. Similarly, as prepositional elements, they will be combined with the non-verbal elements.

As it is a common feature of most of the elements in the same category to be directly attached to verbs to construct a subordinate clause, the elements are added to verbs as far as they are concerned to play the role of a conjunction.

Their most essential function is introducing all possible nouns which indicate a certain place or an undefined area without mention of any additional place name. With this regard, they can be generally keep the concept of the adverb ‘where’.[3] The word ‘place’ may also sporadically appear with ‘where’ jointly or being combined with other place prepositions.

Textual evidence:

4.7.1.1. ኀበ፡ ሀሎ፡ ገዳላ፡ ሀየ፡ ይትጋብኡ፡ አንስርት። (Matt. 24:28).

ḫaba hallo gadalā həyya yətgābbə’u ’ansərt

<Conj> <V:Perf.3m.s> <NCom:m^s.s.Nom> <Adv> <V:Imperf.3m.p> <NCom:m^s.p>

‘Where the carcass is, there the eagles will gather together’.

---

1 Dillmann 1907, 38, 394, 683.

2 Leslau 2006, 255.

3 Dillmann 1865, 592, 685; Kidāna Wald Kəfle 1955, 128; Leslau 1989, 39, 113.

Further references: Gen. 8:9, 22:4; Ruth 1:16; 1 Sam. 9:22; Enoch (com.) 12:1; Esther 5:3; Ps. 131:7; Matt. 2:9, 24:28; Luke 9:12; John 1:40; Rev. 11:8; Anap.John (com.) verse 29.

There are five elements that can be attached to the elements initially. They are namely ለ *la*, በ *ba*, እም *'əm*, እስከ *'əska*, እንተ *'ənta* and ውስተ *wəsta*.[1] Among them, ለ *la*, እንተ *'ənta* and ውስተ *wəsta* do not lose their actual meanings. In Dillmann's observation, the combination *'ənta-mangala* is very common.[2] This means the elements will regularly keep the concept 'to'. But the remaining three elements turn their meaning to the conception of 'the place where'.

Textual evidence: with la, 'ənta *and* wəsta

4.7.1.2. ለኀበ፡ እለ፡ ይትሜክሑ፡ ለገጽ፡ ወአኮ፡ በልብ። (2 Cor. 5:12).

la-ḫaba 'əlla yətmekkəḥu la-gaṣṣ

<Prep-Prep> <PRel> <V:Imperf.3m.p> <Prep-NCom:unm.s.Nom>

wa-'akko ba-ləbb

<Conj-PartNeg > <Prep-NCom:unm.s.-Nom>

'To those who take pride in appearance but not in heart'.

4.7.1.3. ወኀሠሡ፡ እንተ፡ ኀበ፡ ይቀትልዎ። (Mark 11:18).

wa-ḫaśaśu 'ənta ḫaba yəqattələww-o

<Conj-V:Perf.3m.p> <PRel> <Conj> <V:Imperf.3m.p-PSuff:3m.s>

'They seek a place where they may kill him'.

4.7.1.4. ለእለ፡ ይቀርቡ፡ ኀበ፡ እግዚአብሔር፡ እንተ፡ መንገሌሁ። (Heb. 7:25).

la-'əlla yəqarrəbu ḫaba 'əgzi'abḥer 'ənta mangale-hu

<Prep-PRel> <V:Imperf.3m.p> <Prep> <NCom:m.s.Nom> <PRel> <Prep-Psuff:3m.s>

---

[1] Tropper 2002, 147.
[2] Dillmann 1907, 399.

'Those who come close to God through him'.

Textual evidence: with *ba, 'əm* and *'əska*

4.7.1.5. ወሮጸ፡ ብእሲ፡ ብንያማዊ፡ እም፡ ኀበ፡ ይትቃተሉ፡ ወበጽሐ፡ ውስተ፡ ሴሎም። (1 Sam. 4:12).

wa-roṣa bə'si bənyāmāwi 'əm

<Conj-V:Perf.3m.s> <NCom:m.s.Nom> <NProp:pl.s-Part> <Prep>

ḫaba yətqāttalu wa-baṣḥa wəsta selom

<Conj> <V:Imperf.3mp> <Conj-V:Perf.3m.s> <Prep> <NProp.pl.s. Nom>

'And a man of Benjamin ran from the place where they were fighting each other and arrived in Shiloh'.

Further references: Josh. 4:10; 2 Sam. 1:1; Anap. Nicean (com) verse 20.

The initial attachment of *ba* to *ḫaba* enables it to keep the notion of 'everywhere or anywhere', if it is attached to a verb.

Textual evidence:

4.7.1.6. ወአድኀኖ፡ እግዚአብሔር፡ ለዳዊት፡ በኀበ፡ ሖረ። (2 Sam. 8:7).

wa-'adḫan-o 'əgzi'abḥer la-dāwit

<Conj-V:Perf.3m.s-PSuff:3m.s> <NCom:m.s.Nom> <Prep-NProp:m.s.Nom>

ba-ḫaba ḥora

<Prep-Conj> <V:Perf.3m.s>

'And the Lord saved David wherever he went'.

ኀበ *ḫaba* can be exclusively used as a distributive conjunction in its multiple occurence (ኀበ ኀበ *ḫaba-ḫaba*). The aim is mainly to show how the action, or the incidence affirmed through the verb happens progressively or frequently.

Textual evidence:

4.7.1.7. ቤተ፡ ሳኦል፡ ኀበ፡ ኀበ፡ የሐጽጽ፡ ሖረ፡ ወቤተ፡ ዳዊት፡ ኀበ፡ ኀበ፡ ይመልዕ። (1 Sam. 3:1).

beta sā'ol ḫaba ḫaba yaḥaṣṣəṣ

<NCom:m^{s}.s.ConSt> <NProp:m.s.Nom> <Conj> <Conj> <V:Imperf.3m.s>

ḥora wa-beta dāwit

<V:Perf.3m.s> <Conj-NCom:m^{s}.s.ConSt> <NProp:m.s.Nom>

ḫabaḫaba yəmall'ə

<Conj> <Conj> <V:Imperf.3m.s>

'The house of Saul goes to be (more and more) less, but the house of David goes to be (more and more) full'.

By a combination with a verb in present or past, it may urge sometimes the verb to keep a gerund form in meaning.

Textual evidence:

4.7.1.8. ርእያሃ፡ ለእብን፡ ኀበ፡ አንኰርኰረት። (Mark 16:4).

rə'yā-hā la-'əbn ḫaba 'ank^{w}ark^{w}arat

<V:Perf:3f.p-PSuff:3f.s > <Prep-NCom:f^{s}.s.Nom > <Conj> <V:Perf.3f.s >

'They saw the stone rolled up'.

Not far from the scope, it might be necessary to mention that there are some uncommon usages of *ḫaba* that can be found in some written texts. For instance, if we have a look at the passage አስተበቍዐክሙ፡ አኃዊነ፡ አነ፡ ጳውሎስ፡ በየውሀት፡ ወበምሕረተ፡ ክርስቶስ፡ እስመ፡ ሶበ፡ እሄሉ፡ ኀቤክሙ፡ መጠነ፡ አነ፡ በገጽ፡ ወበኀበሰ፡ ኢሀሎኩ፡ እተፌ፡ ላዕሌክሙ። (2 Cor. 10:1). *'astabaqq^{w}'a-kkəmu 'aḫāwi-na 'ana p̣āwəlos ba-yawwəhāt wa-ba-məḥrata krəstos maṭana 'ana ba-gaṣṣ wa-ba-ḫaba-ssa 'i-halloku 'ətaffi lā'le-kmu* 'Brethern, I, Paul urge you by the meekness and compassion of Christ as long as I am with you face to face, but when absent, I would write to you'.

In the reading, *ḫaba* took the place of *soba* and attempts to play the role of a time conjunction. However, we cannot assume that it is one of its features since such kind of strange treatment can be applied very rarely or accidentally, and we cannot find more identical readings to ratify it.

4.8. CONJUNCTIONS OF CONDITION

4.8.1. እመ *'əmma* and ሶበ *soba*

We have seen earlier the function of ሶበ *soba* as a time conjunction. Here, we see its further functions which it shares with እመ *'əmma*.[1] Before that, let us discuss about their attachments. Like most conjunctional elements, they are attached to perfectives and imperfectives only whenever they play the role of a conjunction. But when they are employed as prepositional elements, their attachment will be fixed with the non-verbal elements.

ለ *la* can be prefixed to እመ *'əmma* particularly. Likewise, some suffixes such as ሁ *hu*, ሂ *hi*, ሰ *sa*, ኒ *ni* and ኬ *ke* can be suffixed to both elements. This introduces the following phrases: እመሁ *'əmma-hu*, ሶበሁ *soba-hu*, እመሂ *'əmma-hi*, ሶበሂ *soba-hi*, እመሰ *'əmma-ssa*, ሶበሰ *soba-ssa*, እመኒ *'əmma-ni*, ሶበኒ *soba-ni*, ሶበኬ *soba-ke*, and እመኬ *'əmma-ke*.[2] The double suffixation of ሰ *ssa* and ኬ *ke* at the same time may occur as ሶበሰኬ *soba-ssa-ke* and እመሰኬ *'əmma-ssa-ke*. These fixed phrases are quite common. References: Job 3:15.; Ps. 103:29; Luke 16: 31; John 13:32; Rom. 11:6; 2 Cor. 2:2, 11:4; Gal. 1:10.

We can also find እመ *'əmma* while keeping both a prefix and a suffix at the same time in the form of ለእመሁ *la-'əmma-hu*, ለእመሂ *la-'əmma-hi*, ለእመሰ *la-'əmma-ssa* and ለእመኬ *la-'əmma-ke*. Nevertheless, no change will happen to the meaning or to the role of the element because of the prefixation or the suffixation. References: Matt. 4:9; Acts 5:39, 8:22; 2 Cor 2:9; Anap. Nicean (com) verse 20, 59.

Having said this, let us come to their functions. They are used as:

---

[1] Dillmann indicates that *'əmma* is formed from the interrogative and relative *ma* by prefixing *'a*. Dillmann 1907, 417.

[2] Tropper 2002, 146.

4.8.1.1. Conjunctions in expression of hypothesis or possibility with the meaning ‘if’ or ‘if…then’. [1]

Textual evidence:

4.8.1.1.1. እመ፡ አሕየውኮ፡ ለዝንቱ፡ ኢኮንከ፡ አርኮ፡ ለቄሳር። (John 19:12).

ʾəmma ʾaḥyawk-o la-zəntu ʾi-konka

<Conj> <V:Perf.2m.s-PSuff:3m.s> <Prep-PDem:3m.s.Nom> <PartNeg-V:Perf.2m.s>

ʾark-o la-qesār

<NCom:m.s.Acc-PSuff:3m.s> <Prep-NPro:m.s.Nom>

‘If you release him, you are not Caesar’s friend’.

4.8.1.1.2. ሶበሰ፡ ሀሎከ፡ ዝየ፡ እም፡ ኢሞተ፡ እኁየ። (John 12:21).

soba-ssa hallo-ka zəya ʾəm ʾi-mota ʾəḫ̮u-ya

<Conj-Part> <V:Perf.2m.s> <Adv> <Conj> <PartNeg-V:Perf.3m.s> <NCom:m.s.Nom-PSuff:1c.s>

‘If you had been here, my brother would not have died’.

Further references: Mark 13:22; John 5:46.

4.8.1.2. Conjunctions expressing the concepts ‘even if’ and ‘despite the possibility that’.

እመኒ፡ ኵሎሙ፡ ዐለዉከ፡ አንሰ፡ ኢየዐልወከ፡ ግሙራ። (Matt. 25:33).

ʾəmma-ni kwəll-omu ʿalawu-ka ʾanəsa

<Conj-Part> <ProTot-Psuff:3m.p> <V:Perf.3m.p-PSuff:2m.s> <PPer:1c.s>

ʾi-yyaʿalləwa-kka gəmurā

<PartNeg-V:Imperf.1c.s-PSuff:2m.s> <Adv>

‘Even if all may deny you, I will never deny you’.

Further references: 2 Cor. 4:3, 5:1.

---

[1] Dillmann 1865, 726, 354; Kidāna Wald Kəfle 1955:131; Leslau 1989, 22, 70; Yāred Šiferaw 2009:376.

4.8.1.3. Conjunctions to introduce alternate possibilities with the meaning 'whether'.

This will be realized when the element occurs repeatedly jointed by *wa*. Then, the first will be 'whether' or 'either', and every next element goes to be 'or'.

Textual evidence:

4.8.1.3.1 እመኒ፡ ጳውሎስ፡ ወእመኒ፡ አጵሎስ፡ ወእመኒ፡ ጴጥሮስ። (1 Cor. 3:22).

'əmma-ni p̣āwəlos wa-'əmma-ni 'ap̣əlos wa-'əmma-ni

<Conj-Conj> <NPro:m.s.Nom> <Conj-Conj> <NPro:m.s.Nom> <Conj-Conj-Conj>

p̣eṭros

<NPro:m.s.Nom>

'Whether Paul or Apollos or Peter'.

4.8.1.3.2. እንጃዒ፡ ለእመ፡ ወሀቦሙ፡ እግዚአብሔር፡ ከመ፡ ይነስሑ፡ ለሕይወት። (Acts 11:18).

'əndā'i la-'əmma wahab-omu 'əgziz'abḥer

<AdvUnc> <Prep-Conj> <V:Perf.3m.s-PSuff:3m.p> <NCom:m.s.Nom>

kama yənnassəḥu la-ḥəywat

<Conj> <V:Subj.3m.p> <Prep-NCom: unm.s.Nom>

'I do not know whether God has granted them to repent for life'.

Further references: Luke 22: 33; 2 Cor. 5:9, 10; Jas. 5:12.

4.8.1.4. Conjunctions with the meanings 'or', 'or else' and 'otherwise'.

To play such a role, the elements shall be combined with the negation particle አኮ *'akko*. The used fixed phrase እመ፡ አኮ *'əmma 'akko* is formed out of such a combination.[1]

---

[1] Tropper 2002, 146.

Textual evidence:

4.8.1.4.1. ግበሩ፡ ዕፀ፡ ሠናየ፡ ወፍሬሁኒ፡ ሠናየ፡ ወእመ፡ አኮ፡ ግበሩ፡ ዕፀ፡ እኩየ፡ ወፍሬሁኒ፡ እኩየ። (Matt. 12:33).

gəbaru ʿəśạ śannāya wa-fəre-hu-ni

<V:Impt.2m.p> <NCom:unm.s.Acc>
<NCom:m.s.Acc-Conj>
<Conj-NCom:m^{s}.s.Acc-PSuff:3m.s-Conj>

śannāya wa-ʾəmma

<NCom:m.s.Acc> <Conj-Conj>

ʾakko gəbaru ʿəśa ʾəkkuya

<PartNeg> <V:Inf.2m.p.> <NCom:m.s.Acc>
<NCom:m.s.Acc>

wa-fəre-hu-ni ʾəkkuya

<Conj-NCom:m.Acc-PSuff:3m s-Part>
<NCom:m.s.Acc>

'Make the tree good and its fruit good; otherwise, make the tree bad and its fruit bad'.

4.8.1.4.2. ወእመ፡ አኮ፡ ወይን፡ በለሰ፡ ፈርየ። (Jas. 3:12).

wa-ʾəmma ʾakko wayn balasa farəya

<Conj-Conj> <PartNeg> <NCom:m.s.Nom>
<NCom:m.s.Acc> <V:Inf. Acc>

'Or else, (can) a wine produce a fig?'

Further references: Gen. 30:1; 1 Sam. 2:18, 19:17; Acts 24:17; 1 Cor. 5:10.

Similarly, the combination of *ʾəmma* with ቦ *bo* and አልቦ *ʾalbo* produces the most used fixed phrases እመቦ *ʾəmma-bo* or ለእመቦ *la-ʾəmma-bo* (if there is...), እመ፡ አልቦ *ʾəmma ʾalbo* or ለእመ፡ አልቦ *la-ʾəmma ʾalbo* (if there is no...).

Textual evidence:

4.8.1.4.3. በአይቴ፡ አአምር፡ ለእመ፡ አልቦ፡ ዘመሀረኒ። (Acts 8:31).

ba-ʾayte ʾaʾammər la-ʾəmma ʾalbo za-mahara-nni

<Prep-AInt> <V:Imperf:1c.s> <Prep-Conj> <ExNeg-3m.s> <Prel-V:Perf. 3m.s-PSuff:1c.s>

'How can I know if there is no one who teaches me?'

4.8.1.4.4. ሶበ፡ አኮ፡ እግዚአብሔር፡ ምስሌነ፡... ፡ አሐዝብ፡ ሕያዋኒነ፡ እም፡ ውኅጡነ። (Ps. 124:2).

soba-'akko 'əgzi'abḥer məsle-na ... 'aḥazzəb

<Conj-PartNeg> <NCom:m.s.Nom> <Prep-Psuff:1c.p> <V:Imperf.1c.s>

ḥəyāwani-na 'əm-wəḫṭu-na

<NCom:m.s.Acc-PSuff:1c.p> <Conj-V:Perf.3m.p-PSuff:1c.p>

'If God had not been with us, ... I think that they would have swallowed us'.

4.8.2. ወእደ *wa'əda*

Tropper identified ወእደ *wa'əda* as a preposition, and also showed how it is combined with the preposition *ba*.[1] But in accordance with the *'Aggabāb* tradition, it functions as a conjunction without need of any word attachment. On its origin, Leslau proposed that it is derived from the root for *'əd* 'hand' with a deictic *w*.[2] It is used as a conjunction with the meanings 'as', 'if' and 'since'.[3] In a sentence, it is always attached to verbs directly.

Textual evidence:

4.8.2.1. ወእደ፡ ተናገረ፡ ኢዮብ፡ አውሥአ። (Job 16:1).

wa'əda-tanāgara 'iyyob 'awəśə'a

<Conj-V:Perf.3m.s> <NPro:m.s.Nom> <V:Perf.3m.s>

---

[1] Tropper 2002, 143.
[2] Leslau 2006. 602.
[3] Dillmann 1865, 919; Kidāna Wald Kəfle 1955, 128; Leslau 1989, 164; Yāred Šiferaw 2009,344, 376, 410; Yətbārak Maršā 2002, 157.

'As Job has spoken, he answered'.

Further references: Job 23:10; Prov. (com.) 15:6.

4.9. OTHER CONJUNCTIONS

4.9.1. ህየንተ *həyyanta*, በቀለ *baqala* ተውላጠ *tawlāṭa* and ፍዳ *fəddā*

All these elements share similar concepts expressing causes, replacements, and charges. They are involved in the categories of conjunctions and prepositions with the meanings 'since', 'while', 'instead of', 'in charge of', 'in the ransom of', 'in the place of' and 'in terms of'.[1]

When we come to their origins, በቀለ *baqala,* ተውላጠ *tawlāṭa* and ፍዳ *fəddā* have evident relation with the verbs ተበቀለ *tabaqqala* 'avenge', ወለጠ *wallaṭa* 'change' or 'substitute'[2] and ፈደየ *fadaya* 'pay a charge' respectively. ህየንተ *həyyanta* is believed to have no origin connected with a verb like the other elements. It is supposed to be a combination of ህየ *həyya* 'there' and እንተ *'ənta* 'that', 'which' and 'to', and that the vowel '*ə*' was influenced to disappear because of the combination. But, most of the *Qəne* masters do not agree with this. Dillmann supposed that it originally was ህየተ *həyyata* formed from ህየ *həyya*.[3] On the contrary, Leslau stated in his comparative dictionary of Gəʿəz that it is difficult to consider whether *həyyata* is the original form to *həyyanta* or the original *həyyanta* becomes *həyyata*.[4] Bausi's intermediary observation expresses that *həyyanta* is a variation of *həyyata* with the insertion of the nasal *n*.[5]

Each element is attached to perfectives[6] and imperfectives initially.[7] Most often, ዘ *za* intervenes between the elements and the verbs in the attachment. In such cases, ዘ *za* does not play its main role as a relative pronoun unless as a modifier for the combination of

---

1 Dillmann 1865,13, 890, 1379; Kidāna Wald Kəfle 1955:127-128; Leslau 1989, 3, 159, 245; Yāred, Šiferaw 2009: 381; Yətbārak Maršā, 2002:155.

2 Dillmannn 1907, 404; Leslau 2006, 614.

3 Dillmann: 402-403

4 Leslau 2006, 221-222.

5 "Ancient features of Ancient Ethiopic", Aethiopica 8 (2006), 158 (A. Bausi).

6 Gəʿəz- ቀዳማይ፡ አንቀጽ *qadāmay 'anqaṣ*

7 Gəʿəz- ካልዓይ *kāləʿāy*/ ትንቢት *tənbit*

the two elements. In this case, it is called በር፡ ከፋች *bar kafāč* (lit.: somebody or something that unlocks a door).[1]

Textual evidence:

4.9.1.1. (with the mediation of *za*) ወምንተ፡ ተዐሥዮሙ፡ ህየንተ፡ ዘገብሩ፡ ለከ። (Sir. 7:28).

wa-mənta ta'aśśəy-omu həyyanta za-gabru la-ka

<Conj-PartInt> <V:Imperf.2m.s-PSuff:3m.p> <Conj> <PRel-V:3m.p> <Prep-PSuff:2m.s>

'And what do you pay them instead of what they have done to you?'

4.9.1.2. (without the mediation of *za*) ብፁዕ፡ ዘይትቤቀለኪ፡ በቀለ፡ ተበቀልክነ። (Ps. 137:8).

bəḍuʿə za-yətbeqqala-kki baqala tabaqqalkə-nna

<NCom:m.s.Nom> <PRel-V:Imperf:3m.w-PSuff:2f.s> <Conj> <V:Perf:2f. s-PSuff:1c.p>

'Blessed is the one who avenges you in charge that you avenged us'.

When they function as prepositional elements, they are attached to the non-verbal linguistic elements without the insertion of *za*.

Textual evidence:

4.9.1.3. ህየንተ፡ አበውኪ፡ ተወልዱ፡ ለኪ፡ ደቂቅ። (Ps. 45:16).

həyyanta 'abawə-ki tawaldu la-ki daqiq

<Prep> <NCom:m.p.Nom-PSuff:2f.s> <V:Perf.3m.p> <Prep-PSuff:2f.s> <NCom:m.p.Nom>

'In the place of your fathers, children were born for you'.

4.9.1.4. ዓይን፡ ፍዳ፡ ዓይን፡ ስን፡ ፍዳ፡ ስን። (Exod. 21:24).

'ayn fəddā 'ayn sən

[1] The terminology is given to it to precisely indicate its role as a mediating element.

<NCom:unm.s.Nom> <Prep> <NCom:unm.s.Nom> <NCom:unm.s.Nom>

fəddā sən

<Prep> <NCom:unm.s.Nom>

'Eye in charge of eye, teeth in charge of teeth'.

Further references: Exod. 21:25; Josh. 5:7; Job 8:6; 22:27; Ps. 48:8; 2 Cor. 2: 17; M. Məśṭir 1:19.

4.9.2. መጠነ *maṭana*, አምጣነ *ʾamṭāna* and ዐቅመ *ʿaqma*

መጠነ *maṭana* and አምጣነ *ʾamṭāna* are nouns in status constructus. The nominatives መጠን *maṭan* and አምጣን *ʾamṭān* are originally related with the verb መጠነ *maṭṭana* 'measure' or 'weigh'. ዐቅመ *ʿaqm* is also a noun in status constructus. The nominative ዐቅም *ʿaqm* is etymologically related with the verb ዐቀመ *ʿaqqama* 'measure', 'delimit' and 'decide'.

They are used to express measurement, amount, weight, duration, size, correspondence, distance, capacity, dignity, status, limit, quantity and equality. The following constructed phrases have correspondences with them: 'as much as', 'as long as', 'as far as', 'as often as', 'to such extent', 'as many as', 'as large as', 'in accordance with' and 'as strong as'.[1] References: Josh. 10:13; Ps. 103:33; Prov. (com.) 1:22; Matt. 10:25; Acts 17:26; Rev. 11:6

አምጣነ *ʾamṭāna* has two characteristics like አምሳለ *ʾamsāla*. First, it is the accusative plural form of መጠን *maṭan*. Second, it is an equivalent noun with *maṭan* itself with the same number and meaning.

All the three elements can play the roles of both conjunctional and prepositional elements, they are added to verbs (perfectives and imperfectives). They will also be attached to the non-verbal elements when they function as prepositions. In both cases, they always take the first position in the attachment.

Some elements such as በ *ba*, በበ *babba*, እም *ʾəm* and በከመ *bakama* can be affixed to them initially in all cases to magnify them.[2]

---

[1] Dillmann 1865, 221-222, 975; Kidāna Wald Kəfle 1955, 129; Leslau 1989, 46, 173; Tropper 2002, 148.

[2] Leslau 2006, 373; Tropper 2002, 148.

Textual evidence:

4.9.2.1. ወባሕቱ፡ በአምጣነ፡ ታጸንዕ፡ ልበከ፡ ወኢትኔስሕ፡ ትዘግብ፡ ለከ፡ መቅሠፍተ። (Rom. 2:5).

wa-bāḥəttu ba-'amṭāna tāṣannəʿ ləbba-ka

<Conj-Conj> <Prep-Conj> <V-Imperf.2m.s> <NCom:unm.s.Acc-PSuff:2m.s>

wa-'i-tənessəḥ təzaggəb la-ka

<Conj-PartNeg-V:Imperf.2m.s> <V:Imperf.2m.s> <Prep-PSuff:2m.s>

maqśafta

<NCom:unm.s.Acc>

'But as much as you harden your heart, and not repent, you store punishment for yourself'.

4.9.2.2. እገኒ፡ ለእግዚአብሔር፡ በአምጣነ፡ ሀሎኩ። (Ps. 103:33).

'əganni la-'əgzi'abəḥer ba-'amṭāna halloku

<V:Imperf.1c.s> <Prep-NProp:m.s.Nom> <Prep-Conj> <V:Perf.1c.s>

'I will sing to the Lord as long as I live'.

Further references: Matt. 25:15; Mark 4:33; Anap.John (com.) verse 28.

Apart from this, *maṭana* and *'amṭāna* have individually additional uses and meanings. *Maṭana* is used to magnificently express emotions, feelings and greatness/ hugeness of things or situations accompanied with the interrogative particle ሚ *mi* 'how' or 'what'.

Textual evidence:

4.9.2.3. ሚ፡ መጠን፡ ግርምት፡ ዛቲ፡ ዕለት። (Litu. (com.) verse. 1).

mi maṭan gərəmt zātti ʿəlat

<Int> <Ncom:unm.s.Nom> <Ncom:f.s.Nom> <PPers:f.s.Nom> <Ncom:f^{s}.s.Nom>

'How tremendous is this day!'

This depends, however, on the state of the word which comes after *maṭana*. If ውእቱ *wə'ətu* or ይእቲ *yə'əti* takes the position of a main verb detectably or undetectably, the element tends to have the feature mentioned above. Otherwise, it will have the common function of query concerning quantity or amount with the meaning 'how much?' or 'how many?'

Textual evidence:

4.9.2.4. ሚ፡ መጠን፡ ኅባውዝ፡ ብክሙ። (Matt. 15:34).

mi maṭan ḫabāwəz bə-kəmu

<Int> <NCom:unm.p.Nom> <ExAff-PSuff:2m.p>

'How many loaves do you have?'

It can also be used in the place of ከመ *kama* in some cases.

Textual evidence:

4.9.2.5. ኢትሬኢኑ፡ መጠነ፡ ይበልዕ፡ ወይሰቲ። (Dan. 13:6).

ʾi-təreʾi-nu maṭana yəballəʿ wa-yəsatti

<PartNeg-V:Imperf-2m.s-PartInt> <Conj-V:Imperf.3m.s> <Conj-V:Imperf. 3m.s>

'Do not you see as he eats and drinks?'

When we come to *ʾamṭāna,* we find two more features and meanings which it shares commonly with አኮኑ *ʾakkonu,* እስመ *ʾəsma* and እንዘ *ʾənza.* Like *ʾakkonu* and *ʾəsma,* it is used as a conjunction combining clauses by facilitating the subordinate clause to give up a reason for the action or incidence mentioned in the main clause. This will be discussed in fact later with *ʾakkonu* and *ʾəsma.*

It can keep the notion of the conjunctive phrase 'since'/ 'while' in the place of *ʾənza.* At this point, the only difference between *ʾənza* and *ʾamṭāna* is the limitation of verbal forms which they can be combined with; *ʾənza* is combined only with imperfectives including prepositions, adverbs and nouns; however, it is not added to perfectives since it has an imperfective meaning.

The only perfective verb which is found in texts being combined with *ʾənza* is ሀሎ *hallo* or ሀለወ *hallawa.* But to *ʾamṭāna,* the combination with perfectives and imperfectives is equally possible.

Textual evidence:

4.9.2.6. ኢየኀዝኑ፡ ደቂቁ፡ ለመርዓዊ፡ አምጣነ፡ ሀሎ፡ መርዓዊ፡ ምስሌሆሙ። (Matt. 9:15).

ʾi-yyaḫazənnu daqiq-u la-marʿāwi ʾamṭāna

<PartNeg-V:Imperf.3m.p> <NCom:m.p.Nom> <Prep-NCom:m.s.Nom>

hallo marʿāwi məsle-homu

<Conj> <V:Perf3m.s> <NCom:m.s.Nom> <Prep-PSuff:3m.p>

'The friends of the bridegroom will not be sad since the bridegroom is with them'.

4.9.2.7. አምጣነ፡ ብነ፡ ዕለት፡ ንግበር፡ ሠናየ፡ ለኵሉ። (Gal. 6:10).

ʾamṭāna bə-na ʿəlat nəgbar

<Conj> <ExAff-PSuff:1c.p> <NCom:unm.s.Nom> <V:Subj:1c.p>

śannāya la-k^wəllu

<NCom:unm.s.Acc> <Prep-ProTot:Nom>

'While we have a day, let us do what is good for all'.

The individual particle ሰ *s/ssa* can be attached to the elements as a suffix by splitting their direct connection with verbs or nouns.

Textual evidence:

4.9.2.8. አምጣነሰ፡ ሐዋርያሆሙ፡ አነ፡ ለአሕዛብ፡ እሴብሓ፡ ለመልእክትየ። (Rom. 11:13).

ʾamṭāna-ssa ḥawāryā-homu ʾana la-ʾaḥəzāb

<Conj-Part> <NCom:m.s.Nom-PSuff:3m.p> <PPer:1c.s> <Prep-NCom:m.p.Nom>

ʾəsebbəḥ-ā la-malʾəktə-ya

<V:Imperf.1c.s-PSuff:3f.s> <Prep-NCom:f^s.s.Nom-PSuff:1c.s>

'As much as I am an apostle of Gentiles, I magnify my ministry'.

Like other elements, they can be combined with nominal derivations, nouns, numbers and all other non-verbal linguistic elements while functioning as prepositions. Example: መጠነ፡ ሠለስቱ *maṭana śalastu* (elem. + number), በአምጣነ፡ ቆሙ *ba-ʾamṭāna qom-u* (elem. +. elem. + noun), በዐቅመ፡ ዝንቱ (elem. + Pron) etc.

አምጣነ *ʾamṭāna* has the meaning 'more than' or 'beyond' when *ʾəm* is attached to it initially.

Textual evidence:

4.9.2.9. እስመ፡ ፈድፋደ፡ እም፡ አምጣነ፡ ኀይልነ፡ አመንደቡነ። (2 Cor. 1:8).

ʾəsma fadfāda ʾəm ʾamṭāna ḫaylə-na ʾamandabu-na

<Conj-Adv> <Prep> <Prep> <NCom:unm.s.Nom-PSuff:1c.p> <V:Perf: 3m.p-PSuff:1c.p>

'Because they afflicted us excessively beyond our strength'.

4.9.3. በእንተ *baʾənta*, በይነ *bayna* and እንበይነ *ʾənbayna*

These elements are involved in the categories of conjunction and preposition. As conjunctions, they express reasons with the meanings: 'about', 'because', 'for', 'for the sake of', 'since', 'while', 'on account of' and 'for the reason that'.[1] Dillmann indicated that በእንተ *baʾənta* is a compound of the prepositions *ba* and *ʾənta* and *ʾənbayna* of *ʾən* and *bayna*.[2] Indeed the *ʾAggabāb* tradition asserts the strong connection between *bayna* and *ʾənbayna*, and considers them as variants. But the formation of *baʾənta* is not obviously stated since it has different semantic value than the two components.

Each can be attached initially to verbs (perfectives and imperfectives) followed by the so-called *bar-kafāč* ዘ *za*.

Textual evidence:

4.9.3.1. ነጸረ፡ ዘንተ፡ ግፍዕየ፡ በእንተ፡ ዘፈለጠኒ፡ እም፡ ወልድኪ። (Gdl. Qaw 4:6).

naṣṣəri zanta gəfʿə-ya baʾənta

---

1 Yāred Šiferaw 2009,381, 388.

2 Dillmann 1907, 402, 403.

<V:Impt.2f.s> <PDem.s.Acc> <NCom:m.s.Acc-PSuff:1c.s> <Conj>

za-falaṭa-nni 'əm wald-əki

<PRel-V:Perf.3m.s-PSuff:1c.s> <Prep> <NCom:m.s.Nom-PSuff:2f.s>

'Look at this wrong toward me since he separated me from your son'.

4.9.3.2. በይነ፡[1] ዘሀሎ፡ ዘርዕ፡ ቡሩክ። (Gdl.Qaw 2:10).

bayna za-hallo zar' buruk

<Conj> <PRel-V:Perf.3m.s> <NCom:m.s.Nom> <NCom:m.s.Nom>

'Because there is a blessed offspring'.

4.9.3.3. ወእንበይነ፡[2] ዘነአምር፡ ጽድቀ፡ እግዚአብሔር፡ ወፈሪሆቶ፡ ናአምን፡ ሰብአ። (2 Cor. 5:11).

wa-'ənbayna za-na'ammər ṣədqa 'əgzi'abəḥer

<Conj-Conj> <PRel-V:Imperf.1c.p> <NCom:unm.s.ConSt> <NCom:m.s.Nom>

wa-farihot-o na'ammən sab'a

<Conj-NCom:unm.s.Acc-PSuff:3m.s> <V:Imperf.1c.p> <NColl: Acc>

'And since we know the truth of God and his fear, we persuade men'.

When they get attached to the non-verbal elements to play their secondary role as prepositional elements, the intercession of *za* is not necessary. They can be directly attached.

---

[1] Dillmann attested it frequently with double በ as "በበይነ" or "በበይናተ", its plural form. 1907, 403.

[2] Ibid 1865, 537-538, 775; Kidāna Wald Kəfle 1955,127; Leslau 1989, 142.

Textual evidence:

4.9.3.4. በእንተ፡ ዳዊት፡ ገብርየ። (1 Kgs 11:12).

ba'ənta dāwit gabrə-ya

<Prep> <PPro:m.s.Nom> <NCom:m.s.Nom-PSuff:1c.s>

'For the sake of my servant David'.

4.9.3.5. ወናቅም፡ ርእሰነ፡ በጽድቅ፡ ገሀደ፡ እንበይነ፡ ግዕዘ፡ ኵሉ። (2 Cor. 4:2).

wa-nāqəm rə'sa-na ba-ṣədq

<Conj-V:Subj.1c.p> <NCom:unm.s.Acc> <Prep-NCom:unm.s.Nom>

gahada 'ənbayna-gə'za k^{w}*əllu*

<Adv> <Prep-NCom:unm.s.Nom> <ProTot:Nom>

'But, let us entrust ourselves plainly in truth for the conscience of all'.

The preposition በ *ba* can be added to *bayna* as a prefix in all cases.

Textual evidence (as a conjunctional element):

4.9.3.6. ተናገሩ፡ ሰብዓቱ፡ ነጐድጓድ፡ በበይነ፡ ዘሀለዎ፡ ይጸሐፍ። (Rev. 10:3).

tanāgaru sab'āttu nag^{w}*adg*^{w}*ad ba-bayna*

<V:Perf.3m.p> <NumCa:m^{s}.p.Nom> <NCom:m^{s}.p^{s}.Nom> <Prep-Conj>

za-hallaw-o yəṣṣaḥaf

<PRel-V:Perf.3m.s> <V:Subj.3m.s>.

'The seven thunders uttered about what has to be written'.

Textual evidence (as a prepositional element):

4.9.3.7. በበይነ፡ ኀጢአቶሙ። (Heb. 9:7).

ba-bayna ḫāṭi'at-omu

<Prep-Prep> <NCom:unm.s.Nom-PSuff:3m.p>

'For their sin'.

4.9.4. አምሳለ *'amsāla* and አርአያ *'ar'ayā*

አምሳለ *'amsāla* is a noun in status constructus. The nominative አምሳል *'amsāl* which is etymologically related with the verb መሰለ *masala* 'look like' and 'resemble' has the following meanings: 'example', 'model', 'resemblance', 'form', 'figure', 'parable' and 'story'. In addition to this, *'amsāl* can be the plural form of the noun ምስል *məsl* with the precise meanings 'image', 'figure', 'picture', 'form' and 'idol'.

Similarly, አርአያ *'ar'ayā* is initially related with the verb ርእየ *rə'ya* 'see' or 'watch'. It means 'example', 'image', 'likeness', 'form' and 'model'.

On one side, as conjunctional elements, they are combined with perfectives and imperfectives to make a subordinate clause. On the other side, they are added to the non-verbal lexical elements when they play their additional role of a preposition.[1] Dillmann considered them to be used as prepositions only while Leslau mentioned the function of *'ar'ayā* as a conjunctional element.[2]

In the state of being conjunctions, both equally keep the meanings 'as' and 'though'. But when they are used as prepositions, they determine rather the concept of 'like'.[3]

Textual evidence:

4.9.4.1. ወንሕነሰ፡ አኃዊነ፡ ውሉደ፡ ተስፋ፡ አምሳለ፡ ይስሐቅ። (Gal. 4:28).

wa-nəḥna-ssa 'aḫāwi-na wəluda

<Conj-PPer:c.p.Nom-Part> <NCom:m.p.Nom-PSuff:1c.p> <NCom:m.p.ConSt>

tasfā 'amsāla yəsḥaq

<NCom:unm.s.Nom> <Prep> <NPro:m.s.Nom>

'But we brethren are children of promise like Isaac'.

In this case, it is possible for the elements to have an attachment of the particle በ *ba* in the beginning as to say በአምሳለ፡ ይስሐቅ *ba-*

---

[1] Kidāna Wald Kəfle 1955,131; Yāred Šiferaw 2009,344, 404, 413; Yətbārak Maršā 2002, 158-9.

[2] Dillmann 1907, 404; Leslau 2006, 365, 499.

[3] Dillmannn 1865, 173; Yāred Šiferaw 2009,413; Yətbārak Maršā 2002, 159.

'amsāla yəsḥaq. The meaning will not be affected in terms of the attachment.

About their position in a sentence, there are two different possibilities according to their two different features. When they are employed as accusative nouns, they can precede or follow a verb alone, like አምሳለ፡ ይገብሩ *'amsāla yəgabbəru* or in the other way round ይገብሩ፡ አምሳለ *yəgabbəru 'amsāla*. However, when they function as ACPPIP elements in general, they must be combined initially with the verbs or the non-verbal elements as we have seen in the examples mentioned above.

4.9.5. ብሂለ *bəhila*

Etymologically, it is related with the verb ብህለ *bəhla* 'say', 'mean', 'talk' and 'state'. There can be found two kinds of ብሂል *bəhil* with the same structure but with different meanings and functions, the noun[1] and the infinitive one.

However, the grammatical connection of the ACPPIP element *bəhila* goes to the infinitive ብሂል *bəhil* 'saying'/ 'say' or 'meaning'/ 'mean'.[2]

The infinitive ብሂል *bəhil* 'saying'/ 'say' or 'meaning'/ 'mean'.[3] It is the only infinitive form of a verb which can have a direct attachment to a verb.

It can be employed in two different ways either being attached to other words or without attachment as an individual element. *'Alaqā* Kidāna Wald Kəfle affirms its attachment to the perfective, imperfective and jussive verb forms. Unfortunately, he has provided no explanation about its attachment to other lexical elements. Nevertheless, basing the witnesses of various textual accounts, we can assume that it can be added even to the non-verbal linguistic elements.

---

1 Lit.: 'saying', 'proverb', 'statement', 'oral tradition' and 'oral succession'. Dillmann 1865, 483; Kidāna Wald Kəfle 1955, 138; Leslau 2006, 89.

2 Moreno 1949, 46.

3 Moreno 1949, 46.

Textual evidence:

4.9.5.1. ወብሂለ፡ ኢያእመራሰ፡ ይተረጎም፡ ኀበ፡ አእምሮ፡ ወኀበ፡ ኢያእምሮ። (M.Məśṭir 11:2).

wa-bəħila ʾi-yyāʾmar-ā-ssa yəttaraggʷam ḫaba ʾaʾəmro

<Conj-Conj> <PartNeg-V:Perf-PSuff:3f.s-Part> <V:Imperf:3m.s> <Conj-V:Inf>

wa-ḫaba ʾi-yyāʾəmro

<Conj-Conj> <PartNeg-V:Inf>

'And saying of he did not know her is interpreted by knowing and by not knowing'.

4.9.5.2. ኢይምሰልክሙ፡ ዘታመስጡ፡ በብሂለ፡ አብ፡ አብርሃም፡ ብነ። (Matt. 3:9).

ʾi-yyəmsal-kəmu za-tāmassəṭu ba-bəħila

<PartNeg-V:Impt.2m.p-PSuff:2m.p> <PRel-V:Imperf.2m.p> <Prep-Conj>

ʾab ʾabrəhām bə-na

<NCom:m.s.Nom> <Npro:m.s.Nom> <ExAff-Psuff:1c.p>

'Do not think that you will be saved by saying we have a father, Abraham'.

Further reference: M. Məśṭir 11:9, 12:8.

4.9.6. እም *ʾəm*

እም *ʾəm*[1] is a variant of እምነ *ʾəmənna* which is used as a conjunction and a preposition. Similarly, Dillman calls it a shortened form of *ʾəmənna.* According to his view, *ʾəmənna* is often used than *ʾəm* particularly in old manuscripts[2]

It can be attached to all lexical elements except the imperatives and gerund. However, as a conjunction, it is specifically attached to

---

[1] Dillmann 1865, 191; Kidāna Wald Kəfle 1955, 138, 140; Leslau 1989, 22, 134; Yāred Šiferaw 2009, 351, 404.

[2] Dillmann 1907, 392, 418.

perfectives, imperfectives and subjunctives. It also functions as a preposition being combined with the non-verbal elements.[1] Let us see now how it functions as a conjunctional element.

4.9.6.1.

In a conditional sentence which is constructed with a conjunction 'If', *'əm* can be directly attached to perfectives to express uncertain conditions which might happen in the past.

Textual evidence:

4.9.6.1.1. ሶበሰ፡ በዝንቱ፡ ዓለም፡ መንግሥትየ፡ እም፡ ተበአሱ፡ ሊተ፡ ወዐልየ፡ ከመ፡ ኢይግባእ፡ ለአይሁድ። (John 18:36).

soba-ssa ba-zəntu ʿālam mangəśtə-ya

<Conj-Part> <Prep-Pdem:3m.s.Nom> <NCom:m.s.Nom> <NCom:m.s.Nom-PSuff:1c.s>

'əm tabaasu li-ta waʿalə-ya

<Conj> <V:Perf.3m.p> <Prep-Psuff:1c.s> <NCom:m.s.Nom-PSuff>

kama 'i-yyəgbā'ə la-'ayhud

<Conj> <PartNeg-V:Subj.1cs> <Prep-NPro:unm.p.Nom>

'If my kingdom were of this world, my servants would be fighting so that I would not be handed over to the Jews'.

Further references: Gen. 31:12; John 11:32.

---

[1] *'Əm* is the only conjunctional and prepositional element ending with a sixth order radical. For this special reason, whenever it goes to be combined with any linguistic element which begins with one of the seven orders of the syllable መ *ma*, the ending syllable of *'əm* ም *mə* will automatically disappear from the combination. (This is in fact concerned with the Gəʿəz transliteration only). On the other way round, if a verb or a nominal derivation or a personal name which begins with any one of the seven orders of the issued syllable is directly combined with *'əm,* its first radical absorbs the ending radical of the element *m* and gets geminated. This means double consonants of the same syllable are attested in the transliteration. Example: እም *'əm* + መሰልነ *masalna* = እመሰልነ *'əm-masalna 'əgzi'ə-ya nəguś dāwit ;* እም *'əm* + መንበርከ *manbarə-ka* = እመንበርከ *'əm-manbarə-ka.* 1 Kgs 1:37; Isa. 1:9.

4.9.6.2.

When it is combined with perfectives, it should always have such a role. Otherwise, it must be followed by ከመ *kama* or ዘ *za* to be combined with Perfectives and Imperfectives. So, the combination may consist of three elements (*'əm* + *kama/ za* + verb).

4.9.6.3.

When it is combined with ከመ *kama,* it may have alternate meanings 'as', 'after', 'if', 'when' and 'unless'. But when it is combined with *za,* it may rather reflect the concept of 'since', 'while' and 'after' in expression of time, age or duration of certain things that happened before. See the following textual accounts.[1]

Textual evidence:

(እም *'əm* + ከመ *kama*)

4.9.6.3.1. ወእምከመ፡ ሰምዑ፡ ቃለ፡ ይመጽእ፡ ሰይጣን፡ ሶቤሃ፡ ወይነሥእ፡ እም፡ ልቦሙ፡ ቃለ፡ ዘተዘርዐ። (Mark 4:16).

wa-'əm-kama sam'u qāla yəmaṣṣ'ə

<Conj-Conj-Conj> <V:Perf.3m.p> <NCom:m.s.Acc> <V:Imperf.3m.s>

sayṭān sobehā wa-yənaśś'ə 'əm ləbb-omu

<NCom:m.s.Nom> <Adv> <Conj-V:Imperf.3m.s> <Prep> <NCom:unm.s-Psuff:3m.p>

qāla za-tazar'a

<NCom:m.s.Acc> <PRel-V:Perf.3m.s>

'As they hear the word, Satan comes immediately and takes away the word which has been sown from their heart'.

---

[1] Tropper 2002, 147. Leslau's construction '*la-'əm-kama*' is somehow strange. 2006; 285.

4.9.6.3.2. ተሐውሩ፡ ኀበ፡ ኀለይክሙ፡ እምከመ፡ ግኀሥክሙ፡ ኀበ፡ ገብርክሙ። (Gen. 18:5).

taḥawwəru ḫaba ḫallay-kəmu ʾəm-kama

<V:Imperf.2m.p> <Conj> <V:Perf.2m.p-PSuff:2m.p> <Conj-Conj>

gəḫəś-kəmu ḫaba gabrə-kəmu

<V:Perf.2m.p-PSuff:2m.p> <Prep> <NCom:m.s.Nom-PSuff:2m.p>

'You will go wherever you thought after you enter to (the house of) your servant'.

4.9.6.3.3. እምከመ፡ ሰክረ፡ ልቡ፡ ለአምኖን፡ በወይን፡ እቤለክሙ፡ ቅትልዎ። (2 Sam. 13:28).

ʾəm-kama sakra ləbb-u la-ʾamnon

<Conj-Conj> <V:Perf.3m.s> <NCom:m.s.Nom-PSuff:3m.s> <Prep(g)-NPro:m.s.Nom>

ba-wayn ʾəbela-kkəmu qətələww-o

<Prep-NCom:unm.s.Nom> <V:Imperf.1c.s> <V:Impt.2 m.p-PSuff:3m.s>

'When Amnon's heart is merry with wine, I say to you: kill him!'

Further references: Ps. 103:22, 28; Jas. 1:11.

4.9.6.3.4. እምከመ፡ ሊተ፡ አእመርክሙኒ፡ እም፡ አእመርክምዎ፡ ለአቡየኒ። (John 14:7).

ʾəm-kama li-ta ʾaʾmarkəmu-ni ʾəm

<Conj-Conj> <Prep-Psuff:1c.s> <V:Perf.2m.p-PSuff:1c.s> <Conj>

ʾaʾmarkəməww-o la-ʾabu-ya-ni

<V: Perf.2m.p-PSuff:2m.p-PSuff:3m.s> <Prep-NCom:m.s.Nom-PSuff:1c.s-Part>

'If you had known me, you would have known my Father also'.

Further references: Gen. 12:12; 1 Sam. 20:9; Mark 3:11, 5:28, 13:29; Rom. 5:10.

4.9.6.3.5. እምከመ፡ ኢትትገዘሩ፡ በሕገ፡ ሙሴ፡ ኢትክሉ፡ ሐዩወ። (Acts 15:1).

ʾəm-kama ʾi-tətgazzaru ba-ḥəgga muse

<Conj-Conj> <PartNeg-V:Imperf.2m.p> <Prep-NCom:unm.s.ConSt>

ʾi-təklu ḥayiwa

<Npro:m.s.Nom> <PartNeg-V:Imperf.2m.p> <V:Inf.Acc>

'Unless you are circumcised according to the Law of Moses, you cannot be saved'.

እም *ʾəm* + ዘ *za*[1]

4.9.6.3.6. እስመ፡ ጐንዱይ፡ መዋዕል፡ እምዘ፡ አስሐቶሙ፡ በሥራዩ። (Acts 8:11).

ʾəsma gʷənduy mawāʿəl ʾəmza ʾasḥt-omu

<Conj> <NCom:m.s.Nom> <NCom:m.s.Nom> <Conj> <V:Perf.3m.s-PSuff:3m.p>

ba-śərāy-u

<Prep-NCom:unm.s.Nom-Psuff:3m.s>

'Because it is long time since he deceived them in his magic'.

4.9.6.3.7. ወእምዘ፡ ወፅኡ፡ እሙንቱ፡ አምጽኡ፡ ኀቤሁ፡ ዘጋኔን። (Matt. 9:32).

wa-ʾəmza waṣ̌u ʾəmmuntu ʾamṣ̌əʾu ḫabe-hu

<Conj-Conj> <V:Perf.3m.p> <PPer:3m.p.Nom> <V:Perf.3m.p> <Prep-PSuff:3m.s>

za-gānen

<PRel-NCom:unm.s.Nom>

'After they went out, they brought a demon-possessed man to him'.

---

[1] Ibid; Leslau 2006, 22.

4.9.6.3.8. ወእምዘፈጸመ፡ ፍርየተ፡ ሶቤሃ፡ ይፌኑ፡ ማዕፀደ። (Mark 4:29).

wa-ʾəmza faṣṣama fəryata sobehā yəfennu

<Conj-Conj> <V:Perf.3m.s> <V:Inf.Acc> <Adv> <V:Imperf.3m.s>

māʿḍada

<NCom:m.s.Acc>

'But when it is finished producing a fruit, he immediately puts a sickle'.

Further references: Exod. 19:1; Enoch (com.) 2:1; 1 Kgs 3:19; Ezra 1:1.

4.9.6.4.

The combination with a subjunctive is a direct combination without intercession of any substantive element. In such cases, its meaning will be 'rather than'.

Textual evidence:

4.9.6.4.1. ይኄይሰነ፡ አሐደ፡ ብእሴ፡ ንቅትል፡ ወይሙት፡ ህየንተ፡ ሕዝብ፡ እም፡ ይትኀጐል፡ ኵሉ፡ ሕዝብ። (John 11:50).

yəḫeyyəsa-nna ʾaḥada bəʾse nəqtəl

<V:Imperf.1c.p> <NumCa.m.Acc> <NCom:m.s.Acc> <V:Subj:1c.p>

wa-yəmut həyyanta ḥəzb ʾəm yətḫagʷal

<Conj-V:Subj:3m.s> <Prep> <NCom:unm.p.Nom> <Conj> <V:Subj.3m.s>

kʷəllu ḥəzb

<ProTot:Nom> <NCom:m.s.Nom>

'It is better for us that we may kill one man, and that he shall die instead of the people rather than the whole people would perish'.

Further references: Ps. 50:3; Prov. (com.) 2:19; Jas. 3:6; Gdl.Qaw 1:31.

4.9.6.5.

Sometimes, in the same attachment, the relative pronoun *za* may come first as a prefix being attached to the element. In this case, the meaning that will be found out of the combination is either 'instead of' or 'rather than'.

Textual evidence:

4.9.6.5.1. ወቀተልክዎ፡ በሴቄላቅ፡ ለዝንቱ፡ ዘእም፡ አሀቦ፡ ዐስበ፡ ዜናሁ። (2 Sam. 4:10).

wa-qatalkəww-o ba-seqqelāq la-zəntu

<Conj-V:Perf.1c.s-PSuff:3m.s> <Prep-Npro:pl.s.Nom> <Prep-Pdem:3m.s.Nom>

za-'əm 'ahabb-o 'asba zena-hu

<PRel-Conj> <V:Subj.1c.s-PSuff:3m.s> <NCom:m.s.ConSt> <NCom:unm.s.Nom-PSuff:3m.s>

'I killed him in Ziklag instead that I give him the reward of his news'.

In this sentence, the presence of *za* did not introduce a new idea; it would have kept the same meaning even if *za* was not yet present. Thus, we can perceive that in such a combination, *za* has no impact on the proper meaning of the attachment.

4.9.6.6.

The same way, a particle ነ *na* can be combined with እም *'əm* as a suffix when it plays the role of a preposition. Here again, the presence of the particle does not introduce any grammatical change.

Textual evidence:

4.9.6.6.1. እምነ፡ ዘተርፈ፡ ቃለ፡ መጥቅዖሙ፡ ለሠለስቱ፡ መላእክት። (Rev. 8:13).

'əmənna za-tarfa qāla maṭqə'o-mu

<Conj> <PRel-V:Perf.3m.s> <NCom:unm.s.ConSt> <NCom:unm.s.Nom>

la-śalastu malā'əkt

<Prep()-Num.Ca.Nom> <NCom:m.p.Nom>

'Because of the remaining blast of the trumpet of the three angels'.

4.9.6.6.2. ወብዙኅ፡ ሰብእ፡ ዘሞተ፡ እምነ፡ ምረሮሙ፡ ለማያት። (Rev. 8:11).

wa-bəzuḫ sabə' za-mota 'əmnna

<Conj-NCom:m.s.Nom> <NCom:m^{s}.s.Nom> <PRel-V:Perf.3m.s>

mərar-omu la-māyāt

<Conj> <NCom:unm.s.Nom-Psuff:3m.p> <Prep-NCom: m^{s}.p.Nom>

'And many people died from the bitterness of the waters'.

Further references: Matt. 24:12; Prov. (com.) 1:33, 5:4, 24.

When it functions as a preposition, its English equivalent meaning is 'from'. With this regard, as mentioned in advance, not only some specific elements but various language elements except verbs will be combined with it by taking the second position in the combination. Nouns, pronouns, nominal derivations, numerals, infinitives and other ACPPIP elements are some of the components that take part in such a combination with *'əm.*

Textual evidence:

4.9.6.7. እምኀበ፡ ውሉዶሙኑ፡ ወሚመ፡ እምኀበ፡ ነኪር። (Matt. 17:25).

'əm-ḫaba wəlud-omu-nu wa-mimma

<Prep-Prep> <NCom:m.p.Nom-Psuff:3m.p-PartInt> <Conj-Conj>

'əm-ḫaba nakir

<Prep-Prep> <NCom:m.s. Nom>

'Is it from their children or from foreigners?'

Further references: 1 Kgs 1:37; Matt 17:26, 21:19; Luke 10:30, 24:47; Acts 20:33; Rom. 16: 24, 16:24; 1Tim. 1:19; 2 Cor. 9:2; Rev. 2:5, 7:2, 8:11.

In some combination, *'əm* introduces an additional concept of 'starting from' or 'since', most probably when the combined word is dealing with time.

Textual evidence:

4.9.6.8. እስመ፡ ሰብአ፡ አካይያ፡ አስተዳለዉ፡ እም፡ ቀዳሚ፡ ዓም፡፡ (2 Cor. 9:2).

'əsma saba 'akāyəyā 'astadālawu 'əm

<Conj> <NCom:ms.p.ConSt> <NCom:pl.s.Nom> <V:Perf.3m.p> <Conj>

qadāmi 'ām

<NCom:m.s.Nom> <NCom:m^s.s.Nom>

'For the Achaians have prepared since last year'.

Further references: Ezra 4: 19; Gdl.Qaw 2:11.

Again, in some combinations, *'əm* serves as a reason-providing conjunction with the meaning 'because of' or 'for the reason of/ that'. Have a look at the readings mentioned earlier under 4.9.6.6.1.

4.9.7. እንበለ *'ənbala*

እንበለ *'ənbala* is a linguistic element which plays the roles of a conjunction and a preposition. On its origin, Dillmann affirmed it as a derivation from *'əmbala*. Leslau's suggestion contradicts this; he suggested that it is a composition of *'ən* and *bala*. But he did not indicate the meanings of these separate words.[1]

As a conjunction, *'ənbala* is combined with verbs (perfectives, imperfectives and subjunctives) while its attachment as a preposition is to nominalized verbs, nouns and numbers etc. It cannot occur alone without attachment unless it occurs with suffixes. In every attachment, it keeps the initial position.

The meaning it has and the role it plays as a conjunction is little as compared as its role as a preposition. When it is used as a conjunction, it keeps the meanings 'before', 'unless' and 'without'.[2]

---

[1] Dillmann 1907, 404; Leslau 2006, 27.

[2] Dillmann 1865, 773; Kidāna Wald Kəfle 1955, 230; Leslau 1989, 27; Yāred Šiferaw 2009,344; Yətbārak Maršā 2002, 157.

Textual evidence:

4.9.7.1. ዘእንበለ፡ ይትወለድ፡ አብርሃም፡ ሀሎኩ፡ አነ። (John 8:58).

za-ʾənbala yətwalad ʾabrəhām halloku ʾana

<PRel-Conj> <V:Subj.3m.s> <NPro:m.s.Nom> <V:Perf:1c.s> <PPer:1c.s>

'Before Abraham was born, I am'.

4.9.7.2. ኵሉ፡ ዘይድኅር፡ ብእሲቶ፡ ዘእንበለ፡ ትዘሙ፡ በላዕሌሁ፡ ለሊሁ፡ ረሰያ፡ ዘማ። (Matt. 5:32).

k^wəllu za-yədəḫər bəʾsit-o za-ʾənbala

<PTot.Nom> <PRel-V:Imperf.3m.s> <NCom:f.s.Acc-Psuff:3m.s> <PRel-Conj>

təzzamu ba-lāʿle-hu lalihu rassay-ā

<V:Subj.3f.s> <Prep-Prep-PSuff:3m.s> <PSub:3m.s.Nom> <V:Perf.3m.s-PSuff:3f.s>

zammā

<NCom: unm.s.Acc>

'Everyone who divorces his wife unless she commits adultery against him, he himself makes her become adulteress'.

Further references: Gen. 13:10; PS. 38:13; PS. 38:13; Prov. (com.) 25:5; Eccles. 7:17; Isa. 66:2; Matt. 1:18; Mark 13:30; John 14:6; 1 Cor. 4:5.

There are some ACPPIP elements which occur often with *ʾənbala* being either prefixed or suffixed to it. The elements that are prefixed to it are አምጣነ *ʾamṭāna* and እስመ *ʾəsma* while the elements to which it gets attached are ለ *la*, በ *ba*, አመ *ʾama*, ከመ *kama*, ዳእሙ *dāʾəmu* and ጊዜ *gize*. The only element which can be a prefix or a suffix to it is ዘ *za*. Particularly, when it is combined with perfective or imperfective verbs, *za* or one of the intermediary elements mentioned earlier shall take the medial position in the combination. However, it does not affect the actual meaning and role that it does play.

Its attachment to subjunctives does not need the intercession of *za* as an intermediary element; a direct attachment will be applied. See the evidence provided earlier.

CHAPTER FIVE: PREPOSITIONS

5.1. PREPOSITIONS OF PLACE

In this section, fifty-one various elements are provided in different sub-sections. All these elements serve as prepositions. More than half of the prepositional elements are originally nouns in status constructus. They can be attached to nouns, pronouns, adjectives, and numerals to indicate the relationship between them and the verb in a sentence, and are mainly concerned with place, time and comparison. Let us see each in its own sub-section.

5.1.1. ላዕለ *lāʿla*, መልዕልተ *malʿəlta* and ዲበ *diba*

ላዕለ *lāʿla* and መልዕልተ *malʿəlta* are originally nouns in status constructus that are etymologically related with the verbs ለዐለ *laʿla*/ ተለዐለ *talaʿala*/ ተልዕለ *talʿla* 'be the highest one', 'be superior' and 'rise up'. Similarly, *diba* is a noun in status constructus which is related with the verb ደየበ *dayyaba* 'go up' or 'ascend'.[1] Dillmann interprets it as it is formed from *di* and *ba*. He also gave it a probable meaning 'at - the', and indicated its synonymity with *lāʿla*.[2] All are used as prepositions in expression of position with the meanings 'above', 'on', 'over' and 'upon'.[3] መትሕተ *matḥəta*, ታሕተ *tāḥta* and ታሕቲተ *tāḥtita* are their negative counterparts.

[1] Dillmann 1865, 56, 1103; Kidāna Wald Kəfle 1955, 345.
[2] Dillmann 1907, 398.
[3] Leslau 1989, 12 and 194; Yətbārak Maršā 2002, 166.

When we discussed earlier the functions of *lāʿla* as an adverb, we said that it occurs alone. Here, it is quite the contrary, because there is no prepositional element that occurs alone. Each element shall be attached to the non-verbal language elements initially. The elements *ba* and *ʾəm* are the most essential elements which can be attached to them initially.

Textual evidence:

5.1.1.1. ወኮነ፡ ማየ፡ አይኅ፡ ላዕለ፡ ምድር፡ አርብዓ፡ ዕለተ፡ ወአርብዓ፡ ሌሊተ። (Gen. 7:17).

wa-kona māya ʾayḫ lāʿla

<Conj-V:Perf.3m.s> <NCom:unm.s.CoSt> <NCom:unm.PSt> <Prep>

mədr ʾarbəʿā ʿəlata wa-ʾarbəʿā

<NCom.unm.s.Nom> <NumCa:Acc> <NCom:unm.s.Acc> <Conj-NumCa:Acc>

lelita

<NCom:unm.s.Acc>

‘And the flood came upon the earth for forty days and forty nights’.

5.1.1.2. ወመንፈሰ፡ እግዚአብሔር፡ ይጼልል፡ መልዕልተ፡ ማይ። (Gen. 1:2).

wa-manfasa ʾəgziʾabəḥer yəṣelləl malʿlta

<Conj-NCom.m^{s}.s.ConSt> <NCom:m.s.Nom> <V:Imperf.3m.s> <Prep>

māy

<NCom:unm.s.Nom>

‘And the spirit of God was moving over the water’.

5.1.1.3. ወሰሎሞን፡ ነግሠ፡ ዲበ፡ መንበረ፡ ዳዊት። (1 Kgs 2:12).

wa-salomon nagśa diba manbara dāwit

<Conj-NPro:m.s.Nom> <V:Perf.3m.s> <Prep> <NCom:unm.s.ConSt> <NPro:m.s.Nom>

‘And Solomon sat on David’s throne’.

Further references: Gen. 8:1; 1 Sam. 13:13; Isa. 14:12; Matt. 27:29; John 6:10; 1 Chr. 2:19, 24, 23:29.

Besides, *lāʿla* can be used distinctively as a preposition with the meanings 'against', 'for' and 'to' in the places of *la*, and *mangala* or *ḫaba*.

Textual evidence:

5.1.1.4. ወቆሙ፡ ላዕሌየ፡ ያመንስዉኒ። (Ps. 54:3).

wa-qomu lāʿle-ya yāmansəwu-ni

<Conj-V:Perf.3m.p> <Prep-PSuff:1c.s> <V:Subj.3m.p-PSuff:1c.s>

'And they arose against me to destroy me'.

5.1.1.5. ብፁዕ፡ ዘይሌቡ፡ ላዕለ፡ ነዳይ፡ ወምስኪን። (Ps. 40:1).

bəḍuʿ za-yəlebbu lāʿla nadāy wa-məskin

<NCom:m.s.Nom> <PRel-V:Imperf.3m.s> <Prep> <NCom:m.s.Nom> <Conj-NCom:unm.s.Nom>

'Blessed is the one who has compassion to the poor and to the pity'.

5.1.1.6. እግዚአብሔር፡ ሐወጸ፡ እም፡ ሰማይ፡ ላዕለ፡ ዕጓለ፡ እመ፡ ሕያው። (Ps. 13:2).

ʾəgziʾabəḥer ḥawwaṣa ʾəm samāy lāʿla

<NCom:m.s.Nom> <V:Perf.3m.s> <Prep> <NCom:unm.s.Nom> <Prep>

ʿəg^{w}*āla ʾəmma ḥəyāw*

<NCom:unm.p.ConSt> <NCom:f.s.Nom> <NCom:m.s.PSt>

'The Lord has looked down from heaven to the sons of men'.

Further references: Gen. 4:4, 4:8, 37:2; 2 Sam. 3:29, 7:28, 9:1; 1 Kgs 2:44; Esther 1:17; Ps. 72:3.

In the same way, *diba* is also used in the places of *ba* and *ṭəqqa*.

Textual evidence:

5.1.1.7. አንጐርጐሩ፡ ደቂቀ፡ እስራኤል፡ ዲበ፡ ሙሴ፡ ወዲበ፡ አሮን። (Num. 16:39).

'angwargwaru daqiqa 'əsrā'el diba muse

<V:Perf.3m.p> <NCom:m.p.ConSt> <NPro.pl.Nom> <Prep> <Npro.m.s.Nom>

wa-diba 'aron

<Conj-Prep> <Npro:m.s.Nom>

'The sons of Israel grumbled against Moses and Aaron'.

5.1.1.8. ወነበረ፡ ዲበ፡ ዐዘቅት። (Exod. 2:15).

wa-nabara diba 'azaqt

<Conj-V:Perf.3m.s> <Prep> <NCom.unm.s.Nom>

'And he sat dawn by a wall'.

5.1.2. መትሕተ *matḥəta* and ታሕተ *tāḥta*

An eligible 'explanation on the origin and meaning of መትሕተ *matḥəta* and ታሕተ *tāḥta* and how they function as adverbs is provided in chapter 3.1.4. Hence, we see their functionality as prepositions with the meaning 'under' or 'below' [1] Like the other prepositional elements, they are attached to the non-verbal linguistic elements initially.

Textual evidence:

5.1.2.1. ሖርኩ፡ መትሕተ፡ ሰማይ፡ ወአንሶሰውኩ፡ ኵለሄ። (Job 2:2).

ḥorku matḥəta samāy wa-'ansosawku kʷəllahe

<V.Perf.1c.s> <Prep> <NCom:unm.s.Nom> <Conj-V:Perf.1c.s> <Adv>

'I went under the heaven and walked everywhere'.

---

[1] Dillmann 1865, 554, 556; Kidāna Wald Kəfle 1955, 468, 624; Leslau 1989, 39, 113; 2006, 572.

5.1.2.2. ኢይደልወኒ፡ ትባእ፡ ታሕተ፡ ጠፈረ፡ ቤትየ። (Matt. 8:8).

ʾi-yyədalləwa-nni təbāʾ tāḥta ṭafara

<PartNeg-V:Imperf.3m.s-PSuff:1c.s> <V:Subj.2m.s> <Prep> <NCom:unm.s.ConSt>

betə-ya

<NCom: unm.s. Nom-PSuff:1c.s>

'I am not worthy that you may enter under the roof of my house'.

Further references: Esther 4:20, 5:18; S. of S. 2:3, 6; Matt. 5:15; Haym. (com.) 7:30.

5.1.3. መንገለ *mangala* and ኀበ *ḫaba*

An adequate explanation on their origins, meanings and functions as conjunctions are elaborated in the preceding chapter under the subsections 4.7. Henceforth, we discuss their further grammatical function as prepositional elements with various meanings. In such cases, they are attached always to the non-verbal linguistic elements.

5.1.3.1. (With the meanings 'to' and 'toward')

5.1.3.1.1. ነሐውር፡ ኀበ፡ እግዚእነ። (2 Cor. 5:8.).

naḥawwər ḫaba ʾəgziʾə-na

<V:Imperf.1c.p> <Prep> <NCom:m.s.Nom-PSuff:1c.p>

'We will go to our Lord'.

5.1.3.1.2. ወዝኒ፡ አኮ፡ ዘመንገለ፡ እግዚአብሔር። (2 Cor. 11:17).

wa-zə-ni ʾakko za-mangala ʾəgziʾabəḥer

<Conj-PDem-Part> <PartNeg> <PRel-Prep> <NCom:m.s.Nom>

'But, this is not towards God'.

5.1.3.2. With the meanings 'at', 'through', 'by' and 'near'

ወናሁ፡ ቆምኩ፡ ኀበ፡ ኆኅት፡ ወእጕደጕድ። (Rev. 3:20).

wa-nāhu qomku ḫaba ḫoḫət wa-ʾəgwadaggwəd

<Conj-Partpres> <V:Perf.1c.s> <Prep-NCom:unm.s.Nom> <Conj-V: Imperf.1c.s>

‘And now, I stand at the door and knock’.

5.1.3.3. ቤተ፡ ስምዖን፡ ሰፋዪ፡ ዘመንገለ፡ ባሕር። (Acts 10:5).

beta səmʿon safāyi za-mangala

<NCom:unm.ConSt> <NProp:m.s.Nom> <NCom:m.s.Nom> <PRel-Prep>

bāḥr

<NCom:unm.s.Nom>

‘The house of Simon a tanner which is by sea’.

5.1.3.4. With the meaning ‘via’ or ‘by way of’:

ወእንተ፡ ኀቤክሙ፡ እሑር፡ መቄዶንያ። (2 Cor. 1:16).

wa-ʾənta ḫabe-kəmu ʾəḥur maqedonyā

<Conj-PRel> <Prep-PSuff:2m.p> <V:Subj.1c.s> <NProp:pl.s.Acc>

‘I may pass your way to Mecedonia’.

Further references: Gen. 20:12; Acts 18:17, 18; Rom. 2:22; 2 Cor. 1:7; 1 John 2:1; Anap.John (com.) verse 43; Gdl. Qaw 2:6.

According to Leslau, *ḫaba* can be added to *mangala* to form the phrase *ḫaba-mangala* ‘toward’.[1] But such a combination is not mentioned in the *ʾAggabāb* tradition. Even, the duplication of *mangala* like *ḫaba* as a conjunctional element is not recognised as a correct combination since each element is enough to express the concept ‘toward’, and hence, there is no need of the attachment of other element with the same semantic value.

5.1.4. መንጸረ *manṣara*, መቅድመ *maqdəma*, ቅድመ *qədma*, አንጻረ *ʾanṣāra* and ገጸ *gaṣṣa*

A fair explanation on the origins, meanings and functions of መቅድመ *maqdəma*[2] and ቅድመ *qədma* is presented in chapter three under 3.2.2

[1] Leslau 2006, 349.

[2] Tropper indicates that it is one of the few prepositional elements which are rarely needed. Tropper 2002, 142. This is perhaps because of the little

and chapter four under the sub-section 4.3.2. The preceding chapter also provides some explanations concerning **መንጸረ** *manṣara* and **አንጻረ** *'anṣāra* (3.1.4). For this reason, we skip discussing these aspects here again, and focus on their functionality as prepositional elements including **ገጸ** *gaṣṣa*.

Gaṣṣa is a noun in status constructus which is originally related with the verb **ገጸወ** *gaṣṣawa* 'separate', and 'personify'. Literally, *gaṣṣ* means 'face'. It is used in expression of a position or location like *qədma* and *'anṣāra* with the meanings 'before', 'in front of', 'in the presence of' and 'in the sight of'.[1]

In a sentence, each element is attached to the non-verbal element initially. The particles **በ** *ba*, **እም** *'əm* and **ውስተ** *wəsta* can be affixed to all these elements initially without affecting their actual meanings. Even *qədma* can be added to the remaining elements.

Textual evidence:

5.1.4.1. ዐቢየ፡ ይከውን፡ ውእቱ፡ በቅድመ፡ እግዚአብሔር። (Luke 1:15).

'abiyya yəkawwən wə'ətu ba-qədma 'əgzi'abəḥer

<NCom:m.s.Acc> <V:Imperf.3m.s> <PPer:3m.s.Nom> <Prep-Prep> <NCom: m.s.Nom>

'He will be great in the sight of the Lord'.

5.1.4.2. ኀደጉ፡ ለልየ፡ በእንቲአከሙ፡ በገጹ፡ ለክርስቶስ። (2 Cor. 2:10).

ḫadaggu laləya ba'əntia-kəmu ba-gaṣṣ-u la-krəstos

<V:Perf.1c.s> <PSub> <Prep-PSuff:2m.p> <Prep-Prep-PSuff:3m.s> <Prep –NPro:m.s.Nom>

'I have forgiven for your sake in the presence of Christ'.

---

attestations of the element in this grammatical function. But to ratify its function of a preposition, there is some unambiguous textual evidence such as "መቅድመ፡ ኵሉ፡ ንሰብክ፡ ሥላሴ *maqdəma kwəllu nəsabbək śəllāse* 'Before all things, we preach Trinity'" Haym. (com) 60:2.

[1] Dillmann 1865, 702, 703, 1208; Kidāna Wald Kəfle 1955, 329, 650, 683; Leslau 1989, 90, 130.

5.1.4.3. **እም፡ ገጸ፡ መቅሠፍተ፡ መዐትከ።** (Ps. 101:10).

'əm gaṣṣa maqśafta ma'atə-ka

'From the sight of the indignation of your wrath'.

La can also be accidentally attached to the element in the place of *ba*.

Textual evidence:

ወሠናየ፡ ኅልዩ፡ ለቅድመ፡ እግዚአብሔር፡ ወለቅድመ፡ ሰብእ። (2 Cor. 8:21).

wa-śannāya ḫalləyu la-qədma 'əgzi'abəḥer wa-la-qədma

<Conj-Adv> <V:Imp:2m.p> <Prep-Prep> <NCom:m.s.Nom> <Conj-Prep-Prep>

sab'

<NCom:unm.p.Nom>

'And think what is good in the sight of God and in the sight of man'.

Further references: Enoch (com.) 25:2; Ps. 77:55; Luke 1:19; Acts 10:4.

5.1.5. ማእከለ *mā'əkala*

According to the *'Aggabāb* tradition, ማእከለ *mā'əkala* in such a case is a noun in status constructus which is related with the verb አማእከለ *'amā 'əkala* 'plot a centre'. ማእከል *mā'kal* means 'centre' or 'middle'. But from the perspective of modern Gə'əz studies, the etymological relation of *mā'kal* is with the verb አከለ *'akala* 'be equal', 'be enough'; አማእከለ *'amā'əkala* is a denominative from ማእከል *mā'kal*.[1]

It mostly plays the role of a preposition with the meaning 'between' or 'in the middle of'.[2] In such a case, it is always attached to the non-verbal language elements initially.

1 Dillmann 1907, 401; Leslau 2006, 15, 324.

2 Dillmann 1865, 784; Kidāna Wald Kəfle 1955, 153; Leslau 1989, 39.

Textual evidence:

5.1.5.1. ወኀለፈ፡ ማእከለ፡ ሰማርያ፡ ወገሊላ። (Luke 17:11).

wa-ḫalafa mā'əkala samārəyā wa-galilā

<Conj-V:Perf.3m.s> < Prep> <NPro:pl.s.Nom> <Conj-NPro:pl.s.Nom>

'And he passed between Samaria and Galilee'.

In some text traditions, it occurs twice before each noun. However, its double employment does not make any semantic change.

Textual evidence:

5.1.5.2. ወፈለጠ፡ እግዚአብሔር፡ ማእከለ፡ ብርሃን፡ ወማእከለ፡ ጽልመት። (Gen. 1:4).

wa-falaṭa 'əgzi'abəḥer mā'əkala bərhān

<Conj-V:Perf.3m.s> <NCom:m.s.Nom> <Prep> <NCom:unm.s.Nom>

wa-mā'əkala ṣəlmat

<Conj-Prep> <NCom:unm.s.Nom>

'And God make a separation between the light and (between) the darkness'.

Ba, *'əm*[1] and *wəsta* are the most essential ACPPIP elements which can be added to *mā'əkala* initially.

Textual evidence:

5.1.5.3. ዘካርያስ፡ ወልደ፡ በራክዩ፡ ዘቀተልክምዎ፡ በማእከለ፡ ቤተ፡ መቅደስ፡ ወምሥዋዕ። (Matt. 23:35).

Zakārəyās walda barākəyu za-qatalkəməww-o

<Npro:m.s.PSt> <NCom:m.s.ConSt> <NPro:m.s.Nom> <PRel-V:Perf.2m.p-PSuff:3m.s>

ba-mā'əkala bata maqdas

---

[1] Due to the attachment, the first consonant of *mā'kala* goes to be geminated while the ending syllable of *'əm* is absorbed by (*mā*) and does not appear any more in the fidal transcription. See the textual evidence 5.1.5.4.

<Prep-Prep> <NCom:unm.s.ConSt> <NCom:unm.s.Nom>

wa-məśwāʿ

<Conj-NCom:unm.s.Nom>

'Zechariah the son of Berechiah whom you murdered between the temple and the altar'.

5.1.5.4. **ወይሰጥቆ፡ እማእከሉ፡፡** (Matt. 24:51).

wa-yəsaṭṭəq-o 'əm-mā'kal-u

<Conj-V:Imperf:3m.s-PSuff:3m.s> <Prep-Prep-PSuff:3m.s>

'And he will cut him in pieces'.

5.1.5.5. **እግዚአብሔር፡ ውስተ፡ ማእከላ፡፡** (Ps. 45:5).

'əgzi'abəbḥer wəsta mā'kal-ā

<NCom:m.s.Nom> <Prep> <Prep-Psuff:f.s>

'The Lord is in her midst'.

Notwithstanding, if it occurs alone, it will be considered as an adverb.

Textual evidence:

5.1.5.6. **ወይእቲኒ፡ ብእሲት፡ ትቀውም፡ ማእከለ፡፡** (John 8:9).

wa-yə'əti-ni bə'əsit təqawwəm mā'əkala.

<Conj-PPro:f.s.Nom-Part> <NCom:f.s.Nom> <V:Imperf.3f.s> <Adv>

'And the woman was standing in the midst'.

Further references: 1 Sam. 2:11, 6:6; 2 Sam. 13:34; Ps. 81:1; S. of S. 2:2; Gdl.Qw 1:38.

5.1.6. ማዕዶተ *māʿdota*

ማዕዶተ *māʿdota* is originally the nominal derivation in status constructus which is related with the verb **ዐደወ** *ʿadawa* 'crossover'. It is used as a preposition with the meanings ‘across’ or ‘beyond’.[1] It can be attached to the non-verbal elements only.

Textual evidence:

5.1.6.1. ወሖሩ፡ ማዕዶተ፡ ባሕር፡ ኀበ፡ ቅፍርናሆም። (John 6:17).

wa-ḥoru mā'dota bāḥr ḫaba qəfrənnāhom

<Conj-V:Perf.3m.p> <Prep> <NCom:unm.s.Nom> <Prep> <NPro:pl.s. Nom>

‘And they went beyond the sea to Capernaum’.

Further reference: Mark 8:13; John 6:1, 6:22.

5.1.7. አፍአ *'af'ā*

አፍአ *'af'ā* is originally a linguistic element that can be used as a preposition or as an adverb with the meaning ‘outside’.[2] As a prepositional element, it goes to be attached to the non-verbal elements while as an adverb, it does occur alone. In both occurrences, the notion of some ACPPIP elements such as መንገለ *mangala*, በ *ba*, ኀበ *ḫaba*, እም *'əm*, እንተ *'ənta* and ውስተ *wəsta* are sounded without occurring evidently. These elements can also be prefixed to it.[3]

Textual evidence:

5.1.7.1. (as a preposition) ነዋ፡ ይቀውሙ፡ አቡከ፡ ወእምከ፡ አፍአ፡ ቤተ፡ ክርስቲያን። (Gdl.Qaw 4:30).

nawā yəqawwəmu 'abu-ka wa-'əmmə-ka

<PartPres> <V:Imperf.3m.p> <NCom:m.s.Nom-PSuff:2m.s> <NCom:f.s.Nom-PSuff:2m.s>

'af'ā beta krəstiyān

---

1 Dillmannn 1865, 1013; Kidāna Wald Kəfle 1955, 685; Leslau 1989, 179.

2 Dillmann 1865, 809; Kidāna Wald Kəfle 1955, 236; Leslau 1989, 147. *Mal'aka 'aryam* Yətbārak stated in his grammar and dictionary that *'af'ā* cannot be recognized as ACPPIP element. But, he did not propose a reason for this suggestion. Yətbārak Maršā 2002, 168.

3 Leslau 2006, 9.

<Prep> <NCom:unm.s.ConSt>
<NCom:unm.p.Nom>

'Behold, your father and mother are standing outside the church'.

5.1.7.2. (as an adverb) አውጽእዎ፡ አፍኣ፡ ውስተ፡ ጸናፌ፡ ጽልመት። (Matt. 25:30).

ʾawṣəʾww-o ʾafʾā wəsta ṣanāfe ṣəlmat

<V:Impt-PSuff:3m.s> <Prep> <Prep>
<NCom:unm.s.ConSt> <NCom.unm.s.Nom>

'Send him away into the outer darkness'.

Further references: Job 2:8; Luke 24:50; John 9:34.

5.1.8. እስከ *ʾəska*

እስከ *ʾəska* as a preposition is attached to the non-verbal linguistic elements. On different aspects of the element, a detailed explanation is presented in chapter four under 4.3.3.

5.1.9. እንተ *ʾənta*

Apart from being a relative pronoun, እንተ *ʾənta* has at least two more exclusive functions which are not shared by its fellow elements *za* and *ʾəlla*.

5.1.9.1. It is used as a preposition expressing a diraction with the meaning 'to'.

Textual evidence:

5.1.9.1.1. ፈቀድነ፡ ንሑር፡ እንተ፡ መቄዶንያ። (Acts 16:10).

faqadna nəḥur ʾənta maqedonyā

<V:Perf.1c.p> <V:Subj:1c.p> <Prep> <NPro:pl.s.Nom>

'We wanted to go to Macedonia'.

5.1.9.2. It is used again as a preposition in expression of location with the meanings ‘through’ and ‘by’.

Textual evidence:

5.1.9.2.1. ወልድ፡ እኍየ፡ ፈነወ፡ እዴሁ፡ እንተ፡ ስቍረት። (S. of S. 5:4).

wald ʾəḫu-ya fannawa

<NCom:m.s.Nom> <NCom:m.s.Nom-PSuff:1c.s> <V:Perf.3m.s>

ʾəde-hu ʾənta səqʷrat

<NCom:unm.s.Acc> <Prep> <NCom:m.s.Nom>

‘The son, my brother extended his hand through opening’.

5.1.9.2.2. ወእንተ፡ ካልእት፡ ፍኖት፡ አውፅአቶሙ። (Jas. 2:25).

wa-ʾənta kāləʾt fənot ʾawḍəʾatt-omu

<Conj-Prep> <NCom:f.s.Nom> <NCom:m.s.Nom> <V:Perf.3f.s-PSuff: 3m.p>

‘And she sent them out by another way’.

Further references: Ps. 17:3; Matt. 19:24; Acts 16:28; Rom. 15:28; Eph. 3:17.

5.1.10. ከዋላ *kawālā* and ድኅረ *dəḫra*

The origins of these two elements and their functionalities as adverbial elements are discussed in chapter three, section 3.2.5. Now in this part, we will see how they serve as prepositional elements. Leslau mentioned that they function as adverbs, but did not say anything as to wether or not they can be used as prepositions.[1] In Tropper's opinion, *kawālā* is a rarely needed element for this function.[2]

The grammatical function of *kawālā* and *dəḫra* as prepositions is to express a position with the precise meaning ‘behind’ or ‘at the back of’. In this case, they are attached to the non-verbal language

---

[1] Leslau 2006, 129, 299.

[2] Tropper 2002, 142.

elements. An initial affixation of some ACPPIP elements such as *mangala, ba* and *ʾəm* to the elements is possible.

Textual evidence:

5.1.10.1. ወውእቱሰ፡ መንገለ፡ ከዋላ፡ ሐመር፡ ተተርአሰ። (Mark 4:38).

wa-wəʾətu-ssa mangala kawālā ḥamar tatarasa

<Conj-PPro:m.s.Nom-Part> <Prep> <Prep> <NCom:unm.s.Nom> <V:Perf.3m.s>

'But he lies on the cushion at the back part of the boat'.

5.1.10.2. ወድኅረ፡ ኵሎሙ፡ ሞተት፡ ይእቲ፡ ብእሲት። (Matt. 22:27).

wa-dəḫra kʷəllomu motat yəʾəti bəʾəsit

<Conj-Prep> <PTot.Nom> <V:Perf.3f.s> <PPro:f.s.Nom> <NCom:f.s. Nom>

'And after them all, the woman died'.

Further references: Luke 1:24; John 20:26.

Particularly, the nominative form *dəḫr* can play the same role if a place preposition such as መንገለ *mangala,* በ *ba,* ኀበ *ḫaba,* እም *ʾəm* and እንተ *ʾənta* is attached to it. The actual concepts of the elements added to it may not move on in terms of the attachment. It may rather have the following meanings መንገለ፡ ድኅር *mangala dəḫr*/ ኀበ፡ ድኅር *ḫaba dəḫr* 'towards back'; በድኅር *ba-dəḫr* 'at the back', 'behind'; እም፡ ድኅር *ʾəm dəḫr* 'from behind' and እንተ፡ ድኅር *ʾənta dəḫr* 'backward'.

Textual evidence:

5.1.10.3. ሑር፡ እም፡ ድኅሬየ፡ ሰይጣን፡ እስመ፡ ኮንከ፡ ማዕቀፍየ። (Matt. 16:23).

ḥur ʾəm dəḫre-ya sayṭān

<V:Impt.2m.s> <Prep> <prep-PSuff:1c.s> <NPro:m.s.Nom>

ʾəsma konka māʿəqafə-ya

<Conj> <V:Perf. 2m.s> <NCom:unm.s.Acc-PSuff:1c.s>

'Go away Satan behind me! You became a stumbling block to me'.

5.1.11. ውስተ *wəsta*, ውስጠ *wəsṭa*, ውሳጤ *wəsāṭe* and ውሳጢተ *wəsāṭita*

The elements ውስጠ *wəsṭa*, ውሳጤ *wəsāṭe* and ውሳጢተ *wəsāṭita* are equally affiliated with the verb ወሰጠ *wasaṭa* 'become inside or inner'. ውስተ *wəsta* is also semantically equivalent to each of them. Besides, it is much closer to *wəsṭa*. So, it is possible to consider that *wəsta* is the result of the loss of *ṭ*. In support of this, Leslau claimed as it is a variant of *wəsṭa*.[1] Dillmann also suggested that it is probably from *wəsṭ*.[2]

Even if *wəsta* has exclusively some additional functions, the common grammatical function of all of these elements is to be used as prepositions in expression of position or place with a meaning 'in' or 'inside'.[3] The linguistic elements to which each of these elements goes to be attached are the non-verbal elements. Some other appropriate elements such as *mangala*, *ba*, *ḫaba*, *ʾəm*, *ʾənta* and *za* can be added to them initially.[4] Even *wəsta* is attached to *wəsāṭe* and *wəsāṭita*. But none of them can be attached to *wəsta*.

Textual evidence:

5.1.11.1. በጸጋ፡ እግዚአብሔር፡ አንሶሰውነ፡ ውስተ፡ ዓለም። (2 Cor. 1:12).

ba-ṣaggā ʾəgziʾabəḥer ʾansosawna wəsta

<Prep-NCom:unm.s.Nom> <NCom:m.s.Nom> <V:Perf.1c.p> <Prep>

ʿālam

<NCom:unm.s.Nom>

'In the grace of God, we have walked in the world'.

5.1.11.2. ወአልቦ፡ ዘሀሎ፡ ሰብእ፡ ውስተ፡ ውሳጤ፡ ቤት። (Gen. 39:11).

wa-ʾalbo za-hallo sabʾ wəsta wəsāṭe

<Conj-PartNeg> <PRel-V:Perf.3m.s> <NCom:m.s.Nom> <Prep><Prep>

bet

---

1 Leslau 2006, 620.

2 Dillmann 1907, 396.

3 Dillmann 1865, 908384; Kidāna Wald Kəfle 1955, 345; Leslau 1989, 163.

4 Dillmann 1907, 396; Tropper 2002, 144.

<NCom: unm.s.Nom>

'And there was no man inside the house'.

5.1.11.3. ሀለወከ፡ ታእምር፡ አመ፡ ትበውእ፡ ውስተ፡ ውሳጢተ፡ ውሳጢት። (1 Kgs 22:24).

hallawakka tāʾmər ʾama təbaww ʾ wəsta wəsāṭita

<V:Perf.2m.s> <V:Subj.2m.s> <Prep> <V:Imperf.2m.s> <Prep> <Prep>

wəsāṭit

<NCom:unm.s.Nom>

'You have to know when you enter into the inner room'.

Further references: Gen. 16:6; 1 Kgs 6:19; Esther 4:3; Job 2:5, 8; Isa. 8:1; Rom. 9:33; Gal. 6:8; Rev. 1:11.

If any other prepositional element such as *ʾənta* is attached to *wəsṭ* or *wəsāṭit* (not status constructus), then, in such cases, they are considered as nouns but not as prepositions.

Textual evidence:

5.1.11.4. ወሖረ፡ እንዘ፡ ይርዕድ፡ እንተ፡ ውስጥ። (Acts 16:28).

wa-ḥora ʾənza yərəʿəd ʾənta wəsṭ

<Conj-V:Perf.3m.s> <Conj> <V:Imperf.3m.s> <Prep> <NCom.unm.s>

'And he rushed inside trembling'.

Further references: 1 Kgs 6:13; Jas. 4:9, 13.

Henceforth, we will see the exclusive functions of *wəsta* that cannot be shared by the other elements of the sub-group. As it is yet a preposition in expressing a position, place, site and direction, it is used in the place of *ḫaba*, *ba-ḫaba*, *lāʿla* and *māʾəkala* with the meanings 'to', 'toward', 'in', 'on', 'among', 'within, 'through', 'throughout', 'against' and 'by'.[1]

[1] Leslau 2006, 620; Yāred Šiferaw 2009, 381.

Textual evidence:

5.1.11.5. ሑሩ፡ አንትሙ፡ ውስተ፡ አጸደ፡ ወይንየ፡ ወተቀነዩ። (Matt. 20:7).

ḥuru ʾantəmu wəsta ʾaṣada

<V:Impt.2m.p> <PPer:2m.p:Nom> <Prep> <NCom:unm.s.ConSt>

waynə-ya wa-taqanayu

<NCom:unm.s.Nom-PSuff:1c.s> <Conj-V:Impt.2m.p>

'You may go into my vineyard and work'.

5.1.11.6. ወሦጠ፡ ወይነ፡ ወቅብዐ፡ ውስተ፡ ቊስሊሁ። (Luke 10:34).

wa-soṭa wayna wa-qəbʿa

<Conj-V:Perf.3m.s> <NCom:unm.s.Acc> <Conj-NCom:unm.s.Acc>

wəsta *q^{w}əsali-hu*

<Prep> <NCom:unm .s.Nom-PSuff:3m.s>

'And he poured wine and oil on his wound'.

5.1.11.7. ወአአኀዝዎ፡ ሕለተ፡ ውስተ፡ የማኑ። (Matt. 27:29).

wa-ʾaʾaḫazəww-o ḥəllata wəsta yamān-u

<Conj-V:Perf.3m.p-PSuff:3m.s> <NCom:unm.s.Acc> <Prep> <Com:unm.s.Nom>

'They caused him to take a reed in his right hand'.

5.1.11.8. ወኢይኩኑ፡ እም፡ ውስቴትክሙ፡ ብዙኃን፡ መምህራነ። (Jas. 3:1).

wa-ʾiyyəkunu ʾəm wəstetə-kəmu bəzuḫān

<Conj-PartNeg-V:Subj(Imt).3m.p> <Prep> <Prep-PSuff:2m.p> <NCom:m.p.Nom>

mamhərāna

<NCom:m.p.Acc>

'Let not many among you become instructors'.

5.1.11.9. ወነፍሐ፡ ቀርነ፡ ውስተ፡ ኵሉ፡ ምድር። (1 Sam. 13:4).

wa-nafḫa qarna wəsta *k^{w}əllu mədr*

<Conj-V:Perf.3m.s> <NCom:unm.s.Acc> <Prep> <PTot.Nom> <NCom: unm.s. Nom>

'Then he blew the trumpet throughout the land'.

5.1.11.10. ወአንበሩ፡ አፉሆሙ፡ ውስተ፡ ሰማይ። (Ps. 72:9).

wa-'anbaru 'afu-homu wəsta samāy

<Conj-V:Perf.3m.p> <NCom:unm.s.Acc> <Prep> <NCom:unm.s.Nom>

'They have set their mouth against the heaven'.

5.1.11.11. ወእንዘ፡ ይነብር፡ አሐዱ፡ ወሬዛ፡ ውስተ፡ መስኮት። (Acts 20:9).

wa-'ənza yənabbər 'aḥadu wareẓā

<Conj-Conj> <V:Imperf.3m.s> <NumCa:m.Nom> <NCom:m.s.Nom>

wəst maskot

<Prep> <NCom:unm.s.Nom>

'And while a certain young man was sitting by the window'.

Further references: Gen. 6:4, 18:22, 38:21; Exod. 14:29, 20:21, 31:54; 1 Sam. 2:34, 3:9, 13:17; 2 Sam. 3:38, 7:25, 10:6; 1 Kgs 8:20, 18:42; Esther 3:8; Ps. 18:4, 65:12, 74:8, 78:1 114:7, 138:8; John 6:4, 7:8, 20:6; Rom. 9:24; Jas. 4:9, 13; Rev. 3:21; Haym. (com.) 7:5.

5.1.12. ዐውደ *'awda*

ዐውደ *'awda* does occur alone when it is used as an adverb but when it serves as a preposition, it gets attached to the non-verbal linguistic elements. In such functionality, its English equivalent is 'around'.[1]

Textual evidence:

5.1.12.1. ወድቀ፡ ማእከለ፡ ተዐይኒሆሙ፡ ወዐውደ፡ ደባትሪሆሙ። (Ps. 77:28).

wadqa mā'əkala ta'ayyəni-homu wa-'awda

---

[1] Dillmann 1865, 1000; Kidāna Wald Kəfle 1955, 687; Leslau 1989, 177.

<V:Perf.3m.s> <Prep> <NCom:unm.s.Nom-PSuff:3m.p> <Conj-Prep>

dabātəri-homu

<NCom:unm.s.Nom-PSuff:3m.p>

'It had fall down in the midst of their cam and around their tents'.

Further reference: 2 Sam. 7:1.

5.1.13. ገቦ *gabo*, ጎረ *gora* and ጥቃ *ṭəqā*

ገቦ *gabo* and ጥቃ *ṭəqā* are originally nouns that do not have etymological relations with a verb. On the contrary, ጎረ *gora* is a noun in status constructus which is initially related with the verb ገወረ *gawara/* ተጋወረ *tagāwara* 'be neighbor' and 'be closer'. As a noun, each may have its own specific meaning. *Gabo* means 'waist' or 'side', and *gor* means 'neighbor'. *Ṭəqā* means 'near' and 'closely'.[1] Nevertheless, as prepositional elements, all are used in expressing place or position with the precise meanings 'near', 'by' and 'around'.

As prepositional elements, they are combined with the non-verbal language elements. Some ACPPIP elements such as በ *ba,* እለ *ʾəlla,* እም *ʾəm,* እንተ *ʾənta,* ውስተ *wəsta* and ዘ *za* can also be attached to them initially.[2]

Textual evidence:

5.1.13.1. ቤተፋጌ፡ እንተ፡ ገቦ፡ ደብረ፡ ዘይት። (Matt. 21:1).

betafāge ʾənta gabo dabra zayt

<NPro:pl.s.Nom> <PRel> <Prep> <NCom:unm.s.ConSt> <NCom:unm. s.Nom>

'Bethphage which is near the Mount of Olives'.

---

[1] Dillmann 1865, 1173-1174; Kidāna Wald Kəfle 1955, 295 and 307; Leslau 1989, 216.

[2] Dillmann 1907; 404; Leslau 2006, 595.

5.1.13.2. ወይእዜኒ፡ ሀለውነ፡ ውስተ፡ ቃዴስ፡ ጥቃ፡ ደወለ፡ ብሔርከ። (Num. 20:16).

wa-yəʾəze-ni ḫallawna wəsta-qādes ṭəqā-dawala-bəḥerə-ka

<Conj-Adv-Part> <V:Perf.1c.p> <Prep-NPro:pl.s.Nom> <Prep-NCom-NCom:unm.s.Nom-PSuff:2m.s>

'And now we are at Kadesh near the edge of your territory'.

More than this, *gabo* is used infrequently in the place of በኀበ *ba-ḫaba* or መንገለ *mangala* 'towards' or 'at the direction of'.

Textual evidence:

5.1.13.3. አድባረ፡ ጽዮን፡ በገቦ፡ መስዕ። (Ps. 47:2).

ʾadbāra ṣəyon ba-gabo masʿ

<NCom:unm.p.ConSt> <NPro:pl.s.Nom> <Prep-Prep> <NCom:unm. s.Nom>

'The mountains of Zion are towards the northeast'.

5.2. Prepositions of Time

5.2.1. ሳኒታ *sānitā*

We have seen earlier (3.2.3) how it functions as an adverb. Now, we will see its further function as a preposition. In such a case, it does not occur alone, but is attached to nouns. Its meaning remains the same ('next day').[1]

Textual evidence:

ወይቤላ፡ ንጉሥ፡ ለአስቴር፡ አመ፡ ሳኒታ፡ በዓል፡ ምንተ፡ ኮንኪ፡ አስቴር። (Esther 8:2).

wa-yəbel-ā nəguś la-ʾaster

<Conj-V:Perf.3m.s-Psuff:3f.s> <NCom:m.s.Nom> <Prep-Npro:f.s.Nom>

ʾama sānitā baʿāl mənta konki ʾaster

---

[1] Dillmann 1865, 373; Kidāna Wald Kəfle 1955, 875; Leslau 1989, 73.

<Prep> <Prep> <NCom:unm.s.Nom> <AInt> <V:Perf.2f.s> <NPro:f. s.Nom>

'On the second day of the feast, the king asked Ester, what happend to you, Ester?'

5.2.2. ሶበ *soba*, አመ *'ama*, ዕድሜ *'ədme* and ጊዜ *gize*

The explanations given on the grammatical functions of ሶበ *soba*, አመ *'ama* and ጊዜ *gize* in the previous chapter involves the role of the elements as prepositional elements (4.3.1, 4.8.1). Here, we discuss only the origin, meaning and function of ዕድሜ *'ədme*.

Originally, *'ədme* is related with the verb ዐደመ *'addama* 'fix a time' and 'invite'. It means literally 'age' or 'time'. It does not exist in the preposition lists of all grammarians mentioned in this work (see Table 3). But according to the *'Aggabāb* tradition, it serves as a preposition, and shares the principal concept of አመ *'ama*, ሶበ *soba*, and ጊዜ *gize* in expressing an unfixed time. Indeed, it has a similar meaning with those prepositional elements but in function, it is distinct because it is used often as a noun. Let us see the following reading which is one of the rare readings mentioned as evidence.

5.2.2.1. ወአመ፡ በጽሐ፡ ዕድሜሁ፡ ፈነወ፡ እግዚአብሔር፡ ወልዶ፡ ወተወልደ፡ እም፡ ብእሲት። (Gal. 4:6).

wa-'ama baṣḥa 'ədme-hu fannawa 'əgzi'abəḥer

<Conj-Conj> <V:Perf:3m.s> <Prep-PSuff:3m.s> <V:Perf.3m.s> <NCom:m.s.Nom>

wald-o wa-tawalda 'əm bə'əsit

<NCom:m.s.PSuff:m.s.Acc> <Conj-V:Perf.3m.s> <Prep> <NCom:f.s. Nom>

'And when the time reached, God had sent his son, and he was born from a woman'.

In the given example, *'ədme* with the prenominal suffix of the third person masculine singular *-hu* is used as a noun, and is not playing the role of a preposition. We can take also ዝ፡ ውእቱ፡ ዕድሜ፡ ሣህልኪ። *zə wə'ətu 'ədme śāhələ-ki* 'this is the time of your mercy' (M. Sa'at, 158.) as additional example. But, even in this reading, *'ədme* is a noun. Thus, it is difficult to consider it a preposition while it does not function as a preposition.

5.2.3. አፈ *'afa* and ፍና *fənnā*

አፈ *'afa* is a noun in status constructus. አፍ *'af* means 'mouth'. ፍና *fənnā* is the nominal derivation which is originally related with the verb ፈነወ *fannawa* 'send'. It means literally 'way', 'road' and 'street'. However, in the state of prepositional elements, they are used in expression of time with the meanings 'in' and 'towards'.[1] They are mostly attached to the nouns which express time of the day.

Textual evidence:

5.2.3.1. ወቋዓት፡ ያመጽኡ፡ ሎቱ፡ በአፈ፡ ጽባሕ፡ ኅብስተ፡ ወፍና፡ ሠርከ፡ ሥጋ።[2] (1 Kgs17:5).

wa-qwa'āt yāmaṣṣə'u l-ottu ba-'afa

<Conj-NCom:ms.p.Nom> <V:Imperf.3m.p> <Prep-PSuff:3m.s> <Prep-Prep>

ṣəbāḥ ḫəbəsta wa-fənnā śark

<NCom:unm.s.Nom> <NCom:unm.s.Acc> <Conj-Prep> <NCom:unm.s.Nom>

śəgā

<NCom:unm.s. Acc>

'And the ravens were bringing him bread in the morning and meat towards evening'.

Further references: Gen. 3:8; Esther 3:14; 1 Kgs 18:29.

---

[1] Dillmann 1865, 809, 1373; Kidāna Wald Kəfle 1955, 235, 727; Leslau 1989, 147, 244.

[2] Leslau introduced the combination of *fənnā* with *sark* and *nagh* and formed two phrases *fənnā sark* 'towards evening' and *fənnā nagh* 'towards dawn' Leslau 2006, 163. But practicaly *'afa ṣəbāh* is often used instead of *fənnā nagh* because the metaphorical expression relates to the movment of the sun; when it rises it is said *'af* for *'af* is a starting point. When it goes down, it is said *fənnā* since *fənnā* means 'way', and it shows the journey of the sun. So, the metaphor *fənnā nagh* is as strange as *'afa sark*.

5.3 COMPARATIVE PREPOSITION

5.3.1. መጠነ *maṭana* and አምጣነ *'amṭāna*

መጠነ *maṭana* and አምጣነ *'amṭāna* are among the ACPPIP elements that can deliberately be categorized under the lexical categories of conjunctions and prepositions according to their diverse functions. Thus, an eloquent explanation on their origins and functions is provided in chapter four (See 4.9.2).

5.3.2. አምሳለ *'amsāla* and አርአያ *'ar'ayā*

We have already seen the etymology and meaning of these two elements as well as their grammatical function as conjunctions in 4.9.4. Here, we see how they function as prepositional elements being added to the non-verbal language elements. The preposition 'like' is the most attainable English equivalent of both elements.[1] Nonetheless, the following phrases can also express their notion: 'in the likeness of', 'in resemblance of' 'in the form of' and 'in the image of'. The preposition 'like' can also be its equivalent in some expressions.

Textual evidence:

5.3.2.1. ወንሕነሰ፡ ንትነበል፡ በአምሳለ፡ ክርስቶስ። (2 Cor. 5:20).

wa-nəḥna-ssa nətanabbəl ba-'amsāla krəstos

<Conj-PPro-Part> <V:Imperf.1c.p> <Prep-Prep> <NPro:m.s.Nom>

'And we beg you in the likeness of Christ'.

5.3.2.2. ንግበር፡ ሰብአ፡ በአርአያነ፡ ወበአምሳሊነ። (Gen. 1:26).

nəgbar sab'a ba-'ar'ayā-na wa-ba-'amsāli-na

<V:Subj (Impt).1c.p> <NCom:m.s.Acc> <Prep-Prep-PSuff:1c.p> <Conj-Prep-Prep-PSuff:1c.p >

'Let us create man in our image and in our likeness'.

---

1 Dillmann 1865, 173, 300; Kidāna Wald Kəfle 1955, 613, 816; Leslau 1989, 34 Yāred Šiferaw 2009, 344.

5.3.3. አያተ *'ayāta*

አያተ *'ayāta* is on one hand the plural form of the interrogative adverb አይ *'ay* 'what' and 'which'. On the other hand, it is an individual element that can be used as a preposition with the meaning 'like'.[1] On its origin, Leslau proposed that it is a noun which is connected with the verb *'ayaya* 'make equal'. For *'ayāta*, he gave the meanings 'equally', 'in like manner' and 'like' by considering it as andverb and a preposition.[2]

It is attached to the non-verbal linguistic elements.

Textual evidence:

5.3.3.1. አያተ፡ አዕናቍ፡ እለ፡ ተሰክዓ። (Malkəʿa 'iyyasus Hymn 12).

'ayāta 'aʿnāqʷ 'əlla tasakʿā

<Prep> <NCom:f.p.Nom> <PRel> <V:Perf.f.p>

'Like diamonds which are threaded'.

5.3.4. እም *'əm*

See the explanation under 4.9.6.

5.3.5. ከመ *kama*

The grammatical functions of ከመ *kama* which is one of the most important ACPPIP elements in the category of conjunctions has been discussed in the previous chapter (4.6.2). In this part, we will see only how it is employed as a preposition.

As a preposition, it is attached to the non-verbal linguistic elements. Its meaning is 'like'.[3] In the absence of a visible verb, ውእቱ *wə'ətu* will take the place of a verb to express the similarity of two or more persons or things by comparison.

---

1 Dillmann 1865, 798; Kidāna Wald Kəfle 1955, 215; Leslau 1989, 146; Yāred Šiferaw 2009, 381.

2 Leslau 2006, 51.

3 Dillmann 1865, 826; Kidāna Wald Kəfle 1955, 156; Leslau 1989, 147.

5.3.5.1. ሰብእሰ፡ ከመ፡ ሣዕር፡ መዋዕሊሁ። (Ps. 103:15).

sab'ə-ssa kamaśā'r mawā'əli-hu

<NCom:m.s.Nom-Part> <Prep> <NCom:m.s.Nom> <NCom:m.s.Nom-PSuff:3m.s>

'But a man, his days are like a grass'.

5.3.5.2. ክልኤ፡ አጥባትኪ፡ ከመ፡ ክልኤ፡ ዕጐለ፡ መንታ፡ ዘወይጠል። (S. of S. 4:5).

kəl'e 'aṭbātə-ki kama kəl'e

<NumCa.Nom> <NCom:unm.p-PSuff:2f.s> <Prep> <NumCa.Nom>

'əgʷla mantā za-wayṭal

<NCom:unm.s.ConSt> <NCom:unm.s.PSt> <Part-NCom:unm.s.Nom>

'Your two breasts are like two twin fawns of a gazelle'.

In some cases, it is used to mean 'according to'.

Textual evidence:

5.3.5.3. ወትፈድዮ፡ ለኵሉ፡ በከመ፡ ምግባሩ። (Ps. 61:12).

wa-təfaddəy-o la-kʷəllu ba-kama

<Conj-V:Imperf.2m.s-PSuff:3m.s> <Prep-PTot.Nom> <Prep-Prep>

məgbār-u

<NCom:unm.s.Nom-PSuff:3m.s>

'You recompense everyone according to his deed'.

Further references: Gen. 1:4, 21; Ps. 109:17.

When it is combined with nouns in making a comparison of two things, ከመ *kama* can drag the same verb even after the combination in the translation to make the comparison eligible. In such cases, it is identified as ውጥን ጨራሽ *wəṭṭən čarrāš*.[1]

Textual evidence:

5.3.5.4. ዐገቱኒ፡ ከመ፡ ንህብ፡ መዐረ። (Ps. 118:12).

'agatu-ni kama nəhb ma'ara

<V:Perf.3m.p-PSuff:1c.s> <Prep>
<NCom:unm.s.Nom> <NCom:unm.s.Acc>

'They surrounded me as the bee surrounds the honey.

5.3.5.5. ወኀደረት፡ ውስቴቶሙ፡ ከመ፡ ዝናም፡ በበድው፡ ወከመ፡ ጠል፡ በምድር፡ ፅምዕት። (Enoch (com.) 12:3).

wa-ḫadarat wəstet-omu kama zənām

<Conj-V:Perf.3f.s> <Prep-PSuff:3m.p> <Prep>
<NCom:unm.s.Nom>

ba-badəw wa-kama ṭall ba-mədr

<Prep-NCom:unm.s.Nom> <Conj-Prep>
<NCom:unm.s.Nom> <Prep-NCom:unm.s. Nom>

ḍəmə't

<NCom:f.s.Nom>

'And it abides in them as a rain abides in a remote area,
and as a dew (abides) on the thirsty ground'.

Further reference: Rev. 1:14, 6:13.

5.4 OTHER PREPOSITIONS

5.4.1. ህየንተ *həyyanta*, በእንተ *ba'ənta*, ቤዛ *bezā*, ተክለ *takla* and ተውላጠ *tawlāṭa*

The origins and grammatical functions of ህየንተ *həyyanta*, በእንተ *ba'ənta* and ተውላጠ *tawlāṭa* as the conjunctional elements were discussed in chapter four under 4.9.1 and 4.9.3. The discussions includ-

[1] Amharic phrase with a literal meaning 'someone or something that completes what is incomplete'.

ed comprehensive textual evidence. Thus, we discuss here only ቤዛ *bezā* and ተክለ *takla.*

Bezā is initially related with the verb ቤዘወ *bezawa* 'redeem' and 'rescue'. *Takl* is the root noun of the verb ተከለ *takala* 'plant' in status constructus. They are equally used as prepositions with the meanings 'for', 'for the sake of', 'in charge of', 'instead of', 'in the place of' and 'in terms of'.[1]

As long as they function as prepositions, they have to be attached to the non-verbal language elements only. They do not occur alone. Even in the attachment, they always take the initial position.

Textual evidence:

5.4.1.1. ይፍዲ፡ ላህመ፡ ተክለ፡ ላህሙ። (Exod. 21:36).

yəfdi lāhma takla lāhm-u

<V:Subj (Impt)3m.s> <NCom:unm.s.Acc> <Prep> <NCom.unm.s-PSuff:3m.p>

'He shall pay an ox instead of his ox'.

5.4.2. ለ *la*

ለ *la* has various grammatical functions with different meanings.[2] It is attached to verbs (imperatives and infinitives), ACPPIP elements, nouns, numerals and nominal derivations initially.

The element is identified with various scholarly identifications which are intended to express its roles according to each function. The identifications are originally Amharic terms. From the functions which the elements execute, we can imagine how the identifications are reasonable and fitting. Let us see them individually.

[1] Dillmann 1865, 565; Leslau 1989, 102, 109; Yāred Šiferaw 2009, 381; Tropper 2002, 142.

[2] Dillmann 1865, 22; Kidāna Wald Kəfle 1955, 155, 554; Yāred Šiferaw 2009, 344.

5.4.2.1. ለ la as በቁም ቀሪ *baqum-qari* (lit.: 'something which remains unchangeable').

When it is attached to infinitives, nouns and numbers in the state of being a preposition with the meaning 'for' or 'to', it is called *baqum-qari*. The reason is that in such cases, the Gəʿəz *la* is totally equivalent with the Amharic *la*.

Textual evidence:

5.4.2.1.1. ተአክሎ፡ ለዘከመዝ፡ ዛቲ፡ ተግሣጽ። (2 Cor. 2:6).

ta'akkəl-o la-za-kama-zə zātti tagśāṣ

<V:Imperf.3f.s-PSuff:3m.s> <Prep-PRel-Prep-PDem.3m.s.Nom> <PDem. 3f.s. Nom> <NCom: f[s].s.Nom>

'This punishment is sufficient for such a one'.

5.4.2.2. ለ *la* as ተጠቃሽ *taṭaqqaš* (lit.: 'something which is mentioned or touched').

When a verb in a sentence is with a suffix, the object shall not change its ending vowel. But instead, *la* gets attached to it initially. In such cases, *la* will be called '*taṭaqqaš*'

Textual evidence:

5.4.2.2.1. ለንጉሥክሙኑ፡ እሰቅሎ። (John 19:15).

la-nəguśə-kəmu-nu 'əsqəll-o

<Prep-NCom:m.s.Nom-PSuff:2m.p-PartInt> <V:Subj(Impt)-PSuff:3m.s>

'Shall I crucify your king?'

5.4.2.3. ለ *la* as አቀብሎ፡ ሻሺ *'aqabbəlo-šaši* (lit.: 'someone who gives something and gets away').

When a jussive functions as an imperative, *la* can be added to it initially without introducing any semantic change.[1] In such a case, *la* is

[1] Dillmann 1907, 389, 391; Leslau 1989, 5.

called *ʾaqabbəlo-šaši*. Some call it ታይቶ፡ ጠፊ *tāyto ṭafi* (lit.: s/th that disappears after appearing) since it does appear only in the Gəʿəz reading.

Textual evidence:

5.4.2.3.1. እመቦ፡ ዘይቴክዝ፡ ለይጸሊ። (Jas. 5:13).

ʾəmma-bo za-yətekkəz la-yəṣalli

<Prep-V:Perf.3m.s> <PRel-V:Imperf.3m.s> <Conj-V:Subj (Impt).3m.s>

'If there is anyone who is sad, he shall pray'.

Further references: Gen. 1:9, 12, 20, 6:20; 1 Sam. 3:17, 18, 12:24; 1 Kgs 4:23; Esther 10:25; Ps. 62:10, 69:2, 102:1; Rom. 11:13, 21; 1 Chr. 2:23; Eph. 4:12; Phil 1:16; Jas. 4:11, 12.

Besides, it is used as a preposition in expression of direction, place and position with the meanings 'to', 'in' and 'upon'.

Textual evidence:

5.4.2.3.2. (to) አሐዱ፡ ብእሲ፡ ይወርድ፡ እም፡ ኢየሩሳሌም፡ ለኢያሪኮ። (Luke 10:30).

ʾaḥadu bəʾəsi yəwarrəd ʾəm

<NumCa.Nom> <NCom:m.s.Nom> <V:Imperf.3m.s> <Prep>

ʾiyyarusālem la-ʾiyyāriko

<NPro:pl.s.Nom> <Prep-NPro:pl.s.Nom>

'A man was going down from Jerusalem to Jericho'.

5.4.2.3.2. (in)

ወሠናየ፡ ኀልዩ፡ ለቅድመ፡ እግዚአብሔር። (2 Cor. 8:21).

wa-śannāya ḫalləyu la-qədma ʾəgziʾabəḥer

<Conj-NCom:m.s.Acc> <V:Impt.2m.p> <Prep-Prep> <NCom:m.s. Nom>

'And you may think what is good in the sight of God'.

5.4.2.3.3. (upon)

> **አሌ፡ ለክሙ፡ እለ፡ ትሰፍሕዋ፡ ለእኪት፡ ለቢጽክሙ።** (Enoch (com.) 38:14).
>
> *'alle la-kəmu 'əlla təsaffəḥəwwā la-'əkkit la-*
>
> <Intr> <Prep-PSuff:2m.p> <PRel> <V:Imperf.2m.p-PSuff:3f.s> <Prep-NCom:f.s.Nom>
>
> *biṣə-kəmu*
>
> <Prep-NCom:m.s.Nom-PSuff:2m.p>
>
> 'Woe to you who stretch out to the evil upon your friends'.
>
> **Further references: Acts 19:22; Enoch (com.) 15:13, 21:26; Haym. (com.) 1:9.**

Its double occurrence expresses the distributives 'each' and 'every'.[1]

Textual evidence:

5.4.2.3.4. **ለለአሐዱ፡ ይትከሠት፡ ምግባሩ።** (1 Cor. 3:13).

> *lalla-'aḥadu yətkaśśat məgbār-u*
>
> <Prep-NumCa.Nom> <V:Imperf.3m.s> <NCom:m^{s}.s.Nom-PSuff:3m.s>
>
> 'Each man's work will become evident'.
>
> **Further references: Esther 2:1; Gdl.Gmq, 149.**

When it is combined with a verb, it will be translated as 'whenever', 'every time' (e.g.: **ለለወሀበ** *lalla-wahaba* 'whenever he gives', **ለለነገደ** *lalla-nagada* 'whenever he goes').

5.4.3. ምስለ *məsla*

ምስለ *məsla* has a clear etymological relation with **አምሳለ** *'amsāla*. It is a noun in status constructus which is related with the verb **መሰለ** *masala* 'look like' or 'resemble'. Its main function is to be used as a preposition in expression of unity and togetherness with the mean-

---

[1] Belay Mekonen 2007, 4; Yāred Šiferaw 2009, 344.

ing 'together ... with'.[1] Interestingly, it can also be used to express an opposition with the meaning 'against'. Leslau expressed it as an element expressing reciprocity.[2]

Furthermore, with the same treatment, it functions in the place of *la* 'to' and 'for' as it can be used seldom to express similarity and comparability in the place of *kama* 'like'.[3] However, in all cases, it is attached only to the non-verbal linguistic elements at the beginning. *Za* is an essential element to be attached to *məsla* initially without making any change.

5.4.3.1. Textual evidence: as used as 'with, together ... with'

ወእምከመ፡ ሠረቀ፡ ፀሐይ፡ ምስለ፡ ላህቡ፡ ያየብሶ፡ ለሣዕር። (Jas. 1:21).

wa-'əm kama śaraqa ḍaḥay məsla lāhəb-u

<Conj-conj> <Conj> <V:Perf.3m.s> <NCom:ms.s.Nom> <Prep>

yāyabbbəs-o la-śāʿər

<NCom:unm.s.Nom-PSuff: 3m.s> <V:Imperf.3m.s-PSuff:3m.s> <Prep-NCom:ms.s.Nom>

'But when the sun rises with its heat will cause the grass to wither'.

5.4.3.2. Textual evidence: as used as 'against'

ወአኀዘ፡ ኢዮአብ፡ ወኵሉ፡ ሕዝብ፡ ዘምስሌሁ፡ ይትቃተሉ፡ ምስለ፡ ሶርያ። (2 Sam. 10:14).

wa-'aḫaza 'iyyo'ab wa-kwəllu ḥəzb

<Conj-V:Perf.3m.s> <NPro:m.s.Nom> <Conj-PTot.Nom> <NCom.m.p.Nom>

za-məsle-hu yətqātalu məsla soryā

<PRel-Prep-PSuff:3m.s> <V:Subj.3m.p> <Prep> <NPro:pl. Nom>

---

[1] Belay Mekonen 2007, 40; Dillmann 1907, 400; Leslau 1989, 34

[2] Leslau 2006, 365.

[3] Kidāna Wald Kəfle 1955, 256

'Then Joab and the people who were with him started to fight against the Syrians'.

5.4.3.3. Textual evidence: as used as 'like'

ወይእዜሰኬ፡ እለ፡ የአምኑ፡ ይትባረኩ፡ ምስለ፡ አብርሃም፡ ምእመን። (Gal. 3:9).

wa-yə'əze-ssa-ke 'əlla ya'ammənu yətbārraku məsla

<Conj-Adv-Part> <PRel> <V:Imperf.3m.p> <V:Imperf.3m.p> <Prep>

'abrəham mə'man

<NPro:m.s. Nom> <NCom:m.s.Nom>

'And those who believe today are blessed like the faithful Abraham'.

5.4.3.4. Textual evidence: as used as 'to' or 'for'

እገብር፡ ምሕረተ፡ ምስለ፡ ሐኖን፡ ወልደ፡ ናኦስ። (2 Sam. 10:2).

'əgabbər məḥrata məsla hanon

<V:Imperf.1c.s> <NCom:unm.s.Acc> <Prep> <NPro:m.s.Nom>

walda nāos

<NCom:m.s.ConSt> <NPro:m.s.Nom>

'I will show kindness to Hanun the son of Nahash'.

Further references: 2 Sam. 7:12; 1 Kgs 1:21, 2:10; Prov (com.) 22:4; Mark 5:7; John 6:3; 1 Chr. 33:15.

5.4.4. በ *ba*

በ *ba* plays an essential role in the language. It functions as a preposition with the meanings 'by', 'in', 'with', 'at', 'because of', 'out of' and 'from'.[1] It can be attached only to the non-verbal language elements.

[1] Dillmann 1865, 478; Kidāna Wald Kəfle 1955, 154, 250; Leslau 1989, 94.

Textual evidence:

5.4.4.1. ወኀደገ፡ አልባሲሁ፡ በእዴሃ፡ ወጐየ። (Gen. 39:12).

wa-ḫadaga ʾalbāsi-hu ba-ʾəde-hā

<Conj-V:Perf.3m.s> <NCom:unm.p.Acc-PSuff:3m.s> <Prep-NCom:unm.s.Nom-PSuff:3m.s>

wa-gʷayya

<Conj-V:Perf.3m.s>

'He left his garments in her hand and fled'.

5.4.4.2. ወለእመኒ፡ መጽአቶ፡ ኀጢአቱ፡ እጌሥጾ፡ በበትረ፡ ዕደው። (2 Sam. 7:14).

wa-la-ʾəmma-ni maṣatt-o ḫaṭiʾat-u

<Conj-Prep-Prep-Part> <V:Perf.3f.s-PSuff:3m.s> <NCom:f^s.s.Nom-PSuff:3m.s>

ʾəgeśśəṣ-o ba-batra ʿədaw

<V:Imperf.1c.s-PSuff:3m.s> <Prep-NCom:unm.s.ConSt> <NCom: m.p.Nom>

'And if he commits a sin, I will correct him with the rod of men'.

Again, it is used in the places of ምስለ *məsla* (with).
Textual evidence:

5.4.4.3. ናሁ፡ ይመጽእ፡ በአእላፊሁ፡ ቅዱሳን፡ መላእክት። (Jude 1:14).

nāhu yəmaṣṣəʾə ba-ʾaʾlāfi-hu qəddusān

<Adv> <V:Imperf.3m.s> <Prep-NumCa.unm.p-PSuff:3m.s> <PPar:m.p.Nom>

malāʾəkt

<NCom:m.p.Nom>

'Behold, he will come with many thousands of his holy angels'.

5.4.4.4 ወታቀንተኒ፡ ኀይለ፡ በጸብዕ። (Ps 17:39)

wa-tāqannta-nni ḫayla ba-ṣabʿə

<Conj-V:imperf.1m.s-PSuff:1c.s> <Nom:c.s.Acc> <Prep-Nom:c.s.Nom>

'You gird me at war'.

Further references: Num. 10:35; Luke 7:46.

In the case of nominal sentences where *ba* is attached to a noun, a fitting verb is added in the translation to make the attachment provide a full and clear message.

Textual evidence:

5.4.4.5. ከልብኑ፡ አነ፡ ከመ፡ ትምጻእ፡ ኀቤየ፡ በበትር፡ ወአእባን። (1 Sam. 17:43).

kalbə-nu 'ana kama təmṣā'

<NCom:unm.s.Nom-PartInt> <PPro:1.c.s.Nom> <Conj> <V:Subj.2m.s>

ḫabe-ya ba-batr wa-'a'bān

<Prep-PSuff:1c.s> <Prep-NCom:unm.p.Nom> <Conj-NCom:unm.s.Nom>

'Am I a dog that you come to me taking a stick and stones?'

Consider that the verb ነሥአ *naś'a* 'take' is added in the translation for the comprehensibility of the sentence, it is just because of the engagement of the element.

Its duplication expresses the distributives 'every...'and 'each ...' or 'each by one'.[1]

Textual evidence:

5.4.4.6. ወእምነ፡ ኵሉ፡ ዘሥጋ፡ ታበውእ፡ ውስተ፡ ታቦት፡ በበክልኤቱ። (Gen. 6:19).

wa-'əmənna kʷəllu za-śəgā tābawwə'

<Conj-Prep> <PTot:m.Nom> <PRel-NCom:unm.s.Nom> <V:Imperf>

---

[1] Belay Mekonen 2007, 89; Dillmann 1907, 374-90, Leslau 2006, 82.

wəsta tābot babba-kəlʾettu

<Prep> <NCom:unm.s.Nom> <Prep-NumCa>

'And of every living thing of all flesh, you bring two of every kind into the ark'.

5.4.4.7. ወሤሞሙ፡ ዳዊት፡ በበዕብሬቶሙ፡ ለደቂቀ፡ ሌዊ። (1 Chr. 23:6).

wa-śem-omu dāwit babba-ʿəbret-omu

<Conj-V:Perf.3m.s-PSuff:3m.p> <NPro:m.s.Nom> <Prep-NCom:unm.s.Nom-PSuff: 3m.p>

la-daqiqa lewi

<Prep-NCom:m.p.ConSt> <NPro:m.s.Nom>

'And David asigned the sons of Levi according to their turn'.

Further references: 2 Sam. 6:18 Enoch (com.) 21:2; Matt. 21: 41, 24: 7; Acts 25:3; Rom. 14:6; Heb. 9:7; Rev. 10:3; Gdl.Gmq, 123.

5.4.5. እንበለ *ʾənbala*

We have seen its etymology and grammatical function as a conjunctional element in the previous chapter (4.9.7). When we come to its importance and usage as a preposition, we find it being rather multifunctional with various meanings.

5.4.5.1. ('But' and 'instead').[1]

ወአጥባዕነ፡ ለመዊት፡ ከመ፡ ኢንትአመን፡ በርእስነ፡ ዘእንበለ፡ በእግዚአብሔር ። (2 Cor. 1:9).

wa-ʾaṭbāʿna la-mawit kama-ʾi-nətʾaman

<Conj-V:Perf.1c.p> <Prep-V:Inf.Nom> <Conj-PartNeg-V:Subj.1c.p>

ba-rəʾsə-na za-ʾənbala ba-ʾəgziʾabəḥer

<Prep-NCom:unm.s.Nom-Psuff:1c.p> <PRel-Prep> <Prep-NCom:m.s. Nom>

---

1 Dillmann 1865, 773; Kidāna Wald Kəfle 1955, 230; 141.

'We took courage to die so that we should never trust in ourselves, but instead in God'.

5.4.5.2. ('Beyond' and 'despite').

ወዘእንበለ፡ ብዙኅ፡ ባዕድ፡ ዘረከበኒ፡ ኵሎ፡ አሚረ፡ እንዘ፡ እኄሊ፡ ቤተ፡ ክርስቲያናት።[1] (2 Cor. 11:28).

wa-za-'ənbala-bəzuḫ bā'd za-rakaba-nni

<Conj-PRel-Prep-NCom:m.s.Nom> <NCom:m.s.Nom> <PRel-V:Perf.3m.s-PSuff:1c.s>

kwəllo 'amira 'ənza 'əḫelli beta

<PTot.Acc> <Adv> <Conj> <V:Imperf.1c.s> <NCom:unm.s.ConSt>

krəstiyānāt

<NCom:unm. ps.Nom>

'Beyond many strange things happened to me all the time since I think for the churches'.

5.4.5.3. ('Apart from').

አርእየኒኬ፡ ሃይማኖተከ፡ ዘእንበለ፡ ምግባሪከ። (Jas. 2:18).

'ar'əya-nni-ke haymānota-ka za-'ənbala

[1] The pluralization of combined terms has three features. First, only the initial word of the combination gets pluralized while the second word remains singular. Example: አጽድ፡ ወይን *'aṣada wayn* → አእጻዳተ፡ ወይን *'a'ṣādāta wayn*; እመ፡ ገዳም *'oma gadām* → አእዋመ፡ ገዳም *'a'wāma gadām*. Second, the second term will be pluralized while the initial term remains singular. Example: ሊቀ፡ ብርሃን *liqa bərhān* → ሊቀ፡ ብርሃናት *liqa bərhānāt*, ርእሰ፡ መኰንን *rə'sa makwannən* → ርእሰ፡ መኳንንት *rə'sa makwānənt*. Third, both terms can be equally pluralized. Example: ቤተ፡ ጣዖት *beta ṭa'ot* → አብያተ፡ ጣዖታት *'abyāta ṭā'otat;* ቤተ፡ ንጉሥ *beta nəguś* → አብያተ፡ ነገሥት *'abyata nagaśt*. According to this perspective, the way how the reconstructed term ቤተ፡ ክርስቲያን *beta krəstiyān* was pluralized is not to be condemned. Nevertheless, as one of the well-known and widely used terms, it seems incredibly strange since the most practicable plural forms for the combined term ቤተ፡ ክርስቲያን *beta krəstiyān* is either አብያተ፡ ክርስቲያን *'abyāta krəstiyān* or አብያተ፡ ክርስቲያናት *'abyāta krəstiyānāt* Acts 9:1.

<V:Impt.2m.s-PSuff:1c.s-Part> <NCom:m.s.Acc-PSuff:2m.s> <PRel>

məgbāri-ka

<Prep-NCom:unm.s.Nom-PSuff:2m.s>

'Then, show me your faith apart from your deed'.

5.4.5.4. ('Except' and 'excluding').

5.4.5.4.1. ኢታድልዉ፡ ለርእስክሙ፡ ዘእንበለ፡ ለቢጽክሙ። (1 Cor. 10:24).

ʾi-tādləwu la-rəʾsə-kəmu za-ʾənbala

<PartNeg-V:Subj.2m.p> <Prep-NCom:unm.s.Nom-PSuff:2m.p> <Prel-Prep>

la-biṣə-kəmu

<Prep-NCom:m.s.Nom-Psuff:2m.p>

'Do not be partial for yourselves but for your friends'.

5.4.5.4.2. ወእለሰ፡ በልዑ፡ ዕደው፡ የአክሉ፡ አርብዓ፡ ምዕት፡ ብእሲ፡ ዘእንበለ፡ አንስት፡ ወደቅ። (Matt. 15:38).

wa-ʾəlla-ssa balʿu ʿədaw yaʾakkəlu

<Conj-PRel-Part> <V:Perf.3m.p> <NCom:m.p.Nom> <V:Imperf.3m.p>

ʾarbəʿā məʾt bəʾsi za-ʾənbala

<NumCa.Nom> <NumCa.Nom> <NCom:m.s.Nom> <PRel-Prep>

ʾanəst wa-daqq

<NCom:f.p.Nom> <Conj-NCom:unm.p^{s}. Nom>

'And the people who ate were about four thousand men excluding women and children'.

5.4.5.5. ('Including' and 'without skipping').

ኀምሰ፡ ቀሠፉኒ፡ አይሁድ፡ በበአርብዓ፡ ዘእንበለ፡ አሐቲ። (2 Cor. 11:24).

ḫəmsa qaśafu-ni ʾayhud

<NumCa:Acc(Adv)> <V:Perf.3m.p-PSuff:1c.s> <NCom:ms.p.Nom>

babba-'arbə'ā za-'ənbala 'aḥatti

<Prep-Prep-Num.Ca.Nom> <PRel-Prep>
<NumCa.Nom>

'The Jews have beaten me five times, forty times by each without skipping one'

5.4.5.6. ('Without').

አልቦ፡ ባዕድ፡ ሕግ፡ ዘእንበለ፡ አሚን። (Rom. 3:27).

'albo bā'd ḥəgg za-'ənbala 'amin

<CopuNeg> <NCom:unm.s.Nom>
<NCom:unm.s.Nom> <PRel-Prep>
<NCom:unm.s.Nom>

'There would be no Law without faith'.

5.4.5.7. ('Unless').

ኢተቀብዐት፡ በቅብዕ፡ ዘእንበለ፡ በደመ፡ ቅቱላን። (2 Sam. 1:21).

'i-taqb'at ba-qəb' za-'ənbala ba-dama

<PartNeg-V:Perf.3f.s> <Prep-NCom:unm.s.Nom>
<PRel-Prep> <Prep-NCom:unm.s.ConSt>

qətulān

<NCom:m.p.Nom>

'Saul's shield was not anointed with oil unless with the blood of the slains'.

Further references: Ezra 2:64; Matt. 6:18; Prov. (com.) 7:2; Heb. 7:20, 11:40; Rev. 3:7.

※ ※ ※

CHAPTER SIX: INTERROGATIVE PRONOUNS, RELATIVE PRONOUNS AND INTERJECTIONS

This chapter consists of three sub-lexical categories Interrogative Pronouns, Relative Pronouns and Interjections. The elements involved in the chapter divided in three sub-categories are fourteen all in all. According to the *ʾAggabāb* tradition, none of them is originally related with a verb except the interjection *wayle* (see 6.4.1). In a sentence, only three elements of the second sub-category (relative pronoun) are attached to verbs or nouns; the elements of the remaining sub-categories occur alone.

The grammatical importance of the elements of the first sub-category is to be used to ask questions with the meanings 'who', 'what' and 'which'; and of the second sub-category is to be used to give information about the noun in a sentence. The elements of the third sub-category are used to express an emotion such as 'sadness', 'happiness' and so on. Now, we will see them more in detail.

6.1. INTERROGATIVE PRONOUNS: መኑ *MANNU*,[1] ሚ *MI*, ምንት *MƎNT* AND አይ *ʾĀY*[2]

These elements are the most exploitable interrogative elements in Gəʿəz language with the meanings 'who', 'how', 'what', 'why' and 'which'.[3] Nevertheless, each has its own special focus and character.

መኑ *mannu* is employed specifically with regard to human beings for all genders and numbers. Its precise meaning is 'who?' The particles ሂ *hi* and መ *ma* can be suffixed to them. However, their attachment makes no change. The attachment of the relative pronoun እለ *ʾəlla* to መኑ *mannu* at the beginning forms the plural fixed phrase እለ፡ መኑ *ʾəlla-mannu*.[4]

Textual evidence:

6.1.1. (singular) መኑ፡ ይሴብሖ፡ ለልዑል፡ በመቃብር። (Sir. 17:27).

mannu yəsebbəḥ-o la-ləʿul ba-maqābər

<AInt:m^{s}.s.Nom> <V:Imperf.m.s-PSuff:3m.s> <Prep-NCom:m.s.Nom> <Prep-Ncom:unm.s.Nom>

'Who praises to the Most High in the grave?'

6.1.2. (plural) ወመኑ፡ አንትሙ፡ ዕደው፡ እለ፡ ተሐንፅዋ፡ ለዛቲ፡ ሀገር። (Ezr 5:4).

wa-mannu ʾantəmu ʿədaw ʾəlla

<Conj-AInt:m^{s}.p.Nom> <PPer:2m.p.Nom> <NCom:m.p.Nom> <PRel>

taḥannəḍəww-ā la-zātti hagar

<V:2m.p-PSuff:3f.s> <Prep-ProDem.f.s.Nom> <NCom:unm.s.Nom>

'But who are you men who build that land?'

---

[1] Leslau described it as a composition of *man* and *-nu*. It seems to say *-nu* is an interrogative particle; but what about *man*? Its origin or affiliation, again, its meaning is not indicated. Leslau 2006, 348.

[2] This can also be transcribed as ዓይ *ʿay*.

[3] Dillmann 1865, 186, 188, 794; Kidāna Wald Kəfle 1955, 142, 143; Leslau 1989, 28, 37, 38, 145.

[4] Dillmann 1907, 333-5; Leslau 2006, 348.

6.1.3. (*'əlla* + Par) ወእለ፡ መኑ፡ እለ፡ ሰምዑ፡ ወአምረርዎ። (Heb. 3:16).

wa-'əlla mannu 'əlla samʿu wa-'amrarəww-o

<Conj-PRel> <AInt:m^{s}. p.Nom> <PRel> <V:3m.p> <Conj-V:Perf.3m.p-PSuff:3m.s>

'And who are those who heard but not believed in him'.

Further references: Gen. 27:18; Sir. 43:3; Matt. 12:48; Luke 22:27, 64.

The accusative form of መኑ *mannu* is obviously መነ, and this is considered as the standard form even if the replacement of the ending vowel '*u*' into '*a*' is a bit stranger.[1] However, according to the tradition of almost all written texts, the accusative particle ሃ *hā* can be added to መነ *manna* at the end. As a result, a double standard accusative form መነሃ *manna-hā* comes into existence. In supporting this, Leslau stated that it is found rarely in this form.[2]

Textual evidence:

6.1.4. (without outer object-marker).

ለነሰ፡ ኢይከውነነ፡ ንቅትል፡ ወኢመነሂ። (John 18:31).

la-na-ssa 'i-yykawwəna-nna nəqtəl

<Prep-PSuff:1c.p-Part> <PartNeg-V:Imperf.1c.p-PSuff:1c.p> <V:Subj.1c.p>

wa-'i-manna-hi

<Conj-PartNeg-AInt.unm.s.Acc-Conj>

'But for us, it is not permitted to put any one to death'.

6.1.5. (with additional object-marker) መነሃ፡ ፈራህኪ። (Isa. 51:12).

manna-hā farāhki

<AInt.unm.s.Acc-PartAcc> <V:Perf:2f.s>

'Whom have you feared?'

---

[1] The regular replacement of '*u*' in terms of pattern is into '*o*'. Example, ቤቱ *bet-u* → ቤቶ *bet-o*, ሕዝቡ *ḥəzb-u* → ሕዝቦ *ḥəzb-o*. However, this kind of replacement is very rarely or may be accidentally employed.

[2] Leslau 2006, 348.

Further references: Josh. 6:10; Wis (com.) 8:12; Job 26:3; Isa. 37:23; Luke 20:2, 22: 24; John 1:22, 18:4, 7.

Mannu is used to form the usual inquiry for personal names 'what is your/ his/ her ...... name?' with or without the occurrence of copula.

Textual evidence:

6.1.6. መኑ፡ ስምከ። (Gen. 32:27).

mannu sǝmǝ-ka

<PInt:unm.s.nom> <NCom:unm.s.Nom-PSuff:2m.s>

'What is your name?'

The questions concerned with possessions of things and actions can be constructed based on the combination of particles or nouns and *mannu*. In any combination, *mannu* takes regularly the second position.

Textual evidence:

6.1.7. (particle + *mannu*) ለመኑ፡ እንከ፡ ይከውን፡ ዘአስተዳለውከ። (Luke 12:20).

la-mannu ʾǝnka yǝkawwǝn za-ʾastadālawka

<Prep-AInt:unm.Nom> <Adv> <V:Imperf.3m.s> <PRel-V:Perf.2m.s>

'To whom will be then what you have prepared?'

6.1.8. (noun + *mannu*) በመባሕተ፡ መኑ፡ ዘንተ፡ ትገብር። (Matt. 21:23).

ba-mabāḥta mannu tǝgabbǝr zanta

<Prep-NCom:unm.s.ConSt> <AInt:unm.Nom> <V:Imperf.2m.s> <Pro Dem:m.s.Acc>

'By whose authority are you doing this?'

Further references: Gen. 24:23; Heb. 1:5, 3:18.

ሚ *mi* is specifically concerned with the untouchable things such as measurements, amounts and feelings. Its actual meaning or concern is easily known by the character of the word which follows it. For example, if it precedes መጠን *maṭan* or መጠነ *maṭana*, we can simply understand that it concerns about measurement, amount or continuance.[1]

Textual evidence:

6.1.9. ሚ፡ መጠን፡ እማንቱ፡ መዋዕሊሁ፡ ለገብርከ። (Ps118:84).

mi maṭan ʾəmmāntu mawāʿli-hu la-gabrə-ka

<AIntNom> <PPer:3f.p> <NCom:unm.p.NomPSt-PSuff:3m.s> <Prep-NCom:m.s.NomPSt-PSuff:2m.s>

'How many are the days of your servant'.

6.1.10. ሚ፡ መጠነ፡ ንክል፡ አእኰቶቶ። (Sir. 44:28).

mi maṭana nəkl ʾaʾəkʷətot-o

<AInt.Acc> <V:Imperf.1c.p> <V:Inf-PSuff:3m.s>

'How much can we praise him?'

Further references: 1 Kgs 22:15; Job 13:23, 35:5; Ecl 8:26; Matt. 23:36, 26:15; Luke 13:34; Acts 21:20.

But if it is followed by ለ *la* or ላዕለ *lāʿla* taking pronominal suffixes, it is concerned with feelings or situations. In such cases, it keeps a notion of 'how' or 'what'.

Textual evidence:

6.1.11. ሚ፡ ላዕሌከ፡ ወአንተሰ፡ ትልወኒ። (John 21:22).

mi lāʿle-ka wa-ʾanta-ssa təlwa-nni

<AInt> <Prep-PSuff:2m.s> <Conj-PPer:2m.s.Nom-Part> <V:Impt.2m.s-PSuff:1c.s>

'What is up to you? But you follow me!'

Exlusively, ሚ *mi* has neither an accusative form nor goes to be combined with other elements. In fact, it has unique features to occur in the same structure, but for different genders and numbers

---

[1] Dillmann1907, 361; Yətbārak Maršā 2002, 184.

with different range of motives. Let us see the following textual reading as an instance:

6.1.12. ሚ፡ ሊተ፡ ወሚ፡ ለከ፡ ብእሴ፡ እግዚአብሔር። (1 Kgs 17:17).

mi li-ta wa-mi la-ka bəʾəse

<AInt> <Prep-PSuff:1c.s> <Conj-AInt> <Prep-PSuff:2m.s> <NCom:m.s.ConSt>

ʾəgziʾabəḥer

<NCom:m.s.Nom>

'What is up to me, and what is up to you, the man of God?'

In the sentence mentioned above, ሚ *mi* remains the same in both cases of first and second person singulars. Even the meaning basically is similar 'what is up to me?', 'what is up to you?' It occurs the same way in all other cases, only the pronominal suffixes attached to the preposition *la* change their endings to address the right person (ሚ *mi* ... ሎቱ/ ላዕሌሁ *l-ottu/ lāʿle-hu,* ለከ/ላዕሌከ *la-ka/ lāʿle-ka,* ላቲ/ ላዕሌሃ *l-ātti/ lāʿle-hā,* ለኪ/ ላዕሌኪ *lā-ki/ lāʿle-ki,* ሎሙ/ ላዕሌሆሙ *l-omu/ lāʿle-homu,* ለክሙ/ ላዕሌክሙ *la-kəmu/ lāʿle-kəmu,* ሎን/ ላዕሌሆን *l-on/ lāʿle-hon,* ለክን/ ላዕሌክን *la-kən/ lāʿle-kən,* ሊተ/ ላዕሌየ *l-ita/ lāʿle-ya* and ለነ/ ላዕሌነ *la-na/ lāʿle-na*).

Notwithstanding, beyond the meanings and importance that we discussed up to now, the particle is used to express emotions, admirations and appreciations having been combined with adjectival phrases.

Textual evidence:

6.1.13. እግዚኦ፡ ሚ፡ በዝኁ፡ እለ፡ ይሣቅዩኒ። (Ps. 3:1).

ʾəgziʾo mi bazḫu ʾəlla yəśāqqəyu-ni

<PartVoc> <AInt> <V:Perf:3m.p> <PRel> <V:Imperf.3m.p-PSuff:1c.s>

'Lord, how would have increased those who trouble me!'

6.1.14. ሚ፡ አዳም፡ አጥባትኪ፡ እኅትየ፡ መርዓት። (S. of S. 4:10).

mi ʾaddām ʾaṭbātə-ki

<AInt> <NCom:unm.s.Nom> <NCom:unm.p.NomPSt-PSuff:2f.s>

ʾəḫtə-ya marʿāt

<NCom:f.s.Nom.PSt-PSuff:1c.s> <NCom:f.s.Nom>

'How beautiful are your breasts, my sister the bride!'

ምንት *mənt* and አይ *ʾāy* are concerned with human beings, and other creations all, natural and artificial things, events and situations. ምንት *mənt* is used either in its nominative (ምንት *mənt*) or in its accusative form (ምንተ *mənta*) for both genders and numbers like መኑ *mannu* with the meanings 'what?' and 'why?'

Textual evidence:

6.1.15. (m.s.Nom) ምንት፡ ተአምሪሁ፡ ለምጽአትከ። (Matt. 24:3).

mənt taʾammari-hu la-məṣʾatə-ka

<AInt> <NCom:unm.s.Nom-PSuff:3m.s> <Prep-NCom:unm.s.Nom-Psuff:2m.s>

'What is the sign of your coming?'

6.1.16. (f.S.Nom) ወምንት፡ ይእቲ፡ ጥበብ። (Ecl (com.) 5:21).

wa-mənt yəʾəti ṭəbab

<Conj-AInt> <Copu.f.s> <NCom:f^{s}.s.Nom>

'And what is a wisdom?'

6.1.17. (c.sing.) ወጻድቅሰ፡ ምንተ፡ ገብረ። (Ps. 10:4).

wa-ṣādəqə-ssa mənta gabra

<Conj-NCom:m.s.Nom-Part> <AIntAcc> <V:Perf.3m.s>

'But what did a righteous?'

6.1.18. (m.P.Nom) አርእየኒ፡ ምንት፡ እሙንቱ። (Job 13:23).

ʾarʾəya-nni mənt ʾəmmuntu

<V:Impt.2m.s-PSuff:1c.s> <AInt> <Copu:3m.p>

'Show me what they are ...'

6.1.19. (f.p.Nom) ምንት፡ እማንቱ፡ ሕለሚሁ። (Gen. 37:20).

mənt ʾəmmāntu ḥəlami-hu

<AInt> <Copu:3f.p> <NCom:unm.p.NomPSt-PSuff:3m.s>

'What were his dreams?'

Further references: Gen. 29:15, 38:6, 16; Josh. 4:20, 1 Kgs 1:16, 18:9; 2 Kgs 2:29; Neh. 4:2; Job 4:2, 15:12; Ps. 29:9, 138:4; Is 39:3; Hos. 6:4; Mark 10:17, 14:63; Acts 21:33.

When *mənt* functions with the meaning 'why', the following three features are shown clearly.

First, it is followed by a verb that has an initial attachment of the relative pronoun ዘ *za*. Second, particles such as ሀየንተ *həyyanta*, ለ *la*, በ *ba*, በእንተ *ba'ənta*, በይነ *bayna,* and እንበይነ *'ənbayna* are initially added to it. Third, it can take an ending attachment of the interrogative particle ኑ *nu*.

In such cases, the particle can have the following meanings 'why', 'for what reason', 'in what/ which case'.

Textual evidence:

6.1.20. ለምንት፡ ትቴክዚ፡ ነፍስየ፡ ወለምንት፡ ተሐውክኒ። (Ps. 42:5).

la-mənt tətekkəzi nafsə-ya

<Prep-AInt> <V:Imperf.2f.s> <NCom:unm.s.NomPSt-PSuff:1c.s>

wa-la-mənt taḥawwəkə-nni

<Conj-Prep-AInt> <V:Imperf.2f.s>

'Why are you in despair, O my soul, and why do you trouble me?'

6.1.21. ወእመሰ፡ ጼው፡ ለስሐ፡ በምንትኑ፡ ይቄስምዎ። (Matt. 5:13).

wa-'əmma-ssa ṣew lasḥa ba-mənt-nu

<Conj-Conj-Part> <NCom:m^{s}.s.Nom> <V:Perf.3m.s> <Prep-AInt-PartInt>

yəqessəməww-o

<V:Impef.3m.p>

'But if salt has become tasteless, by what do they season it?'

6.1.22. ወበእንተ፡ ምንት፡ ምስለ፡ ርእሰ፡ መዋዕል፡ የሐውር። (Enoch (com.) 12:22).

wa-baʾənta mənt məsla rəʾsa mawāʿl

<Conj-Prep> <AInt> <Prep> <NCom:m.s.ConSt> <NCom:unm.s.Nom>

yaḥawwər

<V:Imperf.3m.s>

'And for what reason does he go together with the old one?'

Further references: Gen. 25:22, 32, 29:25, 26:27; 2 Kgs 4:23; Ps. 51:1; Job 3:11, 12; Hos. 10:13; Acts 1:8 |particle + *mənt* + *nu*/*ni* ወለምንትኑ *wa-la-məntə-nu*, ወለምንትኒ *wa-la-məntə-ni*, ለምንትኬ *la-məntə-ke*, ወእስከ፡ ምንትኑ *wa-ʾəska məntə-nu*: Gen. 34:31; Job 7:19, 20, 8:2; Ps. 41:5; Prov. (com.) 1:23; Lam. 5:20; Matt. 26:8, 10; Luke 12:57, 19:23, 33; John 18:23.

The particles መ *ma*, ኑ *nu*, and ኒ *ni* are the most frequently attested particles that can be attached to the nominative ምንት *mənt* or to the accusative ምንተ *mənta* without an introduction of any grammatical change. To be precise, መ *ma* is most regularly attached to the accusative ምንተ *mənta*, but the other two particles are attached to it in both forms. There is also a trend to use an attachment of double particles ኑ *nu* and መ *ma* in both forms of the element.

Textual evidence:

6.1.23. (Nom. + *nu*) ምንትኑ፡ አነ፡ ከመ፡ ትምጽኢ፡ ኀቤየ። (Luke 1:43).

məntə-nu ʾana kama təmṣəʾi ḫabe-ya

<AInt-PartInt> <PPer:1c.s> <Conj> <V:Subj.2f.s> <Prep-PSuff:1c.s>

'What am I so that you may come to me?'

6.1.24. (acc. + *nu*) ምንተኑ፡ አዐሥዮ፡ ለእግዚአብሔር። (Ps115:3).

mənta-nu ʾaʿaśśəy-o la-ʾəgziʾabəḥer

<AIntAcc-PartInt> <V:Imperf.1c.s-PSuff:3m.s> <Prep-NCom.m.s.Nom>

'What shall I render to the Lord?'

6.1.25. (Nom. + *ni*) **አልብኪ፡ ነውር፡ ወኢምንትኒ፡ ላዕሌኪ።** (S. of S. 4:7).

'albə-ki nawr wa-'i-məntə-ni lāʿle-ki

<PartNeg-Prep-Psuff:2f.s> <NCom:unm.s.Nom> <Conj-PartInt-AintPart > <Prep-PSuff:2f.s>

'You are immaculate, and there is no blemish in you'.

6.1.26. (acc. + *ni*) **ወኢተሠጥዎ፡ እግዚእ፡ ኢየሱስ፡ ወኢምንተኒ።** (Mark 15:5).

wa-'itaśaṭw-o 'əgzi' 'iyyasus

<Conj-PartNeg-V:Perf.3m.s-PSuff:3m.s> <NCom:m.s.Nom> <NPro.m.s.Nom>

wa-'i-mənta-ni

<Conj-PartNeg-AInt.Acc-Part>

'But Jesus did not answer to him, nothing'.

6.1.27. (Nom. + *nu* + *ma*) **ምንትኑመ፡ ጽሑፍ፡ ዘይብል።** (Luke 20:17).

məntə-nu-mma ṣəḥuf za-yəbl

<AInt-PartInt-Part> <NCom:m.s.Nom> <PRel-V:Imperf.3m.s>

'What then is this that written'.

6.1.28. (acc. + *nu* + *ma*/ *mma*) **ወምንተኑመ፡ መጻእክሙ፡ ትርአዩ።** (Matt. 11:9).

wa-mənta-nu-mma maṣā'kəmu tər'ayu

<Conj-AInt-Acc-PartInt-Part> <V:Perf.2m.p-PSuff:2m.p> <V:Subj.2m.p>

'What did you go out to see?'

Further references: Gen. 21:29, 23:15, 26:10; Ps. 8:4; S. of S. 6:1; Dan. 13:57; Luke 7:25-26, 18:36; John 14:22, 15:5, 8:29; Philem. 1:14; Heb. 2:6.

With regard to a number, አይ *'āy* is exactly used to form a question about the manner of somebody or something that has a singular number with the meanings 'what' and 'which'. For two or more numbers, its plural forms አያት *'āyāt* (nominative) and አያተ *'āyāta* (accusative) are used instead.

Textual evidence:

6.1.29. ወአይ፡ ሰብእ፡ ዘይጸድቅ፡ በተግባሩ። (Job 4:17).

wa-ʾāy sabʾ za-yǝṣaddǝq ba-tagbār-u

<Conj-AInt> <NCom:m^s.s.Nom> <PRel-V:Imperf.3m.s> <Prep-NCom: unm.s.Nom-PSuff:3m.s>

'Which man is to be just in his deed?'

6.1.30. ወይቤሎ፡ አያተ። (Matt. 19:18).

wa-yǝbel-o ʾāyāta

<Conj-V:Perf.3m.s-PSuff:3m.s> <AInt.Acc>

'And he said to him, 'which ones?'

Many prepositional elements whose ending vowel is '*a*' such as ሀየንተ *hǝyyanta*, ለ *la*, ላዕለ *lāʿla*, መንገለ *mangala*, በ *ba*, በእንተ *baʾǝnta*, በይነ *bayna*, ታሕተ *tāḥta*, ኀበ *ḫaba*, እም *ʾǝm*, እስከ *ʾǝska*, እንበይነ *ʾǝnbayna*, ውስተ *wǝsta*, and ዲበ *diba* can be attached to *ʾāy* including the remaining elements except ሚ *mi* to make the questions more objective. In the attachment, they always take the second position in their nominative forms.

Textual evidence:

6.1.31. (*ba* + *ʾāy*) ወኢተገብረ፡ ዘከማሁ፡ ወኢበአይ፡ መንግሥት። (1 Kgs 10:20).

wa-ʾi-tagabra za-kamā-hu ba-ʾāy

<Conj-PartNeg-V:Perf.3m.s> <PRel:c-Prep-PSuff:3m.s> <Conj-PartNeg-Prep-AInt>

mangǝśt

<NCom:unm.s.Nom>

'And nothing like it was made during any other kingdom'.

6.1.32. በአይ፡ ሥልጣን፡ ትገብር፡ ዘንተ። (Matt. 21:23).

ba-ʾāy śǝlṭān tǝgabbǝr zanta

<Prep-AInt> <NCom:unm.s.Nom> <V:Imperf.2m.s> <PDem.2m.s.Acc>

'By what authority are you doing this?'

In the accusative sentences, they should keep an accusative form, including the nouns to which they refer.

Textual evidence:

6.1.33. አየኑ፡ ቤተ፡ ተሐንጹ፡ ሊተ። (Acts 7:49).

'āya-nu beta taḥannəṣu li-ta

<AInt-PInt> <NCom:unm.s.Acc> <V:Imperf.2m.p> <Prep-PSuff:1c.s>

'What kind of house will you build for me?'

The interrogative particle ኑ *nu* can join both the nominative *mənt* and the accusative *mənta.* Any verb can appear together; it is optional. Nonetheless, no syntactical change occurs due to the attachment.

Textual evidence:

6.1.34. አይኑ፡ ትእዛዝ፡ የዐቢ፡ በውስተ፡ ኦሪት። (Matt. 22:36).

'āyə-nu tə'əzāz ya'abbi ba-wəsta 'orit

<AInt-PartInt> <NCom:unm.s.Nom> <V:Imperf.3m.s> <Prep-Prep> <NCom:unm.s.Nom>

'Which is the great commandment in the Law?'

6.2. RELATIVE PRONOUNS

6.2.1. እለ *'əlla*, እንተ *'ənta* and ዘ *za*

None of them has an origin related with verbs or nouns. Both are originally independent elements formed to be used as relative pronouns.[1]

They share almost similar functions with similar concepts. This can be pragmatically observed by the following few generalizations and supplementary examples.

---

[1] Dillmann 1865, 774, 1028, 1030; Kidāna Wald Kəfle 1955,135; Leslau 1989, 132, 142, 182.

6.2.1.1.

They play the role of relative pronouns and determinative adjectives referring to nouns. It seems that each is formed originally to be utilized for different gender and number, ዘ *za* for masculine, and እንተ *ʾənta* for feminine singular whereas እለ *ʾəlla* is to be used as the plural form for both ዘ *za* and እንተ *ʾənta*.[1] But in practice, this is not fully preserved as a common rule since we find *za* as used as a determinative or a relative pronoun for both genders and numbers and *ʾənta* as used for both genders in singular numbers.

From the perspective of modern Gəʿəz study, *ʾənta* is used for masculine singular only in poetry since the abundant readings in such cases is found in hymns and in Gəʿəz poetry (*Qəne*). But rarely, we find also the same reading in non-poetry litratures (see 6.2.1.1.4).

With this regard, a number of textual accounts can be presented as evidence. We can see the following readings:

6.2.1.1.1. ዘ ***za*** in the case of masculine singular

ወኵሉ፡ ዘወሀበኒ፡ አቡየ፡ ይመጽእ፡ ኀቤየ። (John 5:37).

wa-kʷəllu za-wahaba-nni ʾabu-ya

<Conj-PTot.Nom> <PRel-V:Perf.3m.s-PSuff.1c.s> <NCom:m.s.Nom-Psuff:1c.s>

yəmaṣṣəʾ ḫabe-ya

<V:Imperf.3m.s> <Prep-PSuff:1c.s>

'All that my father gives me comes to me'.

6.2.1.1.2. ዘ ***za*** - in the case of feminine singular:

ወይእቲ፡ ብእሲት፡ ዘዴወውናሃ፡ ዮም ...። (Gdl.Qaw 1:24).

wa-yəʾəti bəʾəsit za-ḍewawnā-hā yom

<Conj-PPer.f.s.Nom> <NCom:f.s.Nom> <PRel-V:Perf.1c.p-PSuff:3f.s> <Adv>

'And that woman whom we captured today...'

[1] Leslau 1989, 182

6.2.1.1.3. **ዘ *za*** - in the case of masculine plural:

ዘአመከሩኒ፡ አበዊክሙ፡ ፈተኑኒ። (Heb. 3:9).

za-'amakkaru-ni 'abawikə-mu fatanu-ni

<PRel-V:Perf.3m.p-PSuff:1c.s> <NCom:m.p.Nom-PSuff:2m.p> <V:Perf. 3m.p-PSuff:1c.s>

'Your fathers who tried me tested me'.

6.2.1.1.4. **እንተ *'ənta*** in the case of masculine singular:

ተዘከር፡ ሥጋ፡ እንተ፡ ነሣእከ፡ እም፡ ቅድስት፡ ድንግል፡ ከመ፡ ውእቱ፡ ሥጋ፡ ዘቆመ፡ ቅድመ፡ ጲላጦስ። (Anap. Nicean (com) verse 121).

tazakkar śəgā 'ənta naśā'ka 'əm qəddəst

<V:Imp.2m.s> <NCom:ms.s.Acc> <PRel> <V:Perf.2m.s> <Prep> <NCom:f.s.Nom>

dəngəl kama wə'tu śəgā za-qoma-

<NCom:fs.s.Nom> <Conj> <NCom:Ppro.m.s.Nom> <NCom:m.s.Nom>

qədma p̣ilāṭos

<PRel-V:Perf.s> <Prep> <NPro:m.s.Nom>

'Remember the body which you took from the holy Virgin as the one which has been standing before Pilate was that body'.

6.2.1.1.5. **እንተ *'ənta*** in the case of feminine singular:

ወለልሳን፡ እንተ፡ ተዐቢ፡ ነቢበ። (Ps. 11:3).

wa-la-ləssān 'ənta ta'abbi nabiba

<Conj-Prep-NCom:f.s.Nom> <PRel> <V:Imperf.3f.s> <V:Inf.Acc>

'And to the tongue that speaks proudly'.

6.2.1.1.6. **እለ *'əlla*** in the case of masculine plural:

ወቦ፡ እለ፡ ይቤሉ፡ ኄር፡ ውእቱ። (John 7:12).

wa-bo 'əlla yəbelu ḫer wə'ətu

<Conj-ExAff:3ms.ps> <PRel> <V:Perf.3m.p> <NCom:m.s.Nom> <Copu>

'There were some who said: He is a good man'.

6.2.1.1.7. እለ *'əlla* in the case of feminine plural:

ወክልኤ፡ ዕጐላተ፡ እለ፡ ተበከራ፡ ዘእንበለ፡ ዕጐሊሆን። (1 Sam. 6:7).

wa-klə'e 'əgwalāta 'əlla tabakwra za-'ənbala

<Conj-NumCa.Acc> <NCom:f.p.Acc> <PRel> <V:Perf.3f.p> <PRel-Prep>

'əgwali-hon

<NCom:unm.p.Nom-PSuff:3f.p>

'And two young cows that became milk cows apart from their calves'.

Further references: Ps. 71:18 1, 73:19, 78:6; Josh. 5:6; John 4:4; Rom. 9:23; Anap. Nicean (com) verse 144.

Hence, the following relative pronouns and demonstrative adjectives are considered to be their English equivalents: 'who', 'whom', 'which', 'that', 'what', 'whomever', 'whoever' and 'whatever'. In a sentence without a clear subject or an object, they keep the status of a subject or an object; otherwise, they may remain demonstrative adjectives referring to someone or something that makes something or happens.

Textual evidence:

6.2.1.2. Referring to the subject or an object → demonstrative adjective:

6.2.1.2.1. እኩት፡ እግዚአብሔር፡ ዘዘልፈ፡ የዐቅበነ። (2 Cor. 2:14).

'əkkut 'əgzi'abəḥer za-zalfa ya'aqqəba-nna

<NCom:m.s.Nom> <NCom:m.s.Nom> <PRel-Adv> <V:Imperf.3m.s-PSuff:1c.p>

'Blessed is the Lord who protects us always'.

6.2.1.2.2. ኢየሩሳሌም፡ ኢየሩሳሌም፡ እንተ፡ ትቀትሎሙ፡ ለነቢያት። (Matt. 23:37).

'iyyarusālem 'iyyarusālem 'ənta təqattəl-omu

<NPro:pl.s.Nom> <NPro:pl.s.Nom> <PRel> <V:Imperf.3f.s-PSuff:3m.p>

la-nabiyāt

<Prep-NCom:m.p.Nom>

'Jerusalem, Jerusalem who kills the prophets'.

6.2.1.2.3. ወትዌግሮሙ፡ ለሐዋርያት፡ ለ[1] እለ፡ ተፈነዉ፡ ኀቤሃ። (Matt. 23:37).

wa-tәweggәr-omu la-ḥawārәyāt la-'әlla

<Conj-V:Imperf.3f.s-PSuff:3m.p> <Prep-NCom:m^{s}.s.Nom> <Prep-PRel>

tafannawu ḫabe-hā

<V:Perf.3m.p> <Prep-Psuff:3f.s>

'And (she) who stones the Apostles who were sent to her'.

6.2.1.3. Taking the position of a subject or an object → relative pronoun

6.2.1.3.1. ወዘፈጠራሁ፡ ለዓይን፡ ኢይሬእይኑ። (Ps. 93:9).

za-faṭarā-hu la-'āyәn 'i-yyәre'y-nu

<Conj-PRel-Perf.3m.s-PSuff:3m.s> <Prep-NCom:m^{s}.s.Nom> <PartNeg-V:Imperf.3m.s-PartInt>

'He who formed the eye, does he not see?'

6.2.1.3.2. ወኅሪት፡ ይእቲ፡ ለእንተ፡ ወለደታ። (S. of S. 6:9).

wa-ḫәrit yә'әti la-'әnta waladatt-ā

<Conj-NCom:f.s.Nom> <Copu> <Prep-PRel> <V:Perf.3f.s-PSuff:3f.s>

'And she is the elect of the one who bore her'.

---

[1] It seems to be a trival employment since there is already the same element as attached to the noun '*ḫawārәyāt*'. We understand that *'әlla* refers to '*ḫawārәyāt*' only for the reason that the sentence is not interrupted by a conjunction ወ *wa*. If it were disconnected by a conjunction, it would have been rather a relative pronoun. Though, it does not make any sense as far as it is the effect of unnecessary duplication of the same element for a single case. Compare it with the same reading stated at Luke 13:34.

6.2.1.3.3. ወጸውዐ፡ እለ፡ ፈቀደ፡ ወመጽኡ፡ ኀቤሁ። (Mark 3:13).

wa-ṣawwəʿa ʾəlla faqada wa-maṣʾu ḫabe-hu

<Conj-V:Perf.3m.s> <PRel> <V:Perf.3m.s> <Conj-V:Perf.3m.p> <Prep-PSuff:3m.s>

'And he summoned those whom he wanted, and they came to him'.

Further references: Ps. 68:26, 31, 72:27; Prov (com.) 6:18; S. of S. 3:1; Mark 3:34; 2 Cor. 2:6, 15, 4:16, 13:2; Heb. 3:3.

As it can be clearly seen in the given examples, all of the elements can play double roles as demonstrative adjectives and relative pronouns. In the first group of examples, each element functions as an adjective to give some additional information about the subject or the object. In the second group of examples, they take the position of the subject or the object itself since there is no mention of a specific subject or an object in the sentences. So, in such cases, they are obviously playing the role of relative pronouns.

Not apart from this, if we carefully see their position in a sentence, we find a profound difference according to the role they play in a sentence. In the first group of examples when they are used as demonstrative adjectives, they often come after the subject or the object. In fact, there is no restriction on them not to follow subjects or objects. We can also read the same examples in the other way round as እኩት፡ ዘዘልፈ፡ የዐቅበነ፡ እግዚአብሔር *ʾəkkut za-zalfa yaʿaqqəbanna əgziʾabḥer*. But they cannot be used to begin a sentence by taking the initial position of a sentence unless when they are used as relative pronouns (Phil. 3:19).

6.2.1.4.

The following elements can be suffixed to all the elements: ሂ *hi*, ሰ *ssa*, ኒ *ni* and ኬ *ke*. During suffixation with one of the elements, they occur peculiarly without having an attachment of other words; each is pronounced like an individual fixed phrase as ዘሂ *za-hi*, እንተሂ *ʾənta-hi*, እለሂ *ʾəlla-hi*, ዘሰ *za-ssa*, እንተሰ *ʾənta*-ssa, እለሰ *ʾəlla-ssa*, ዘኒ *za-ni*, እንተኒ *ʾənta-ni*, እለኒ *ʾəlla-ni*, ዘኬ *za-ke*, እንተኬ *ʾənta-ke* and እለኬ *ʾəlla-ke*. There is also a possible combination with both ሰ *ssa* and ኬ *ke* together as an individual variant as ዘሰኬ *za-ssa-ke*, እንተሰኬ *ʾənta-ssa-ke* and እለሰኬ *ʾəlla-ssa-ke* (Matt 5:19; 2 Cor. 5:15; 1 Tim. 5:17, 6:2; 2 Tim 2:6; M. Məśṭir 1:48).

6.2.1.5.

In nominal sentences where one of these three elements is combined with the prepositions ለ *la*, በ *ba*, እም *ʾəm*, and ከመ *kama*, the verbs which are preferred to express the concept are mainly ደለወ *dalawa*/ ይደሉ *yədallu* (*la* and *məsla*) ሀሎ/ ሀለወ *hallo*/ *hallawa*/ ይሄሉ *yəhellu* (*ba*), ተረክበ *tarakba*/ ይትረከብ *yətrakkab* (*ʾəm*), ወፅአ *waḍa*/ ይወፅእ *yəwaḍḍʾ* (*ʾəm*), መጽአ *maṣa*/ ይመጽእ *yəmaṣṣʾ* (*ʾəm*) and መሰለ *masala*/ ይመስል *yəmassəl* (*kama*). Let us see some exmaples in the case of *za*.

6.2.1.5.1. **ለ *la***

ዘሎቱ፡ ስብሐት። (Gal. 1:5).

za-l-ottu səbḥat

<PRel-Prep-Psuff:3m.s> <NCom:unm.s.Nom>

'To whom praise is worthy'.

6.2.1.5.2. **ምስለ *məsla***

እስመ፡ ይበዝኁ፡ እም፡ እለ፡ ምስሌየ። (Ps. 54:18).

ʾəsma yəbazzəḫu ʾəm ʾəlla məsle-ya

<Conj> <V:Imperf.3m.p> <PRep> <PRel> <Prep-Psuff:1c.s>

'Because they are many more than those who are with me'.

6.2.1.5.3. **በ *ba***

አቡነ፡ ዘበሰማያት ። (Matt. 6:9).

ʾabu-na za-ba-samāyāt

<NCom:m.s.Nom-Psuff:1c.p> <PRel-Prep-NCom:unm.p.Nom>

'Our Father who is in heavens'.

6.2.1.5.4. **እም *ʾəm***

ብርሃን፡ ዘእም፡ ብርሃን ። (Liturgy (com). sec. 2, verse 32).

bərhān za-ʾəm bərhān

<NCom:unm.s.Nom> <PRel-PRep>
<NCom:unm.s.Nom>

'A light which comes out of a light...'

6.2.1.5.5. **ከመ *kama*:**

አልቦ፡ ዘከማሁ፡ በዲበ፡ ምድር። (Job 1:11).

ʾalbo za-kamā-hu ba-diba mədr

<ExNeg> <PRel-Prep-PSuff:3m.s> <PRep-PRep>
<NCom:unm.s.Nom>

'There is no one who is like him on the earth'.

Further references: Prov. (com.) 3:9; Luke 22: 49; Acts 16:2, 13; Rom. 16:26; Eph. 1:1; Heb. 8:3; Haym. (com.) 5:14; Anap. John (com.) verse 57.

It is the same to *ʾənta* and *ʾəlla*. This is what we can find in any Gəʿəz text. But some other combinations and results occurring rarely might be found indeed. Let us look at the following example.

6.2.1.5.6. ወኢኮነ፡ ሐሰተ፡ ቃልነ፡ ዘኀቤክሙ። (2 Cor. 1:18).

wa-ʾi-kona ḥassata qālə-na

<Con-ExNeg-V:Perf.3m.s> <NCom:unm.s.Acc>
<NCom:ms.s.Nom-PSuff:1c.p>

za-ḫabe-kəmu

<PRel-Prep-PSuff:2m.p>

'And our word that was spoken to you was not wrong'.

The predicative word 'was told' is not stated in the original statement, but it appears in the translation. Without its appearance, the statement would have been too complicated to be translated.

When they are combined with various place prepositions such as ላዕለ *lāʿla*, መንገለ *mangala*, ቅድመ *qədma*, ታሕተ *tāḫta*, ኀበ *ḫaba*, ውስተ *wəsta*, ዲበ *diba* and ድኅረ *dəḫra*, again, in such cases, the verb which is mainly preferred to be added in translation is ሀሎ *hallo*/ ሀለወ *hallawa* or ይሄሉ *yəhellu* (see examples from Num. 24:6; Josh. 11:16; Enoch (com.) 17:32; Matt 5:12; Heb. 5:13 Jas. 5:14 Haym. (com.) 7:17, 29).

The verb which is needed for such cases in the case of nominal sentences is not always *hallo*. Some other verbs which fit the nature and status of the combined word can occur in the place of *hallo*. For example, if we have a reading like ወነጸርኩ፡ ኰሎ፡ ዘበጸፍጸፈ፡ ሰማይ። *wa-naṣṣarku kwəllo za-ba-ṣafṣafa samāy*, it will be definitely better to take the verb ተጽሕፈ *taṣḥəfa* 'be written' or ተነበ *tanabba* 'be read' because ጸፍጸፍ *ṣafṣaf* is an object to write something on. With this respect, the sentence goes to be translated as either 'And I read that could be read from the tablet of the sky' or 'And I saw/ read whatever written on the tablet of the sky' (see Luke 22:37).

6.2.1.6.

A verb to which one of the elements is attached cannot be a final verb in a sentence. Even if no verb is mentioned in a sentence at which the element is used as a relative pronoun, the final verb will be a copula.

Textual evidence:

> ዛ፡ አንቀጽ፡ እንተ፡ እግዚአብሔር። (Ps. 117:20).
>
> *zā 'anqaṣ 'ənta 'əgzi'abəḥer*
>
> <PDem:Nom> <NCom:m.s.Nom> <PRelNPro:m.s.Nom>
>
> 'That is the gate of the Lord'.

6.2.1.7.

They do not follow after one another in a single sentence. Indeed, repetition might occur as ዘዘ *za-za*, እንተ፡ እንተ *'ənta-'ənta* or እለ፡ እለ *'əlla 'əlla* if necessary according to the number of verbs employed in the sentence.[1]

6.2.1.8.

They can take a medial position in a combination. But, the verb to which they are affixed cannot affect the object which is placed before the combination if the initial element of the combination is an AC-

[1] Dillmann 1907, 313; Leslau 2006, 629.

PPIP element. For this reason, the object occurs regularly just after the combination being directly close to the verb.

Example:

አንበሳ፡ ከመ፡ ዘቀተለ

ʾanbasā kama za-qatala

object preposition relative pronoun verb

The rough translation of this section is 'a lion, like someone who killed', and this is obviously incorrect. So, to have the correct statement, the object must follow the verb like ከመ፡ ዘቀተለ፡ አንበሳ *kama za-qatala ʾanbasā* 'like someone who killed a lion'.

Notwithstanding, at least two exceptional features of *ʾənta* can be understood basing its usages in some readings.

6.2.1.8.1. It is used as a time conjunction with the meaning 'when'.

Textual evidence:

ወነፍስ፡ ርኅብት፡ እንተ፡ ጸገበት፡ ተአኵተከ። (M. Ziq II, 3).

wa-nafs rəḫəbt ʾənta ṣagbat taʾakkwəta-kka

<Conj-NCom:fs.s.Nom> <NCom:f.s.Nom> <Conj>
<V:Perf.3f.s> <V:Imperf.3f.s-PSuff:2m.s>

'And a hungry body will praise you when it is satisfied'.

6.2.1.8.2.

It is used to express frequent occurrence with the meanings 'time to time', 'step by step' or 'day by day'. This specifically occurs in a combination with a verb ጸብሐት *ṣabḥat*.

Textual evidence:

ወእንተ፡ ጸብሐት፡ ይዌስክ፡ እግዚአብሔር፡ ዲቤሆሙ፡ ለእለ፡ የሐይዉ።
(Acts 2:47).

wa-ʾənta-ṣabḥat yəwessək ʾəgziʾabəḥer dibe-homu

<Conj-Conj-V:Perf.3f.s> <V:Imperf.3m.s>
<NCom:m.s.Nom> <Prep-Psuff:3m.p>

la-'əlla yaḥayyəwu

<Prep-PRel> <V:Imperf. 3m.p >

'And the Lord was adding to them day by day those who were being saved'.

Further reference: Acts 16:5.

Likewise, ዘ *za* can be used as a conjunction introducing a clause that claims actions or occurrences.

Textual evidence:

6.2.1.8.3. ምንተ፡ ኮንኪ፡ ባሕር፡ ዘጐየይኪ። (Ps. 113:5).

mənta konki bāḥr za-gʷayayki

<Aint:Acc> <V:Perf.2f.s> <NCom:f^{s}.s.Nom> <PRel(conj)-V:Perf.2f.s>

'What happened to you, O, sea that you fled?'

6.2.1.8.4. ወሠናየ፡ ገበርከ፡ ዘመጻእከ። (Acts 10:33).

wa-śannāya gabarka za-maṣā'ka

<Conj-NCom:m.s.Acc> <V:Perf.2m.s> <Prel(Conj)-V:Perf.2m.s>

'And you did good that you came'.

እለ *'əlla* is exclusively used to refer several members of a certain group by mentioning only the name of a single member.

Textual evidence:

6.2.1.8.5. ወእምዝ፡ ኀለፉ፡ እለ፡ ጳውሎስ፡ እምነ፡ ጳፉ። (Acts 13:6).

wa-'əmzə ḫalafu 'əlla p̣āwəlos 'əmənna p̣āfu

<Conj-Prep> <V:Perf.3m.p> <PRel> <NPro:m.s.Nom> <PRep> <NPro: pl.s.Nom>

'And then Paul and his mates moved from Paphos'.

This is not about Paul alone; as far as *'əlla* is attached to Paul, we understand that there are some more people behind him; that is why a plural verb is employed in the sentence. There might be two or more persons; however, the sentence deals with all of them even if the name of an individual person is mentioned alone. According to this theory, if we have a certain group of twelve members, and want to say something about their activity by mentioning a personal name, we do not need to mention each member; but instead, it will be enough to mention just one name combining with *'əlla.* The Amharic እነ *'ənna* also plays the same role in Amharic.

While taking suffixes, the ending vowel '*a*' tends to be replaced by '*i*'. The possessive pronouns ዚአሁ *zi-'ahu* 'his', ዚአከ *zi- 'aka* 'yours'... are also formed the same way.

When they receive suffixes, they can occur either by being combined with other words or alone. In the combination, they always keep the last position even if the combination consists of more than two words.

Examples:

In a simple combination:

6.2.1.8.6. ወልደ፡ እንቲአሃ *walda 'ənti'a-hā* - the son of her/ her own son

6.2.1.8.7. ሕዝበ፡ እሊአሆሙ *ḥəzba 'əlli'a-homu* - the people of them/ their own people

6.2.1.8.8. ቤተ፡ ዚአየ *beta zi'a-ya* - the house of mine/ my own house

In a combination of more than two words:

6.2.1.8.9. መስኮተ፡ ቤተ፡ ዚአየ፡ *maskota beta zi'a-ya* - 'The window of the house of mine/ the window of my house'

6.2.1.8.10. ፍቅረ፡ ልበ፡ ሰብአ፡ ዚአሁ *fəqra ləbba zi'a-hu* - 'The love of the heart of the people of him/ the love of his peoples' heart'.

6.2.1.8.11. ሰላመ፡ ቤተ፡ እንቲአኪ *salāma beta 'ənti'a-ki* - 'The peace of the house of yourself/ the peace of your house'

When they occur alone as combined with suffixes, the final verb will be a copula.

Textual evidence:

6.2.1.8.12. ዚአየ፡ ገለዓድ፡ ወዚአየ፡ ምናሴ። (Ps. 59:7).

ziʾa-ya galaʿād wa-ziʾa-ya mənāse

<PPoss-Psuff:1c.s> <NPro:m.s.Nom> <Conj-PPoss-PSuff:1c.s> <NPro:m .s.Nom>

'Gilead is mine, and Manaseh is also mine'.

6.2.1.8.13. እንቲአነ፡ ሥጋ፡ አኮ፡ እም፡ ሰማያት፡ ዘአውረድከ። (Anap. Nicean (com) verse 120).

ʾəntiʾa-na śəgā ʾakko ʾəm samāyāt

<PPoss-PSuff:1c.p> <NCom:m.s.Nom> <PartNeg> <Prep> <NCom:unm.p.Nom>

za-ʾawrad-ka

<PRel-V:Perf.2m.s>

'It is our body, not that you brought down from the heavens'.

6.2.1.8.14. ዚአከ፡ ሰማያት፡ ወዚአከ፡ ምድር። (Anap. Nicean (com) verse 108).

ziʾa-ka samāyāt wa-ziʾa-ka mədr

<PPoss-Psuff:2m.s> <NCom:m.p.Nom> <Conj-PPoss-Psuff:2m.s> <NCom: m.s.Nom>

'The heavens are yours, and the earth (also) is yours'.

ዘ *za* can be attached to all possessive pronouns at the beginning as ዘዘ *za-za...*, ዘዘዚአሁ *za-za-ziʾa-hu*, ዘዘእንቲአኪ፡ *za-za-ʾəntiʾa-ki*, ዘዘእሊአሃ *za-za-ʾəlliʾa-hā* etc. (Num. 28:3, 9, 19; Prov. (com.) 9:3). The attachment of a single *za* changes neither the positions of the units nor affects their meanings. It is about either connecting them with other words or bolding them. But the engagement of double *za* might introduce additional ideas such as 'each', 'different', 'every' and 'own'.

Textual evidence:

6.2.1.8.15. ወለለ፡ አሐዱ፡ ዘርዐ፡ ዘዘዚአሁ፡ ነፍስቱ። (1 Cor. 15:38).

wa-lalla ʾaḥadu zarʿ za-za-ziʾa-hu

<Conj-Prep> <NumCa:m.s.Nom>
<NCom:unm.s.Nom> <PRel-PRel-PPoss-PSuff:3m.s>

nafsət-u

<NCom:m.s.Nom-PSuff:3m.s>

'And to each seed (there is) its own body'.

6.3. INTERJECTIONS

6.3.1. Exclamations of Joy

6.3.1.1. እንቋዕ *ʾənqʷāʿ*

It has no nominal origin. It is used as an exclamation of joy and appreciation with the meaning 'aha'.[1] The exclamatory elements of sad and sorrow ሰይ *say*, አሌ ***ʾalle***, ወይ *way* and ወይሌ *wayle* are its counterparts. In a sentence, it occurs alone. Though, it can be employed more than once to express the high degree of joyment.

Textual evidence:

6.3.1.1.1 ወይቤሉ፡ እንቋዕ፡ እንቋዕ፡ ርኢናሁ፡ በአዕይንቲነ። (Ps. 34:21).

wa-yəbelu ʾənqʷāʿ ʾənqʷāʿ rəʾinā-hu ba-ʾaʿəyyənti-na

<Conj-V:Perf.3m.p> <Intr> <Intr> <V:Perf.1c.p-PSuff:3m.s> <Prep-NCom:unm.p.Nom-PSuff:1c.p>

'They said, aha, aha, we have seen him with our eyes'.

6.3.2. Exclamations of Pain, Sorrow and Anxiety

6.3.2.1. ሰይ *say*, አህ *ʾah*, አሌ *ʾalle*, ወይ *way*, ወይሌ *wayle* and ዬ *ye*

All are originally the linguistic elements which are not related with verbs or nouns with the exception of *wayle*. *Wayle* has an etymological relation with the verb *waylawa* 'cry', 'mourn'. Leslau claimed it to be a denominative from *way*. Similarly, he affirmed *say* as the origin of *sayl* 'misfortune'. But Dillmann kept both as variants.[2]

---

[1] Dillmann 1865, 772; Kidāna Wald Kəfle 1955,146; Leslau 1989, 141.
[2] Dillmann 1865, 392; Leslau 2006, 521, 522, 623.

Their grammatical function is to be used as exclamations of distress, pain, sorrow, sadness, unhappiness and anxiety.[1]

አህ *'ah* is mostly used in expression of pain and sorrow; its English equivalent is 'Ah!'

ሰይ *say,* አሌ *'alle* and ወይሌ *wayle* are mainly used in expression of anxiety, sorrow and allusion or warning of destructive occurrences that took or may take place at a certain point of time. Each is followed by the preposition *la* with suffixes to identify the person that it refers to. It is as follows:

ሰይ/ አሌ/ ወይ ሎቱ፡ *say/ 'alle/ way l-ottu* (3m.s)
ሰይ/ አሌ/ ወይ ለከ *say/ 'alle/ way la-ka* (2m.s)
ሰይ/ አሌ/ ወይ ላቲ *say/ 'alle/ way l-ātti* (3f.s)
ሰይ/ አሌ/ ወይ ለኪ *say/ 'alle/ way la-ki* (2f.s.)
ሰይ/ አሌ/ ወይ ሎሙ *say/ 'alle/ way l-omu* (3m.p)
ሰይ/ አሌ/ ወይ ለክሙ *say/ 'alle/ way la-kəmu* (3m.p)
ሰይ/ አሌ/ ወይ ሎን *say/ 'alle/ way l-on* (3f.p)
ሰይ/ አሌ/ ወይ ለክን *say/ 'alle/ way la-kən* (2f.p)
ሰይ/ አሌ/ ወይ ሊተ(ልየ) *say/ 'alle/ way l-ita* (1c.s)
ሰይ/ አሌ/ ወይ ለነ*say/ 'alle/ way la-na* (1c.p)

References: Num 28:3, 19; 1 Sam. 4:7; 1 Kgs 4:7; Job 19:5; Gdl.Gmq, 275.

In the case of the third person masculine singular and third person feminine singular, ሎ *l-o* is fairly used in the place of *l-ottu,* and ላ *l-ā* instead of *l-ātti* especially with *'alle* Job 31:3.

In addition to this, the nouns or the relative pronouns that come after the phrases are described will frequently be preceded by *la* in a proper attachment as አሌ፡ ሎቱ፡ ለይሁዳ *'alle l-ottu la-yəhudā*; ወይ፡ ሎሙ፡ ለእለ፡ ክህዱ *way l-omu la-'əlla kəhdu*; አሌ፡ ሊተ፡ ለገብርከ *'alle l-ita la-gabr-əka.* However, no difference appears in the translation; it usually goes to be translated as: 'woe is to/ on/ upon him, woe to you ...'.

---

[1] Dillmann 1865, 392, 718, 928; Kidāna Wald Kəfle 1955,145; Leslau 1989, 76, 132, 166.

Textual evidence:

6.3.2.2. እንዘ፡ ይብል፡ ሰይ፡ ልየ፡ ማኅደርየ፡ ርኁቀ።[1] (Maḫ. ṣəge (com.) verse 181).

ʾənza yəbl say lə-ya māḫədarə-ya

<Conj> <V.Imperf.3m.s> <Intr> <Prep-PSuff:1c.s> <NCom:unm.s.Nom-PSuff:1c.s>

rəḫqa

<V:Perf.3m.s>

'While saying, Woe to me for my dwelling place is far'.

6.3.2.3. አሌ፡ ለክሙ፡ ለዕደው፡ ኃጥአን፡ እለ፡ ኃደግሙ፡ ሕጎ፡ ለልዑል። (Sir. 41:8).

ʾalle la-kəmu la- ʿədaw ḫaṭəʾan

<Intr> <Prep-PSuff:3m.p> <Prep-NCom:m.p.Nom> <NCom:m.p.Nom>

ʾəlla ḫadaggəmu ḥəgg-o la-ləʿul

<PRel> <V:Perf.m.p> <NCom:unm.s-Psuff:3m.s> <Prep-NCom:m.s. Nom>

'Woe to you the sinners who left the commandment of the Most High'.

6.3.2.4. ወይ፡ ሎሙ፡ ለእለ፡ የኃድጉ፡ ፍናወ፡ ርቱዐተ። (Prov. (com.) 2:13).

way l-omu la-ʾəlla yaḫaddəgu fənnāwa rətuʿata

<Intr> <Prep-PSuff:3m.p> <Prep-PRel> <V:Imperf.3m.p> <NCom: unm.p.Acc> <NCom:f.p.Acc>

'Woe is to those who leave the right paths'.

---

[1] Dillmann has provided the interjection in his lexicon in the forms of 'ሰይል *sayl*, ሰይሌ *sayle* and ሰይልየ *saylə-ya* 1865, 392. In the psalterium Davidis of Hiob Ludof, it is ascribed as 'ሴልየ *seləya*' 119, 5.

6.3.2.5. ወልድየ፡ ለመኑ፡ ወይሌ። (Prov. (com.) 23:29).

waldə-ya la-mannu wayle

<NCom:m.s:Nom-PSuff:1c.s> <Prep-AInt> <Intr>

'My son, to whom is deserved woe?'

Further references: Job 19:5; Matt. 23:13-16.

ዬ *ye* is also to be determined the same way; it is however used as an exclamation of lamentation to lament on somebody's death or something's destruction. Leslau described it as an exclamation of admiration and grief or pain. But the *'Aggabāb* tradition recognizes it as an exclamation of pain or sorrow only.[1]

In a sentence, it can be used once or more than once. Most of the writers used to mention it not less than three times even in a very short verse while it is believed that the extent of its frequent usage reflects the degree of the sorrow.

Textual evidence:

6.3.2.6. ዬ፡ ዬ፡ ዬ፡ አማኑኤል፡ አምላክነ። (Anap.Jh.chr (com.) verse 60).

ye ye ye 'amānu'el 'amlākə-na

<Intr> <Int> <Int> <NPro:m.s.Nom>
<NCom:m.s.Nom-PSuff:1c.p>

'Woe, woe, woe, Immanuel our Lord'.

---

[1] Leslau 2006, 625.

CHAPTER SEVEN: PARTICLES

This chapter deals with the linguistic elements comprised in the lexical category of Particles. Twenty-eight individual elements are provided in ten sub-sections. Their grammatical function is to be used as interrogative, affirmative, vocative, negative and accusative particles as well as the particles expressing uncertainty and indicating the genitive relation of nouns. Each particle has no origin related with a verb or a noun. Let us see each in detail.

7.1. INTERROGATIVE PARTICLES

7.1.1. ሁ *hu* and ኑ *nu*

ሁ *hu* and ኑ *nu* are used as interrogative particles to present questions.[1] Tropper claimed *nu* to be mostly used and stronger in expression than *hu*.[2] But *'Aggabāb* considers both equally valuable and attestable. They are attached to verbs, nouns, numerals and other elements. A sentence which involves a combined word with either *hu* or *nu* is quite often considered as an interrogative sentence.

Textual evidence:

7.1.1.1. (Verb + *hu*) ኢ.ተአምንሁ፡ ከመ፡ አነ፡ በአብ። (John 14:10).

'i-ta'ammənə -hu kama 'ana ba-'ab

---

[1] Dillmann 1865, 629; Kidāna-Wald Kəfle 143; Leslau 1989, 1, 119.

[2] Tropper 2002, 153.

<PartNeg-V:Imperf.2m.s-PartInt> <Conj> <PPer:1.c.s> <Prep-NCom: m.s.Nom>

'Do you not believe that I am in the Father?'

7.1.1.2. (Conj. + *hu*) እስመሁ፡ እንጋ፡ ኢያፈቅረከሙ። እንከሰ፡ እግዚአብሔር፡ የአምር፡ ዘንተ። (2 Cor. 11:11).

ʾəsma-hu ʾəngā ʾi-yyāfaqqəra-kkəmu ʾənka-ssa

<Conj-PartInt> <Part> <PartNeg-V:Imperf.1c.s-PSuff:2m.p> <Adv-part>

ʾəgziʾabəḥer yaʾammər zanta

<NCom:m.s.Nom> <V:Imperf.3m.s> <PDem:m.s.Accu>

'Is it perhaps since I do not love you? Then, God knows this'.

7.1.1.3. (Prep.+ Conj + *hu*) ወሐተቱ፡ ለእመሁ፡ ስምዖን፡ ዘተሰምየ፡ ጴጥሮስ፡ በህየ፡ የኀድር። (Acts 10:18).

wa-ḥatatu la-ʾəmma-hu səmʿon za-tasamya

<Conj-V:Perf.3m.p> <Prep-Conj-PartInt> <NPro:m.s.Nom> <PRel:m.s-V:Perf.3m.s>

peṭros ba-həyya yaḫaddər

<NPro:m.s.Nom> <Prep-Adv> <V:Imperf.3m.s>

'And they searched whether Simon who was called Peter was staying there'.

7.1.1.4. (verb + *nu*) ኢይቤኑ፡ ለሊሁ፡ ዳዊት፡ ይቤሎ፡ እግዚእ፡ ለእግዚእየ፡ ንበር፡ በየማንየ። (Acts 2:34).

ʾi-yyəbe-nu lalihu dāwit yəbel-o

<PartNeg-V:Perf.3m.s-PartInt> <PSub:3m.s> <NPro:m.s.Nom> <V:Perf.3m.s-PSuff:3m.s>

ʾəgziʾ la-ʾəgziʾə-ya nəbar ba-yamānə-ya

<NCom.m.s.Nom> <Prep-N:m.sNom> <V:Impt.2m .s> <PrepNCom:unm.s.PSt-NSuff.1c.s>

'Did not David himself say: Lord said to my Lord, sit down at my right?'

7.1.1.5. (Pron. + *nu*) አንተኑ፡ ውእቱ፡ ክርስቶስ፡ ወልዱ፡ ለቡሩክ። (Mark 14:61).

ʾanta-nu wəʾətu krəstos wald-u la-buruk

<PPer:2m.s-PartInt> <copu> <NPro:m.s.Nom> <NCom:m.s.NomPSt> <Prep-NCom:m.s.Nom>

'Are you the Christ, the son of the blessed one?'

7.1.2. (PartNeg. + *nu*) አኮኑ፡ ዐሠርቱ፡ ወክልኤቱ፡ ሰዓቱ፡ ለዕለት። (John 11:9).

ʾakko-nu ʿaśśartu wa-kəlʿettu saʿāt-u la-ʿəlat

<PartNeg-PartInt> <NumCa> <Conj-NumCad> <NCom:unm-PSuff: 3m.s> <Prep-NCom:unm.s.Nom>

'Are not twelve the hours of the day?'

Further references: Job 19:5; 1 Kgs 18:17; Isa. 36:5, 37:23; Jer. 7:17, 19; Ezek. 16:2, 18:25, 24:18; Dan. 6:20; Matt. 25:26; John 7:17, 13:23, 15:12; 1 Chr. 10:2, 11:22.

When the interrogative sentence involves two or more verbs or direct objects, *hu* or *nu* can occur only once having been added to the preceding verb. Otherwise, it can appear repeatedly as many times as the verbs.

Textual evidence:

7.1.1.7. .(single employment) እዛለፍከኑ፡ ወእቁም፡ ቅድመ፡ ገጽከ። (Ps. 49:22)

ʾəzyālaf-ka-nu wa-ʾəqum qədma gaṣṣə-ka

<V:Subj.1c.s-PSuff:2m.s-PartInt> <Conj-V:Subj.1c.s> <Prep> <NCom: unm.s.NomPSt.-PSuff:2m.s>

'Shall I reprove you, and stand before you?'

7.1.1.8. (frequent employment) ታማስኖሙኑ፡ ወኢታሐዩኑ፡ በእንተ፡ ፶፡ ጻድቃን፡ ኵሎ፡ ብሔረ። (Gen. 18:24).

tāmāssəno-mu-nu wa-ʾi-tāḥayyu-nu

<V:2m.s-PSuff:3m.p-PartInt> <Conj-PartNeg-V:Imperf.2m.s-PartInt>

ba-ʾənta-50 ṣādqān kʷəllo bəḥera

<Prep-NumCa> <NCom:unm.p.Nom> <PTot.Acc> <NCom:unm.s.Acc>

'Would you chastise them, and not save all the cities in terms of fifty righteous?'

If an adverbial phrase precedes a verb, the interrogative particles *hu* and *nu* are mostly attached to the adverbial phrases instead of the verbs. However, the syntactical change does not alter the meaning. Let us see the following textual readings in different possibilities.

ጥቀኑ፡ ትቴክዝ፡ አንተ።

ṭəqqa-nu təteklkəz 'anta

<Adv-PartInt> <V:Imperf.2m.s> <PPer:2m.s>

We can have this reading in different syntactical arrangements as follows:

7.1.1.9. ትቴክዝኑ፡ አንተ፡ ጥቀ።

təteklkəzə -nu 'anta ṭəqqa

<V:Imperf.2m.s-PartInt> <PPer:2m.s> <Adv>

7.1.1.10. አንተኑ፡ ትቴክዝ፡ ጥቀ

'anta-nu təteklkəz ṭəqqa

<PPer:2m.s-PartInt> <V:Imperf.2m.s> <Adv>

7.1.1.11. አንተኑ፡ ጥቀ፡ ትቴክዝ።

'anta-nu ṭəqqa təteklkəz

<PPer:2m.s-PartInt> <Adv> <V:Imperf.2m.s>

Nevertheless, each possible interrogative sentence introduces the same question 'Are you going to be extremely sad?' See John 4:4.

The same will happen when a subject precedes a verb.

Textual evidence:

7.1.1.12. ዓውሎኑ፡ ይቀጠቅጠኒ። (see Job 4:12, 9:17).

'awlo-nu yəqaṭaqqəṭa-nni

<NCom:unm.s.Nom-PartInt> <V:Imperf.3m.s-PSuff:1c.s>

'Does a whirlwind strike me?'

Again, we can have this reading with different syntactical arrangement as:

ኢተአምሩኑ፡ አኀዊነ፡ ሕገ፡፡ (Rom. 7:1)

ʾi-taʾammәru-nu ʾaḫawi-na ḥәgga

<NPart-V:Imperf.2m.p-PartInt> <NCom:m.p.Nom-PSuff:1c.p> <NCom :m.p.Acc>

'Do you not know law, brethren?'

In the case of nominal interrogative sentences where *nu* is combined with the non-verbal language elements such as nouns, pronouns, adjectives or other kind of nominal derivation, the verb will be a copula.

Textual evidence:

7.1.1.13. (Part + *nu*) ምንትኑ፡ ዝንቱ፡ ዘእሰምዕ፡፡ (Luke 15:26).

mәntә-nu zәntu za-ʾәsammәʿ

<PartInt-PartInt> <PPer:m.s.Nom> <PRel:m.s-V:Imperf.1c.s>

'What is this I hear?'

7.1.1.14. (Part + *nu*) ምንትኑ፡ ዕፁ፡ በኀበ፡ ረከብኮሙ፡፡ (Dan. 14:29).

mәntә-nu ʿәḍ-u ba-ḫaba rakab-komu

<AInt-PartInt> <NCom:unm.s.Nom-PSuff:3m.s> <Prep-Prep> <V:2m.s-PSuff:3m.p>

'What was the tree under which you met them?'

Further references: Neh. 2:19; Job 6:11, 7:17, 35:2; Ps. 26:1.

Despite this, the particles (ሁ *hu* in particular) are used as external particles attached to other ACPPIP elements, supporting them to occur apart from a direct attachment without introducing a new concept. According to the tradition of the schools, the particles in such cases are called ትራስ *tәrās*[1] for the reason that they are employed

[1] Literal meaning: 'head cushion'.

just to keep the ease of the attachment even if there is no direct contact between the ACPPIP elements and the other component. In modern linguistic thoughts, this is expressed as the reinforcement of a conditional sentence.[1]

Textual evidence:

7.1.1.15. ሶበሁ፡ ሖርከ፡ ፍኖተ፡ እግዚአብሔር፡ እም፡ ነበርከ፡ ለዓለም። (Bar. 3:13).

soba-hu ḥor-ka fənota 'əgzi'abəḥer

<Conj-Part> <V:Perf.2m.s-PSuff:2m.s> <NCom:unm.s.ConSt> <NPCom:m.s.Nom>

'əm nabar-ka la-'ālam

<Conj> <V:Perf.2m.s-PSuff:2m.s> <Adv>

'If you have walked on the way of the Lord, you would have been living forever'.

Further references: Job 16:6; Ps. 43:20; Luke 22:67.

7.2. AFFIRMATIVE PARTICLES

7.2.1. እወ *'əwwa*

It is a particle which is used in expression of affirmation, recognition and agreement with the meaning 'yes'.[2] አልቦ *'albo*, ሐሰ *ḥassa* and ኢኮነ *'i-kona* are its negative counterparts.

As an affirmative reply to the questions that require an affirmation, it can be said alone without being followed by additional phrases which can clearly show how the speaker is kind and polite. Indeed, even in such circumstances, to address the enquiring person by mentioning his personal name or the right proper noun is traditionally believed as the correct way of politeness. But unfortunately, as far as it can be seen from the dialogues mentioned in many texts, this might not be kept frequently.

---

[1] Dillmann 1907, 550; Leslau 2006, 213.
[2] Dillmann 1865, 781; Kidāna Wald Kəfle 1955,207; Leslau 1989, 144.

Its frequent attestation (እወ፡ እወ *ʾəwwa ʾəwwa*) or the engagement of polite phrases such as ኦ *ʾo* and እግዚኦ *ʾəgziʾo* just after mention of the particle is recognized as the highest standard level of recognition or agreement.

Textual evidence:

7.2.1.1. እወ፡ አነ፡ ውእቱ። (1 Kgs 18:8).

ʾəwwa ʾana wəʾətu

<PartAff> <PPer:1c.s> <Copu>

'Yes it is me'.

7.2.1.2. እወ፡ እግዚእ፡ አንተ፡ ተአምር፡ ከመ፡ አነ፡ አፈቅረከ። (John 21:16).

ʾəwwa ʾəgziʾo ʾanta taʾammər kama ʾana

<PartAff> <PartVoc> <PPer:2m.s> <V:Imperf.2m.s> <Conj> <PPer:1c.s>

ʾafaqqəra-kka

<V:Imperf.1c.s-PSuff:2m.s>

'Yes Lord, you know that I love you'.

Further references: Matt. 5:37; Luke 11:51.

7.2.2. ኦሆ *ʾoho*

ኦሆ *ʾoho* is initially a particle which is used as an interjection in expression of agreement and acceptance with the precise meaning 'ok'. Its counterpart is እንብየ *ʾənbəya*.[1]

If we try to deeply trace its genetic relation, we find አሀ *ʾah* which has average graphic and phonetic similarity with it. It is in fact used as an exclamation of pain or sorrow. Human beings articulate such sounds when they are in painful situations or due to bad internal emotions. Thus, hypothetically, it might have been reformed by changing their ending vowels from 'a' and 'ə' into 'o' to express their agreement or acceptance in contrast.

---

[1] Dillmann 1865, 716; Kidāna Wald Kəfle 1955,206; Leslau 1989, 132.

In a sentence, it mostly comes after a command or a question as an affirmative reply. Logically, without a discernible command or inquiry, አሆ *'oho* may not appear whether in a dialogue or in a literary text. In text tradition, it sometimes goes to be employed without a command just to express one's subjection. In such a case, the particle is followed by a noun preceded by the preposition ለ *la*.

Textual evidence:

7.2.2.1. አሆ፡ በልዎ፡ ለእግዚአብሔር፡ ወእንብየ፡ በልዎ፡ ለጋኔን፡፡ (Jas. 2:7).

'oho ballәww-o la-'әgzi'abәḥer wa-'әnbә-ya

<PartVoc> <V:Impt.2m.s-PSuff.:3m.s> <Prep-NCom:m.s.Acc> <Conj-PartVocNeg>

balәww-o la-gānen

<V:Impt.2m.p><Prep-Npro:m.s.Acc>

'You may submit to God and resist the devil'.

Further References: Job 4:17, 19:4; Eph. 4:2.

7.2.3. ጓ *gʷā*

ጓ *gʷa* has no etymological relation with any verb. It is used as an affirmative particle in expression of certainty with the meanings 'even', 'just', 'indeed' and 'at least'.[1] It comes mostly after a verb or a noun as an individual element. All forms of verbs with all possible numbers and genders can follow it as equipped to occur with.

Textual evidence:

7.2.3.1. ከለባትኒ፡ ጓ፡ ይበልዑ፡ እም፡ ፍርፋራት፡ ዘይወድቅ፡ እማዕደ፡ አጋእዝቲሆሙ፡፡ (Matt. 15:27).

kalabāt-ni gʷā yәballә'u 'әm fәrfārāt

<NCom:unm.p.Nom-Part> <Part> <V:Imperf.3m.p> <Prep> <NCom:unm.p.Nom>

za-yәwaddәq 'әm-mā'әdda 'agā'әzti-homu

[1] Leslau 2006, 174.

<PRel-V:Imperf.3m.s> <Prep-NCom:unm.s.Nom>
<NCom: m.p.Nom-PSuff:3m.p>

'Even the dogs eat the crumbs which fall down from the table of their masters'.

7.3. PRESENTATIONAL PARTICLES

7.3.1. ነያ *nayā*, ነዋ *nawā* and ናሁ *nāhu*

These particles are often used to draw attention of the hearers before introducing the main point. The following phrases can express them 'now', 'here is/ are' and 'behold'.[1] On their origin, Leslau indicated that each element is the result of the combination of ነ *na* with suffix pronouns.[2]

By using these particles at the beginning of the speech, a speaker can be able to express his respect for the message that he addresses and for his audiences while these particles are considered as the right elements expressing sincerity and genuineness. None of them is employed in a sentence which publicizes an uncertain or an ambiguous message.

Theoretically, ነያ *nayā* seems to have been originally proposed to refer to a feminine gender while ነዋ *nawā* refers to masculine. Even at present, there are some scholars who still keep this kind of supposition, and mention the following reading as a serious reference: ነዋ፡ ወልድኪ፡ ... ወነያ፡ እምከ። *nawā waldǝ-ki... wa-nayā ʾǝmmǝ-ka* (Woman, behold, your son! ... Behold, your mother!) John 19:26.

Nonetheless, we find the attestations of *nawā* for both genders like *nāhu*.

Textual evidence:

7.3.1.1. (*nawā*, m.s) ነዋ፡ ዘበአማን፡ እስራኤላዊ፡ ዘአልቦ፡ ጽልሑት። (John 1:48).

nawā za-ba-ʾamān ʾǝsrāʾelāwi za-ʾalb

---

[1] Dillmann 1865, 630; Kidāna Wald Kǝfle 1955, 632; Leslau 1989, 127; Yǝtbārak Maršā 2002,193.

[2] Leslau 2006, 380.

<PartPres> <PRel-Prep-Adv> <NCom.m.s.Nom> <PRel-ExNeg-V:Perf.c>

ṣəlḥut

<NCom: unm.s.Nom>

'Behold, an Israelite indeed, in whom there is no deceit'.

7.3.1.2. (*nāhu*, m.s) ናሁ፡ መርዓዊ፡ መጽአ። (Matt. 25:7).

nāhu mar'āwi maṣ'a

<PartPres> <NCom:m.s.Nom> <V:Perf.3m.s>

'Behold, the bridegroom has come'.

7.3.1.3.(*nawā*, f.s) ነዋ፡ ርእዪ፡ ከመ፡ ሐይወ፡ ወልድኪ። (1 Kgs 17:22).

nawā rə'əyi kama ḥaywa waldə-ki

<PartPres> <V:Impt.2f.s> <Conj> <V:Perf.3m.s> <NCom:m.s.Nom-PSuff:2f.s>

'Now, see that your son is alive'.

7.3.1.4. (*nāhu*, f.s) ናሁ፡ ድንግል፡ ትፀንስ፡ ወትወልድ፡ ወልደ። (Isa. 7:14).

nāhu dəngəl təḍannəs wa-təwalləd walda

<PartPres> <NCom:c.s.Nom> <V:Imperf.3f.s> <Conj-V:Imperf.3f.s> <NCom.m.s.Acc>

'Behold a virgin shall conceive and bear a son'.

7.3.1.5. (*nawā*, m.p) ነዋ፡ ሀለዉ፡ ኀቤነ፡ ክልኤቱ፡ መጣብሕ፡ ዝየ። (Luke 22:38).

nawā hallawu ḫabe-na kəl'ettu maṭābəḥ zəya

<PartPres> <V:Perf.3m.p> <Prep-PSuff:1c.p> <NumCa:Nom> <NCom: unm.p.Nom> <Adv>

'Behold, there are two swords here with us'.

7.3.1.6. (*nāhu*, m.p) ናሁ፡ እም፡ ይእዜሰ፡ ያስተበፅዑኒ፡ ኵሉ፡ ትውልድ። (Luke 1:48).

nāhu 'əm yə'əze-ssa yāstabaḍə'u-ni kʷəllu təwlədd

<PartPres> <Prep> <Adv-Part> <V:Imperf:3m.p-PSuff:1c.s> <Ptot.Nom> <NCom:m^{s}.p.Nom>

'From now on, all generations will bless me'.

Further references: Ps. 51:7; Matt. 8:3, 12:28, 17:23, 18:28, 31; John 1:29.

7.4. PARTICLES OF UNCERTAINITY

7.4.1. እንዳዒ *'əndāʿi* and እንጋ *'əngā*

Both are originally particles formulated to be used as an adverb in expression of uncertainty, probability and unfamiliarity with the rough meanings 'maybe', 'perhaps', 'probably' and 'most likely'.[1] On the origin of *'əngā*, Leslau supposed that it is formed out of the combination of *'ən* and *gā*. But he did not explain what these elements are for pattern and what their meaning is.[2]

It is not possible to precisely determine their position in a sentence since they do not keep a consistent engagement in every case. But in fact, in an interrogative sentence, they follow immediately after the interrogative particles.

Textual evidence:

7.4.1.1. እፎኑ፡ እንጋ፡ ናዐብዮ፡ ለዘሩባቤል። (Sir. 49:11).

'əffo-nu 'əngā nāʿabbəy-o la-zarubābel

<AInt-PartInt> <Part> <V:Imperf.1c.p> <Prep-NPro:m.s.Nom>

'How could we extol Zerubbabel?'

7.4.1.2. ቦኑ፡ እንጋ፡ ከመ፡ አብድ፡ ዘገበርኩ። (2 Cor. 1:17).

bo-nu 'əngā kama 'abd za-gabarku

<ExAff-PartInt> <Part> <Prep> <NCom:unm.s.Nom> <PRel-V:Perf.1c.s>

'Is there something that I perphas did like a foolish?'

እንጋ *'əngā* is exceptionally used to give emphasis with the meanings 'then', 'indeed' and 'in fact'.

---

1 Dillmann 1865, 779, 1077; Kidāna Wald Kəfle 1955, 145; Leslau 1989, 143.

2 Leslau 2006, 28.

Textual evidence:

7.4.1.2. እንጋ፡ አግዐዝያንኑ፡ እሙንቱ፡ ውሉዶሙ፡፡ (Matt. 17:26).

ʾəngā ʾagʿazəyānə-nu ʾəmmuntu wəlud-omu

<Part> <NCom:m.p.Nom-PartInt> <PPer:3m.p> <NCom:m.p.Nom-PSuff:3m.p>

'Then, are their children maybe free?'

Further references: Luke 18:8; Heb. 4:4.

7.5. VOCATIVE PARTICLE

7.5.1. ኦ *ʾo*

It is an exclamation of integrity and uprightness which is regularly spoken before calling a personal or a proper name of the addressee. The particle in graphic structure and grammatical aspects has a strong affiliation with the English interjection 'o'.[1]

Among the other Semitic languages of Ethiopia which are believed to be mostly related with the Gəʿəz language, Təgrəññā preserves the interjection with the same structure and use. Its Amharic equivalent ሆይ *hoy* is also supposed to have a connection with it.

The particle does not change its structure due to the number or gender of the succeeding noun or pronoun; it is on a regular basis used as fitting as to all genders and numbers. According to the perspectives of various modern scholars of the language, *ʾo* is either prefixed or suffixed to a noun.[2] It is also customary to get it prefixed to a noun in some texts. But the *ʾAggabāb* tradition does not recommend this at all. I also preferred to keep it alone like its relative element *ʾəgziʾo*.

[1] Dillmann 1865, 144; Kidāna Wald Kəfle 144: 142; Leslau 1989, 132.
[2] Dillmann 1907, 319, 320; Leslau 2006, 1.

Textual evidence:

7.5.1.1. (3m.s) ኦ፡ ዝንቱ፡ ምሥጢር፡ ዘኢይትፌከር። (Anp. Jh.chr (com.) verse 82)

ʾo zəntu məśṭir za-ʾi-yyətfekkar

<PartVoc> <PDem:m.s.Nom> <NCom:unm.s.Nom> <PRel-PartNeg-V:Imperf:3m.s>

'O that mystery which cannot be interpreted'.

7.5.1.2. (2m.s) ኦ፡ አባ፡ ቅዱስ፡ ዕቀቦሙ፡ በስምከ። (John 17:11).

ʾo ʾabbā qəddus ʿəqabb-omu

<PartVoc> <NCom:m.s.Nom> <NCom:m.s.Nom> <V:Impt:2m.s>

basəmə-ka

<Prep-NCom:unm.s.Nom-PSuff:2m.s>

'O Holy Father, you may keep them in your name'.

7.5.1.3. (3f.s) ኦ፡ ዛቲ፡ ዕለት፡ እንተ፡ ባቲ፡ ሙቁሓን፡ ተፈትሑ። (Anp. Ath (com.) verse 67).

ʾo zātti ʿəlat ʾənta b-ātti muquḥān tafatḥu

<PartVoc> <PDem:f.s:Nom> <PRel> <Prep-PSuff:3f.s> <NCom:m.p.Nom> <V:Perf.3m.p>

'O that day by which the prisoners became released'.

7.5.1.4. (2 c.) ኦ፡ ድንግል፡ አምሳል፡ ወትንቢት፡ ዘነቢያት። (Anp. Mary (com.) verse 37).

ʾo dəngəl ʾamsāl wa-tənbit

<PartVoc> <NCom:unm.s.Nom> <NCom:unm.s.Nom> <Conj-NCom:unm.s.Nom>

za-nabiyāt

<PRel-NCom:m.p.Nom>

'O Virgin, (you are) the parable and the prophecy of the prophets'.

7.5.1.5. (3f.p) ኦ፡ ዘአሜሃ፡ ትውልድ፡ ዖራ፡ አዕይንቲሆሙ። (Anap. Nicean (com) verse 80).

'o za-'amehā tǝwlǝdd ʿorā 'aʿyǝnti-homu

<PartVoc> <PRel-Adv> <NCom:unm.p> <V:Perf.3f.p> <NCom.unm .p.Nom-PSuff:3m.p>

'O the generation of that time, their eyes were blind'.

7.5.1.6. (2m.p) ኦ፡ አንትሙ፡ ሕዝበ፡ ክርስቲያን፡ በከመ፡ ተጋባእክሙ፡ በዛቲ፡ ዕለት...። (Anp. Mary (com.) verse 153).

'o 'antǝmu ḥǝzba kǝrstiyān ba-kama tagābā'kǝmu

<PartVoc> <PPer:2m.p> <NCom:unm.p.ConSt> <Prep-Conj> <V:Perf:2m.p>

ba- zātti ʿǝlat

<Prep-PDem:f.s> <NCom:unm.s.Nom>

'O you the Christian (people), as you gathered this day...'

7.5.1.7. (3f.p) ኦ፡ አእዳው፡ እለ፡ ለሐኰሁ፡ ለአዳም፡ ተቀነዋ፡ በቅንዋተ፡ መስቀል። (Anp. śallastu (com.) verse 95).

'o 'aʿǝdāw 'ǝlla laḥakʷā-hu la-'addām

<PartVoc> <NCom:unm.p.Nom> <PRel> <V:Perf.3f.p-PSuff:3m.s>

taqannawā ba-qǝnnǝwāta masqal

<Prep-NPro:m.s.Nom> <V:Perf:3f.p> <Prep-NCom:unm.p.ConSt> <NCom:unm.s.Nom>

'O the hands that fashioned Adam, they were nailed with the nails of the cross'.

Further references: Gen. 3:19; Prov (com.) 1:10; Wis (com) 9:1; Dan. 5:18; Matt. 1:20, 15:28, 25:21, 27:40; Luke 1:3, 10:25, 12:29, 32, 13:12; John 2:4, 8:10, 19:26; Acts 1:1.

The grammatical function of the particle is however not fixed only with kindly and humbly addressing statements for the highly favored or honorable personalities; it also is used to fairly blame or criticize persons or other natures and incidents due to the faults they did or due to their weakness.

Textual evidence:

7.5.1.8. ኦ፡ ሔዋን፡ ምንተኑ፡ ረሰይናኪ፡ ናሁ፡ ይበክያ፡ ኵሎን፡ አዋልድኪ። (Anp. Ath (com.) verse 29).

ʾo ḥewān mənta-nu rassaynā-ki nāhu

<PartVoc> <NPro:f.s:Nom> <AIntAcc> <V:Perf.1c.p-PSuff:2f.s> <PartPres>

yəbakkəyā kʷəllon ʾawālədə-ki

<V:PImperf.3f.p> <PTot:f.p> <NCom:f.p.Nom-PSuff:2f-s>

'O Eve, what wrong did we do against you, now all your daughters lament'.

Again, it is used to rebuke or disgrace persons due to their guilt.

Textual evidence:

7.5.1.9. ኦ፡ አብዳን፡ ሰብአ፡ ገላትያ፡ መኑ፡ አሕመመከሙ፡ ከመ፡ ኢትእመኑ፡ በጽድቅ። (Gal. 3:1).

ʾo ʾabdān sabʾa galātəyā

<PartVoc> <NCom:m.p.Nom> <NCom.c.p.ConSt> <NProp:s.Nom>

mannu ʾaḥmama-kkəmu kama ʾi-təmanu

<AIntc.Nom> <V:Perf.3m.s-PSuff:2m.p> <Conj> <PartNeg-V:Subj.2m.p>

ba-ṣədq

<Prep-NCom:unm.s.Nom>

'O, you foolish Galatians, who has bewitched you not to believe in truth?'

Further references: Matt. 3:7, 8:26, 17:17; Luke 11:40, 12:20.

Apart from this, the particle is used once more as an exclamation of anxiety, regret and sorrow[1] as a variant of **እግዚኦ** *ʾəgziʾo* without being connected with personal or proper names.

---

[1] Ibid.

Textual evidence:

7.5.1.10. ወይቤ፡ ኦ፡ ኦ፡ መኑ፡ የሐዩ፡ አመ፡ ይገብሮ፡ እግዚአብሔር፡ ለዝንቱ። (Num. 24:22).

wa-yəbe 'o 'o mannu yaḥayyu 'ama-

<Conj> <V:Perf.3m.s> <PartVoc> <PartVoc> <AInt.Nom> <V:Imperf.3m.s>

yəgabbər-o 'əgzi'abḥer la-zəntu

<Conj-V:Imperf.3m.s-Psuff:3m.s> <NCom:m.s.Nom> <Prep-PDem.m.s.Nom>

'And he said, O, O, (O Lord) who will be saved when the Lord will do this?'

Further reference: Zech. 2:7.

At the same time, it can be used as an exclamation of admiration and appreciation as a variant of 'how', preceding the adjectival phrases.

Textual evidence:

7.5.1.11. ኦ፡ ዕሙቅ፡ ብዕለ፡ ጥበቡ፡ ለእግዚአብሔር። (Wed. Mar (com.) Thursday).

'o 'əmuq ṭəbab-u la-'əgzi'abḥer

<PartVoc> <NCom:m.s.Nom> <NCom:unm.s.ConSt> <Prep-NCom:unm.s.Nom>

'How great is the richness of God's wisdom!'

7.5.1.12. ኦ፡ ፍቅር፡ ዘመጠነ፡ ዝ፡ አፍቅሮተ፡ ሰብእ። (Anp. Jh.chr (com.) verse 52).

'o fəqr za-maṭana zə 'afqərota

<PartVoc> <NCom:unm.s.Nom> <PRel-Prep> <PDem:m.s.Nom> <V:Inf.ConSt>

sab'

<NCom:unm.p.Nom>

'How great is the love, loving of human beings to such extent!'

7.6. PARTICLE OF SINCERITY AND SUPPLICATION

7.6.1. እግዚኦ *ʾəgziʾo*

According to the perspective of modern linguistic study *ʾəgziʾo* is a vocative form of the noun እግዚእ *ʾəgziʾ* 'master', 'governor' or 'Lord'.[1] The tradition of *ʾAggabāb* accepts its affiliation with the noun *ʾəgziʾ*. However, it considers it as an individual ACPPIP element.

Its function is to be used as an exclamatory phrase of disappointment, atonement, supplication, devotion, surprise and adoration with the meaning 'O' or 'O Lord'.

Its status in a sentence can be specifically decided in terms of the state and the general impression of the sentence.

On its usage, it cannot be attached to other language element, and not restricted to take a position either before or after a verb. It does not change its form due to diverse gender and number aspects.

Textual evidence:

7.6.1.1. (supplication) እግዚኦ፡ አድኅኖ፡ ለንጉሥ። (Ps. 19:10).

ʾəgziʾo ʾadḫənn-o la-nəguś

<PartVoc> <V:Impt.2m.s-PSuff:3m.s> <Prep-NCom:m.s:Nom>

'O Lord, save the king'.

7.6.1.2. (devotion) ተዘከር፡ እግዚኦ፡ ከመ፡ መሬት፡ ንሕነ። (Ps. 102:14).

tazakkar ʾəgziʾo kama maret nəḥna

<V:Impt.2m.s> <PartVoc> <Prep> <NCom:unm.s.Nom> <PPer:1c.p>

'Lord, (please) remember that we are dust'.

7.6.1.3. (veneration) የአክለኒ፡ ዘረከብኩ፡ ሞገሰ፡ በቅድሜከ፡ እግዚኦ። (Gen. 33:15).

yaʾakkəla-nni za-rakab-ku mogasa

[1] Dillmann 1865, 1191; Kidāna Wald Kəfle 1955, 307.

<V:Imperf.3m.s-PSuff:1c.s> <PRel-V:Perf.1c.s-PSuff:1c.s> <NCom:unm.s.Acc>

ba-qədme-ka 'əgzi'o

<Prep-Prep-PSuff:2m.s> <PartVoc>

'It is enough to me that I got favor in your sight, O, Lord'.

Further references: Neh. 5:19; Ps. 20:1, 21:19, 25:8, 101:12; Hos. 9:14; Luke 17:37, 19:18, 20; Heb. 1:8.

The recurrence of the particle expresses the high degree of the surprise or sorrow of the speaker.

Textual evidence:

7.6.1.4. እግዚኦ፡ እግዚኦ፡ አንተ፡ ውእቱ፡ እግዚአብሔር። (2 Sam. 7:28).

'əgzi'o 'əgzi'o 'anta wə'ətu 'əgzi'abəḥer

<PartVoc> <PartVoc> <PPro> <Copu> <NCom:m.s.Nom>

'Lord, Lord, you are God'.

Further references: Job 5:17; Amos 7:5.

7.7. NEGATIVE PARTICLES

7.7.1. አል *'al* and ኢ *'i*

These elements are originally formed to be used as negative particles in expression of negation, prohibition and renunciation with the meanings 'no', 'not', 'nothing' and 'without'. They can be represented by the negation-making elements 'un…', 'dis…' and 'in…'.[1]

አል *'al* is mostly used in Amharic; but in Gəʿəz, it is implemented only to negate ቦ *bo* ('exist', 'be present') (አል *'al* + ቦ *bo* → አልቦ *'albo* which means 'no', 'not', 'nothing, 'let it not be').[2]

[1] Dillmann 1865, 715, 717; Kidāna Wald Kəfle 1955,147; Leslau 1989, 132.
[2] Dillmann 1907, 381; Tropper 2002, 149.

Textual evidence:

7.7.1.1. ወአልቦ፡ እም፡ ውስተ፡ ሕዝብ፡ እለ፡ የአምኑ፡ ቃለ፡ ይባቤ። (Ezr 3:13).

wa-ʾal-bo ʾəm-wəsta ḥəzb

<Conj-PartNeg-ExAff(=ExNeg):m.p> <Prep-Prep> <NCom:unm.p.Nom>

ʾəlla yaʾammənu qāla yəbbābe

<PRel> <V:Imperf.3m.p> <NCom:unm.s.ConSt> <NCom:unm.s.Nom>

'And among the people, nobody knows jubilating'.

7.7.1.2. (renunciation) ወይቤሎ፡ አዴር፡ አልቦ፡ ዳእሙ፡ ፈንዎ፡ ፈንወኒ። (1 King 11:22).

wa-yəbel-o ʾader ʾal-bo

<Conj-V:Perf.3m.s-PSuff:3m.s> <NPro:m.s.Nom> <PartNeg-ExAff (=Ex Neg)>

dāʾmu fannəwo fannəwa-nni

<Conj> <V:Inf.Acc> <V:Impt.2m.s-PSuff:2m.s>

'And Ader said him: no, but you may send me out'.

7.7.1.3. (prohibition) ደቂቅየ፡ አልቦ፡ ዘያስሕትክሙ።[1] (1 Jh 3:7).

daqiqə-ya ʾal-bo za-yāsəḥətə-kəmu

<NCom:m.p-PSuff:1c.s> <PartNeg-ExAff(=ExNeg):m.s> <PRel-Imperf. 3m.s-PSuff: 2m.p>

'My children, no one shall deceive you'.

Further references: Gen. 18:15, 19:19.

---

[1] Here the ending consonant of the verb *ta* is followed by the vowel *ə*. Normally, in the cases of almost all reciprocal verbs, the vowel before the prenominal suffix is *a* (ዘያከብረክሙ *za-yākabbəra-kkəmu*, ዘያነሥአክሙ *za-yānaśśʾa-kkəmu*, ዘያኀድረክሙ *za-yāḫaddəra-kkəmu*). This seems to be one of some exceptional verbs keeping this unique form. The verb in such a form indicates the state of the sentence that it is nominative. If it was an accusative senetence, the vowel would have been *a* (ዘያስሕተክሙ). This occurs in the case of second person masculine and feminine imperfective and jussive in singular and plural.

The most used negation particle is ኢ *ʾi*. In a sentence, it always exceeds the verbs, or nominals that it may negate. It can be attached to all verb forms excluding gerund.[1] Conceptually, its attachment to gerund can also be possible but it is difficult to find evidence. However, the particle can be attached not only to verbs, but rather to all members of all language classes.

Textual evidence:

7.7.1.4. (*ʾi*+ perf.) ዘበጡኒ፡ ወኢሐመምኩ። (Prov. (com.) 23:35).

zabaṭu-ni wa-ʾi-ḥamamku

<V:Perf.2m.p-PSuff:1c.s> <Conj-PartNeg-V:Perf.1c.s>

'They struck me, but I did not become ill'.

7.7.1.5. (*ʾi*+ imperf.) ኢይመውት፡ ዘእንበለ፡ ዘአሐዩ። (Ps. 117:17).

ʾi-yyəmawwət za-ʾənbala-za-ʾaḥayyu

<PartNeg-V:Imperf.3m.s> <Conj-PRel-V:Imperf.1c.s>

'I will not die, but I will live'.

7.7.1.6. (*ʾi* + subj.) ወንጼሊ፡ ኀበ፡ እግዚአብሔር፡ ኢይግበር፡ እኩየ፡ ላዕሌክሙ። (2 Cor13:7).

wa-nəṣelli ḫaba-ʾəgziʾabəḥer ʾi-yyəgbar

<Conj-V:Imperf.2Sc.p> <Prep-NCom:m.s.Nom> <PartNeg-V:Subj.3m.s>

ʾəkkuya lāʿle-kəmu

<NCom:unm.s.Acc> <Prep-PSuff:2m.p>

'And we pray towards the Lord so that he may not do evil on you'.

7.7.1.7. (*ʾi*+ inf.) እስመ፡ ኢተመይጦቶሙ፡ ለአብዳን፡ ትቀትሎሙ። (Prov 1:32).

ʾəsma ʾi-tamayəṭot-omu la-ʾabdān təqattəl-omu

---

[1] "sie kann vor Verben (alle Modi) und (seltener) auch vor Nomina stehen". Tropper 2002, 148.

<Conj> <PartNeg-V:Inf-PSuff:3m.p> <Prep-NCom:m.p:Nom> <V:Impe rf.3f.s>

'For the waywardness of the fools will kill them'.

7.7.1.8. (*'i* + gernd.) አናሕስዮ፡ ኀጢአቶሙ፡ ወኢነጺሮ፡ ጌጋዮሙ። (2 Cor. 5:19).

'anāḫəsyo ḫaṭi'at-omu wa-'i-naṣṣiro

<V:Gern.3m.s> <NCom:unm.s.Acc-PSuff:3m.p> <Conj-PartNeg-V:Gern.3m.s>

gegāy-omu

<NCom:unm.s.Acc:-PSuff:3m.p>

'Forgiving their sin, even not imputing their trespasses'.

7.7.1.9. ዑቅ፡ አልቦ፡ ዘትሔሊ፡ ላዕለ፡ ቍልዔየ፡ ኢዮብ። (Job 1:8).

'uq 'al-bo za-təgabbər lā'la

<V:Impt.2m.s> <PartNeg-(=ExAff)> <PRel-V:Imperf.2m.s> <Prep>

qʷəl'e-ya 'iyyob

<NCom:m.s.Nom-PSuff:1c.s> <NPro.m.s.Nom>

'Take head; do not think anything against my servant Job'.

7.7.1.10. (*'i*+ Part) ወኢትትገኀሥ፡ ኢለየማን፡ ወኢለጸጋም። (Prov. (com) 4:27).

wa-'i-tətgaḫaś 'i-la-yamān

<Conj-PartNeg-V:Imperf.2m.s> <PartNeg-Prep-NCom:unm.s.Nom>

wa-'i-la-ṣagām

<Conj-PartNeg-Prep-NCom:unm.s.Nom>

'Turn neither to the right nor to the left'.

7.7.1.11. (*'i* + nominal derivation) ወኢንክል፡ ተዋሥኦ፡ ኢሠናየ፡ ወኢእኩየ። (Gen. 24:50).

wa-'i-nəkl tawāśə'o 'i-śannāya

<Conj-PartNeg-V:Imperf.1c.p> <V:Inf.Acc> <PartNeg-NCom:unm.s.Acc>

wa-'i-'əkkuya

<Conj-Part-Neg-NCom:unm.s.Acc>

'And we cannot say good or bad'.

7.7.1.12. ወኢአሐዱሂ: እምኔክሙ። (John 16:5).

wa-'i-'aḥadu-hi 'əmənne-kəmu

<Conj-PartNeg-Num-Part> <Prep-PSuff:PSuff:2m.p>

'And no one among you/ none of you'.

Further references: Gen. 18:15, 19:19, 24:50, 32:28; Ezra 10:6; Prov (com.) 3:7, 5:3, 23:10, 24:1; Wis (com.) 1:18, 2:18; Sir. 3:10, 21, 4:1; Hos. 13:4; John 8:39, 44, 14:4, 5, 17, 15:15; 16:7; 1 Pet. 2:5 1; 1 John 2:15.

When it negates the non-verbal language elements, the state of the element either a nominative or an accusative form never affects the invariable structure of the particle to have something new or an extra mode. In all cases, it remains the same.

Textual evidence:

7.7.1.13. ኢውእቱ: አበሰ: ወኢአዝማዲሁ። (John 9:3).

'i-wə'ətu 'abbasa wa-'i-'azmādi-hu

<PartNeg-PPers.m.s.Nom> <V:Perf.3m.s> <Conj-PartNeg-NCom:unm .p-PSuff:3m.s>

'Neither this man nor his parents sinned'.

7.7.1.14. እስመ: ኢየአምርዎ: ለአብ: ወኢኪያየ። (John 16:3).

'əsma 'i-yya'ammərəww-o la-'ab

<Conj> <PartNeg-V:Imperf.3m.p-PSuff:3m.p> <Prep-NPro:m.s.Nom>

wa-'i-kiyāya

<Conj-PartNeg-PObj:1c.s>

'Because they do not know the Father nor me'.

In a negative sentence, *'i* can be employed more than once, even sometimes as much as the verbs or the nouns that keep negative concepts.

Textual evidence:

7.7.1.15. ኢንጉሥ፡ ወኢመኰንን፡ ወኢመስፍን፡ ተናጽሮ፡ ምስሌከ፡ ኢይክል። (Ecl (com.) 8:16).

ʾi-nəguś wa-ʾi-makʷannən wa-ʾi-masfən

<PartNeg-NCom:m.s.Nom> <Conj-PartNeg-NCom:m.s.Nom> <Conj-PartNeg-NCom:m.s.Nom>

tanāṣəro məsle-ka ʾi-yyəkl

<V:Inf.Acc> <Prep-PSuff:2m.s> <PartNeg-V:Imperf.3m.s>

'Neither a king nor a judge nor a governor is able to see you face to face'.

The ACPPIP elements which are attached initially to *ʾi* will keep their own meaning in translation. For example, the attachment of ለ *la*, ኀበ *ḫaba*, እስመ *ʾəsma* and ዘ *za* to the particle can produce constructed negative phrases (e.g.: ለኢአሚን *la-ʾi-ʾamin*, ኀበ፡ ኢያእምሮ *ḫaba-ʾi-yyāʾməro*, እስመ፡ ኢቀተለኒ *ʾəsma-ʾi-qatala-nni*, ከመ፡ ኢይኩን *ka-ma-ʾi-yyəkun*, ዘኢቆመ *za-ʾi-qoma*). Nonetheless, the affixed elements do not lose their own common concepts due to the attachment. Uniquely, በ *ba* is treated in two ways. In some cases, it keeps its own notion 'in' or 'by', and in some other cases, it loses its initial meaning and keeps the function of እንበለ *ʾənbala* 'without'.

Textual evidence:

7.7.1.16. ትስሕቱ፡ በኢያእምሮ፡ መጻሕፍት። (Matt. 22:29).

təsəḫətu ba-ʾi-yyāʾməro maṣāḥəft

<V:Imperf.2m.p> <Prep-PartNeg-V:Inf.Nom.ConSt> <NCom:unm.p. Nom>

'You are mistaken by not knowing the scriptures'.

አልቦ *ʾalbo* can receive pronominal suffixes and keep the concept of 'not to have'.

Textual evidence:

7.7.1.17. ወወልደ፡ እጓለ፡ እመ፡ ሕያው፡ አልቦቱ፡ ኀበ፡ ያሰምክ፡ ርእሶ። (Matt. 8:20).

wa-la-walda ʾəgʷāla ʾəmma

<Conj-NCom:m.s.ConSt> <NCom:unm.p.ConSt> <NCom:f.s.ConSt>

ḥəyāwə-ssa 'albo-ttu ḫaba yāsammək

<NCom:m.s.Nom-Part> <PartNeg-PSuff:3m.s> <Conj> <V:Imperf.3m.s>

rə's-o

<NCom:unm.s.Acc>

'But the son of man has nowhere to lay himself'.

7.7.1.18. አልብየ፡ ምት። (John 4:17).

'albə-ya mət

<PartNeg-PSuff:1c.s> <NCom:m.s.Nom>

'I have no husband'.

7.7.2. አኮ *'akko* 'not' and እንብ *'ənb* 'no'

አኮ *'akko* is the negation of the copula ውእቱ w*ə'ətu* or ይእቲ *yə'əti* . እንብ *'ənb* is also the negative counter part of the affirmative vocative *'oḫo*. *'Akko* serves to negate nouns of all genders and numbers. It occurs alone before the noun to negate.

Textual evidence:

7.7.2.1. (*'akko* - singular) አኮ፡ ስምዐ፡ ሰብእ፡ ዘእፈቅድ። (John 5:34).

'akko səm'a sabə' za-'əfaqqəd

<PartNeg> <NCom:unm.s.m.ConSt> <NCom:unm.p.Nom> <PRel-V-Imperf.1c.s>

'I am not the one who wants the testimony of people'.

7.7.2.2. (*'akko* - plural) አኮ፡ ኵልክሙ፡ ንጹሓን። (John 13:11).

'akko kʷəllə-kəmu nəṣuḥan

<PartNeg> <PTot:PSuff:2m.p> <NCom:m.p.Nom>

'You are all not clean'.

'Ənb receives always pronominal suffixes. See the textual evidence 7.2.2.1.

7.8. ACCUSATIVE PARTICLE

7.8.1. ሃ *hā*

As a particle, it is used as an object marker.[1] ለ *la.* also serves as an object marker in different form. However, the following two factors make them different from one another.

First, *hā* is attached particularly to personal names[2] while *la* is combined with all types of nouns and numerals.[3] Second, *la* keeps the initial position in the attachment while *hā* is commonly suffixed. Furthermore, *hā* is mostly treated along with a verb without a suffix.

Textual evidence:

7.8.1.1. ወወሀበቶ፡ ባላሃ፡ ትኩኖ፡ ብእሲተ። (Gen. 30:4).

wa-wahabatt-o bālā-hā təkunn-o bəʾəsita

<Conj-V:3f.s> <NPro.f.s-Part> <V:Subj.3f.s> <NCom.f.s.Acc>

'Then, she gave him Bilhah so that she shall be to him a wife'.

7.8.1.2. ወነሥአ፡ ዮሴፍ፡ ክልኤ፡ ደቂቆ፡ ምናሴሃ፡ ወኤፍሬምሃ። (Gen. 48:1).

wa-naś'a yosef kəlʾetta daqiq-o

<Conj-V:Perf.3m.s> <NPro.m.s.Nom> <NumCa.Acc> <NCom:m.p-PSuff:3m.s>

mənāse-hā wa-ʾefrem-hā

<NPro.m.s-Part> <Conj-NPro.m.s-Part>

'And Joseph took his two sons Manasseh and Ephraim with him'.

---

1 Kidāna Wald 1955,364; Leslau 1989, 1.

2 Leslau 2006, 213.

3 Theoretically, the constructed personal names such as ተክለሃይማኖት *takla hāymānot*, ገብረመንፈስቅዱስ *gabra manfas qəddus*, ዜናማርቆስ *zenā mārqos* do not need the attachment of *hā* to stand in an accusative state. In the case of a verb with a pronominal suffix (ቀደሶ *qaddas-o*, ባረኮ *bārak-o*, ቀጥቀጦ *qaṭqaṭ-o*), ለ *la* shall be added to them initially. But, in the case of the verb without a suffix, they can be employed as objects without an object marker.

7.9. PARTICLES INDICATING GENITIVE RELATION

7.9.1. ለ *la* as, እለ *'əlla*, እንተ *'ənta* and ዘ *za*

These particles are used to express a genitive case relationship by indicating references.[1] When they serve as relative pronouns, they keep either direct or indirect attachments to verbs, but in this feature, their attachment is devoted to non-verbal elements. With this regard, the elements keep different designations that indicate how the relation is expressed. See the following examples. For their ratification, some additional readings are presented as evidence at the end of this section.

7.9.1.1. ዘርፍ፡ አያያዥ *zarf-'ayyāyyāž* (lit.: 'connector of a fringe').

Examples (noun - part.+ noun):

7.9.1.1.1. ታቦቱ፡ ለእግዚአብሔር።

tābot-u la-'əgzi'abəḥer

<NCom:unm.s.Nom-PSuff:3m.s> <Prep-NCom: m.s. Nom>

This means: ታቦተ፡ እግዚአብሔር - 'the temple of the Lord'.

7.9.1.1.2. አምላክ፡ ዘሰማይ።

'amlāk za-samāy

<NCom:m.s.Nom> <PRel(g)[2]-NCom:unm.s.Nom>

This means: አምላክ፡ ሰማይ - 'The God of heaven'.

Further references: Prov (com.) 1:24; Heb. 9:10; Gdl.Qaw 2:26.

7.9.1.1.3. አንቀጽ፡ እንተ፡ እግዚአብሔር።

'anqaṣ 'ənta 'əgzi'abḥer

<NCom:m.s.Nom> <PRel (g)> <NCom:m.s.Nom>

This means: አንቀጸ፡ እግዚአብሔር - 'The gate of the Lord'.

Further reference: Ps. 117: 20.

---

[1] Dillmann 1865, 774, 1028, 1030; Kidāna Wald Kəfle 1955,135; Leslau 1989, 37.
[2] Expressing a genitive relationship.

7.9.1.1.4. ደቂቅ፡ እለ፡ እስራኤል።

deqiq ʾəlla ʾəsrāʾel

<NCom:m.s.Nom> <PRel(g)> <NPro:m.s.Nom>

This means ደቂቀ፡ እስራኤል - 'The sons of Israel'.

7.9.1.2. **ዘርፍ ደፊ *zarf-dafi*** (lit.: 'altering a subsequent from back to front').

In this case, the noun to which the elements are attached precedes the other component.

Examples (Prep.+ noun - noun):

7.9.1.2.1. ለእግዚአብሔር፡ ምሕሮቶ።

la-ʾəgziʾabəḥer məḥrot-o

<Prep-NCom:m.s.Nom> <NCom:unm.s.Acc-PSuff:3m.s>

This means: ምሕሮተ፡ እግዚአብሔር - 'Lovingkindness of the Lord'.

7.9.1.2.2. ዘጳውሎስ፡ ሰይፈ።

za-p̣āwlos sayfa

<Part-NPro:m.s.Nom> <NCom:unm.s.Acc>

This means: ሰይፈ፡ ጳውሎስ - 'The sword of Paul'.

7.9.1.2.3. እንተ፡ ኤልያስ፡ ደመና።

ʾənta ʾeləyās dammanā

<Part> <NPro:m.s.Nom> <NCom:unm.s.Nom>

This means: ደመና፡ ኤልያስ - 'The cloud of Elijah'.

7.9.1.2.4. እለ፡ ቤል፡ ነቢያተ።

ʾəlla bel nabiyāta

<PRel(g)> <NPro:m.s.Nom> <NCom:unm.s.Acc>

This means: ነቢያተ፡ ቤል - 'The prophets of Beal'.

Further references: Ps. 76:11, 107:15, 117: 20; Gdl.Gmq p. 160.

7.9.1.3. ዘርፍ ጠምዛዥ *zarf-ṭamzāž* (lit.: 'the one that bends a fringe').
This involves only *za* and *'əlla.*
Examples (noun + prep.- noun):

7.9.1.3.1. ቃለ፡ ዘሰሎሞን፡ መጽሐፍ።

qāla za-salomon maṣḥaf

<NCom:m.s.ConSt> <PRel (g)-NPro:m.s.Nom> <NCom:m.s.Nom>

This means: ቃለ፡ መጽሐፈ፡ ሰሎሞን - 'The word of the book of Solomon'.

7.9.1.3.2. ሰይፈ፡ እለ፡ ሮምያ፡ ሰብእ።v

sayfa 'əlla romǝyā sab'

<NCom:unm.s.ConSt><PRel(g)> <NPro:m.s.Nom> <NCom:m.s.Nom>

This means: ሰይፈ፡ ሰብአ፡ ሮምያ - 'The sword of the people of Rome'.

Further references: Num. 23:10; Josh. 5:6; Prov (com.) 4:23; 2 Sam. 9:7; Ps. 102:17; Isa 52:7, 53:1; Matt. 20:25; John 12:38, 18:33; Acts 11:16; Rom. 10:15, 10:16; 2 Cor. 1:3, 3:7.

7.10. OTHER PARTICLES

7.10.1. መ *ma*, ሰ *sa*, ሶ *so*, አ-ኣ *'a - 'ā* and ኬ *ke*

These particles are used to give emphasis through the word to which they are attached in expression of sincerity, pledge, undertaking and promise.[1] With regard to a position that they most probably keep in a sentence, we can rearrange them in two sub-divisions.

The first sub-division encloses the particle which can be attached directly only to the verbs while the second one involves the particles that are attached to both the verbal and the non-verbal linguistic elements.

---

1 Dillmann 1865, 141, 321, 714, 811; Kidāna Wald Kəfle 1955,143, 147, 517; Tropper, 2002, 152; Leslau 1989, 26, 64, 132, 148; 2006, 323.

The only particle which goes to the first sub-category is ሶ *so.* It is directly attached to the imperative verbs at the end (e.g.: ግበርሶ *gəbar-so,* ሐውጽሶ *ḥawwəṣ-so,* ተመየጥሶ *tamayaṭ-so*).

The remaining particles namely መ *ma,* ሰ *sa,* አ/ ኣ *'a/ 'ā* and ኬ *ke* are included in the second sub-category. This means they can be combined with any language element of all word classes. In the combination, each particle takes the ending position.

Regarding with their meanings, each may have its own special expression. However, in most cases, the concepts of the auxiliaries 'may', 'must' and 'shall'; and of the adverbs 'just', 'exactly', 'precisely' are sounded as a result of the combination at which they individually or two of them are engaged together.

Textual evidence:

7.10.1.1.(Subj. verb + *ma/ mma*) ወከመ፡ ኢንበልመ፡ ነኪርኑ፡ ትስብእቱ ...። (M. Məsṭir 14:13).[1]

wa-kama 'i-nəbalə-mma nakirə-nu təsbə't-u

<Conj-Conj> <PartNeg-V:Subj.1c.p-Part> <NCom:m.s.Nom-PartInt> <NCom:unm.s.NomPSt-PSuff:3m.s>

'Again, so that we should not say, is his incarnation unique...?'

7.10.1.2. (non-verb. + *ma/mma*) እፎኑመ፡ ትክሉ።

'əffo-nu-mma t əklu

'How could you?'

---

[1] According to the known practice in the tradition of *Qəne* schools, መ *ma* is attached to the nouns, numerals and particles (e.g: አሐዱመ *'aḥadu-mma,* መኑመ *manu-mma,* ምንተመ *mənta-mma,* ምንተኑመ *mənta-nu-mma* see 7.10.1.2), and indeed to the different forms of verbs, when the question marker ኑ *nu* interferes between the verb and the particle (e.g.: አብደኑመ *'abda-nu-mma,* ሐመኑመ *ḥamma-nu-mma,* ገደፎኑመ *gadaf-o-nu-mma*). However, a direct attachment of *ma/ mma* to a verb occurs very rarely. This is perhaps one of the few attestations that can be found in literary sources.

7.10.1.3. (verb + *ke*) ዑቅኬ፡ ለቍልዔየ፡ ኢዮብ። (Job2:3).

ʿuqə-ke la-qʷəlʿe-ya ʾiyyob

<V:Impt.2m.s-Part> <Prep-NCom:m.s-PSuff:1c.s> <NPro:m.s.Nom>

'Take care of my servant Job'.

7.10.1.4. (nom + *ke*) ወራሲሁኬ፡ ለእግዚአብሔር፡ አንተ። (Gal. 4:7).

warāsi-hu-ke la-ʾəgziʾabəḥer ʾanta

<NCom:m.s.NomPSt-PSuff:3m.s-Part> <Prep-NCom:m.s.Nom> <PPer: 2m.s>

'And you are just the heir of God'.

7.10.1.5. (nom + *a*) ጻድቅአ፡ በአሚን፡ የሐዩ። (Rom. 1:17).

ṣādəq-ʾa ba-ʾamin yaḥayyu

<NCom:m.s.Nom-PartQuet> <Prep-NCom:unm.s.Nom> <V:Imperf.3m .s>

'Behold the righteous shall live by faith'.

7.10.1.6. (Part + *ke*) ወእፎኬ፡ ንሰርቅ፡ እም፡ ቤትከ፡ ወርቀ፡ አው፡ ብሩረ። (Gen. 44:8).

wa-ʾəffo-ke nəsarrəq ʾəm betə-ka

<Conj-AInt-Part> <V:Imperf.1c.p> <Prep> <NCom:unm.s.Nom>

warqa ʾaw bərura

<NCom:unm.s.Acc> <Conj> <NCom:unm.s.Acc>

'How do we steal gold or silver from your house?'

Further references: Gen. 44:8; 2 Kin 1:3; Ezr 9:11; Job 1:12; Prov (com.) 1:31; Isa. 7:14; Matt. 26:5; Acts 23:27; Rom. 11:5; Gal. 4:7.

ሶ *so* and አ/ ኣ *ʾa/ ʾā* are equally used to state a message being attached to the imperative verbs. Example: ተመየጥሶ *tamayaṭ-so*, አድኅንሶ *ʾadḫən-so*. When the message is given by a superior one and addresses his inferior, they will be translated keeping the same meaning mentioned above ('may'/ 'just').

But if the communication is in the vice versa, they should be translated as 'please' since the person that speaks should use them only to express his sincerity and humbleness.

Examples:

7.10.1.7. ኦ፡ እግዚኦ፡ አድኅንሶ። (Ps. 117:24).

ʾo ʾəgziʾo ʾadḫən-so

<PartVoc> <PartVoc> <V:Impt.2m.s-Part>

'O Lord, please save (us)'.

7.10.1.8. መንግሥተ፡ ምድርአ፡ ሀበኒአ፡ እግዚአብሔርአ፡ እግዚአ፡ ሰማይአ። (Ezr 1:2).

mangəśta mədr-ʾa haba-nni-ʾa

<NCom:unm.s.ConSt> <NCom:unm.s.Nom-PartQuet> <V:Impt.2m.s-PartQuet>

ʾəgziʾabḥer-ʾa ʾəgziʾa samāy-ʾa

<NCom:m.s.Nom-PartQuet> <NCom:m.s.ConSt> <NCom: unm.s.Nom-PartQuet>

'God the Lord of the heaven gave me kingdom of the world'.

Further references: Gen. 38:25; Ezr 1:4, 4:13, 7:18; Ps. 79:14; Gdl. Gmq, 130.

Beyond this, ሰ *sa* and ኬ *ke* have distinctively some additional functions that cannot be shared by the remaining elements. ሰ *sa* can function as a conjunction being combined with all parts of speech with the meanings 'but', 'however', 'nevertheless' and 'nonetheless'. Similarly, ኬ *ke* functions as an adverb with the meaning 'then'. It is also used to call attention of the hearer. In such cases, it may sound like 'Behold'.

Textual evidence:

7.10.1.9. (Part. + *ssa*) ወዘሰ፡ አዝለፈ፡ ትዕግሥቶ፡ ውእቱ፡ ይድኅን። (Matt. 24:13).

wa-za-ssa ʾazlafa təʿgəśt-o wəʾətu

<Conj-PRel-Part> <V:Perf.3m.s> <NCom:unm.s.Acc>
<PPer:3m.s.Nom>

yədəḫən

<V:Imperf.3m.s>

'But the one who ever keeps patience, he will be saved'.

7.10.1.10. (noun + *ssa*) ወኀሬሰ፡ አድምዐ፡ ወእለሰ፡ ተርፉ፡ ዖሩ። (Rom. 11:7).

wa-ḫəre-ssa ʾadməʿawa-ʾəlla-ssa tarfu

<Conj-NPro:m.s.Nom-Part> <V:Perf.3m.s>
<Conj-PRel-Part> <V:Perf.3m.p>

ʿoru

<V:Perf.3m.p>

'However, Israel has obtained but the rest were blinded'.

7.10.1.11. (pron. + *ssa*) አንትሙሰ፡ ኩኑ፡ ፍጹማነ። (Matt. 5:48).

ʾantəmu-ssa kunu fəṣṣumāna

<V:Impt.2m.p-Part> <PPer:Nom-Part>
<NCom:m.p.Acc>

'But you, be perfect'.

7.10.1.12. (verb + *ssa*) ዘሞተሰ፡ አዕረፈ፡ ወባሕቱ፡ ግበር፡ ሎቱ፡ ተዝካሮ። (Sir. 37:23).

za-mota-ssa ʾaʿrafa wa-bāḥəttu gəbar l-ottu

<PRel-V:3m.s-Part> <V:Perf.3m.s> <Conj-Adv>
<V:Impt.2m.s> <Prep-PSuff:3m.s>

tazkār-o

<NCom:unm.s.Acc>

'But the one who died got rest. However, you shall make to him his remembrance'.

7.10.1.13. (part. + *ke*) ወእመሰኬ፡ ወልድ፡ አንተ፡ ወራሲሁኬ፡ ለእግዚአብሔር፡ አንተ። (Gal.4:7).

wa-ʾəmma-ssa-ke wald ʾanta warāsi-hu-ke

<Conj-Conj-Part-Part> <NCom:m.s.Nom> <PPer:2m.s> <NCom:m.s.NomPSt-PSuff:3m.s>

la-'əgzi'abəḥer 'anta

<Prep-NCom:m.s.Nom> <PPer:2m.s>

'If you are a son, then you are the hire of God'.

7.10.1.14. (verb + *ke*) አእመረኬ፡ ፈጣሪ፡ ከመ፡ ኢይትቄደስ፡ ሰብእ፡ በቍርባነ፡ ሥጋሁ፡ ለሰብእ። (M. Məsṭir 1:48).

'a'mara-ke faṭāri kama 'i-yyətqeddas

<V:Perf.3m.s-Part> <NCom:m.s.Nom> <Conj> <PartNeg-V:Imperf.3m.s>

sab' ba-qʷərbāna śəgā-hu

<NCom:m^{s}.s.Nom> <Prep-NCom:unm.s.NomPSt> <NCom:unm. s.NomPSt-PSuff:3m.s>

la-sab'

<Prep-NCom:unm.s.Nom>

'Behold, the Lord has known that man would never be sanctified by the sacrifice of human flesh'.

Further references: Gen. 34:31; 1 Kgs 5:1, 7:39, 12:7; 1 Kgs 1:1, 15, 7:39, 11:25; Ps. 48: 12; Prov. (com.) 17:21; Sir. 18:13; John 16:31, 21:29; Acts 16:1, Rom. 11:6; Rev. 6:6; M. Məsṭir 1:48.

At the combination of two or more different language elements, ሰ *sa* and ኬ *ke* can change their position due to the nature of the initial element. If the element that leads the combination is an ACPPIP element, they will be often combined with the elements themselves by splitting up the combination while the possibility to be combined at the end of the combination is still preserved. But in all other cases, the particles (*ma* and *sa*) keep the ending position.

Textual evidence:

7.10.1.15. (part. + *ssa* - verb) ወዘሰ፡ ነበበ፡[1] ጽርፈተ፡ ላዕለ፡ መንፈስ፡ ቅዱስ...። (Luke 12:10).

wa-za-ssa nababa ṣərfata lāʿla manfas

<Conj-PRel-Part> <V:Perf.3m.s> <NCom:unm.s.Acc> <Prep> <NCom:m.s.Nom>

qəddus

<NCom:m.s.Nom>

'But whoever blasphemes against the Holy Spirit ....'

7.10.1.16. (noun + noun + *ssa*) ወሰብእ፡ ሀገሩሰ፡ ይጸልዕዎ። (Luke 19:14).

wa-sab'a hagar-u-ssa yəṣallʿə-wwo

<Conj-NCom:m[s].p.ConSt> <NCom:unm.s.Nom-PSuff:3m.s-Part> <V: Imperf:3m.p>

'But his citizens hate him'.

7.10.1.17. ወበእንተ፡ ዝንቱኬ፡ በዘከመዝ፡ እትሜካሕ። (2 Cor. 12:5).

wa-ba'ənta zəntu-ke ba-za-kama zə 'ətmekkāḥ

<Conj-Prep> <PDem-Part> <Prep-PRel-Prep> <PDem> <V:Imperf.1c.s>

'Therefore, on behalf of such a man I will boast'.

Concerning the pronouncing mode, መ *ma* and ሰ *sa* exclusively affect the original pronunciation mode of a word to which they are added. Let us first see ሰ *sa*, it affects it in two specific ways:

7.10.1.18.

If it is attached to nouns, particles and numerals ending with the first, second, third, fourth, fifth or seventh order letters, it causes

[1] The insertion of *sa/ssa* splits the direct combination of *za* and *nababa* (ወዘነበበ).

their mode of pronunciation to be changed from *wadāqi nəbāb* into *tanaš nəbāb*.[1]

7.10.1.19.

If it is attached to verbs and personal or place names ending with the sixth order syllable that are originally pronounced with a stronger tone, pushing out the air powerfully then, it makes their mode of pronunciation change to the so-called *wadāqi nəbāb*. The original mode of pronunciation of such kinds of language elements is known in the tradition as ሰያፍ፡ ንባብ *sayyāf nəbāb*.[2]

According to this theory, the attachment of ሰ *sa* changes the pronunciation mode of *wadāqi nəbāb* into *tanaš nəbāb* and of *sayyāf nəbāb* into *wadāqi nəbāb*.

Example: *wadāqi nəbāb + sa-ssa* = *tanaš nəbāb*

ዘ + ሰ *za + sa/ssa* — ዘሰ *za-ssa*
ቤቱ + ሰ *betu + sa/ssa* — ቤቱሰ *betu-ssa*
መዋቲ + ሰ *mawāti + sa/ssa* — መዋቲሰ *mawāti-ssa*
ደብተራ + ሰ *dabtara + sa/ssa* — ደብተራሰ *dabtara-ssa*
ቅዳሴ + ሰ *qəddāse + sa/ssa* — ቅዳሴሰ *qəddāse-ssa*
መሰንቆ + ሰ *masanqo + sa/ssa* — መሰንቆሰ *masanqo-ssa*

sayyāf nəbāb + sa/ssa = *wadāqi nəbāb*
ይገብር + ሰ *yəgabbər + sa/ssa* — ይገብርሰ *yəgabbərə-ssa*
ትጹም + ሰ *təṣum + sa/ssa* — ትጹምሰ *təṣumə-ssa*
ኤልያስ + ሰ *ʾəlәyās + sa/ssa* — ኤልያስሰ *ʾəlәyāsə-ssa*

---

[1] See the details from section 3.1.1; Glossary.

[2] The pronunciation mode ተነሽ *tanaš* has almost the same phonetic feature with the so-called *sayyāf nəbāb*. The only difference is that it includes all verbs and nouns that end with the second, third, fourth and seventh order letters but not the nouns and verbs ending with sixth order such as ዲዲሞስ *didimos* አብርሃም *ʾabrhām*, ቶማስ *tomās*, ይቄድስ *yəqeddəs*, ትርከብ *tərkab* and ይቁም *yəqum*. In the same way, *sayyāf nəbāb* does not include the verbs and nouns that do not end with sixth order.

Examples in textual reading: wadāqi nəbāb + sa sayyāf nəbāb

7.10.1.19. (2nd order + *sa-ssa*) ወምክሩሰ፡ ለእግዚአብሔር፡ ይሄሉ፡ ለዓለም። (Prov. (com.) 19:21).

wa-məkru-ssa la-'əgzi'abəḥer yəhellu la-'ālam

<Conj-NCom:ms.s.PSt-Psuff:3m.s-Part> <Prep-NCom.m.s.Nom> <V: Imperf.3m.s> <Adv>

'But the council of Lord will stand'.

7.10.1.20. (7th order + *sa-ssa*) ወዘይዌህኮሰ፡ ይኤብስ፡ ላዕለ፡ ነፍሱ። (Prov. (com.) 20:2).

wa-za-yəwehək-o-ssa yə'ebbəs lā'la nafs-u

<Conj-Prel-V:Imperf.3m.s-PSuff:3m.s-Part> <V:Imperf.3m.s> <Prep> <NCom:unm.s.Nom.PSt-Psuff:3m.s>

'But he who provokes him to anger forfeits his own life'.

However, መ *ma* changes mainly the *wadāqi nəbāb* into *tanaš nəbāb*. Therefore, the attachment of መ *ma* to verbs and nouns that originally keep the *wadāqi nəbāb* just like that of ሰ *sa*, changes the pronunciation mode into *tanaš nəbāb*.

Examples in textual reading: (wadāqi nəbāb + sa → tanaš nəbāb)

7.10.1.21. (2nd order + *ma*) ኦ፡ አዳም፡ ምንተኑመ፡ ረሰይናከ። (Anp. Ath (com.) verse 27).

'o 'addām manta-nu-mma rassaynā-ka

<PartVoc> <NPro:m.s.Nom> <AInt.Acc-PartInt-Part> <V:Perf.2m.s-PSuff:2m.s>

'O, Adam what evil did we do on you?'

7.10.1.22. (3rd order + *ma*) ዓዲመ፡ እስመ፡ ምክንያቶሙ፡ ስፉሕ። (Ecl (com.) 8:43).

'adi-mma 'əsma məknəyāt-omu səfuḥ

<Adv-Part> <Conj> <NCom:unm.s.Nom-PSuff:3m.p> <NCom:m.s>

'Their reason is still much'.

7.10.1.23. (7th rad. + *ma*) ወእፎመ፡ ኢክህሉ፡ ይርከብዎ፡ ለእግዚአ፡ እሉ፡ ፍጡራን። (Ecl (com.) 8:45).

wa-ʾəffo-mma ʾi-kəhlu yərkabə-wwo

<Conj-PartInt-Part> <PartNeg-V:Perf.3m.p> <V:Subj.3m.p-PSuff.3m.p>

la-ʾəgziʾa ʾəllu fəṭurān

<Prep-NCom:m.s.ConSt> <PDem:m.p> <NCom :m.p.Nom>

'And how are they unable to meet to the Lord of these creations?'

* Notice that because of the attachment, መ *ma* and ሰ *sa* are quite often geminated.

7.10.2. ያ *yā* and ዮ *yo*

Leslau described *yo* as a particle expressing admiration, grief and pain.[1] But according to Dillmann, both are suffixes which are assumed by the verbs that may govern two accusatives.[2] The *ʾAggabāb* tradition considers them as particles which are suffixed to the subjunctive and imperative verbs in expression of sincerity, eagerness, and humbleness.[3] *Yā* is employed with a feminine and *yo* with a masculine noun or pronoun. Due to the attachment, the ending syllable of the verb changes to a sixth order radical. Though it is not consistent.

The attachment of the elements to verbs does not make any change in the lexical meaning of the verbs. However, their employment shows that the sentence is more polite.

Textual evidence:

7.10.2.1. ጸግዉንያ፡ ለዛቲ፡ አበሳየ። (2 Cor. 12:13).

ṣaggəwun-yā la-zātti ʾabasā-ya

---

1 Leslau 2006, 625.

2 Dillmann 1907, 351.

3 Kidāna Wald Kəfle 1955, 512.

<V:Impt.2m.p-PSuff:1c.s-Part> <Prep-PDem:f.s.Nom> <NCom:unm.s.Nom.PSt-PSuff:1c. 1c.s>

'Forgive that guilt of mine'.

7.10.2.2. **ወእቤሎ፡ ከመ፡ የሀበንያ፡ ለይእቲ፡ መጽሐፍ።** (Rev. 10:9).

wa-'əbel-o kama yahabannə-yā la-yə'əti

<Conj-V:Perf.1c.s> <Conj> <V:Subj.3m.s-PSuff:1c.s-Part> <Prep.PPer:f.s.Nom>

maṣḥaf

<NCom:unm.s.Nom>

'And I told him so that he may give me that book'.

7.10.2.3. **እግዚእየ፡ ሀበንዮ፡ እም፡ ውእቱ፡ ማይ።** (John 4:15).

'əgzi'ə-ya habann-yo 'əm

<NCom:m.s.Nom-PSuff:1c.s> <V:Impt:2m.s-PSuff:1c.s-Part> <Prep>

wə'ətu māy

<PPer:m.s.Nom> <NCom:unm.s.Nom>

'Sir, give me from this water'.

7.10.2.4. **ሀቡኒያ፡ ለዛቲ፡ ወለት።** (Gen. 34:12).

habu-ni-yā la-zātti wallat

<V:Impt.2m.p-PSuff:1c.s-Part> <Prep-PDem:f.s.Nom> <NCom:f.s.Nom>

'Give me this girl'.

※ ※ ※

CHAPTER EIGHT: CONCLUSION

8.1. CONCLUDING OBSERVATIONS ON *'AGGABĀB* AND ITS ISSUES

Gəʿəz is a classical Ethiopian language which ceased to be spoken in the late thirteenth century CE. Until the coming of Amharic literature in the ninetieth, it served being the leading language of literature.[1] Even today, it is used for liturgical and academic purposes.

In Ethiopia, the most important academic centers which are highly devoted to the study of Gəʿəz are *Qəne* schools. Since the fifteenth century, the schools have the leading local institutes at which the language is intensively studied. One of the two major parts of the study in the schools, *Sawāsəw*, is specifically concerned with grammatical studies while the other part *Qəne* is just about composing and reciting *Qəne* the highly esteemed Gəʿəz poetries.

Sawāsəw comprises at least four basic grammatical courses which are offered to the students in different levels. The first three courses *gəśś*, *rəbā gəśś* and *rəbā qəmr* are relatively less complicated than the fourth one which is *'Aggabāb*. Particularly, *rəbā gəśś* and *rəbā qəmr* are small in size (pp. 3, 12). Scholarly approaches confirm the conceptual connection of *Sawāsəw* with the grammatical tradition applied in the Coptic-Arabic vocabulary.[2]

From the context of Ethiopian language studies, the Amharic term *'Aggabāb* refers to the grammatical study of a language. It can

---

1 Ullendorff 1955, 5, 7.

2 Goldenberg 2013, 60, "Sawāsəw", *EAe*, IV (2010), 562 (M. Mulugetta).

be used in the case of any language. But practically, it is mostly known as a title of the significant part of the grammatical study of Gəʿəz in the *Qəne* Schools.

'Aggabāb is the major part of the grammatical study to which a high concentration is given due to its large scope and tough issues. It is concerned with various linguistic elements that are used such as Adverbs, Conjunctions, Prepositions, Relative Pronouns, Interrogative Pronouns, Interjections and Particles. Discussing the etymologies, meanings and grammatical functions of these elements is the main objective of *'Aggabāb*. It also deals with the right position of each element in a sentence.

The number of linguistic elements involved in the study of *'Aggabāb* is varied from one school to the other due to the inclusion and exclusion of various words which do not belong to the aforementioned lexical categories. However, the non-controversial ACPPIP elements which are accepted by most of the schools are about two hundred thirty-four. All these elements are included in this research work in those lexical categories.

On the classification of the elements, the tradition held in the *Qəne* Schools is evidently different from the perspective of modern language study. In accordance with the *'Aggabāb* tradition, the elements are categorized in three categories. The categories are called *ʿAbiyy 'Aggabāb*, *Nəʿus 'Aggabāb* and *Daqiq 'Aggabāb*. The criteria are basically related with the position and the roles that the elements can play in a sentence.

The first category of *ʿAbiyy 'Aggabāb* consists of forty-eight individual elements. Three of them are the relative pronouns እለ *'əlla*, እንተ *'ənta* and ዘ *za* while the fourth one is an adverbial element ዓዲ *ʿādi* 'again'. The remaining forty-four elements are conjunctional elements. As to the tradition, all these elements excluding ባሕቱ *bāḥəttu* 'but', አኮኑ *'akkonu* 'because', and ዳእሙ *dā'əmu* 'however' are directly attached to verbs, and this is the common linguistic feature that the elements of the category share equally.

Thus, if we put aside *ʿādi*, we can compare this *'Aggabāb* category with the lexical categories of Conjunctions and Relative Pronouns.

In the so-called *Nəʿus 'Aggabāb* which is the second category in the given order, and the largest category in terms of the number of elements, about one hundred thirty-five linguistic elements are included. Out of them, ninety-six elements are used as Adverbs while eleven elements are Interrogatives and Interjections. The remaining twenty-eight elements of the category are used as Particles. According to the *'Aggabāb* tradition, all these elements occur alone in a sentence, and this is the major criteria to put them together in the same category.

The third and last *'Aggabāb* category *Daqiq 'Aggabāb* comprises fifty-one individual elements which are used as Prepositions. The tradition tells that being prefixed to nouns and numerals is the main linguistic feature that the elements of the category keep in common.

Based on these observations and the grammatical functions of the elements, we can assume that *Nəʿus 'Aggabāb* is parallel with the lexical categories of Adverbs, Interrogatives, Interjections and Particles. Similarly, *Daqiq 'Aggabāb* is compared with the lexical category of Prepositions.

The lexical category of Adverbs is the largest category which consists of ninety-seven adverbial elements. Among them, only the following seventeen elements are initially adverbs:

ሀየ *həyya* 'there'
ማእዜ *mā'əze* 'when?'
እስኩ *'əsku* 'let...'
እንካ *'ənka* 'now on'
እንጋ *'əngā* 'then indeed'
እፎ *'əffo* 'how'
ካሃ *kahā* 'away'
ከንቱ *kantu* 'in vain'
ከመ *kəmma* 'the same'
ኵሉሄ *kʷəllahe* 'wherever' or 'whenever'
ዝየ *zəya* 'here'
ዓዲ *ʿādi* 'yet'
ይእዜ *yə'əze* 'today'
ዮም *yom* 'today'
ዮጊ *yogi* 'yet'
ጌሠም *geśam* tomorrow
ግሙራ *gəmurā* 'ever'

Again, the following six elements are formed from two or three different components

በሕቁ *baḥəqqu* 'considerably'
በምልኡ *baməlʿu* 'fully'
ቦኑ *bonu* 'indeed?'
እምድሩ *'əmmədru* 'completely'
እስፍንቱ *'əsfəntu* 'how much'
ዕራቁ *ʿərāqu* 'alone'
ለዝላፉ *lazəlāfu.* 'always'

All these elements except *bonu* and *ʿərāqu* are formed to be used as adverbs by means of prefixation of the preposition ለ *la* or በ *ba* and of the suffixation of the pronominal suffix *-u*. *ʿƎrāqu* received the suffixation of the pronominal *suffix -u*, but there is no prefix in it like the other elements. *Bonu* is also a compound of ቦ *bo* and the interrogative particle ኑ *nu*. The remaining adverbial elements are originally substantives.[1]

While functioning as adverbs, many of the elements having nominal origins are used always in their accusative forms. For example, the nominative በክ *bakk* 'idle' can serve as an adverb when it is employed in the accusative form as በከ *bakka* 'idly'. Similarly, the nominatives ዳግም *dāgəm* 'second' and ፍጹም *fəṣṣum* 'perfect' can play the role of adverbial elements if they are used in the accusative form as ዳግመ *dāgəma* 'again' and ፍጹመ *fəṣṣuma* 'perfectly'.[2]

The remaining adverbial elements are employed in two different ways. Some of them are employed in their original form. The elements are the following:

ቀዲሙ *qadimu* 'earlier'
ቀዳሚ *qadāmi* 'before'
ባሕቲቱ *bāḥətitu* 'alone'
ትማልም *təmāləm* 'yesterday'
ትካት *təkāt* 'in old time'
አማን *'amān* 'truly'
አይቴ *'ayte* 'where?

ዓዲ *'ādi* 'yet'
ዕራቁ *'ərāqu* 'alone'
ዮም *yom* 'today'
ዮጊ *yogi* 'yet'
ግብር *gəbr* 'must'
ደኃሪ *daḫāri* 'later'
ድልወት *dəlwat* 'worthy'

Some other elements such as ርቱዕ *rətu'* 'worthy', እስፍንቱ *'əsfəntu* 'how much', ከንቱ *kantu* '(in) vain' and ዘልፍ *zalf* 'every day' are used either in their accusative forms (*rətu'a*, *'əsfənta*, *kanto* and *zalfa*) or with the prefixation of a preposition such as *la*, *ba* or *'əm*.

Many adverbial elements can be used interchangeably due to the same concept and grammatical function that they share in common. On the other hand, the concepts of various adverbs can be expressed by two or more adverbial elements. Let us see how the following concepts can be expressed by different elements.

The concept 'everyday' or 'always' can be expressed by either one of the following five elements:

---

[1] Dillmann 1907, 383, 385, 386.
[2] Ibid.

ለዝሉፉ *lazəlufu*	ዘልፍ *zalf*
ዘልፈ *zalfa*	ውቱረ *wəttura*
ወትረ *watra*	

An old time or the initial moment of any event can be expressed by the following five adverbial elements with the meanings 'earlier', 'before', 'first' and 'in the beginning'.

ቀዲሙ *qadimu*	አቅዲሙ *ʾaqdimu*
ቅድም *qədm*	ቅድመ *qədma*
ቀዳሚ *qadāmi*	

Similarly, ደኃሪ *daḫāri* and ድኅረ *dəḫra* can replace each another since both are expressing the same concept 'later'.

The concept 'largely', 'much' or 'abundantly' can be expressed by one of the following four adverbial elements:

ብዙኀ *bəzuḫa*	ይሙነ *yəmuna*
ብዝኀ *bəzḫa*	ፈድፋደ *fadfāda*

The following four elements can equally express the concept 'together' or 'jointly' (pp. 111):

ኁባሬ *ḫubāre*	አሐተኔ *ʾaḥattane*
ኅቡረ *ḫəbura*	ድርገተ *dərgata*

The concepts 'silently', 'secretly' or 'in secret' can be expressed by either one of the following five elements:

ኅቡዐ *ḫəbuʿa*	ጽሚተ *ṣəmmita*
ድቡተ *dəbbuta*	ጽምሚተ *ṣəməmita*
ጽመ *ṣəmma*	

Likewise, በከ *bakka* and በከንቱ *kantu* or ከንቶ *kanto* express the concept 'idly' or 'in vain'.

Among the entire forty-four conjunctional elements, seventeen elements such as አምሳለ *ʾamsāla* 'as', አምጣነ *ʾamṭāna* 'as long as' and አርአያ *ʾarʾayā* 'as' are formed in status constructus from nominal origins while the other twenty-two do not have an etymological relation with verbs or nouns.

The elements are mentioned as follows:

ሂ *hi* 'also'
ህየንተ *həyyanta* 'instead of'
ለ *la* 'let...'
ኒ *ni* 'also'
ሰ *sa* 'but'
ሶበ *soba* 'when'
በይነ *bayna* 'about'
ባሕቱ *bāḥəttu* 'but'
ኀበ *ḫaba* 'toward'
አላ *'allā* 'but'
አመ *'ama* 'when'

አው *'aw* 'or'
እመ *'əmma* 'if'
እም *'əm* 'from'
እስመ *'əsma* 'because'
እስከ *'əska* 'until'
እንበለ *'ənbala* 'without'
እንበይነ *'ənbayna* 'about'
እንዘ *'ənza* 'while'
ወ *wa* 'and'
ወእደ *wa'əda* 'if'
ዳእሙ *dā'əmu* 'nonetheless'

The lexical category includes four more elements which are formed from two different components. The elements are ሚመ *mimma* 'otherwise',[1] አኮኑ *'akkonu* 'because', በእንተ *ba'ənta* 'since' or 'for' and በዘ *baza* 'that'. Precisely, *mimma* is formed from the interrogative *mi* and the particle *ma* as *'akkonu* is likely formed from the negation particle አኮ *'akko* and the interrogative particle ኑ *nu*. *Baza* is a composition of the preposition በ *ba* and the relative pronoun ዘ *za*. *Ba'ənta* is also formed from the preposition *ba* and the relative pronoun እንተ *'ənta*.

The remaining one is the exceptional element ብሂል *bəhil* 'meaning'[2] which is originally an infinitive verb and used as a conjunctional element. When it functions as an adverbial element, it is used in status constructus and directly attached to verbs.

The conjunctional elements are employed in three different ways. Five elements አኮኑ *'akkonu*, አላ *'allā*, አው *'aw*, ባሕቱ *bāḥəttu* and ዳእሙ *dā'əmu* occur alone while ሂ *hi* and ኒ *hi* are suffixed to verbs as all the remaining conjunctional elements are prefixed to verbs. The only conjunctional element which can be directly attached to a Jussive verb is ለ *la*[3] Due to the attachment, that Jussive

1 Dillmann 1907, 378.
2 Leslau 2006, 89.
3 Dillmann 1907, 406; Leslau 2006, 303

verb functions as an Imperative. All the remaining elements of the lexical category are mainly attached to Perfective and Imperfective verbs. The direct attachment to Infinitive verbs is quite possible.

There are some conjunctional elements that share identical concept and function. For instance, አመ *'ama*, ጊዜ *gize* and ሶበ *soba* are used similarly as time conjunctions with the same concept 'when'. አምሳለ *'amsāla*, አርአያ *'ar'ayā* and ከመ *kama* also share the same meaning 'as'. Similarly, አምጣነ *'amṭāna*, አኮኑ *'akkonu* and እስመ *'əsma* are used for the same purpose with the concept 'because' or 'since'.

There are also some other conjunctional elements corresponding each other due to identical meaning and grammatical function like አላ *'allā* and ባሕቱ *bāḥəttu* with the meaning 'but', በይነ *bayna* 'about' and እንበይነ *'ənbayna* with the meaning 'about', 'for' and ሂ *hi* and ኒ *hi* with the meaning 'also'.

The lexical category of Prepositions is the second largest category with the sum of fifty-one elements.[1] The majority of the elements are initially nouns which are treated in status constructus due to their attachment to nouns (ዐውደ *'awda* 'around', ዲበ *diba* 'above' or 'upon', and ኀረ *gora* 'near'...).[2] The only prepositional element which is formed from two elements is በእንተ *ba'ənta* 'about' or 'for' which is also used as a conjunctional element. August Dillmann added also ህየንተ *həyyanta* 'instead of' and እንበይነ *'ənbayna* 'about'.[3]

Among the elements of this lexical category, about fifteen elements are initially prepositions since they do not have origins that are related with verbs or nouns.

The elements are the following:

---

[1] Dillmann 1907, 389.

[2] Tropper 2002, 140.

[3] Dillmann 1907: 402-403.

ሀየንተ *həyyanta* 'instead of'
ለ *la* 'to'
ምስለ *məsla* 'with'
ሶበ *soba* 'when'
በ *ba* 'in', 'by'
በይነ *bayna* 'about'
ኀበ *ḫaba* 'toward'
አመ *'ama* 'since'
አፈ *'afa* 'during'
እስከ *'əska* 'till'
እም *'əm* 'from'
እንበይነ *'ənbayna* 'about'
እንበለ *'ənbala* 'without'
ከመ *k*ama 'like'
ገቦ *gabo* 'near'
ጊዜ *gize* 'during'
ጥቃ *ṭəqā* 'near'

While functioning as prepositional elements, each element is attached to nouns, nominalized verbs or numbers. There is no prepositional element that gets attached to verbs directly or indirectly. Among all prepositional elements እም *'əm* 'from' can exclusively be added to the following time and place prepositions:

አመ *'ama* 'since'
ኀበ *ḫaba* 'toward'
ገቦ *gabo* 'near'
ጊዜ *gize* 'during'
ላዕለ *lā'əla* 'above' or 'over'
ማዕዶተ *mā'ədota* 'beyond'
ማእከለ *mā'əkala* 'between'
መልዕልተ *mal'əlta* 'upon'
መቅድመ *maqdəma* 'before'
መትሕተ *matḥəta* 'under'
መንገለ *mangala* 'to'
ቅድመ *qədma* 'before'
ሳኒታ *sānitā* 'on the next day of'
ታሕተ *tāḥta* 'under'
ጥቃ *ṭəqā* 'near'
ውስተ *wəsta* 'in' or 'to'
ውሳጤ *wəsāṭe* 'in'

The other prepositional element which can be possibily prefixed to many prepositional elements is ba. It can be added to the prepositional elements mentioned above except *maqdəma* and *mangala.*

The linguistic elements included in the remaining lexical categories of Interrogative Pronouns (four), Relative Pronouns (three), Interjections (seven) and Particles (twenty-eight) do not have origins which are affiliated with nouns or verbs with the exception of the interjection ወይሌ *wayle* and the vocative particle እግዚኦ *'əgzi'o. Wayle* is etymologically related with the verb ወይለወ *waylawa* 'cry' or 'mourn' while *'Əgzi'o* is formed from the substantive እግዚእ *'əgzi'* 'Lord'.

In use, none of the interrogative pronouns and the interjections are attached to nouns or verbs; they always occur alone. እለ *'Əlla,* አንተ

ʾənta and ዘ *za* are prefixed directly or indirectly to verbs when they are used as Relative Pronouns, and to nouns when they serve to indicate a genitive relation of nouns.

Similarly, the elements ቅድመ *qədma* and ድኅረ *dəḫra* are exclusively used in three different ways for three distinctive grammatical functions. When they serve as Adverbs, they occur alone, and as the conjunctional elements, they are attached to verbs. Again, when they play the role of prepositional elements, they are prefixed to nouns, nominalized verbs and numbers.

Among the elements provided in the category of Particles አ *ʾa* '!', ሁ *hu* 'is…?', መ *ma* '!', ኑ *nu* 'is?', 'shall?', ሰ *sa* '!' and ኬ *ke* '!' are always suffixed to verbs and nouns while the attachment of ሶ *so* '!',[1] ያ *yā* '!' and ዮ *yo* '!' is fixed only to the Imperative verb. The negation particle አል *ʾal* is attached to the existential particle ቦ *bo* while ኢ *ʾi* 'non', 'dis-' or 'un-' is always prefixed to verbs and nouns.[2] The accusative particle ሃ *hā* '-' is added to proper nouns only. The employment of ሚ *mi* 'how' and ኦ *ʾo* 'O!' is still controversial; some would say that they must be affixed to words, and others would suggest placing them alone. Although, the *ʾAggabāb* tradition supports the second suggestion.

8.2. GENERAL REMARKS ABOUT THE STUDY

As mentioned frequently, *ʾAggabāb* is a classical grammatical study of Gəʿəz with an approximate age of five hundred years. It is presumed that it has been progressively developed and many changes occurred to it through time. The methodology applied in the *Qəne* Schools can be considered as one of the factors for the occurrences of changes in a positive or a negative context since it is based on oral lecture. The changes may continue in the future too.

Studying and analysing all the issues comprised within the *ʾAggabāb* outline is one of the recommendable ways to preserve the legacy of *ʾAggabāb* and to keep the knowledge growing.

---

1 Dillmann 1907, 381.
2 Dillmann 1907, 380; Tropper 2002, 149.

Researches show that there is no methodical study on *'Aggabāb* which has been done before.[1] So, this research is believed to become the first methodical research on it. Its major objective is to introduce what *'Aggabāb* is about and to discuss its issues. By examining its narrations and explanations, one can easily understand that *'Aggabāb* is a high-level grammatical study of Gəʿəz language in the *Qəne* schools which deals with various lexical categories. Beside introducing its origin, tradition and the methodology by which *'Aggabāb* is studied, the research helps to acquire the opportunity to preserve the knowledge in general.

If we compare it to modern grammars done by both local and European scholars in terms of content, then, we observe that it holds several important issues and observations which are not provided in other works, and of course, that it also lacks some insights that are presented in other grammars. If we take the lexical category of Adverbs as an example, among ninety-seven adverbial elements comprised in *'Aggabāb*, thirty-four elements are not available in the same category of Dillmann. Likewise, it consists of fourteen conjunctional and ten prepositional elements which are not included in Dillmann.

Likewise, thirty-five elements that exist in the *'Aggabāb* category of Adverbs are not included in the same category of Kidāna Wald Kəfle. Such a difference is encountered in most of the remaining categories. This is however to indicate precisely that *'Aggabāb* provides a number of ACPPIP elements which are excluded in different grammars with clear explanations about their origins, meanings and uses.

Moreover, the scholarly implication on the same element is sometimes different from one another. Nonetheless, this work provides all possible analysis, observations and remarks on the etymologies, concepts and grammatical functions of each linguistic element comprised in the study of *'Aggabāb* from all sides. So, it is possible to conclude that this research contributes to widen our understanding of all linguistic elements provided in the study by observing and comparing various perspectives.

---

[1] Andualem Muluken Sieferew 2013, 5.

Its other contribution is the provision of substantial textual evidence for each theory or grammatical analysis. The importance of textual evidence is not only for the acceptance or the recognition of explanations. It is also necessary to provide an evidence to show the grammatical functions of the elements practically and specifically. To be honest, this task is hesitated in many grammars, excluding that of Dillmann and of Kidāna Wald Kəfle. However, this research provides frequently appropriate evidence quoted from various texts with grammatical annotations and translations.

SUMMARY

In Ethiopia, the *Qəne* Schools are the most important centres for the study of Gəʿəz language. The study has two major parts called *Sawāsəw* and *Qəne*. *Sawāsəw* deals with the grammatical aspects of the language while *Qəne* is specifically concerned with composing and reciting *Qəne* 'Gəʿəz poetry'.

Sawāsəw also has four distinct divisions which are known as *gəśś*, *rəbā qəmr*, *rəbā gəśś* and *'Aggabāb*. According to the attainable tradition of the schools, *'Aggabāb* is the final and the most essential part of the grammatical study of Gəʿəz. It deals with various linguistic elements which can play decisive roles in the language. In the *Qəne* Schools, studying *'Aggabāb* is one of the five requirements to be graduate of *Qəne* and Gəʿəz language.

In this work, two hundred thirty-four linguistic elements are comprised in various divisions and sub-divisions. In accordance with the tradition of *'Aggabāb*, the elements are intentionally categorized in three categories called *ʿAbiyy 'Aggabāb*, *Nəʿus 'Aggabāb* and *Daqiq 'Aggabāb*.

But from the perspective of modern Linguistics, these elements can be categorized into seven lexical categories, namely Adverbs, Conjunctions, Prepositions, Relative Pronouns, Interrogative Pronouns, Interjections and Particles. The purpose of conducting this research is to discuss what *'Aggabāb* is and to bring its issues into light. Thus, to make the study achievable, the elements are re-categorized and analyzed according to the Linguistic perspective.

The particular focus of *'Aggabāb* is to deal with the etymologies, meanings and grammatical functions of the elements included in the categories mentioned earlier. It also touches upon several language rules with regard to sentence structure, mode of pronunciation, word construction, prefixation and suffixation of these linguistic elements.

The other important feature of the study is that it provides often supportive evidence or examples for the ratification of each theory. Of course, the evidence are mostly mentioned without sources, and this is hard to follow comfortably. Thus, one of the challenging tasks in the making of this work was to find out the correct sources of a considerable number of quotations that are mentioned in the study and to provide fitting textual evidence for the theories without evidence. Finally, to make the study more transparent and understandable, a relevant textual evidence is given for each theory or analysis.

The tradition held in the schools tells that the introduction of the existing Gəʿəz grammar *'Aggabāb* goes back to the scholars of fifteenth century. For all these reasons, it can be identified as a classical grammar of Gəʿəz.

The knowledge reached our time through oral succession. Even today, the methodology which is applied in the schools is based on oral lecture. This is supposed to be one of the factors that caused slight differences to occur between the *Qəne* schools with regard to the number and function of some elements.

Zusammenfassung

ʾAggabāb ist der letzte und wichtigste Bestandteil der grammatischen Studien im Gəʿəz-Unterricht in den äthiopischen *Qəne*-Schulen. Es behandelt verschiedene linguistische Elemente, die eine entscheidende Rolle in der Sprache spielen. Der Tradition der *Qəne*-Schulen zufolge geht die Einführung des *ʾAggabāb* auf die Gelehrten des 15. Jahrhunderts zurück. Somit kann *ʾAggabāb* als klassische Grammatik des Gəʿəz bezeichnet werden.

Dieses Wissen hat wurde bis in unsere Zeit mündlich überliefert. Bis heute basiert die Methode der Schulen auf mündlichem Unterricht, was wohl einer der Faktoren ist, die dazu beigetragen haben, dass geringe Unterschiede hinsichtlich der Anzahl, Ursprung und Funktion einiger Elemente entstanden sind.

Die Anzahl der im *ʾAggabāb* untersuchten linguistischen Elemente variiert von einer Schule zur nächsten. In dieser Arbeit werden zwei hundert drei und dreißig linguistische Elemente in verschiedenen Unterteilungen behandelt. Der Tradition des *ʾAggabāb* zufolge werden diese Elemente grob in die drei Gruppen *ʿabiyy ʾaggabāb*, *nəʿus ʾaggabāb* und *daqiq ʾaggabāb* unterteilt. Die Kriterien dafür hängen mit der Position und Funktionen, die die Elemente in einem Satz haben können, zusammen. In die erste Gruppe *ʿabiyy ʾaggabāb* werden Elemente, die Verben angehängt und deren Status beeinflussen können, zusammengefasst. Elemente, die anderen Elementen angehängt werden können, sind in *daqiq ʾaggabāb* zusammengefasst, während die größte Gruppe, *nəʿus ʾaggabāb*, hauptsächlich Elemente, die alleine stehen können, umfasst.

Aus moderner linguistischer Sicht können diese Elemente in die sieben lexikalischen Kategorien Adverbien, Konjunktionen, Präpositionen, Relativpronomen, Interrogativpronomen und Partikeln eingeteilt werden. Das Ziel dieser Forschungsarbeit ist es, zu untersuchen, worum es sich bei *'Aggabāb* handelt und zu seiner Bekanntheit beizutragen. Um diese Untersuchung möglich zu machen, werden die Elemente nach moderner linguistischer Auffassung neu kategorisiert und analysiert.

Bei einem Vergleich mit modernen Grammatiken einheimischer und europäischer Wissenschaftler wird deutlich, dass *'Aggabāb* in anderen Werken nicht beschriebene bedeutende Konzepte und Beobachtungen beinhaltet, wie ihm auch verschiedene Erkenntnisse anderer Grammatiken fehlen. Diese Arbeit soll alle Analysen, Beobachtungen und Bemerkungen zu Etymologien, Konzepten und grammatikalischen Funktionen aller relevanter linguistischer Elemente in der von diesen beiden Perspektiven ausgeführten Untersuchung des *'Aggabāb* umfassen. Jeder Theorie oder Analyse folgt ein relevanter Textbeleg, was die Verständlichkeit und Anschaulichkeit der Untersuchung erhöht.

List of References

ʾAdmāsu Ǧambbare (Malʾāka bərhan) 1970. *መጽሐፈ፡ ቅኔ (maṣḥafa Qəne)*(Addis Ababa: Tənśāʾe za-gubāʾe publishing house, 1970).

ʾAfawarq Zawde (ʾAlaqā) 1995. *ሀገረ፡ መጻሕፍት፡ ሰዋሰው ግዕዝ፡ ወአማርኛ* (*hagara maṣāḥəft _ sawāsəw Gəʿəz wa-ʾamārərññā*) (Addis Ababa: 1995).

ʾAklila Bərhān Walda Qirqos (Liqa ṭabbabt) 1950. *መርሐ፡ ልቡና (marḥa ləbbunā)*(Addis Ababa: Holy Trinity Theological Institute, 1950).

Asfaw Damte "Haddis ʿAlämayyähu" in Siegbert Uhlig, ed., *Encyclopaedia Aethiopica* II (Wiesbaden: Harrassowitz Verlag, 2005) 959.

__ "Märse Ḫazan Wäldä Qirqos" in Siegbert Uhlig, ed., *Encyclopaedia Aethiopica* III (Wiesbaden: Harrassowitz Verlag, 2007) 798.

ʾAsrāda Bayābel (Liqa ṭabbabt) 2005. *ማኅሌተ፡ ጽጌ ንባቡና፡ ትርጓሜው (māḫleta ṣəge, text and commentary)*(Addis Ababa: 2005).

Bachmann, P.J. 1892. *Dodekapropheton Aethiopum* oder die zwölf kleinen Propheten der aethiopischen Bibelübersetzung nach handschriftlichen Quellen herausgegeben und mit textkritischen Anmerkungen versehen (Halle (Saale): Max Niemeyer, 1892).

__ 1893. ሰቆቃው፡ ኤርምያስ፡ ነቢይ። (*Saqoqāwa ʾErməyās nabiy*) Die Klagelieder Jeremiae in der aethiopischen Bibelübersetzung. (Halle a. S.: Max Niemeyer, 1893).

__ 2013. *Der Prophet Jesaia Nach Der Aethiopischen Bibeluebersetzung*(US: Nabu Press, 2013).

Bausi, A. 1995. *Il Sēnodos etiopico.* Canoni pseudoapostolici: Canoni dopo l'Ascensione, Canoni di Simone il Cananeo, Canoni Apostolici, Lettera di Pietro, 552, 553, Scriptore Aethiopic, 101, 102 (Lovanii: Peeter, 1995).

__ 1989. “I manoscritti etiopice di J.M”, RSE 33, Wansleben nella Biblioteca Nazionale Centrale die Firenze” (1989), 5-33.

__ 2006. ‘Ancient features of ancient Ethiopic’, in M. Moriggi, ed., *XII Incontro Italiano di Linguistica Camito-Semitica (Afroasiatica) [Ragusa - Ibla, 6-9 giugno 2005]*, Medioevo Romanzo e Orientale, Colloqui, 9 (Soveria Mannelli: Rubbettino, 2006), 263–268.

__ 2008. ‘“Philology” as Textual Criticism: “Normalization” of Ethiopian Studies’, 1/1 (2008), 13–46.

Baye Yemam 1992. ‘Response to Prof. Tilahun’s Article’, *Wyiyit*- ‘Dialogue’, I, number 1 (1992).

Belay Mekonen (Liqa ḫ̮əruyān) 2006. ሕያው፡ ልሳን ግዕዝ - አማርኛ፡ መዝገበ፡ ቃላት (*həyāw ləssān gəʿəz -ʾamārəññā mazgaba qālāt*) (Addis Ababa: 2006).

Conti Rossini, C. 1941. *Grammatica elementare della lingua etiopica*, Pubblicazioni dell’Istituto per l’Oriente (Roma: Istituto per l’Oriente, 1941).

Crummey, D. 2005. “Ethiopia”, in Siegebrt Uhlig, ed., *Encyclopaedia Aethiopica*, II (Wiesbaden: Harrassowitz Verlag, 2005), 393.

Dillmann, C.F.A. 1857. *Grammatik der äthiopischen Sprache* (Leipzig: T.O Weigel, 1857).

__ 1865. *Lexicon linguae aethiopicae*, cum indice latino. Adiectum Esther vocabularium tigre dialecti septentrionalis compilatum a W. Munziger (Lipsiae: T. O. Weigel, 1865).

__ 1853. *Biblia Veteris Testamenti Aethiopica* (Lipsiae: Sumptibus Fr. Chr. Guil. Vogelii, Typis Guil. Vogelii, Filii, 1853).

__ 1861. *Biblia Veteris Testamenti Aethiopici Tomus Secundus*, sive Libri Regum, Paralipomenon, Esdrae, Esther. Pars 1: Regum I et II (Lipsiae: Vogel, 1861).

__ 1907. *Ethiopic Grammar*, ed. C. Bezold (London: Williams and Norgate, 1907).

Ethiopian Orthodox Tewahido Church Tənśāʾe za-gubāʾe publisher 1994. ‘መጽሐፈ፡ ዚቅ *maṣḥafa ziq* (The Book of Hymn)’ (Addis Ababa: Tənśāʾe za-gubāʾe publishing house, 1994).

Ethiopian Orthodox Tewahido Church Scholars’ Council 1995. ‘ቅዳሴ፡ ማርያም *qəddāse marəyām* (The Anaphora of Mary)’, in

መጽሐፈ፡ ቅዳሴ ንባቡና፡ ትርጓሜው maṣḥafa qəddāse nəbābunnā tərgʷāmew (The Book of Liturgy, text and commentary) (Addis Ababa: Tənśāʾe za-gubāʾe publisher, 1995).

__ 1995. ‘ቅዳሴ፡ ሠለስቱ፡ ምዕት *qəddāse śalastu məʿt* (The Anaphora of the Nicean Fathers)’, in *መጽሐፈ፡ ቅዳሴ ንባቡና፡ ትርጓሜው maṣḥafa qəddāse nəbābunnā tərgʷāmew (The Book of Liturgy, text and commentary)* (Addis Ababa: Tənśāʾe za-gubāʾe publisher, 1995).

__ 1995. ‘ቅዳሴ፡ አትናቴዎስ *qəddāse ʾatnātewos* (The Anaphora of Athanasius)’, in *መጽሐፈ፡ ቅዳሴ ንባቡና፡ ትርጓሜው maṣḥafa qəddāse nəbābunnā tərgʷāmew (The Book of Liturgy, text and commentary)* (Addis Ababa: Tənśāʾe za-gubāʾe publisher, 1995).

__ 1995. ‘ቅዳሴ፡ ኤጲፋንዮስ *qəddāse ʾepifanəyos* (The Anaphora of Epiphany)’, in *መጽሐፈ፡ ቅዳሴ ንባቡና፡ ትርጓሜው maṣḥafa qəddāse nəbābunnā tərgʷāmew (The Book of Liturgy, text and commentary)* (Addis Ababa: Tənśāʾe za-gubāʾe publisher, 1995).

__ 1995. ‘ቅዳሴ፡ ዮሐንስ፡ አፈወርቅ *qəddāse yoḥannəs ʾafa warq* (The Anaphora of John Chrysostom)’, in *መጽሐፈ፡ ቅዳሴ ንባቡና፡ ትርጓሜው maṣḥafa qəddāse nəbābunnā tərgʷāmew (The Book of Liturgy, text and commentary)* (Addis Ababa: Tənśāʾe za-gubāʾe publisher, 1995).

__ 1995. ‘ቅዳሴ፡ ዮሐንስ፡ ወልደ፡ ነጐድጓድ *qəddāse yoḥannəs wald nag wadgwād* (The Anaphora of John)’, in *መጽሐፈ፡ ቅዳሴ ንባቡና፡ ትርጓሜው maṣḥafa qəddāse nəbābunnā tərgʷāmew (The Book of Liturgy, text and commentary)* (Addis Ababa: Tənśāʾe za-gubāʾe publisher, 1995).

__ 1995. ‘ቅዳሴ፡ ዲዮስቆሮስ *qəddāse diyosqoros* (The Anaphora of Dioscurus)’, in *መጽሐፈ፡ ቅዳሴ ንባቡና፡ ትርጓሜው maṣḥafa qəddāse nəbābunnā tərgʷāmew (The Book of Liturgy, text and commentary)* (Addis Ababa: Tənśāʾe za-gubāʾe publisher, 1995).

__ 1995 ‘ቅዳሴ፡ ጎርጎርዮስ *qəddāse gorgorəyos* (The Anaphora of Gregory)’, in *መጽሐፈ፡ ቅዳሴ ንባቡና፡ ትርጓሜው maṣḥafa qəddāse nəbābunnā tərgʷāmew (The Book of Liturgy, text and commentary)* (Addis Ababa: Tənśāʾe za-gubāʾe publisher, 1995).

__ 1995. ‘ቅዳሴ፡ ባስልዮስ *qəddāse bāsləyos* (The Anaphora of Basil)’, in *መጽሐፈ፡ ቅዳሴ ንባቡና፡ ትርጓሜው maṣḥafa qəddāse nəbābunnā tərgʷāmew (The Book of Liturgy, text and commentary)* (Addis Ababa: Tənśāʾe za-gubāʾe publisher, 1995).

Ezrā Ḥaddis (Liqa liqāwənt) 2013. ሃይማኖተ፡ አበው ንባቡና፡ ትርጓሜው (*haymānota*
'abaw, text and commentary) (Gondar: 2013).

Fuhs, H.F. 1968. *Die äthiopische Übersetzung des Propheten Micha*, Bonner biblische Beiträge, 28 (Bonn: Hanstein Verlag, 1968).

Gabra Mikā'el ('Abbā) 1886. *መጽሐፈ፡ ሰዋስው (maṣḥafa sawāsəw)* (Keren: 1886).

Gleave, H.C. 1951. *The Ethiopic version of the Songs of Songs* (London: Taylor's Foreign press, 1951).

Goldenberg, G. 1998. *Studies in Semitic Lingustics* (Jerusalem: Magnes Press,
Hebrew University, 1998).

__ 2013. *Semitic Languages* (Oxford: Oxford University Press, 2013).

Grèbaut, S. 1932. *Les Paralipomènes, livres I et II*, Patrologia Orientalis, t. 23, 4. (Paris - Genève: Firmin-Didot, 1932).

Hetzron, R. 1972. *Ethiopian Semitic* (Cambrige: Manchester University Press, 1972).

Hiruie Ermias 2007. መጽሐፈ፡ ምሥጢር፡ ዘአባ፡ ጊዮርጊስ፡ ዘጋሥጫ (*maṣḥafa məśṭir of 'abbā giyorgis za-gaśəčč̣ā*) (Addis Ababa: Alem Printing house, 2007).

__ 2015. *ገድለ፡ ቀውስጦስ* (*gadla qawəsṭos*) (Advent Publishing P.L.C, 2015).

__ , scribe, 1993. *Unpublished 'Aggabāb* cosisting of various grammatical treatises. (written by hand 1993), 1-85, 98-200.

Hudson, G. 1977. 'Language classification and the Semitic Prehistory of Ethiopia', in *Folia Orientalia*, 18 (1977), 120–166.

Kaplan, S. "Həruy Wäldä Śəllase" in Siegbert Uhlig, ed., *Encyclopaedia Aethiopica* III (Wiesbaden: Harrassowitz Verlag, 2007), 20.

Kaśāte Bərhan Tasammā 1958. *አማርኛ፡ መዝገበ፡ ቃላት ('amārəññā mazgaba qālāt)* (Addis Ababa: Artistic Publishing press, 1958).

Kidāna Wald Kəfle ('Alaqā) 1955. መጽሐፈ፡ ሰዋስው፡ ወግሥ፡ ወመዝገበ፡ ቃላት፡ ሐዲስ (*maṣḥafa sawāsəw wa-mazgaba-qālāt ḥaddis*) (Artistic Publishing press, 1955).

Kleiner, M. "Dillmann, Christian Friedrich August", in Siegbert Uhlig, ed., *Encyclopaedia Aethiopica* II (Wiesbaden: Harrassowitz Verlag, 2005) 160.

Knibb, M.A. 2015. *The Ethiopic Text of the Book of Ezekiel*: A Critical Edition (Oxford: Oxford University Press, 2015).

Leslau, W. 1989. *Concise Dictionary of Ge'ez (Classical Ethiopic)* (Wiesbaden: Harrassowitz Verlag, 1989).

__ 2006. *Comparative Dictionary of Geez* (Wiesbaden: Harrassowitz Verlag, 2006).

Löfgren, L.A.V. 1930. *Jona, Nahum, Habakuk, Zephanja, Haggai Sacharja und Maleachi Ätiopisch* (Uppsala: Parigi Champion, 1930).

Ludolf, H. 1701. መጽሐፈ፡ መዝሙራት፡ ዘዳዊት - Psalterium Davidis aethiopice et latine cum duobus impressis & tribus MSStis codicibus diligenter collatum & emendatum, nec non variis lectionibus & notis philologicis illustratum, ut in præfatione pluribus dicetur. Accedunt Æthiopicè tantùm Hymni et Orationes aliquot Vet. et Novi Testamenti, item Canticum Canticorum, cum variis lectionibus & notis. (Francoforti ad Moenum: Prostat apud Johannem David Zunner et Nicolaum Wihelmum Helwig, 1701).

Marrassini, P. 2003. *"Vita", "Omelia", "Miracoli" del Santo Gabra Manfas Qeddus'*, Scriptores Aethiopic, 597–598 (Lovanii: CSCO, 2003).

Meley Mulugetta 2010. "Sawāsəw", in Siegbert Uhlig with Alessandro Bausi, ed., *Encyclopaedia Aethiopica*, IV (Wiesbaden: Harrassowitz Verlag, 2010), 562-564.

Mittwoch, E. 1926. *Die traditionelle Aussprache des Äthiopischen*, Abessinische Studien, 1 (Berlin: Walter de Gruyter, 1926).

Moreno, M. M. 1949. "Struttura e terminologia del *Sawāsĕw*", RSE 8 (1949), 12-62.

Muluken Andualem Sieferew 2013. *Comparative Classification of Gəʿəz Verbs in the Three Traditional Schools of the Ethiopian Orthodox Church* (Aachen: Shaker Verlag, 2013).

Pankhrust, R. 2005. "Dabra Tābor Iyasus", in Siegbert Uhlig, ed., *Encyclopaedia Aethiopica*, II (Wiesbaden: Harrassowitz Verlag, 2005), 49–50.

Pereira, F.M.E. 1905. *Le livre de Job : version éthiopienne*, 5th, xii, Patrologia Orientalis (Paris : 1905).

__ 1911. *Le livre d'Esther : version éthiopienne*, Patrologia Orientalis, t. 9, Fascc. 1= no. 41 (Paris : Firmin-Didot, 1911).

__ 1917. 'O livro do profeta Amós e a sua versão etiópica', in *Boletin do Segunda Classe*, XI (Coimbra: Academia das sciêncas de Lisboa, 1917).

__ ed., 1918a. *Le Trorsieme Livre de Ezra*, Patrologia Orientalis (Paris: 1918).

__ 1918b. 'Le Trorsieme Livre de Ezra', in *Patrologia Orientalis*, Tome XIII Fasclule 5, 66, (Brepols.) (Paris: 1918).

Platt, T.P., ed., 1830. *Novum Testamentum Domini et ServatorIsa.* Jesu Christi Aethiopice (London: Impressit R. Watts, 1830).

Richter, R. 2007. "Language Policy", in U. Siegbert, ed., *Encyclopaedia Aethiopica*, III (Wiesbaden: Harrassowitz Verlag, 2007), 505.

Rici, L. "Conti Rossini, Carlo", in Siegbert Uhlig, ed., *Encyclopaedia Aethiopica* I (Wiesbaden: Harrassowitz Verlag, 2003) 791.

Shiferaw Bekele "Interfece between Philology and History", *Ethiopian Philology* Vol. I, Number I (Addis Ababa: 2008), 52.

Sohier, E. "Käbbädä Mika'el" in Siegbert Uhlig, ed., *Encyclopaedia Aethiopica* III (Wiesbaden: Harrassowitz Verlag, 2007), 315.

Tāya Gabra Maryām ('Alaqā) 1925. *መጽሐፈ፡ ሰዋሰው (maṣḥafa sawāsəw)* (Monkullo Swedish Mission, 1925).

Tropper, J. 2002. *Altäthiopisch: Grammatik des Ge'ez mit Übungstexten und Glossar*, Elementa Linguarum Orientis (Münster: Ugarit-Verlag, 2002).

Uhlig, S. "Abušākər", in Siegbert Uhlig, ed., *Encyclopaedia Aethiopica*, I (Wiesbaden: Harrassowitz Verlag, 2003), 57.

__ "Hiob Ludolf" in Siegbert Uhlig, ed., *Encyclopaedia Aethiopica* III (Wiesbaden: Harrassowitz Verlag, 2007) 601.

Voigt, R. and Siegbert Uhlig 2005. "Ethio-Semitic", in *Encyclopaedia Aethiopica*, II (Wiesbaden: Harrassowitz Verlag, 2005), 440–443.

Weninger, S. 1999. *Ge'ez (Classical Ethiopic)*, Languages of the World, Materials, 1, (2nd edition.) (München: Lincom Europa, 1999).

__ 2005. "Gəʿəz", in Siegbert Uhlig, ed., *Encyclopaedia Aethiopica*, II (Wiesbaden: Harrassowitz Verlag, 2005), 732.

Wion, A. 2005. "Gonǧ Tewodros", in Siegbert Uhlig, ed., *Encyclopedia Aethiopica*, II (Wiesbaden: Harrassowitz Verlag, 2005), 848.

Yāred Shiferāw (Liqa liqāwənt) n.d. መጽሐፈ፡ ሰዋስው መርኆ፡ መጻሕፍት (*maṣḥafa sawāsəw, marḫo maṣāḥəft*) (Bahər Dar: n.d).

Yemānabərhān Getāhun (Maggābe ḫəruyān) 2010. መጽሐፈ፡ ሰዐታት (*maṣḥafa sa'atat*) (Addis Abeba: Akotet Publishers, 2010).

Yətbārak Marshā (Mal'āka 'aryām) 1999. ሰዋሰወ፡ ግዕዝ (*sawāsəwa Gə'əz*) (Addis Abeba: Bərhanənnā salām Printing press, 1999).

Zabolotskikh, M. "Yoftahe Nəguśe" in Siegbert Uhlig, ed., *Encyclopaedia Aethiopica* V (Wiesbaden: Harrassowitz Verlag: 2014), 66.

Zar'a Dawit Adḫanom (Mamhər) 2003. መርኆ፡ ሰዋስው (*marḫo sawāsəw*) (Addis Ababa: Holy Trinity Theological College, 2003).

GLOSSARY

መወድስ *mawaddəs*: Name of the eleventh type of *Qəne* with eight lines which is taken from the name of St. Yāred's hymn. Its literal meaning is 'praise' or 'the one who praises'.

ሚ በዝኁ *mi-bazḫu*: Name of the fourth type of *Qəne* with three lines, it is taken from the first line of the third psalms of David. It is translated literally as 'how they have increased!'

ሥላሴ *śəllāse*: Name of the eighth type of *Qəne* with five lines which is taken from the name of the Holy Trinity.

ርባ ቅምር *rəbā qəmr*: One of the four major lessons in the study of Gəʿəz grammar (*sawāsəw*) in the *Qəne* schools. The term is formed from *rəbā* 'conjugation', or 'declination' and *qəmr* 'measurement' or 'calculation'.

ርባ ግሥ *rəbā-gəśś*: One of the four major lessons in the study of Gəʿəz grammar (*sawāsəw*) in the *Qəne* schools. Its literal meaning is 'Conjugation of a verb'.

ሰዋስው *sawāsəw*: A broad name of all grammatical studies in the *Qəne* schools which means literally 'ladder'.

ሰያፍ፡ ንባብ *sayyāf nəbāb*: Mode of pronunciation for the names or verbs that end with the sixth order radicals and are pronounced by pushing out the air at the ending point. Literally, *sayyāf* means 'perpendicular', 'sharp' or 'radical', and *nəbāb is* 'reading'.

ቀዳማይ፡ አንቀጽ *qadāmāy ʾanqaṣ*: A term which refers to the perfective verbs. Literally, it means 'the leading gate'.

ቅኔ *qəne*: A Gəʿəz poetry with multiple messages in methaphoric expressions.

ቅኔ፡ ቆጠራ *qəne qoṭara*: The act of composing *Qəne* 'Gəʿəz Poetry'.

ቅኔ፡ ቤት *qəne-bet:* A school where *sawasəw* and *Qəne* are studied.

በር፡ ከፋች *bar-kafāč*: An Amharic phrase which means literally 'someone or something that unlocks a door'. In the *sawāsəw* tradition, it expresses the role of *za* when it is employed as a mediating element occurring between *həyyanta* or *ba'ənta* and verbs.

በቋም ቀሪ *baqum-qari*: An Amharic phrase which means 'someone or something which remains unchangeable'. In the tradition of *sawāsəw*, it expresses the role of *la* or *ba* when they keep their initial meanings in the translation.

ተነሽ ንባብ *tanaš nəbāb*: Mode of pronunciation which is applied in the pronunciation of verbs and nouns ending with first, second, third, fourth and seventh order radicals and are pronounced by pushing out the air at the ending point. *Tanaš* means 'someone or some thing which arises, or is to be raised'.

ተጠቃሽ *taṭaqqāš*: An Amharic word which means 'someone or something which is mentioned or addressed'. In the tradition of *sawāsəw*, it expresses the role of *la* when it is attached to an object following a declining verb.

ታይቶ፡ ጠፊ *tāyto ṭafi*: An Amharic adjectival phrase with the literal meaning of 'something or some body that disappears after appearing awhile'. In the tradition of *sawāsəw*, it expresses the grammatical function of *la* when it is attached to jussive verbs.

ትራስ *tərās*: An Amharic word which compares with the Gəʿəz *tər'as* 'cushion'. According to the tradition of *sawāsəw*, it is the designation of some single particles such as *sa*, *so*, *'a* and *ke* that can be suffixed to verbs.

ትንቢት *tənbit*: An alternative name of the imperfective verbs in the *Qəne* schools. Its literal meaning is 'prophecy'.

ነባር አንቀጽ *nabbār 'anqaṣ*: An Amharic phrase which means 'an immovable gate'. In the tradition of *sawāsəw*, *wə'ətu, 'akko, bo* and *'albo* are known as *nabbār 'anqaṣ* for the reason that they can keep the position of verbs but are not declined like verbs.

ነጠላ፡ ግሥ *naṭalā*[1] *gəśś*: An Amharic phrase refering to a verb which is originated from a verbal root called *zar* 'seed' or 'root'.

---

1 Amharic, lit.: 'single'.

ነበር፡ ግሥ *nabbār*[1] *gəśś*: A phrase refering to the substantives which are not originated from verbal root, i.e., *zar*.

ንዑስ፡ አገባብ *Nəʿus ʾAggabāb*: The second division of *ʾAggabāb*. It also indicates each element involved in the division. *Nəʿus* means 'little', 'small' or 'mini'.

አርኬ *ʾarke*: A hymnodic treatise in a poetic form with five lines.

አቀብሎ፡ ሻሺ *ʾaqabbəlo-šaši*: An Amharic adjectival phrase which means 'someone who gives somebody something and vanishes'. In the context of *sawāsəw*, it expresses the grammatical function of *la* when it is attached to the jussive verbs. The reason is that it appears in the text but neither appears in the translation nor makes any influence.

አንቀጽ፡ ግሥ *ʾanqaṣ gəśś*: An alternate term of *naṭalā*[2] *gəśś* which refers a verb in the perfective form of the third person singular masculine.

አገባብ *ʾAggabāb*: A grammatical study of Language. The word is initially an Amharic word which means 'right' or 'way of entering'. In the tradition of *sawāsəw*, the final and most important part of the grammatical study is called *ʾAggabāb*. All Gəʿəz elements that can be used as adverbs, conjunctions, prepositions, interjections, interrogatives and exclamatory elements are also known in common as *ʾAggabāb*.

ካልዓይ አንቀጽ *kāləʿāy ʾanqaṣ*: Name of the imperfective verbs. *Kāləʿāy* means 'the second one', 'other' or 'next'.

ክብር ይእቲ *kəbr-yəʾəti*: Name of the fourteenth type of *Qəne* with four lines which is performed during the Liturgy soon before the dissemination of the Holy Communion.

ወዳቂ ንባብ *wadāqi-nəbāb*: Mode of pronunciation which is applied by the pronunciation of nouns ending with the first, second, third, fourth, fifth and seventh order radicals that are pronounced by declining the ending syllable. *Wadāqi* means 'someone or something that falls down'.

---

1 Amharic, lit.: 'immovable'.
2 Amharic, lit.: 'single'.

ዋዌ *wāwe*: A grammatical term which refers to *hi*, *ni* and *wa* when they are used as conjunctions.

ዋዜማ *wāzemā*: Name of the fifth type of *Qəne* with five lines. It literally means 'Eve/ a day before any festive day'.

ዋሸራ *wāšarā*: Name of place which is in the province of Goǧǧām. At the same time, it is known as the name of one of the three *Qəne* houses.

ዋድላ *Wādlā*: Name of place which is in the province of Wallo. It is also the name of one of the three *Qəne* houses.

ውጥን ጨራሽ *wəṭṭən čarrāš*: An Amharic adjectival phrase with the literal meaning 'someone who completes what is incomplete'. In the tradition of *sawāsəw*, the term indicates *wa* and *kama* while they are able to draw the conception of the verb in the main clause to the subordinate clause which is a nominal clause.

ዐቢይ አገባብ *'Abiyy 'Aggabāb*: A lesson topic of the first division of *'Aggabāb*. All the ACPPIP elements involved in the division are also called *'Abiyy 'Aggabāb*. *'Abiyy* means 'great', 'main', 'major', 'big' and 'dominant'.

ዕጣነ ሞገር *'əṭāna-mogar*: Name of the thirteenth type of *Qəne* with seven or eleven lines. *'Əṭān* means 'insence', and *mogar* is to mean 'fumigation'.

ዘርፍ አያያዥ *zarf-'ayyāyyāž*: An Amharic adjectival phrase with the literal meaning 'connector of fringe'. In the tradition of *sawāsəw*, it expresses *la*, *'əlla*, *'ənta* and *za* when they are used to indicate a genitive case relation occurring between two components. The word *zarf* 'fringe' refers always to the succeeding component.

ዘርፍ ደፊ *zarf-dafi*: An Amharic adjectival phrase which means 'the one that overturns a fringe'. In the study of *sawāsəw*, the elements *la*, *'əlla*, *'ənta* and *za* are known by this term when they are employed to indicate a genitive relation occurring before two components.

ዘርፍ ጠምዛዥ *zarf-ṭamzāž*: An Amharic adjectival phrase with the literal meaning of 'the one that bends a fringe'. According to the tradition of *sawāsəw*, the elements that can be known by this term are *'əlla* and *za* when they indicate a genitive case relation of three nouns preceding the second and third nouns.

ዘንድ፡ አንቀጽ *zand 'anqaṣ*: Name of the jussive verb in the *Qəne* School.

ዘይእዜ *za-yə'əze*: Name of the tenth type of *Qəne* with six lines. Its literal meaning is 'today's'.

የቅኔ፡ ዜማ፡ ልክ *ya-qəne zemā ləkk*: A lesson in the *Qəne* Schools which is about the measurements of syllables of words in the lines of *Qəne*.

የቅኔ፡ ጎዳና *ya-qəne godānā*: A lesson about different styles of *Qəne*.

ጉት *gutt*: A term which is used as an alternative of *ya-qəne godānā*.

ግሥ *gəśś*: *A* collective noun which refers to all verbs and nouns. It is divided into *'anqaṣ gəśś* (verb) and *nabbār gəśś* (substantive).

የግሥ ምስክር *ya-gəśś məsəkkər*: An Amharic term which means 'an evidence of *gəśś*'. In the study of *sawāsəw*, it is part of the lesson *rəbā-gəśś* which deals with conjugation of verbs and with the textual evidence of further meanings of some polysemantic verbs.

ደቂቅ፡ አገባብ *daqiq 'Aggabāb*: A lesson topic of the third divison of *'Aggabāb*. Again, each ACPPIP element involved in the group is known as *daqiq 'Aggabāb. Daqiq* means 'small', 'little', 'child' and 'children'.

ጎንጅ *gonǧ*: Name of place which is in the province of Goǧǧām. It is also the name of one of the three *Qəne* houses.

INDEX